MILITARY ME

Holly Furneaux is Professor of Engl
She is author of *Queer Dickens: Ero*.
University Press, 2009). She is also co-editor, with Sally Ledger, of *Dickens in Context* (Cambridge University Press, 2011), and editor of John Forster's *Life of Dickens* (Sterling, 2011).

Praise for *Military Men of Feeling*

'Hugely ambitious in its aim not merely to uncover a neglected masculine figure of the period and complicate our historical understanding of the relationship between warfare, reform, and gender in the process, but to do so in such a way as to shed light on wider debates around the nature of conflict... this book is one not simply to relish but to be inspired by.'

American Historical Review

'This work of Victorian studies [is] as relevant to interdisciplinary researchers of present-day militarism as it will be to gender historians of Victorian Britain: *Military Men of Feeling* succeeds in drawing together the work of historians of masculinity and emotion with current feminist scholarship on twenty-first-century war in order to start fulfilling what is already a latent promise, the emergence of a historical as well as present-minded Critical Military Studies.'

Critical Military Studies

'*Military Men of Feeling* is an insightful and highly readable piece of work that makes a very significant contribution to our understandings of military masculinities, the affective experience of war in general, and the cultural history of the Crimean War in particular.'

Literature and History

'Pointedly and provocatively challenges... received wisdom... Furneaux's rich argument ranges well beyond the Crimea, from the eighteenth-century culture of sensibility to contemporary defenses of military engagements as humanitarian projects.'

Victorian Studies

'Historians of the military, of the emotions, gender, and of the family will all find Furneaux's study a hugely rewarding and conceptually stimulating book.'

Journal of Victorian Culture

Military Men of Feeling

*Emotion, Touch, and Masculinity
in the Crimean War*

HOLLY FURNEAUX

OXFORD
UNIVERSITY PRESS

Great Clarendon Street, Oxford, OX2 6DP,
United Kingdom

Oxford University Press is a department of the University of Oxford.
It furthers the University's objective of excellence in research, scholarship,
and education by publishing worldwide. Oxford is a registered trade mark of
Oxford University Press in the UK and in certain other countries

© Holly Furneaux 2016

The moral rights of the author have been asserted

First published in 2016
First published in paperback in 2021

All rights reserved. No part of this publication may be reproduced, stored in
a retrieval system, or transmitted, in any form or by any means, without the
prior permission in writing of Oxford University Press, or as expressly permitted
by law, by licence or under terms agreed with the appropriate reprographics
rights organization. Enquiries concerning reproduction outside the scope of the
above should be sent to the Rights Department, Oxford University Press, at the
address above

You must not circulate this work in any other form
and you must impose this same condition on any acquirer

Published in the United States of America by Oxford University Press
198 Madison Avenue, New York, NY 10016, United States of America

British Library Cataloguing in Publication Data
Data available

Library of Congress Cataloging in Publication Data
Data available

ISBN 978–0–19–873783–4 (Hbk.)
ISBN 978–0–19–285580–0 (Pbk.)

Links to third party websites are provided by Oxford in good faith and
for information only. Oxford disclaims any responsibility for the materials
contained in any third party website referenced in this work.

For my mum, Margaret Barton, and in loving memory of my stepdad, John Barton. In recognition of everyday heroism.

Acknowledgements

I am grateful to the Arts and Humanities Research Council and the University of Leicester for funding which supported the research for this book.

This book was written in very generous company. A range of people introduced me to areas of military history that were new to me, shared previously unstudied materials, and helped me to hone my arguments. My greatest thanks go to Alastair Massie at the National Army Museum, who encouraged this work from the outset and guided me through NAM's fantastic Crimean War collections. I am grateful to Rachel Bates, Pip Dodd, Lara Kriegel, and Sue Prichard for inspiring conversations about things Crimean, and to George Boyce and Glenn Fisher, with whom I am preparing a collection of Crimean War infantry letters, for sharing their expertise and for introducing me to some of the soldier correspondents discussed here. My thanks to Laura Blishen, Patrick Roe, and Marigold Somerset for allowing me to quote from their private collections of the letters of Henry Blishen, George Roe, and William Pechell, respectively. David Rymill and David Bond helped with my work at Hampshire Record Office.

I have been supported by rich research cultures in war and peace studies, Victorian studies, and the history of emotion. Special thanks to my colleagues at the University of Leicester in the War and Literature research group, particularly Phil Shaw and Mark Rawlinson, and to those in the Victorian Studies Centre. I am also deeply thankful for exchanges of ideas with Carolyn Burdett, David Clark, Thomas Dixon, Eli Dryden, Katherine Inglis, Melisa Klimaszewski, Martin Halliwell, Wendy Parkins, Anne Schwan, Paul White, and Ben Winyard. Adam and Stanley Broughton, amongst others, helped me keep going. Thank you Adam for extraordinary love, care, and creative inspiration.

Parts of this book have previously been published in other forms, and I am grateful to their editors for permission to rework that material here. An early version of chapter 1 appeared as 'Victorian Masculinities, or Military Men of Feeling: Domesticity, Militarism, and Manly Sensibility', in *The Oxford Handbook of Victorian Literary Culture*, ed. Juliet John (Oxford: Oxford University Press, 2014). Parts of chapters 2 and 3 were first published as, respectively, '*Household Words* and the Crimean War: Journalism, Fiction and Forms of Recuperation in Wartime', in *Charles*

Dickens and the Mid-Victorian Press, ed. John Drew (Buckingham: University of Buckingham Press, 2013), pp. 245–60, and 'Children of the Regiment: Soldiers, Adoption, and Military Tenderness in Victorian Culture', *Victorian Review*, special issue 'Extending Families', ed. Kelly Hager and Talia Schaffer, 43 (2014), pp. 67–84.

Contents

List of Illustrations xi

Introduction 1

1. 'The company of gentlemen': Thackeray's Military Men of Feeling and Eighteenth-Century Traditions 27

2. Princes of War and of Peace: Secular and Spiritual Redemption in Dickens and Kingsley 54

3. Children of the Regiment: Narratives of Battlefield Adoption 87

4. 'Our poor Colonel loved him as if he had been his own son': Family Feeling in the Crimea 121

5. Sharing the Stuff of War: Soldier Art, Textiles, and Tactility 147

6. Reparative Soldiering and its Limits: Cultures of Male Care-Giving 187

Afterword: The Ballad of the Boy Captain 217

Bibliography 221
Index 237

List of Illustrations

1. F. A. Fraser, Captain Taunton, and Private Doubledick, 'Seven Poor Travellers', 1871, reprinted in the Library Edition of Dickens's works, 1911. Reproduced with permission from the Charles Dickens Museum.   57
2. Charles Green, Corporal Theophile, and Bebelle, 'Somebody's Luggage', 1874, reprinted in the Library Edition of Dickens's works, 1911. Reproduced with permission from the Charles Dickens Museum.   101
3. John Everett Millais, *The Random Shot* or *L'enfant du Régiment* (1854–5, exhibited 1856). Reproduced with permission from the Yale Centre for British Art.   107
4. Lempriere family notebook, cover and detail. Reproduced with permission from the National Army Museum.   127
5. John Luard, *A Welcome Arrival*, 1857. Reproduced with permission from the National Army Museum.   148
6. Lempriere family notebook, sketch of camp. Reproduced with permission from the National Army Museum.   158
7. Thomas Harvey, 'The Trenches at Midday', *Illustrated Times*, 18 August 1855. Reproduced from author's own collection.   161
8. Lempriere family notebook, Russian medal ribbon and on facing page memorial poem 'The Past'. Reproduced with permission from the National Army Museum.   166
9. Patchwork bedcover, 17th Regiment of Foot, c.1856. Reproduced with permission from the National Army Museum.   177
10. Thomas William Wood, *Portrait of Private Thomas Walker*, 1856. Reproduced with permission from the Hunterian Museum at the Royal College of Surgeons.   183
11. J. A. Benwell, *Florence Nightingale in the Military Hospital at Scutari*, 1856. Reproduced with permission from the National Army Museum.   194
12. Jerry Barrett, *The Mission of Mercy*, 1857. Reproduced with permission from the National Portrait Gallery.   207

Introduction

In Leo Tolstoy's *War and Peace* (1868–9) the young officer Nikolai Rostov is asked by his fellow cavalry men for an account of how and where he had been wounded. He immediately gives the narrative of the battle his listeners expect, 'the usual version' complete with 'how he had felt himself burning with excitement, stormed the enemy's square defences, oblivious to everything, hacked his way in, mown men down right, left and centre, tasted blood with his sabre before collapsing from exhaustion, and all the rest'.[1] Although he does not wish to tell a falsehood, both Rostov and his soldier audience find this a more relatable form of war story than the admission that his battle was cut short by a fall from his horse and a scramble for the woods. Tolstoy had previously explored this kind of revised battle story in *Sebastopol Sketches* (1855–6), drawn from his participation, as a Russian artillery officer, in the Crimean War. In 'Sebastopol in May' Pest, whose blood-soaked greatcoat provokes questions from his fellow officers about his part in the latest exchange, 'found himself boasting in spite of himself', describing 'how he, Pest, had bayoneted a Frenchman and how, had it not been for him, the day would have been lost, and so on, and so forth'.[2] He omits the unheroic experiences of confusion, a feeling of having been 'lost in the fog of oblivion' and the floundering randomness of the killing (p. 92). Like Pest, Rostov tells a normalized hyper-aggressive tale, storming, hacking, and mowing, of belligerent emotional and sensory experience. Rostov's own 'burning excitement' and battle oblivion—the phrase 'oblivious to everything' suggesting total unawareness of his own suffering and that of others—is even communicated to his sabre as it 'tasted blood'. As Kate McLoughlin argues in her reading of this scene, 'Rostov yields to a stronger more established version of belligerent events.' Through a 'swerve', typical of war writers (as McLoughlin demonstrates), Rostov draws on many

---

[1] Leo Tolstoy, *War and Peace*, translated by Anthony Briggs (London: Penguin, 2007), p. 257.
[2] Leo Tolstoy, *Sebastopol Sketches*, translated by David McDuff (London: Penguin, 1986), p. 92.

centuries' worth of 'prior versions' to deliver an 'ur-war story'.[3] This ur-war story is, however, in complete contrast to the tales that many mid-Victorian soldiers, authors, and artists felt compelled to tell. In the narratives explored in this book, a very different rhetorical and narratological impulse is at work, in which tales of war violence are swiftly rerouted into ameliorative stories of healing and restoration, physical and emotional.

Margaret Goodman, a volunteer nurse who worked at Scutari hospital with Florence Nightingale during the Crimean War (1854–6), summarizes the kind of narrative swerve with which this book is concerned. Goodman reflects on the types of 'yarn' popular amongst her soldier patients:

> Deeds of cruelty or wickedness were never boasted of, and, if related of others, they were invariably held up to execration and strongly animadverted upon by the whole group; while, not only acts of courage, but acts of mercy, were applauded: such as when, on the taking of Sebastopol, a man, at the risk of his life, rescued a Russian child from the bayonet of an intoxicated Frenchman, and, restoring the boy to his mother, guided them both to a spot which appeared less exposed; or when a wounded soldier, lying on the field of Alma, shared that inestimably precious treasure, under such circumstances, the water in his calabash, with one of the enemy near, whose sufferings appeared more intense than his own.[4]

In their sentimental climax in the self-sacrificing relief of others' suffering (regardless of their side in the conflict), these tales share a widespread narratological commitment to heroic presentations of the military man of feeling. The restoration of vulnerable children and relief of the wounded are, as we shall see, typical plots in representations of, and around, the Crimean War. This book explores the reasons why mid-Victorian British war writing by soldiers and professional writers and artists alike eschews violence in favour of 'acts of mercy'. It considers the range of cultural work performed by the gentle soldier, a figure which demands a reconsideration of the connections between manliness, violence, emotional eloquence, tactile care, and domesticity. The military man of feeling is also used in the service of, variously, social reform and warmongering. The first three chapters of the book are focused on the work of major novelists of

---

[3] Kate McLoughlin, *Authoring War: The Literary Representation of War from the Iliad to Iraq* (Cambridge: Cambridge University Press, 2011), p. 2, p. 6. Rosemary Edmond's 1957 translation which McLoughlin quotes uses a slightly different vocabulary of violence of rushing—the oblivion of Briggs's rendering is here the action of a 'hurricane'—hacking and slashing and sabre tasting 'flesh', quoted by McLoughlin, p. 1.

[4] Margaret Goodman, *An English Sister of Mercy* (London: Smith, Elder, and Co., 1862), p. 180. Further references to this, and other frequently quoted primary texts, are given in parenthesis.

the period, William Makepeace Thackeray, Charles Dickens, Charles Kingsley, and Charlotte Yonge, while the final three chapters examine material produced by those directly involved in the Crimean War, soldiers, their families, and nurses. These diverse texts speak to continuing questions about the relationships between manliness, militarism, and emotion. The mid-Victorian military man of feeling draws together eighteenth-century debates around sensibility and the action it might elicit with discussions that remain urgent about emotional and ethical responses to war.

THE CRIMEAN WAR: RENEGOTIATING HEROISM

On 28 March 1854 Britain joined France and Turkey, usually referred to as the Ottoman empire, in war against Russia. Piedmont-Sardinia later joined the allies. The war, as Orlando Figes summarizes, was 'the major conflict of the nineteenth century', 'the first "total war"', killing at least half a million Russian soldiers and a quarter of a million in the allies' armies as well as uncounted civilian casualties.[5] The ostensible catalyst for this conflict was Russia's assertion of its protectorate of Orthodox Christians in the Holy Lands, and for Tsar Nicholas I the religious motive for war was substantial. Disputes over the keys to the churches of Jerusalem and Bethlehem were underpinned by the Eastern Question: what to do with Turkey, known as 'the sick man of Europe', whose independence had been repeatedly threatened from the Greek War of Liberation (ended 1830) onwards. How this question was answered would have significant effects on the balance of power in Europe. A pressing reason for Britain's participation, which was widely discussed at the time, was the protection of British trade routes to India and the preservation of this colonial 'possession'.[6] Nurse Goodman, for example, explains that Britain 'entered into the war because she deemed the acquisition of Turkey by Russia would open to this encroaching empire a highway to our Indian possessions' (p. 75). Goodman's language of an 'encroaching' Russia is indicative of wider feeling about the war, which received strong, indeed almost

---

[5] Orlando Figes, *Crimea* (London: Penguin, 2010), p. xix.
[6] Following a historical neglect of the complex religious, ideological, and commercial factors contributing to the Crimean War, which had long been misperceived as a pointless and under-motivated conflict, numerous recent histories of the Crimean War detail its causes. Of these I have found Alastair Massie, *The National Army Museum Book of the Crimean War: The Untold Stories* (Basingstoke: Macmillan, 2005) a particularly engaging starting point. Another good introduction is Paul Kerr, *The Crimean War* (London: Boxtree, 1997).

unanimous, public support in Britain, as a welcome opportunity to check Russian expansionism.

Support was typically voiced in terms which presented the war as a legitimate and necessary exercise of manly energy, as just muscle. It was seen, variously, as a righteous crusade against a despotic power, bringing relief to those states suffering under what Karl Marx was calling the Russian empire's 'prison of nations', and as an opportunity to spread Britain's preferred broadly liberal political model and to secure its military dominance in Europe.[7] Ironically, given the significance of concerns about the protection and expansion of free trade in the British decision to go to war, active combat was also viewed as a timely antidote to the enervations of trade, mercantilism, and material comfort. The *British Quarterly Review* argued that war was needed to prevent nations from 'becoming effeminate with ease and luxury'.[8] The threats of mammonism and capitalism are explored from a different angle in Alfred Tennyson's less famous Crimean War poem, 'Maud' (1855). The poem's monodramatist, a character Tennyson described as his 'madman', explains his decision to fight in the Crimea as a waking 'to the higher aims / Of a land that has lost for a little her lust of gold / And love of a peace that was full of wrongs and shames'.[9] These 'wrongs and shames' include the 'lust of gain' driving a 'civil war' of capitalist exploitation and swindling which causes the narrator's father's ruin and probable suicide (part 1, lines 23 and 27, p. 218). Tennyson refused to fully clarify his position, which was interpreted as both pro-peace and pro-war, or that of his dramatic monologist: 'I do not mean that my madman does not speak truths too.'[10] Others of less dubious sanity also propounded this argument. As Elizabeth Barrett Browning put it, 'if we cannot fight righteous and necessary battles, we must leave our place as a nation, and be satisfied with making pins'.[11] Regretful descriptions of British national character as mercantile

---

[7] See Martin Ceadel, *Semi-Detached Idealists: The British Peace Movement and International Relations, 1854–1945* (Oxford: Oxford University Press, 2000) for a discussion on popular support for the Crimean war as 'a war of principle', p. 39. See also Hugh Small, *The Crimean War* (Stroud: Tempus, 2007) on Marx and free trade arguments, p. 23; Olive Anderson's influential study *A Liberal State at War: English Politics and Economics during the Crimean War* (London: Macmillan, 1967); and Jonathan Parry, *The Politics of Patriotism: English Liberalism, National Identity and Europe, 1830–1886* (Cambridge: Cambridge University Press, 2006).

[8] *British Quarterly Review*, quoted in Ceadel, *Semi-Detached Idealists*, p. 39.

[9] Alfred Tennyson, 'Maud', in *Selected Poems*, ed. Christopher Ricks (London: Penguin, 2007). Tennyson's discussion of the poem in a letter of 6 December 1855 is quoted on p. 353; part 3, lines 38–40, p. 266.

[10] Quoted by Ricks, ed., Alfred Tennyson, *Selected Poems*, p. 353.

[11] Quoted by Stefanie Markovits in the context of wider views of war as a relief from a 'long and dreary commercial period', *The Crimean War in the British Imagination* (Cambridge: Cambridge University Press, 2009), p. 93.

rather than martial reflected the changes associated with mass industrialization and resultant social shifts in class power.

The assertion of a supposedly British brand of energetic manliness through involvement in war was, predictably, contrasted to the national characters attributed to the other participants. This followed a well-established tradition of distinguishing a home brand of heroism from the supposedly inferior masculinities and constitutions (political and physical) of both allies and enemies.[12] In a wealth of Crimean War cartoons the British lion appeared in flattering contradistinction to the foppish French cockerel, the Russian bear, and the effeminate, enfeebled Ottoman empire, often depicted as a menaced turkey.[13] Of course firsthand experiences complicated these stereotypes and soldiers reported a range of feelings of amity and enmity along national lines, many respecting Russian enemies as fellow Christians who were seen as more familiar than the often distrusted Turkish, predominantly Muslim, allies. The French reputation for emotional excess was seen as both a national weakness, and, as discussed in chapter 3, a characteristic to celebrate and emulate.[14] While individual perceptions of allies and enemy varied widely, comparisons were often drawn that emphasized the British soldier's superior gentlemanliness, specifically his dedication to fighting fair and chivalrous capacity for relieving the suffering.[15]

British concerns about national character, class, and masculinity coalesced in the Crimean War. Typically described as the first media war, failures of government and army administration and management were widely reported by a vocal press. The war was a pivotal point in the shaping of British attitudes to military masculinity, as the public engaged

[12] See Linda Colley, *Britons: Forging the Nation, 1707–1837* (London: Pimlico, 1992), pp. 311–12, and Catriona Kennedy, 'John Bull into Battle: Military Masculinity and the British Army Officer during the Napoleonic Wars', in *Gender, War and Politics: Transatlantic Perspectives, 1775–1830*, ed. Karen Hagerman, Giselda Mettele, and Jane Rendall (Basingstoke: Palgrave, 2010), pp. 127–46, p. 140.

[13] Examples include [John Tenniel], 'Paws Off Bruin', *Punch*, 4 June 1853; 'The Peace Polka', NAM 1983-10-97.

[14] The different national negotiations of masculinity in the other countries involved in the Crimean War are, sadly, beyond the scope of this book. Together with Rachel Anchor and Alastair Massie I organized a conference and edited a resulting collection that strives to offer a broader range of national perspectives, 'Charting the Crimean War: Contexts, Nationhood, Afterlives', *19: Interdisciplinary Perspectives on the Long Nineteenth Century* 20 (2015), as did the workshop led by Gavin Williams, 'Theatres of the Crimean War: Sound, Affect and Media in the Production of Wartime', King's College London, 2014.

[15] In her discussion 'Traits of National Character' Goodman asserts: 'Without partiality, I think it must be asserted that the Englishman was the greatest favourite with the inhabitants of those foreign countries in which the allied army was stationed: unbounded trust was reposed by Greeks, Turks, and even Russians in the kind-heartedness of the English soldier', p. 173.

with the progress and infamous 'blunders' of the conflict and reflected on appropriate soldierly behaviour across ranks, forms of heroism, the physical suffering of the troops, military management, and the need for army reform. Stefanie Markovits has explored the ambivalence around renegotiated 'ideas of heroism and patriotism during a campaign distinguished more by blunder than by glory'.[16] Traditional aristocratic leadership was found wanting and middle-class and working-class heroes were seen as a solution to the disillusionment. As Michael Brown puts it, 'from the "Thin Red Line" of Balaclava to the "Soldier's Battle" of Inkerman, it was subalterns, non-commissioned officers and private soldiers who were generally credited with snatching victory from the jaws of defeat, [in] a "democratization" of heroism'.[17] This acknowledgement of the bravery and sacrifice of the soldier of the ranks continued a rehabilitation of this figure.[18] Although the Duke of Wellington famously called the soldiers who made up his army 'the scum of the earth', there was, as Michael Snape has shown, already in the army a 'significant evangelical subculture' which advocated a moral code of temperance and restraint prior to the widespread interest in the soldier's spiritual condition that flourished from the mid-1850s.[19] Debates about the character of the soldier of the ranks

---

[16] Markovits, *The Crimean War*, p. 2.

[17] Michael Brown, '"Like a Devoted Army": Medicine, Heroic Masculinity, and the Military Paradigm in Victorian Britain', *Journal of British Studies* 49.3 (2010), pp. 592–622, p. 607. Markovits summarizes the radical shift in the cultural image of the military man: 'Before the war, the stereotypical soldier was an aristocratic fop. After it, he was a brave private', *The Crimean War*, p. 4.

[18] The sailor was less in need of cultural rehabilitation. Nineteenth-century Britain was primary a naval power and the navy, unlike a standing army which might be used to suppress the people, was seen as a safe repository for patriotic enthusiasm. As Kennedy argues, 'much of the nation's psychological investment in the armed forces was focused on the navy, which provided exemplars of masculine patriotism in the form of the plain-speaking ordinary seaman, "Jack Tar", and through the figure of the admiral hero, most notably Horatio Nelson', p. 120. See also Robert McGregor, 'The Popular Press and the Creation of Military Masculinities in Georgian Britain', in *Military Masculinities: Identity and the State*, ed. Paul Higate (Westport, CT: Praeger, 2003), pp. 143–57, and Joanne Bailey's forthcoming *A Manly Nation: Making and Breaking Masculinities, 1750–1918*. The popularity of the Jack Tar figure, which, as McGregor suggests, offered an exemplary masculinity that transcended class barriers, persisted through the Victorian period in charismatic characters like Dickens's former naval officer, Tartar, in *Edwin Drood* (1870), who combines physical vigour with an aptitude for shipshape homemaking. While this book concentrates on the distinctive cultural history of the soldier, there are important parallels with representations of the sailor and debates around class, manliness, physicality, emotional literacy, domesticity, and citizenship, which could fruitfully be considered in further work.

[19] See Carolyn Steedman for a discussion of the class prejudice which 'dwelt consistently on the vices of the unskilled labouring poor, on their brutality, illiteracy and immorality, in making a composite picture of the early Victorian common soldier', *The Radical Soldier's Tale: John Pearman, 1819–1908* (London and New York: Routledge, 1988), p. 37. Michael Snape, *The Redcoat and Religion* (Abingdon: Routledge, 2005), p. 118.

came into sharp focus in the Crimean War, as his suffering in the campaign was exposed. In calling the public to relieve privations through contributions to the paper's newly created 'Sick and Wounded Fund', a *Times* article of 12 October 1854 reassured readers that 'soldiers and sailors are not the savage, murderous, ravaging, and destroying creatures they are sometimes imagined'.[20] Representations of the working-class soldier's gentlemanliness, often expressed as emotional and tactile forms of gentle manliness, directly challenged established perceptions of his brutish violence. Many texts (as discussed in chapters 2 and 3) written during and after the war used the military man of feeling to call for army reforms to allow more opportunities for progression on merit and provide better working conditions for soldiers of the ranks.

Representations of this war and of soldiers in the mid-Victorian period (the earliest text I consider in detail is Charlotte Yonge's *Kenneth* of 1850) also participate, as we shall see further through this book, in broader debates about the extension of the franchise, and cultural discussions about the move from aristocracy to meritocracy. From the late eighteenth century the case was increasingly made that those willing to fight for the country should be full members of its political process.[21] Debates about the relationship between combatancy and gendered citizenship had a particular urgency in the joint context of working-class soldiers' contribution to the Crimean War and reform debates which had gained ground in the early 1850s. As the Chartist organization the National Reform League put it particularly baldly in summer 1855: a 'Parliament in which you are not represented has no right to tax you, nor to claim military service from you, nor to involve you in costly and bloody wars designed to increase the slavery and poverty of your class'.[22]

Renegotiations of class extended through the social strata as value systems based on ability and hard work replaced outmoded aristocratic ideals of birthright, dash, and valour. There was widespread concern with, as James Eli Adams describes it, 're-imagining heroism in an age that seemed to have little place for it'.[23] In 1827 the essayist William Hazlitt lamented the contrast between the action heroism of medieval knights and

---

[20] [Thomas Chenery] *The Times*, 12 October 1854, p. 6.
[21] See Colley, *Britons*, pp. 318–19, and Stefan Dudink and Karen Hagemann, 'Masculinity in Politics and War in the Age of Democratic Revolutions, 1750–1850', in *Masculinities in Politics and War: Gendering Modern History*, ed. Stefan Dudink, Karen Hagemann, and John Tosh (Manchester: Manchester University Press, 2004), pp. 3–21.
[22] 'The Chartists and the War', *The Empire*, 23 June 1855, p. 471. Such arguments continued, as Graham Dawson shows, in the Indian uprising of 1857, *Soldier Heroes: British Literature, Empire and the Imagining of Masculinities* (London and New York: Routledge, 1994), p. 109.
[23] James Eli Adams, *A History of Victorian Literature* (Oxford: Wiley-Blackwell, 2009), p. 158.

the men of feeling of the present day. Voicing ideas which became increasingly popular in a broader chivalric revival, in which authors and artists including Tennyson, Charles Kingsley, John Ruskin, and William Morris were enthusiastic participants, Hazlitt argued that knights of old

> did not merely sigh and smile and kneel in the presence of their mistresses—they had to unhorse their adversaries in combat, to storm castles, to vanquish giants and lead armies. So far, so well. In the good old times of romance and chivalry, favour was won and maintained by the bold achievements and fair fame of the chosen knight... instead of depending, as in more effeminate times, on taste, sympathy, and a refinement of sentiment and manners, of the delicacy of which it is impossible to convey any idea by words or actions.[24]

For many, the Crimean War and the British response to the Indian uprising or so-called 'mutiny' of 1857 offered opportunities for the reformation of these 'effeminate times' of over-'refinement', 'sentiment', and 'delicacy'. As Samuel Smiles put it in his 1859 *Self-Help*: 'Notwithstanding the wail which we occasionally hear for the chivalry that is gone, our own age has witnessed deeds of bravery and gentleness—of heroic self denial and manly tenderness—which are unsurpassed in history. The events of the last few years have shown that our countrymen are as yet an undegenerate race.'[25] Smiles presents gentle manliness in warfare as the strongest evidence that 'chivalry is not dead' (p. 331). In the Crimean War, for Smiles and many other advocates of greater social mobility by endeavour, 'men of all classes proved themselves worthy of the noble inheritance of character which their forefathers have bequeathed to them'; similarly Smiles argues for an egalitarian national nobility of character in the Indian uprising: 'even the common soldiers proved themselves gentlemen under their trials' (p. 331). Smiles participates in an energetic redefinition of gentlemanliness, fully discussed in chapter 1, in which physical acts of care and emotional tenderness were privileged over social status. Smiles's cross-class conjunctions of 'bravery and gentleness', heroism and 'manly tenderness', are, as we shall see, the typical components of the ideal soldier, across ranks, in the period.[26]

---

[24] William Hazlitt, *Sketches and Essays* (London: John Templeman, 1839, first published 1827), p. 261. My thanks to David Clark for sharing his insights on this nostalgia for medieval manliness. There is some excellent work on the Victorian chivalric revival. See especially Mark Girouard, *The Return to Camelot: Chivalry and the English Gentleman* (Yale: Yale University Press, 1981) and Ingrid Hanson, *William Morris and the Uses of Violence, 1856–1890* (London: Anthem Press, 2013).
[25] Samuel Smiles, *Self-Help* (Oxford: Oxford University Press, 2002), p. 331.
[26] This combination of 'the gentle and the brave' is also the keynote of Smiles's glowing report of the self-sacrifice of officers and men on the wrecked *Birkenhead* in 1852, who remained to sink with the ship in order not to overweigh the lifeboats of women and children, p. 332.

In his 1851–3 *A Child's History of England* Charles Dickens reflects on the appeal of accounts, like those favoured by the soldiers in Nurse Goodman's care, of acts of gentleness in wartime. In this otherwise intensely bloodthirsty account of monarchical violence, Sir Philip Sidney's battlefield mercy in the 1586 Battle of Zutphen stands out as a powerful counterexample. Sidney is introduced as 'one of the best writers, the best knights, and the best gentlemen of that or any age', and Dickens recounts the tale that, when fatally injured, he passed on 'some water for which he had eagerly asked' to a 'poor badly wounded common soldier lying on the ground', saying 'thy necessity is greater than mine'.[27] Goodman's Crimean soldier patients also quote Sidney's famous dying words; in their stories of the British wounded offering refreshment to their suffering enemies care does not only transcend barriers of class, as in Sydney's attention to the common soldier, but extends beyond national allegiance. Dickens's admiring account of Sidney concludes that 'this touching action of a noble heart is perhaps as well known as any incident in history—it is as famous far and wide as the bloodstained Tower of London... So delightful is an act of true humanity and so glad are mankind to remember it' (p. 270). An example of the continuing appeal of this narrative as an assurance of 'true humanity' persisting amidst violence is offered by the work of First World War correspondent Philip Gibbs:

> A friend of mine carried a water jar to some of the wounded and held it to their lips. One of them refused. He was a tall, evil-looking fellow, with a bloody rag round his head—a typical 'Hun' I thought. But he pointed to a comrade who lay gasping beside him and said, in German, 'He needs it first.' This man had never heard of Sir Philip Sidney, who at Zutphen, when thirsty and near death, said, 'His need is greater than mine,' but he had the same chivalry in his soul.[28]

Gibbs continues a championing, which flourished in the mid-Victorian period, of a different form of chivalry to that nostalgically craved by Hazlitt. Gibbs, like Dickens, Smiles, Goodman, and many others of the Crimean period, sees the best example of chivalry in acts of battlefield care rather than in a heroics of violence. This brief example shows the continuation of a sensibility that applauded wartime gentleness from the Elizabethan period, through the Victorian, and into the twentieth

---

[27] Charles Dickens, *A Child's History of England* (London: Odhams, no date), p. 270.
[28] Philip Gibbs, *Now It Can Be Told* (New York: Harper, 1920), p. 181. For a discussion of the Elizabethan popularity of Sidney's dying actions see Charles Carlton, *Going to the Wars: The Experience of the British Civil Wars, 1638–1651* (London: Routledge, 1992), p. 216.

century. What this book seeks to determine is why Sidney-like masculinity became the dominant, or perhaps the only, acceptable form of soldierly manliness in the mid-Victorian period, and what historical, political, and social factors resulted in the unprecedented celebration of the military man of feeling.

MANLY TOUGHS AND STIFF UPPER LIPS? CONJUNCTIONS OF MILITARISM AND MASCULINITY

The Times leader quoted in the previous section shows the continuation of ideas about the murderous savagery of the soldier of the ranks; at the other end of the class scale, a stereotype of the hard-drinking, gaming, womanizing landed officer also persisted through the period, notably in the bestselling fiction of George Lawrence. Lawrence is typically grouped with the Muscular Christian school, though his work does not share the concern of that movement with social reform, instead 'lamenting the feminizing ethos of a sedentary middle class'.[29] The eponymous hero of his *Guy Livingstone, or Thorough* (1857) is from a line of distinguished warrior ancestors, 'a race that ever died hard and dangerously' from King Richard's Crusades, through Naseby to the Peninsular wars, in which Guy's father is killed. Guy, a man of 'vast proportions', admired for his 'size and sinews', exhibits 'the rarest union of activity and strength'.[30] Though Guy is not shown in military action, indeed early in the novel he sells out of the Life Guards, as 'even the light restraint of service in the Household Brigade had begun to bore him' (p. 167), he triumphs in the fields of sport (pugilism, hunting, horse racing) and, at least by some measure, love. The characterizations of Guy and his close soldiering friends Charley Forrester, with whom he initially shares regimental quarters, and Colonel Mohan bear out such cliches as 'the tender mercies of the light dragoon are cruel' (p. 209): '[Guy] lives very much like other men in the Household Brigade; plays heavily, though not regularly; but he always has two *affaires de cour*, at least, on hand at once' (p. 47).

The only direct tempering of their valuing of affairs of the heart backed by violence as the central tenet of manliness is voiced by the novel's villain,

---

[29] Charlotte Mitchell, 'George Lawrence', *ODNB* (Oxford: Oxford University Press, 2004), http://www.oxforddnb.com/view/article/16175. See Mitchell on the popularity of Lawrence's fiction.

[30] George Lawrence, *Guy Livingstone, or Thorough* (London: The Daily Telegraph, no date), p. 37, p. 48, p. 30.

the disappointed lover and cowardly murderer Bruce. In a conversation about Paris' flight from Menelaus, Bruce suggests, 'might not remorse at the sight of the man he had injured have something to do with his flight?' This perspective is quickly dismissed as contrary cant: 'He was full of moral sentiments—that man. Only you could not look at him without fancying that they sprang more from an inclination to be contradictious and disagreeable than from any depth of principle' (p. 120). Though the principal cast are firmly set against 'moral sentiments', they are all forced to learn painful moral lessons, apparently against the grain of the novel's energetic commitment to an ideal of taciturn, drinking, playing, and fighting hard masculinity. Mohan has become a misanthropic recluse after the married woman he loves and absconds with dies of her guilt, Forrester is murdered by the jilted man whose fiancé he has courted and married, and Guy is consumed by 'great sorrow' after his infidelity costs him the woman he loves, Constance. On her deathbed Constance urges Guy's reformation: 'Try to be gentler to others first; and with every act of unselfish kindness you will have gained something' (p. 278). This encouragement of gentleness and kindness is a surprising moral centre for a novel famous for its military swagger. As with the wider legacy of Victorian soldierly masculinity, Livingstone's advocacy of the manly tough is less secure than it first appears.

The wealth of gentle soldiers which this book considers is somewhat at odds with persistent perceptions of Victorian men, particularly military men, as strong and silent types, enduring hardship without complaint, and keeping their emotions to themselves. In part as a result of the privations experienced by soldiers of all ranks (though to differing extents) through the inadequacy of supply lines and medical provision, the Crimean War has been widely seen as exemplifying Victorian emotional restraint. In a 2012 BBC documentary, for example, the war was presented as the moment at which the stiff upper lip became democratized as officers and men were commended for their stoicism.[31] The programme positioned the Crimean conflict as the start of a hardening of feeling, which has been considered an essential component of imperial toughness, through the second half of the nineteenth century. Heather Streets traces a shift in this period towards 'the increasingly desirable masculine virtues of loyalty, reckless bravery, strength and willingness to fight'.[32] Narratives

---

[31] *Ian Hislop's Stiff Upper Lip: An Emotional History of Britain*, Episode 2, 'Heyday', BBC 2, 9 October 2012. The strapline for this episode, 'How the Victorians made the stiff upper-lip a genuinely national characteristic' (http://www.bbc.co.uk/programmes/b01n7rh4), is a neat shorthand for the received view of the emotional history of the period.

[32] Heather Streets, *Martial Races: The Military, Race, and Masculinity in British Imperial Culture* (Manchester: Manchester University Press, 2004), p. 13. Similarly Graham

of imperial aggression have tended to dominate perceptions of the military man throughout the century, eclipsing more ambivalent formulations. This book traces a number of tropes and experiences of military feeling that persist through the late nineteenth century (including chapter 1's consideration of Colonel Newcome's popularity in the First World War, chapter 3's discussion of narratives of soldier adoption, and chapter 5's exploration of battlefield collecting). These continuities raise questions about the generally accepted trajectory towards a more explicitly aggressive masculinity. My arguments about the popularity of the gentle soldier, though, do not necessarily suggest that the Victorian age was less bellicose than we have believed. I argue instead that in overlooking the continuing significance of the military man of feeling through the nineteenth century we have misunderstood the cultural tactics by which supposedly civilized nations become reconciled to their participation in war.

I am inspired by recent work on the mid-Victorian period, notably by Matthew Bevis, John Reed, Trudi Tate, and Susan Walton, which attends to the ambivalence within war writing and seeks 'to debunk', as Ingrid Hanson puts it, 'the assumption, set up by the modernists, of the Victorians' unequivocal glorification of battle'.[33] Much of this work draws upon a broader rethinking, also crucial to my work, of Victorian masculinity as less emotionally stifled, more domesticated, and more concerned with hands-on care than we once thought. John Tosh's attention to male familial roles and on the blurred lines between civilian public and private life has been at the centre of scholarship recognizing the diversity of Victorian masculinity.[34] Tosh's work on soldiering, though, like most other scholarship directly concerned with Victorian military masculinity, has reinforced rather than challenged a separate spheres model, presenting

---

Dawson dates an emphasis on 'military virtues' comprising 'aggression, strength, courage, and endurance' to the mid- to late century, *Soldier Heroes*, pp. 1–2. This chronology is considered in more detail in chapter 3.

[33] Hanson, *William Morris*, p. xiii. Bevis reclaims the mixed messages of nineteenth-century war poetry from the legacies of Victorians' 'lips compressed' or 'cavalier' avoidance of the realities of war. He argues that 'as the First World War comes to be seen as heralding a break between Victorian and modern conceptions of conflict, so a series of neat poetic oppositions emerges—the glorious versus the gruesome, the heroic versus the hellish, the romantic versus the realistic'. 'Fighting Talk: Victorian War Poetry', in *British and Irish War Poetry*, ed. Tim Kendall (Oxford: Oxford University Press, 2007), pp. 7–33, p. 8, p. 9.

[34] See especially John Tosh, *A Man's Place: Masculinity and the Middle-Class Home in Victorian England* (New Haven and London: Yale University Press, 1999). Examples of excellent, more recent work on domestic Victorian masculinities, inspired in part by Tosh, include Margaret Markwick, *New Men in Trollope's Novels: Rewriting the Victorian Male* (Ashgate: Aldershot, 2007); Valerie Sanders, *The Tragi-Comedy of Victorian Fatherhood* (Cambridge: Cambridge University Press, 2009); Julie-Marie Strange, *Fatherhood and the British Working Class, 1865–1914* (Cambridge: Cambridge University Press, 2015).

the military as anti-domestic. In one of the few extended discussions of the relationship between soldiering and manliness in this period, Graham Dawson argues that fighting to protect women and children at home was structured by forms of masculinity presented as other to the values of home, while Tosh influentially presented imperial soldiering as a 'flight from domesticity': 'Empire was actively embraced by young men as a means of evading or postponing the claims of domesticity.'[35] These 'claims of domesticity' involve heterosexual courtship, marriage, and fatherhood. By yoking a concept of domesticity to marital and procreative relationships, Tosh's formulation suggests that all male spaces are inherently anti-domestic, whereas, as we will see in this book, many soldiers made strenuous practical and imaginative efforts to connect themselves with the structures of home life—its rhythms, routines, relationships, and even architecture. In the Crimean War the distance between civilian and martial spheres was also reduced through a communications network that newly facilitated regular exchanges of letters and objects and allowed soldiers and those at home to participate in significantly overlapping communities of feeling.

The extent to which militarism is an inherently masculine tendency, and the relationship between violence and social constructions of masculinity, has long been debated. In her 1938 epistolary essay *Three Guineas*, in answer to the question of how to prevent war, Virginia Woolf famously presents war as an exclusively male interest. She argues that men find 'some glory, some necessity, some satisfaction in fighting' which women 'have never felt or enjoyed': 'For though many instincts are held more or less in common by both sexes, to fight has always been the man's habit, not the woman's. Law and practice have developed that difference, whether innate or accidental.'[36] Socially constructionist understandings of gender difference have underpinned more recent explorations of the cultural production of 'habit', 'law and practice' in the militarization of men.[37] Some feminist scholars have continued Woolf's analysis of how

---

[35] Dawson, *Soldier Heroes*, p. 2. Dawson both interrogates and confirms the separation between military and domestic spheres in nineteenth-century fiction and biography: 'If adventure and domestic narratives are seen, not just as simple alternatives but as dynamically inter-related through the splitting of cultural imaginaries, then the domestic imaginary may be read as adventure's political unconscious', p. 76. Tosh, *A Man's Place*, p. 177.

[36] Virginia Woolf, *Three Guineas*, in *A Room of One's Own and Three Guineas* (London: Hogarth, 1984), p. 113.

[37] Marcia Kovitz counters the continuing view that there is an 'innate disposition in men to wage war and to engage in what is seen as its core practice, combat' with evidence that 'inducing and sustaining combativeness in men is difficult' and with examples of warrior women that dispel 'the notion that the military is masculine because women innately lack the requisite characteristics'. She concludes that 'a uniform military masculinity is carefully

the gendered power imbalance in patriarchal societies contributes to violence and war.[38] And various recent commentators, as Santanu Das has noted, have rearticulated a belief given authority by Sigmund Freud in his essays 'Thoughts for the Times on War and Death' (1915) and 'Beyond the Pleasure Principle' (1920): 'The tendency to aggression is an innate, independent instinctual disposition in man.'[39] While most recent work is sceptical about an absolute biological essentialism or 'innate' gender difference, the binaries of masculinity/femininity, war/peace, violence/gentleness, killing/healing have 'stuck', to use Claire Duncanson's language.[40] Duncanson is concerned with the 'stickiness' of gender binaries, which draw on and reaffirm millennia-long associations of masculinity with warfare and violence, and with scholarship that sees little opportunity for transformation. In her work on current peacekeeping she proposes a 'regendering' of military masculinity as one means of disrupting these binaries. My book suggests that the more tender and nurturing forms of soldiering that Duncanson sees as potentially

constructed through deliberate practice' to enable the waging of war, 'ensuring the obedience of potentially resistant practitioners'. 'The Roots of Military Masculinity', in *Military Masculinities: Identity and the State*, ed. Paul Highgate (Westport: Praeger, 2003), pp. 1–14, p. 5, p. 9. Kimberly Hutchings argues similarly that there is a formal and functional, rather than natural or inevitable, association between masculinity and war that renders war 'both intelligible and acceptable', 'Making Sense of Masculinity and War', *Men and Masculinities* 10.4 (2008), pp. 389–404, p. 389.

[38] In *Sexism and the War System* (New York: Syracuse University Press, 1996, first published 1985) Betty Reardon asserts that 'patriarchy invented and maintains war to hold in place the social system it spawned', p. 12. For a development of this view, more attentive to historical and geographical differences, see Cynthia Cockburn, 'Gender Relations as Causal in Militarism and War: A Feminist Standpoint', in *Making Gender: Making War: Violence, Military and Peacekeeping Practices*, ed. Annica Kronsell and Erika Svedberg (London: Routledge, 2012), pp. 19–34. Cockburn argues that 'patriarchal gender relations are among the "root causes" of militarism and war', p. 30.

[39] Freud, quoted by Santanu Das, *Touch and Intimacy in First World War Literature* (Cambridge: Cambridge University Press, 2005), p. 101 and by Niall Ferguson, *The Pity of War* (London: Penguin, 1998), p. 358. For another recent reassertion of the view that 'men like fighting, and women like men who are prepared to fight on their behalf' see Martin van Creveld, *Transformation of War* (New York: The Free Press, 1991), p. 221. Klaus Theweleit draws on Freud in a psychoanalytic reading of the hyper-aggression against others—women, communists, non-Arian races—in the fascist Freikorps, *Male Fantasies*, 2 vols (Minneapolis: University of Minnesota Press, 1987, 1989).

[40] Claire Duncanson, *Forces for Good? Military Masculinities and Peacebuilding in Afghanistan and Iraq* (Basingstoke: Palgrave, 2013), p. 141. She builds on work on regendered military masculinities by Cynthia Cockburn and Meliha Hubic, 'Gender and the Peacekeeping Military: A View from Bosnian Women's Organizations', in *The Postwar Moment: Militaries, Masculinities and International Peacekeeping*, ed. Cynthia Cockburn and Dubravka Zarkov (London: Lawrence & Wishart, 2012), pp. 103–21. See also Dawson, *Soldier Heroes*, for a critique of the perpetuation of 'dichotomies of gender' within nationalist and radical feminist discourses in which 'a conception of the fundamentally martial nature of masculinity remained in place', p. 17.

transformative have a long, but unacknowledged, prehistory in the military man of feeling.

My contribution to this debate is supported by a confluence of developments in military studies, towards a more social, experiential, 'face of battle' approach, and in literary and historical studies, towards affect and the history of emotion.[41] This conjunction has been a notable feature in the 2014 bumper year of events, inspired in part by the centenary of the beginning of the First World War, including 'Battlefield Emotions', Ghent, March; 'Sensing War', London, June; and 'War: An Emotional History', London, July. While these conferences featured plenty of work on pre-nineteenth-century conflicts and the First World War and after, the Victorian period was minimally represented. This gap follows the distribution of inspiring, existing scholarship on war and affect which clusters in the Romantic period—Mary Favret, Neil Ramsey, Philip Shaw, Jenny Uglow—and in the First World War—Joanna Bourke, Santanu Das, Jessica Meyer, and Michael Roper.[42] The tactile and emotional experience of Victorian military men, by contrast, has been ignored, overshadowed by perceptions of compressed Victorian lips, as Bevis puts it, firmly separated civilian and military spheres, and emotionally dysfunctional empire-building. This book offers a different history of Victorian masculinity and Victorian militarism by attending to that pivotal period, almost chronologically, and in many ways conceptually, equidistant between the Napoleonic and First World Wars.

---

[41] John Keegan, *The Face of Battle* (London: Pimlico, 2004, first published 1976) pioneered a shift from 'the study of generals and generalship' (p. 27), considering the battle experience of the regular soldier. For a summary of the now well-established 'new military history' see Catriona Kennedy and Matthew McCormack, 'New Histories of Soldiering', in *Soldiering in Britain and Ireland, 1750–1850: Men of Arms*, ed. Catriona Kennedy and Matthew McCormack (Basingtoke: Palgrave, 2013), pp. 1–14.

[42] Mary Favret, *War at a Distance: Romanticism and the Making of Modern Wartime* (Princeton: Princeton University Press, 2010); Neil Ramsey, *The Military Memoir and Romantic Literary Culture, 1780–1835* (Burlington, VT: Ashgate, 2011); Philip Shaw, *Sentiment and Suffering in Romantic Military Art* (Farnham: Ashgate, 2013); Jenny Uglow, *In These Times: Living in Britain through Napoleon's Wars* (London: Faber, 2014); Joanna Bourke, *Dismembering the Male: Men's Bodies, Britain and the Great War* (London: Reaktion, 1996); Das, *Touch and Intimacy*; Jessica Meyer, *Men of War: Masculinity in the First World War in Britain* (Basingstoke: Palgrave, 2009); Michael Roper, *The Secret Battle: Emotional Survival in the Great War* (Manchester: Manchester University Press, 2009). Throughout I draw upon this inspiring scholarship on the two ends of the long nineteenth century, and on the affective history of other conflicts including the American Civil War and more recent wars. Without eliding the major contextual differences between these conflicts, I want to allow such parallels to resonate in order to propose the wider applicability of some of the arguments made here specifically in relation to the mid-Victorian British context.

OTHER MILITARY MEN OF FEELING: TRADITIONS FROM ANTIQUITY TO THE 1800S (SELECTED HIGHLIGHTS)

In a longer view encompassing classical accounts of warfare, it comes as little surprise that soldiering creates male intimacy and that some soldiers (of all periods) have felt deeply and expressed their emotions eloquently. As Brian Joseph Martin puts it, for nineteenth-century Europeans classical and biblical accounts had established the 'notion that to serve one's country was to live and die in the service of other men', and that both classical and nineteenth-century texts juxtapose 'the violence and brutality of war with the tenderness of... mourning warriors'.[43]

Notable examples, well known to Victorian officers, include Achilles' lament for his beloved Patroclus in Homer's *Iliad*—'my dearest companion is dead, Patroclus, who was more to me than any other of my men, whom I loved as much as my own life' (book 18, lines 80–2)—and Nisus' response to the death of Euryalus and Aeneas' mourning for Pallas in Virgil's *Aeneid*.[44] Nisus' comradeship with the 'lovely youth' Euryalus, 'a boy with the first signs of manhood on his cheeks as yet unshaven', has some parallels with the stories circulated in the Crimean War about 'the boy captain' discussed in chapter 4. Though an experienced 'formidable warrior', Virgil's Nisus is powerless to prevent the death of his friend; he succeeds in killing Volcens, who killed Euryalus—'the only thought in his mind'—and is able to reach Euryalus' body before he is himself killed: 'So in the moment of his own dying, he cut off the breath of his enemy. Then, pierced through and through, he hurled himself on the dead body of his friend and rested there at last in the peace of death' (book 9, lines 180–2 and 446–8, p. 192, p. 199). In each case a determination for vengeance is the product of grief. Homer's Achilles, for example, vows to kill and dishonour the body of Hector who has killed Patroclus in battle, and rejects Hector's pleas for mercy: 'You dog, don't entreat me by the knees or my parents. I only wish I could summon up the will to carve and eat you raw myself, for what you have done to me' (book 22, lines 45–7, p. 390).[45] Though classical expressions of love and loss in battle resonate

---

[43] Brian Joseph Martin, *Napoleonic Friendship: Military Fraternity, Intimacy and Sexuality in Nineteenth Century France* (Durham, NH: University of New Hampshire Press, 2011), p. 2, p. 4.
[44] Homer, *The Iliad*, translated by E. V. Rieu (Oxford: Oxford University Press, 2003), p. 321; Virgil, *The Aeneid*, translated by David West (Oxford: Oxford University Press, 2003).
[45] For a discussion of the emotional complexity of the *Iliad* and its elaboration of the ethical cost of war via the effects of force on both those who wield and are wounded by it see

with accounts of the grief of Victorian soldiers, these models are not explicitly invoked in any accounts I have seen of Crimean War loss, perhaps because the revenge narrative is firmly repudiated, as we shall see, in Victorian debates about the (in)compatibility of war with Christianity and civilized society.[46] As Charles Kingsley put it in his 1854 address to soldiers and sailors in the Crimea, 'You are to kill for the sake of victory, but never to kill for the sake of killing... If any of you are maddened by hearing of the enemy murdering some of your wounded—recollect that revenge is one of the devil's works.'[47] Though it receives a particular inflection from Kingsley's energetic brand of so-called 'muscular' Christian socialism, this sentiment was widespread in Victorian warfare. Heroic models of vengeance for the deaths of beloved comrades are replaced by expressions of grief that can be shared by mourning soldiers and civilians.

Victorian discussions about the particular state of heart and mind required for righteous killing continued eighteenth-century debates about the appropriate composition of the man of feeling, the connections between emotional response and right action, and whether the man of feeling might also be a man of war. Ideal men of feeling, such as Samuel Richardson's Sir Charles Grandison of his 1753–4 novel, combined an acute responsiveness to the pain and needs of others with benevolent action. The extent to which such figures could also incorporate forms of (morally justified) aggression was less clear, a concern played out through a plethora of duelling plots; Grandison's heroism is famously proved by his refusal to fight a duel. At the same time the suffering veteran (rather than active, potentially belligerent) soldier was a typical figure of sympathetic response in the developing culture of sensibility.[48] Lawrence Sterne combines these concerns in his eminently gentle disabled veterans, Captain Toby Shandy and his servant Corporal Trim, in *Tristram Shandy* (1759–67). Uncle Toby literally cannot hurt even a fly and he and Corporal Trim are represented as wounded rather than wounding,

---

Simone Weil, 'The Iliad, or the Poem of Force', first published 1940–1, translated by Mary McCarthy, *Chicago Review* 18.2 (1965), pp. 5–30.

[46] On the gentler reworking of the bellicosity of seventh-century BC Greek martial poet Tyrtaeus during the Crimean War see Tai Chun Ho, 'Civilian Poets and Poetry of the Crimean Conflict: The War at Home', PhD thesis, University of York, 2015, chapter 1.

[47] Charles Kingsley, 'Brave Words for Brave Soldiers and Sailors', collected in *True Words for Brave Men* (London: Kegan Paul, 1885), p. 209. Kingsley's position is considered in detail in chapter 2.

[48] See Shaw, *Sentiment and Suffering*, and Julie Ellison, *Cato's Tears and the Making of Anglo-American Emotion* (Chicago: University of Chicago Press, 1999), p. 18, for discussions of the cultural centrality of the veteran soldier as the 'object of sympathy' in the eighteenth century.

famously devoting their time as injured veterans to the bloodless military strategy of fortifying the bowling green.[49]

As Philip Shaw has shown, representations of wounded soldiers could produce divergent pro- and anti-war sentiment, providing opportunities 'for the exercise of private virtue' as well as an 'uncomfortable encounter with the underlying matter of war; its investment in waste and ruin and reciprocal destruction of human beings'.[50] Edward Penny's 1764 painting *The Marquis of Granby Giving Alms to a Sick Soldier and his Family* visualizes the cost of war in the figure of the sick soldier requiring sympathy and relief, and approves the soldierly nobility of the marquis in his act of charitable care. Similarly, Henry Mackenzie's *The Man of Feeling* (1771) presents the physical and emotional suffering of the veteran soldier as a test case for sympathetic reaction. In Mackenzie's own favourite, much anthologized, passage, Harley, the landowning man of feeling, is reunited with his old friend Edwards, who having taken his press-ganged son's place in the army in India, returns a poor, injured veteran. Moved by Edwards's life story, Harley responds with tears and a gift of land. Edwards's account includes his own self-sacrificing emotional and benevolent response to the distress of a brutally mistreated Indian prisoner:

> Oh! Mr Harley, had you seen him as I did, with his hands bound behind him, suffering in silence, while the big drops trickled down his shriveled cheeks, and wet his grey beard, which some of the inhuman soldiers plucked in scorn! I could not bear it, I could not for my soul... I found means to let him escape. (p. 70)

Here Mackenzie also begins to explore the regular soldier's own capacity for sympathy, even for the 'enemy', which can incite gentle, nurturing responses rather than fuelling further violence. James Hogg's 1832 short story 'The Adventures of Captain John Lochy' continues Mackenzie's emphasis on the soldier's compulsion to care. Hogg's murderous and battle-thirsty mercenary captain is transformed by his reaction to his

---

[49] As Tristram describes it, Toby is both 'a man of courage' and 'of a peaceful, placid nature,—no jarring element in it,—all was mixed up so kindly within him; my uncle Toby had scarce a heart to retaliate upon a fly', Lawrence Sterne, *The Life and Opinions of Tristram Shandy, Gentleman* (London: Penguin, 2003), p. 100. Uncle Toby takes on Corporal Trim as a personal servant after his injury in combat, which predates Toby's groinal battle wound at Namur. This wound is a major component in the novel's descriptions of Toby's body and character and the pain of Toby's and Trim's injuries punctuates the text. These eighteenth-century models of sensibility are further discussed in chapter 1.

[50] Philip Shaw, 'Wars of Seeing: Suffering and Sentiment in Joseph Wright's "The Dead Soldier"', in *Soldiering in Britain and Ireland*, pp. 76–95, p. 89.

wounded enemy. Seeing a Russian officer 'dying of thirst' dragging himself over the ground between them, Lochy, badly injured himself, 'began to feel an inclination to assist him', which, like Edwards's feeling of being unable to 'bear it', grows to a powerful impulse: 'I could not resist the inclination to assist him.'[51] This meeting catalyses, with similar compulsion, Lochy's critique of the conflict: 'I could not help reflecting on the horrible system of warfare in which I was engaged, which allowed no time either for looking after the wounded or the dead, but still hurrying, hurrying on in the work of further destruction' (p. 110). He resists this destructive momentum, instead saving the Russian officer's life, and becoming his lifelong friend, through the mixed sustenance of water, wound dressing, hand holding, and 'mutual sympathy' (p. 111).

The work of Hogg's friend and sometime literary collaborator Walter Scott, well loved by the Victorian authors considered here, offers rich consideration of the characteristics of the military man of feeling.[52] Scott's *Waverley* (1814), dedicated to Mackenzie, is set in the Jacobite uprising of 1745 and, like Hogg and Mackenzie, questions military allegiance and feeling for a cause. The characteristically vacillating hero Edward Waverley wavers between the opposed sides, serving in both armies and admiring men of deep, apparently equally right, feeling in both armies, notably Charles Stuart himself, and Colonel Talbot and Waverley's former commander, Colonel G____. Waverley's reported contribution to the Battle of Prestonpans is entirely concerned with his efforts to save the lives of these two British officers, and while he succeeds with Talbot he fails to reach Colonel G____ in time, and is haunted by the colonel's dying expression.[53] Hogg's and Scott's work begins a shift, completed by Victorian authors, from the late eighteenth-century emphasis on the suffering soldier—usually the wounded veteran—as a figure inciting sympathy, towards a focus on the fine feelings of the soldier himself. Components observable in depictions of the military in eighteenth- and early nineteenth-century texts concerned with the man of feeling—notably a compulsion to cure not kill, soldierly sympathy, and the arbitrary and emotionally slippery nature of amity and enmity—were developed by mid-Victorian writers to become central features of representations of soldierly heroism across classes.

---

[51] James Hogg, 'The Adventures of Captain John Lochy', in *Altrive Tales* (Edinburgh: Edinburgh University Press, 2005), pp. 79–159, p. 110.

[52] For a fuller account of Scott's depictions of honourable soldiering attentive to the physical and emotional well-being of others, including the exhausted adversaries Fitzjames and Roderick Dhu tending each other, sharing food, and sleeping side by side before fighting each other the next day in *The Lady of the Lake* (1810), see Girouard, *The Return to Camelot*, p. 35.

[53] Walter Scott, *Waverley* (London: Penguin, 2011), p. 241.

SENSIBILITY, MILITARISM, AND ETHICS

The same *Times* leader that questioned the brutality of the soldier and exposed his current suffering also characterized its readers as 'indulging in all the sentiment of the affair' from the comfort of their homes but taking little action. Written by the paper's Constantinople correspondent Thomas Chenery, the article argues that for the 'luxurious' 'fireside' spectators, 'the suffering is sadly vicarious': 'Is it fit that the soldier should suffer everything and we not at all?' As Favret has argued, these ethical questions of how to respond to reports of suffering at a distance had already become a concern in the Romantic period. New media brought geographically (and sometimes temporally) distant events affectively close as writers and readers were 'touched and moved by the unaccountable violence of war' and became alert to 'the obstacles to such responsiveness, the negating effects of modern war and modern mediations of war'.[54] For many the Crimean War was felt to be closer still, via photographs, more efficient international postal systems, fast telegraphic communication, and, especially, uncensored reports of soldiers' suffering in a fully established periodical press supplied by dedicated foreign and war correspondents and by soldiers themselves. Chenery's account of the state of the wounded troops caused widespread shock—recorded by many of the authors discussed here, including Thackeray, Dickens, and Kingsley—and such reportage caused a sea change in public opinion about the waging of the war which ultimately led to the toppling of the Aberdeen government.

By establishing a fund to which readers could financially contribute *The Times* offered one possible, partial solution to the ethical problem of how to respond to the pain of others. Campaigning hard for contributions to that fund, the paper also offered an unusually frank consideration of the pleasures of 'devouring' the news of war as 'a very amusing spectacle': 'But, while we are all in the third heaven of martial ecstasy, there is one little consideration that must now and then abate the sublimity of our enjoyment. What are we doing for the cause we have so much at heart? Is it right that these poor fellows should bear the whole of the burden?' Chenery's leader speculates about the emotional response of readers forced to recognize the soldiers' suffering: 'not exactly ashamed' but 'somehow rather smaller than usual'.[55] Rehearsing the problems most thoroughly

---

[54] Favret, *War at a Distance*, p. 233.
[55] Ho argues that 'the phrase "smaller than usual" suggests one effect of perusing such reports is to compromise a civilian's sense of masculinity in the domestic sphere in wartime', *Civilian Poets*, p. 37.

explored in an eighteenth-century literature of sentiment, including Mackenzie's *Man of Feeling* and Sterne's *Tristram Shandy*, the article asks how the luxurious pleasures of empathizing with suffering might be transformed into something close to shame, and a sense of personal diminishment, and how these difficult feelings should be directed into action; it considers the possibility that the scale of the cause will overwhelm the capacity for felt response as 'the amount of suffering is so great that its very magnitude robs it of sympathy'. *The Times* raises these ethical dilemmas in order to offer a solution that will soothe the 'uneasiness of a sensitive mind': 'here is happily provided an occasion for that sympathy, which, as we observed above, the terrible details of warfare ought to awaken'. By contributing to the fund, readers could relieve soldiers' suffering and their own, distinguishing themselves from the shameful position of the fireside pleasure spectator by registering that they had the appropriate response to 'the terrible details of warfare' and 'showing how' their 'hearts beat' for the allies.

The Times leader tackles the same problem, which structured much of the eighteenth-century exploration of sentiment, how to respond appropriately to the pain of others (including the kinds of pain caused by war: penury, illness, wounding, bereavement) and what is the relationship between felt response and action? In the context of the Crimean conflict *The Times* returns to older questions about the cultural role of the suffering soldier and also promises to resolve a perennial, possibly unsolvable, problem that continues to be crucial to war and peace studies: how far can recognizing the horror of war change us at an individual and cultural level? Thinkers like Susan Sontag and Yuval Harari have exposed the fallacy of a widespread hope or presumption that a better understanding of the horror of war and an appreciation of the humanity of the enemy will lead to a reduction or even cessation of belligerence.[56] Tolstoy makes this point in *War and Peace* when the French soldiers take up a wave of laughter from the Russian lines, 'so spontaneously that you would have thought the only thing to do was to unload the guns, blow up the ammunition and get back home as soon as possible. But the muskets remained loaded, the marksmen's slits in buildings and earthworks stared out as ominously as ever, and the big guns stood ready, ranged against each other' (p. 185).[57] Tempering these serious reservations about the limits to

---

[56] Susan Sontag, *Regarding the Pain of Others* (London: Penguin, 2004), p. 12. Yuval Harari, *The Ultimate Experience: Battlefield Revelations and the Making of Modern War Culture, 1450–2000* (Basingstoke: Palgrave, 2008), p. 229, p. 304.

[57] See also Tolstoy's similarly poignant account in 'Sebastopol in May' of how the observation of the humanity and suffering, and in this case broadly shared religion, of the other side during a truce does nothing to prevent the subsequent continuation of the

the transformative power of fellow feeling and sympathy, many thinkers maintain hope that emotional responses to war can change perceptions and behaviour. Judith Butler, for example, presents the ethical obligation to acknowledge shared precariousness as a condition of humanity, and considers how Western war is enabled by a refusal of shared vulnerability—a repudiation of the belligerent power's equal capacity for hurt, fear, loss—and by the devaluation of other populations as worth less.[58]

The swerve towards ameliorative narratives with which this book is concerned is part of a wider pattern of war discourse identified by Elaine Scarry in which wounding drops out of view. Through a plethora of figurative strategies the activity of war is presented as everything other than its core pursuit, injuring. This elision of injuring also obscures the shattering of cultures and ideologies within the dismembered body (in Scarry's elaboration the body and embodied memory, for example, of a bicycle-riding, piano-playing British citizen who has also learnt, in line with the nation's physical practice, to hold her eyebrows slightly elevated—'what is remembered in the body is well remembered'[59]). Although mass wounding is disavowed as the central aim and activity of war, only the visceral inscription of that cultural destruction will legitimate the replacement of the loser's ideologies with the winner's, substantiating the war's outcome. As Scarry puts it, 'the visible and experiencable alteration of injury has a *compelling and vivid reality* because it resides in the human body, the original site of reality, and more specifically because of the "extremity" or "endurance" of the alteration'.[60] Following Scarry's argument that the body remembers, narratives that reroute wounding into stories of nurturing, preserving, and remaking the body, particularly when that body is the enemy's, may not just offer another form of the culturally agreed elision of injuring, but also have a more radical capacity in preserving not only the body, but the body language, the embodied culture of the opposite side, and refusing the intertwined physical, cultural, ideological unmaking of the other. The irresistible compulsion to relieve, nurse, and nurture the suffering, described by Mackenzie and Hogg and developed in Crimean War period narratives, offers a powerful reversal of

---

fighting: 'It might be supposed that when these men—Christians, recognising the same great law of love—see what they have done, they will instantly fall to their knees... Not a bit of it!', *Sebastopol Sketches*, p. 108.

[58] Judith Butler, *Precarious Life: The Power of Mourning and Violence* (London and New York: Verso, 2004), and *Frames of War: When is Life Grievable?* (London and New York: Verso, 2009).

[59] Elaine Scarry, *The Body in Pain: The Making and Unmaking of the World* (Oxford: Oxford University Press, 1985), p. 109.

[60] Scarry, *The Body in Pain*, p. 121.

the capacity for combined physical and cultural shattering on which war relies. In representations of the military man of feeling the impulse presented as natural is to preserve rather than destroy the body. The perceived heroism of soldiers who physically care for allies and enemies—and perhaps care for enemies has the greatest heroic status—exposes cultural discomfort about war. The preference for gentle rather than wounding soldiers has within it the radical potential that the destruction of all bodies/cultures/ideologies be recognized as unacceptable.

Gentle soldiers, or in Joanna Bourke's and Ian Brownlie's terms 'kind-hearted gunmen', also have an opposite potential to legitimate war as a form of humanitarian endeavour.[61] Napoleon used the persona of the caring general to good strategic effect; early histories highlighted details of how 'he used to cry at night for his poor family of soldiers' and he presented his physical presence as a salve to suffering, commissioning paintings that featured him visiting the wounded and showing sympathy to captured enemy soldiers.[62] As Martin argues, the cult of Napoleon's supposedly caring personality and broader appeals to the idea of a military family were ways in which 'the army exploited male intimacy and fraternity as a means of successful integration and a safeguard against desertion'.[63] Infamously the Nazi SS presented themselves as men of feeling, in a particularly jarring extension of many soldiers' expression of sympathy for those they kill, drawing on a long history legitimating killing that is combined with right feeling.[64] Christian theological arguments of this kind, as we shall see in chapter 2, offered powerful, though not uncontested, support for the waging of the Crimean War. Extending from examples of 'sentimentality' 'as entirely compatible with a taste for brutality and worse', Sontag argues that 'it is not necessarily better to be moved'. She points to the ethical problems of feeling for the other both for those who inflict and for those who witness suffering: 'So far as we feel sympathy, we feel we are not accomplices to what caused the suffering. Our sympathy proclaims our innocence as well as our impotence.'[65] The

---

[61] Joanna Bourke, *Wounding the World: How Military Violence and War Play Invade Our Lives* (London: Virago, 2014). Ian Brownlie, 'Thoughts on Kind-Hearted Gunmen', in *Humanitarian Intervention and the United Nations*, ed. Richard B. Lillich (Charlottesville: University Press of Virginia, 1973), pp. 139–48.
[62] Martin, *Napoleonic Friendship*, p. 203, Harari, *The Ultimate Experience*, p. 228. Sarah Knott also discusses Napoleon's plan for a sentimental novel, 'Sensibility and the American War for Independence', *American Historical Review* 10.9 (2004), pp. 19–41, p. 38.
[63] Martin, *Napoleonic Friendship*, p. 34.
[64] Harari discusses the importance that SS members, including Rudolph Höss who commanded Auschwitz, placed on proving that 'they remained decent men-of-feeling despite their horrific "job"', *The Ultimate Experience*, p. 296.
[65] Sontag, *Regarding the Pain of Others*, p. 91.

military man of feeling, then, performs complex and controversial cultural work, raising difficult questions about the functions of expressions of soldiers' feelings, and about civilians' emotional responses to, and sympathy for, soldiers. Clearly the military man of feeling could be put to a whole range of political uses. This figure can offer a justification of violence through, for instance, an appeal of the wounded feelings of the perpetrator; it can also challenge attitudes about the soldier, particularly the working-class soldier, enabling broader shifts of views on manliness and class; and it can contribute to valuable social reforms. A cultural celebration of the gentle soldier might also, to extend Scarry's arguments, entail a remaking of the world in which countries become unwilling to assert their own ideologies through wounding as the destruction of other embodied cultures.

My title *Military Men of Feeling* takes in this complex history, looking back to the significance of the suffering soldier in eighteenth-century debates about sensibility, and emphasizing the continuity of these discussions about the combination of the ethics of feeling and response through the period of the Crimean War. It also seeks to position the book within continuing, broader scholarship about the relationship between emotion, war, and the possible end to war. I believe that these lines of thinking have the potential to change tolerances for war, and that necessary to that thinking is a better understanding of the felt history of war, the ways in which war violence has been made emotionally acceptable for civilians and survivable for some of those engaged in it.

'WAR IS MANY CONTRADICTORY THINGS': SUSPICIOUS AND REPARATIVE STRATEGIES AND THE POLITICS OF AFFECT

War photographer Tim Hetherington captured the range of affective experiences of US soldiers in Battle Company, 173rd Airborne, at war in Afghanistan in 2007–8, including moments of aggression, grieving, machismo, vulnerability, and strategies of home making. His project has similarities to mine in its rejection of persistent stereotypes of macho military masculinity via attention to details of soldiers' emotional and tactile experience. Hetherington concluded that 'war is many contradictory things. There is brutality and heroism, comedy and tragedy, friendship, hate, love and boredom.'[66] Much of the best scholarship on

---

[66] Tim Hetherington, *Infidel* (London: Chris Boot, 2010), p. 240.

nineteenth-century warfare makes a similar point. As John Reed has argued of Victorian war narratives, 'patriotic and imperial impulses jostle with antiwar sentiment, often within the oeuvre of a single writer' and there is 'an uneasy tension between glorifying individual heroics and recognizing war's cost'.[67] These tensions result, in part, from what Brown calls the 'ambivalent place of war in a liberal society'.[68] Markovits documents the equally possible competing interpretations of Tennyson's *Maud* which led to its appropriation by pro-peace and pro-war factions, and recent readings of the Crimean War's most famous text, Tennyson's 'The Charge of the Light Brigade' (1854), have called into question even this poem's apparently straightforward honouring of bellicose willingness to 'do and die'.[69] Bevis draws out Tennyson's 'dual depiction of war as both ennobling and horrifying', and observes how the poem, especially in its persistent iteration of 'err' and 'erred', 'sounds war's heroism, but it also sounds it out'.[70] Bevis's argument that Victorian war poets 'often require us to see double' applies across the wide range of genres I consider in what follows, describing the response needed to work produced by both soldiers and civilians.[71] As we shall see, much of this material simultaneously critiques and romanticizes war, performing contradictory emotional work that encourages the reader, variously, to adopt anti- and pro-war stances.

A method of paranoid/reparative reading structures my navigation of these affectively complex materials, which generate, as is typical of war writing, divergent and competing strands of interpretation. My practice of blending or moving between different interpretative lines follows the inspiration Eve Sedgwick takes from Melanie Klein's theorizing of 'positions', rather than 'ordered stages, stable structures'. Klein advocates a 'flexible to-and-fro movement' between positions, which Sedgwick sees as useful in thinking of 'paranoid and reparative critical practices' 'as changing and heterogenous relational stances'.[72] Paranoid, or suspicious, reading is characterized by a keen critical eye for unveiling hidden power systems and concerned with, as Sedgwick puts it, 'the detection of hidden patterns of violence and their exposure'.[73] Reparative reading provides an

---

[67] John Reed, 'The Victorians and War', in *The Cambridge Companion to War Writing*, ed. Kate McLoughlin (Cambridge: Cambridge University Press, 2009), pp. 135–47, p. 135, p. 145.
[68] Brown, '"Like a Devoted Army"', p. 622.
[69] Markovits, *The Crimean War*, chapter 3, part 2.
[70] Bevis, 'Fighting Talk', p. 14, p. 16. I discuss other nuanced readings of this poem, particularly the important work of Trudi Tate, in chapter 1.
[71] Bevis, 'Fighting Talk', p. 9.
[72] Eve Kosofsky Sedgwick, *Touching Feeling: Affect, Pedagogy, Performativity* (Durham and London: Duke University Press, 2003), p. 128.
[73] Sedgwick, *Touching Feeling*, p. 143.

additional, supplementary position, enabled by the recognition that paranoid reading might not be the only possibility, nor offer a complete account of the material. Sedgwick proposes paranoid-reparative reading as part of an exploration of 'promising tools and techniques for nondualistic thought'.[74] Readings of war literature can be stymied by a dualistic perspective that seeks to establish whether a text's stance is predominantly pro- or anti-war.[75] By contrast, a paranoid-reparative critical practice allows competing interpretations to coexist, overlapping and interrupting each other, and recognizes the intermixture of affective work—enabling and critiquing—performed by war writing.

Many of the texts considered in this book use the gentle soldier as a means to feel better about war, distracting attention away from difficult questions about the justice of the Crimean War or indeed any war, displacing unease via an exemplary military figure that can be celebrated. As will become clear, especially in my accounts of material produced by soldiers themselves, I feel the pull—compelling, moving, ameliorating—of this material. I use a blended method of reading to resist any straightforward experience of feeling better. Instead I draw upon the different sense of feeling better—more intensely, more thoughtfully, oxymoronically more painfully—to argue for an emotionally nuanced, often ambivalent reaction to the culturally powerful figure of the military man of feeling.

[74] Sedgwick, *Touching Feeling*, p. 1.
[75] Catherine Robson notes how criticism of Felicia Hemans's 1826 poem 'Casabianca', about the most famous child casualty of the Battle of the Nile, clashes over whether the poem is imperial and patriarchal or 'antinationalist and feminist', *Heart Beats: Everyday Life and the Memorized Poem* (Princeton and Oxford: Princeton University Press, 2012), pp. 113–16. Similar oppositional readings have preoccupied much work on other nineteenth-century war epics, including Tennyson's 'The Charge of the Light Brigade' (1854) and 'Maud' (1855). See Reed, 'The Victorians and War', on competing interpretations of Tennyson.

1

'The company of gentlemen'

Thackeray's Military Men of Feeling and Eighteenth-Century Traditions

Thackeray's Colonel Newcome is the exemplary Victorian military man of feeling. Protagonist of *The Newcomes* (1853–5), published during the Crimean War and Thackeray's most popular work with Victorian readers, Colonel Newcome draws upon a mixed eighteenth-century literary and historical heritage of prominent men of war and men of feeling and combines this with contemporary deliberations about the composition of the officer and the gentleman. *The Newcomes*, which focuses on the titular family's fortunes, particularly those of the colonel and his son Clive, combines longer debates about sensibility with Victorian class reform concerns. The colonel's gentlemanliness was widely commended throughout the latter half of the nineteenth century. Anthony Trollope, for example, declared that '*The Newcomes* stands conspicuous for the character of the Colonel, who as an English gentleman has no equal in English fiction... Colonel Newcome is the finest single character in English fiction.'[1] Thackeray presents Colonel Newcome's exemplary character as formed by his experiences of reading. The colonel's selection of inspiring books draws on competing eighteenth-century traditions of militaristic masculinity, and of pacifistic sensibility. This chapter considers the rich intertextuality of *The Newcomes*, looking at the books the colonel chooses to take to war, and at the novel's battlefield afterlives in soldiers' (often unexpected) choices of reading material.

Readerly responses to Colonel Newcome, eloquently expressed by Trollope, echoed the enthusiastic appraisals of this figure within the novel.

---

[1] *Cornhill Magazine*, Feb 1864. Quoted in R. D. MacMaster, 'Composition, Publication and Reception', in William Makepeace Thackeray, *The Newcomes*, ed. Peter Shillingsburg (Michigan: University of Michigan Press, 1996), pp. 371–90, p. 385. Other early responses praised the colonel as a 'noble creation'; 'within the whole scope of fiction there is no single character which stands out more nobly'; *The Times*, 29 August 1855; George Smith, *Edinburgh Review*, Jan 1873, both quoted by MacMaster, pp. 384–5.

Despite his shortcomings the colonel incites particular devotion in Arthur Pendennis, the principal narrator and putative editor of the text, and is widely praised by other characters. He is described by fellow military men as 'one of the bravest officers that ever lived' and as 'one of the kindest fellows', while widows are attracted to 'a man so generally liked... with such a good character, with a private fortune of his own, so chivalrous, generous, good looking'.[2] Though closer to an ideal of character than is usual in Thackeray's work—Dobbin, the commended military gentle man of *Vanity Fair* (1847–8) is the other notable exception—the colonel is clearly shown to have faults. These include, perhaps most tragically, his failure to see women for themselves, as he prefers to view romance through an unrealistic chivalric lens. The colonel's excessive idealization of women results in his promotion of his beloved son's disastrous marriage. Given that another of the novel's central critical enquiries is the trading of women as property on the marriage market, the colonel's failure to value women as individuals is presented as a clear character flaw.[3] Reviewers, however, tended to ignore this, instead replicating the adoration expressed for the colonel in the novel.

The beloved colonel often provoked powerful emotional reactions. A *Spectator* review describes the tears shed over Colonel Newcome's death, and popular accounts reported that Thackeray had been found weeping by his housekeeper after writing this scene.[4] Similarly, an account of Thackeray reading the death of Newcome aloud records that 'the tears which had been swelling his lids for some time trickled down his face and the last word was almost an inarticulate sob'.[5] At other times Thackeray, characteristically (as the author committed to the form and philosophy of the 'Novel without a Hero', as he famously put it in the subtitle to *Vanity Fair*), took a more ambivalent view of his leading man, undercutting his own affective response: 'Colonel Newcome' he wrote to a friend, 'is a dear old boy, but confess you think he's rather a twaddler.'[6] Although the

---

[2] William Makepeace Thackeray, *The Newcomes* (London: Dent, 1994), p. 67, p. 55. Further references in parentheses are to this edition.

[3] For readings that identify Thackeray's critique of the marriage market as a central concern of the novel see Michael Lund, *Reading Thackeray* (Detroit: Wayne State University Press, 1988), and Donald Hall, *Fixing Patriarchy: Feminism and Mid-Victorian Male Novelists* (New York: New York University Press, 1997).

[4] Robert Colby, *Thackeray's Canvass of Humanity: An Author and His Public* (Columbus: Ohio State University Press, 1979), note 58, p. 393.

[5] Mario Praz, *The Hero in Eclipse in Victorian Fiction* (Oxford: Oxford University Press, 1956), p. 215.

[6] Quoted by Philip Collins, *From Manly Tear to Stiff Upper Lip: The Victorians and Pathos* (Wellington, New Zealand: Victoria University Press, undated, based on a 1974 lecture), p. 11.

colonel had widespread sentimental appeal, the gentlemanly ideal he represents is far from simple. Celebratory readings (which continued, as we shall see, until at least the First World War) participated in an active debate, to which Thackeray's novel self-consciously contributed, about the characteristics of the ideal Victorian gentleman, and the appropriate components of martial and civil manliness. Via Thackeray's loveable gentle officer, and responses to this character through the long nineteenth century, this chapter considers interrelated discussions about appropriate classed behaviour, democratized manly virtue, military might, and army reform.

'THE COMPANY OF GENTLEMEN', PART 1: *THE NEWCOMES: MEMOIRS OF A MOST RESPECTABLE FAMILY*

Thackeray clearly positions his eminently gentle military man within the wider terms of the contemporary debate about the constitution of the gentleman. The colonel's father is a proto-Smilesean self-made man, his own origins obscure before 'having made his entry into London on a waggon, which landed him and some bales of cloth, all his fortune' (p. 14). Thomas Newcome senior prospers through a combination of industry and upright character, his business in weaving and merchandising flourishing in large part due to the fidelity he shows his first love.[7] The family's priorities, however, shift towards the mercilessly mercenary with the death of the colonel's mother and his father's remarriage, on which he become's partner in the family banking business of his second wife, a shrewd businesswoman who outlives her husband. The family business and fortune passes to the colonel's two younger twin stepbrothers, Brian and Hobson, who treat the colonel with coolness on his return from India and later fail to relieve his financial distress and eventual penury. As in Tennyson's *Maud*, discussed in the Introduction, Thackeray presents banking and speculative capitalism as a form of civil war (adding to these the ruthless social climbing that new money enables), rupturing domestic affections and destroying families. Both texts, responding to the unfolding conflict in the Crimea, suggest that aggressive capitalism inflicts greater cultural damage than war. Thackeray presents the financial sector

---

[7] 'The whole countryside was pleased to think of the prosperous London tradesman returning to keep his promise to the penniless girl whom he had loved in the days of his own poverty; the great country clothiers, who knew his prudence and honesty, gave him much of their business when he went back to London' (p. 16).

as a threat to the values and straightforward martial code of honour embodied by Colonel Newcome, including honesty and a trust of others that is shown to be excessive; the colonel, like the father of Tennyson's monodramatist, loses his fortune in a failed speculation.

Thackeray carefully differentiates the styles of masculinity adopted by the leading Newcomes. The colonel's simplicity is contrasted to the mutually defining roles adopted by his banking stepbrothers. While Hobson 'affected the country gentleman' and was 'pleased to be so taken—for a jolly country squire', Brian 'looked like the "Portrait of a Gentleman at the Exhibition," as the worthy is represented: dignified in attitude, bland, smiling, and statesmanlike, sitting at a table unsealing letters, with a despatch-box and a silver inkstand before him, a column and a scarlet curtain behind' (pp. 61–2). Characteristically Thackeray presents both modes as poses, approximations of recognizable models of manliness.[8] A third major type or style of the period the novel surveys (the late eighteenth century to the 1840s), the dandy, is represented by Brian's son Barnes, 'a fair-haired young gentleman, languid and pale, and arrayed in the very height of fashion' (p. 63). The reliance these men place on costume, self-, and home furnishing is threaded with a characteristically Thackerean irony given their disavowed heritage of weavers and clothiers. In describing these masculine performances Thackeray emphasizes affectation, fashion, looking like, being taken for, and life modelling art. In this he anticipates Butler's, now classic, theoretical work on the inauthenticity of gender. In Hobson's, Brian's, and Barnes's varied performances of gentlemanliness, 'the essence or identity that they otherwise purport to express are *fabrications* manufactured and sustained through corporeal signs and other discursive means'.[9] In the trappings of sober business (letters and despatch box) and furnishings connotative of wealth and social standing (silver inkstand) with which the narrator imaginatively surrounds Brian in the artist's impression, complete with the column and scarlet curtain of the studio, the effortful work of gender fabrication is apparent. Thackeray, then, perhaps more than any of his contemporaries, establishes at the outset of his study of what makes a gentleman that the gentleman is a social construct, a label attached via social consensus rather than arising from any innate or unchanging qualities.

---

[8] The historical significance of stylization and theatricality are emphasized in James Eli Adams's *Dandies and Desert Saints: Styles of Victorian Masculinity* (Ithaca and London: Cornell University Press, 1995). Indeed Adams's title 'points to the importance of this anxious conjunction of discipline and performance in middle-class Victorian constructions of masculinity', p. 10.

[9] Judith Butler, *Gender Trouble: Feminism and the Subversion of Identity* (London: Routledge, 1990), p. 173.

Nonetheless, a quest to identify the qualities and qualifications of the perfect gentleman is a major concern of this tale of social newcomers, and *the* dominant concern in readers' responses to the novel. Colonel Newcome, who for Trollope and many other readers was the authentic 'English gentleman' with 'no equal', has a somewhat contradictory stance on the extent to which the gentleman is born or made, which accurately reflects the broader cultural confusion on this issue. Unlike his pompous stepbrothers, who are attached to a spurious family etymology through which they can trace themselves to a 'surgeon to Edward the Confessor', the colonel is realistic about the recent wealth of his family. The colonel delivers the following major lesson to his young son Clive, in a novel also deeply concerned with forms of education:

> I think every man would like to come of an ancient and honourable race... As you like your father to be an honourable man, why not your grandfather, and his ancestors before him? But if we can't inherit a good name, at least we can do our best to leave one, my boy; and that is an ambition, please God, you and I will both hold by. (p. 71)

Here good birth is desirable but not essential to the possession of a 'good name', which may also be achieved through effort, and is an ideal to which to aspire. For Colonel Newcome the military presents an ideal opportunity to make one's own name. As Robert Colby puts it, 'in emphasising through the colonel that respectability is something transmitted rather than inherited, Thackeray did his part to bring *gentillesse* within the purview of the middle-class'.[10] Elsewhere, though, the colonel is less flexible in his thinking, and he certainly rules out the possibility of a more radical social mobility suggested by the working-class gentleman, a figure explored through characters such as Dinah Craik's *John Halifax, Gentleman* (1856) and Charles Dickens's Pip and Joe (*Great Expectations*, 1860).[11]

Colonel Newcome has a strict code of conduct that he expects those born into the land-owning classes to abide by; deviation from this code is a major cause of his frustration with the coarseness of Fielding, a favourite novelist of Thackeray's: 'If Mr Fielding was a gentleman by birth,' says the colonel, 'he ought to have known better; and so much the

---

[10] Colby, *Thackeray's Canvass of Humanity*, p. 264.

[11] I have explored the centrality of the question of what makes a gentleman to mid-Victorian culture, and the ways in which such literary explorations are often routed through plots of physical and emotional gentleness, particularly via narratives of male nursing, in 'Negotiating the Gentle-Man: Male Nursing and Class Conflict in the "High" Victorian Period', in *Conflict and Difference in Nineteenth Century Literature*, ed. Dinah Birch and Mark Llewellyn (Basingstoke: Palgrave, 2010), pp. 109–25.

worse for him that he did not' (p. 42). Here and throughout the novel Colonel Newcome insists on strict delineation of social and military rank, suggesting that to be a gentleman, here defined by class and occupation, is the 'lot' of some men but not others: 'I am as little proud as many in the world, but there must be distinction, sir; and as it is my lot and Clive's lot to be a gentleman, I won't sit in the kitchen and boose in the servant's hall' (p. 41). Clive expresses an instinctive understanding of such 'distinction', which seems, though Thackeray is explicit that Clive's theory is not fully coherent, to depend on character and personal, rather than social, worth: 'It isn't rank and that; only somehow there are some men gentlemen and some not' (p. 70).[12] By virtue of his nobility of character, Colonel Newcome, as generations of readers enthusiastically maintained, was more of a gentleman than his wealthier, fashionable society banking brothers with their assertions of ancestral pedigree.

The novel's exploration of civilian and military styles of gentlemanliness takes on a distinct urgency in the context of wider debates about whether by being a nation so fit for trade, Britain had become unfit for war. British military prowess was already being tested during the period in which *The Newcomes* was composed and published. Serialization of the novel began in October 1853, at the same time as Russian hostilities against Turkey. The final part was issued in August 1855, a month before the Russians surrendered Sebastopol.[13] During the early part of the Crimean War Thackeray also commented on it directly through a series of squib foreign correspondence sketches for *Punch*, 'Important from the Seat of War! Letters from the East by Our Own Bashi Bouzouk' (June–August 1854). These sketches share central concerns of *The Newcomes* with the value and emotional effects of different forms of reading in wartime, and the appropriate form for documenting war. Though less explicitly responding to the unfolding conflict *The Newcomes* also includes some direct

---

[12] These half-articulated and contradictory ideas represent what Arlene Young has described as a broad concern in the mid-nineteenth century with whether 'manners' could take precedence 'over lineage as the essential defining quality of gentlemanliness'. Arlene Young, *Culture, Class and Gender in the Victorian Novel: Gentlemen, Gents and Working Women* (Basingstoke: Macmillan, 1999), p. 37. See also Robin Gilmour, *The Ideal of the Gentleman in the Victorian Novel* (London: Allen and Unwin, 1981), who sees this topic as 'a major, perhaps the major, concern of Thackeray's fiction', p. 38. Gilmour documents how Thackeray and his contemporaries posed 'testing questions about the constituent elements of the gentleman. How important were birth and breeding in making a gentleman? Was heredity more important than environment...? Could a "natural gentility" exist without the patent of birth, and if so, how much was this a matter of moral qualities and how much a matter of education and fine clothes?', p. 33.

[13] The war officially ended with the Peace of Paris, signed in March 1856.

references to it, such as an analogy with Florence Nightingale and the relief brought to the 'sick and wounded in our private Scutaris' (p. 608), and engages with cultural concerns brought into particular focus by the war. The mismanagement of the war led to widespread calls for reform of government and army, and the formation of the short-lived Administrative Reform Association, of which Thackeray and Dickens (as shall be explored in the next chapter) were members. While the war was the immediate catalyst for the foundation of the association, its aims were wider—the reduction of jobbism in the military and all areas of government, so that roles were allocated according to ability rather than social rank. The resolutions of the association were reported in *The Household Narrative of Current Events*, Dickens's sister publication to *Household Words*:

1. That the disasters to which the country has been subjected in the conduct of the present war are attributable to the Inefficient and practically irresponsible management of the various departments of the state, and urgently demand a thorough change in the administrative system.

The association used the emotive example of the mismanagement of the war to garner support for its wider efforts to end the 'monopoly' of 'aristocratic classes' 'in the councils of the crown' so that roles be allocated to those with the 'practical qualities necessary'.[14] These aims were in line with a broader cultural shift from the Napoleonic Wars through to the 1850s 'from', as John Peck summarizes, 'an aristocratic military dispensation, to a middle-class liberal culture'.[15] This shift was significant, as John Reed argues, in the transformation of approved styles of manliness, as 'the flamboyant aristocratic model inherited from the eighteenth century was gradually rejected and supplanted by a restrained and virtuous middle-class model'.[16] The largely middle-class membership of the Administrative Reform Association promoted the efficiency of industry as more successful than leadership based on aristocratic hierarchy and ability to pay. James Eli Adams has noted the attention that Thackeray gives to a reformist class-based shift in military masculinities in *Vanity Fair*:

Whereas George Osborn envisions himself as a throwback to the traditional, aristocratic gentleman, compounded of martial valour, dashing presence and unlimited credit, William Dobbin incarnates a humbler ideal, more suited to

---

[14] [Anon.], 'Narrative of Parliament and Politics', *The Household Narrative of Current Events*, vol. 6, no. 5 (May 1855), pp. 97–110, p. 110.
[15] John Peck, *War, the Army and Victorian Literature* (Basingstoke: Palgrave, 1998), p. ix.
[16] John Reed, 'Soldier Boy: Forming Masculinity in Adam Bede', *Studies in the Novel*, 33.3 (2001), pp. 268–84.

an emergent middle class...He finds fulfilment in duty (military and domestic) and kindness to the weak.[17]

Like Dobbin, who is briefly resurrected in *The Newcomes* to confirm the colonel's credentials—'there is not a more gallant or respected officer in the service' (p. 132)—the colonel's caring behaviour, informed by the values of home, and domestic fiction, is suitable for a democratized army.

Although wartime is often associated with a restraint of feeling, commended by the *Critic* in 1847 as preferable to the 'social plague' of sentimentalism which is said to gain an ascendancy in peacetime, Colonel Newcome's expansive capacity for emotional response is with the grain of Crimean War period narratives.[18] During this conflict, a wide range of cultural forms presented the military man not as less susceptible to sentiment, but as intensely so. In this climate of supposed increased emphasis on manly restraint, and this period of acute anxiety about the efficiency of the British army, the military figure most applauded was notable, not for a stiff upper lip, but for a particular capacity for feeling. While figures like Thomas Carlyle were carving out spaces for civilian heroism through a transposition of warrior language into civic life, an overhaul of the martial ideal took place through an application of civic ideals, especially domestic and familial ideals, to the soldier. Adams argues that Carlyle's famous phrase 'Captains of Industry' 'gained wide cultural currency because it attached to the economic power of the entrepreneur the status of a traditional martial ideal and thereby solidified the social authority of what had been at best a fragile norm of manhood under an aristocratic ethos contemptuous of trade'.[19] Brown makes a similar point about the application of martial language to the medical profession in the mid-nineteenth century in order to recognize the often self-risking courageousness of doctors, and petition for their greater pay and cultural prestige.[20] During the same period, however, the impetus also went the other way towards the civilizing of the soldier through the transposition of middle-class values into the traditionally aristocratic hierarchy.

Composite of competing traditions of approved manliness, Colonel Newcome reinterprets the aristocratic ideal of the noble officer for a

---

[17] James Eli Adams, *A History of Victorian Literature* (Oxford: Wiley-Blackwell, 2009), p. 118.
[18] 'Sentimentalism', *Critic* 6 (December 1847), p. 370. Carolyn Burdett places this piece in a context of broader journalistic critiques of sentiment at mid-century in her 'Introduction, Sentimentalities', New Agenda section, *Journal of Victorian Culture* 16.2 (2011), pp. 187–94, p. 188.
[19] Adams, *Dandies and Desert Saints*, p. 6.
[20] Michael Brown, '"Like a Devoted Army": Medicine, Heroic Masculinity, and the Military Paradigm in Victorian Britain', *Journal of British Studies* 49.3 (2010), pp. 592–622.

more bourgeois age and for a predominantly middle-class audience, and takes the eighteenth-century man of feeling into an era in which manly restraint and reason was, so the accepted chronology goes, more recommended than manly tears and emotional response. The air of nostalgia and anachronism with which Thackeray imbues this character, who is perceived by others in the novel as old-fashioned, suggests the difficulties of constituting an ideal gentleman in a period which celebrated difficult to reconcile models of masculinity, from domestic sensitivity to imperial aggression. While the colonel draws upon old-fashioned literary models of manliness—he styles himself after *The Spectator*'s 'old English gentleman' Roger de Coverley and Samuel Richardson's Sir Charles Grandison, and is known in India as Don Quixote—his infusion of feeling and of bourgeois civilian values into his admired version of military manliness is, as we shall see, very much of the age.

'THE COLONEL AT HOME': FATHERLY FEELING

Through the figure of a military man, who has served a full career in the East India Company, and whose primary emotional connection is to his son, Thackeray explores the constitution of the gentleman through his public position as servant of empire and domestic role as father. Having decided not to remarry after his own painful experience of being stepmothered, the widowed Colonel Newcome resolves to be 'father and mother too' (p. 56) to Clive.

Though the gentleman was, in one sense, a public category that defined social status, this novel, like many others of the period, is more concerned by the embodiment of gentle manliness within the private sphere. Indeed, the colonel's homecoming inaugurates the narrative.[21] Various connections were made between the identities of father, soldier, and enfranchised citizen in the debates that resulted in the First and Second Reform Acts (1832, 1867). As we shall see in chapter 2, these connections were crucial to the case for the responsibility and respectability of the working man as deserving of the vote. The links between the domestic leadership of the loving father and his capacity for effective public service also advanced the middle-class agenda of the Administrative Reform Association, promoting

---

[21] Colby notes the prevalence of chapter titles, such as 'The Colonel at Home', that direct the reader to the significance of the domestic, and connect the novel to the numbers of contemporary domestic dramas promoted in the accompanying 'Newcomes Advertiser', *Thackeray's Canvass of Humanity*, p. 360.

a bourgeois model of emotionally intelligent hands-on management and care over a more imperious aristocratic mode.

The Newcomes centres on the colonel's efforts to create a more meaningful relationship with his son, now a young man, after a seven-year separation.[22] Colonel Newcome endeavours, to use Tosh's categorization of dominant styles of Victorian fatherhood, to move from the model of 'absent' father, separated, in this case reluctantly, from his children in order to fulfil the professional commitment of an Indian posting, to 'intimate' fatherhood.[23] Indeed, Thackeray anticipates Tosh's scale of diverse fathering modes: 'Our good Colonel was not of the tyrannous but of the loving order of fathers' (p. 199). Following Tosh, a growing body of work has continued to dispel an unhelpful but persistent image of the autocratic Victorian paterfamilias. Valerie Sanders's wonderful study of Victorian fathers through their own testimony of letters and diaries, for example, challenges the stereotype by 'changing the perspective from which' the father 'is viewed'.[24] In Colonel Newcome Thackeray offers a detailed account of the affects of fatherhood as experienced by the father himself, which dwells on the emotional intensity of the colonel's feeling for his son.

Colonel Newcome is bereft at his separation from young Clive. Thackeray describes the colonel's 'constant longing affection', his 'grief and loneliness' at parting, 'his tender and faithful heart'. 'The kind father had been longing' for their reunion 'more passionately than any prisoner for liberty, or schoolboy for holiday'. 'With that fidelity which was an instinct of his nature, this brave man thought ever of his absent child, and longed after him' (p. 54). Thackeray presents the colonel's painful 'longing' for his child as a typical emotional experience of military fathers: 'Strong men, alone on their knees, with streaming eyes and broken accents, implore Heaven for those little ones' (p. 54). Much affected by his early separation from his son, the colonel's fatherly feeling extends beyond biology:

> The experience of this grief made Newcome's naturally kind heart only the more tender, and hence he had a weakness for children which made him the laughing stock of old maids, old bachelors, and sensible persons; but the

---

[22] This has parallels with Thackeray's own early experience. Thackeray was born in Calcutta where his father was secretary to the board of revenue in the East India Company. His father died when Thackeray was four and the following year the boy was sent to England for schooling, his mother remaining in India. See Peter L. Shillingsburg, 'Thackeray, William Makepeace (1811–1863)', *Oxford Dictionary of National Biography* (Oxford: Oxford University Press, 2004); online edn, Oct 2009 [http://www.oxforddnb.com/view/article/27155].

[23] Tosh, *A Man's Place*, p. 87.

[24] Valerie Sanders, *The Tragi-Comedy of Victorian Fatherhood* (Cambridge: Cambridge University Press, 2009), p. 3.

darling of all nurseries, to whose little inhabitants he was uniformly kind: were they the Collector's progeny in their palanquins, or the sergeant's children, tumbling about the cantonment, or the dusky little heathens in the huts of his servants round his gate. (p. 55)

Unlike his other, more firmly delineated, relations the colonel's weakness for children discriminates neither by class nor race, and throughout the novel he is observed forging alliances with children, both related and not: 'Besides his own boy, whom he worshipped, this kind colonel had a score, at least, of adopted children, to whom he chose to stand in the light of a father' (p. 59). This adoptive parenting registers the professional hazard of army life, as the colonel stands father to those children whose parents have died or must remain distant at imperial posts. It also places him in a longer tradition of the paternally sensitive military man, with his forename perhaps referencing Captain Thomas Coram, an exemplar of the fusion of feeling with social commitment. Coram, a retired naval officer, set up the Foundling Hospital after being horrified by the regularity of his encounters with abandoned children on the London streets.[25] In Sterne's exploration of the components of the man of feeling in *Tristram Shandy*, Captain Toby takes some comfort after failing to save the life of fellow military man Le Fever in adopting his son and exercising 'paternal kindness', with the help of Corporal Trim who collects the boy from school at holiday times (p. 389). A capacity to father well, as Matthew McCormack has shown, became a widely accessible basis for calls for political reform, as it 'demonstrates the man's sympathy with others, the basis of political spirit'.[26] Colonel Newcome's refusal to restrict his fatherly feeling to his own offspring goes beyond family feeling to show a capacity for boundless sympathy. Sterne had already made this connection, presenting elective parenting as proof of the military man's benign social care, and this was developed by other mid-Victorian writers.

The soldier as adoptive father was a particularly popular motif during the Crimean War, as we shall see in detail in chapter 3. Paintings like

---

[25] I discuss Captain Coram in the context of tender elective fatherhood in Holly Furneaux, *Queer Dickens: Erotics, Families, Masculinities* (Oxford: Oxford University Press, 2009), chapter 1.
[26] Matthew McCormack, 'Married Men and the Fathers of Families: Fatherhood and Franchise Reform in Britain', in *Gender and Fatherhood in the Nineteenth Century*, ed. Trev Lynn Broughton and Helen Rogers (Basingstoke: Palgrave, 2007), pp. 43–54, p. 48. As William Cobbett put it in his 1829 *Advice to Young Men:* 'to say of a man that he is fond of his family is, of itself, to say that, in private life at least, he is a good and trustworthy man; aye, and in public life too, pretty much; for it is no easy matter to separate the two characters', quoted by McCormack, p. 47.

John Everett Millais's *L'enfant du Régiment* (1854–5) and the revival of Donizetti's opera from which Millais takes his subject (reopened in London 1856) resonate with Newcome's choice to 'stand in light of a father' to numbers of children. Such narratives contributed to a wider focus on, and celebration of, the military man's emotional experience and eloquence. In the colonel's reliance on eighteenth-century models of sensibility, Thackeray explicitly draws the man of feeling into questions not just of what makes a gentleman, but of what constitutes appropriate military masculinity.

Thackeray's paternal delineation of the colonel follows a shift towards an increasing emphasis on an officer's care for the well-being of their men as laid out in mid-nineteenth-century military conduct books, including J. H. Stocqueler's *The British Officer: His Positions, Duties, Emoluments and Privileges* (1851). Thackeray, as Colby has shown, had read this book, and both Colonel Newcome and Stocqueler's ideal officer 'exemplify the aristocratic ideal of chivalry in a modern bourgeois setting'.[27] Stocqueler critiques the insufficiencies of an earlier code of behaviour that omits cross-ranks care:

> The officer who should suppose that due attention to parade drill, orderly duty in quarters, and gallant leading in the field, constitute a full discharge of the obligations imposed upon him by his commission, would, in our opinion, take a very narrow and imperfect view of his position.

Stocqueler goes on to call for the 'moral responsibility' and 'moral influence' of officers, 'whose high qualities excite admiration and awaken attachment'. He advocates a capacity for feeling and pleasure combined with disciplined restraint, prioritizing courtesy, justice, and honour as well as a capacity for well-placed fellow feeling: 'Our ideal, if grave with the grave, should be cheerful with the cheerful; should laugh with the gay and witty, but never with the envious and malicious.'[28]

Stocqueler's central argument, 'It is the character and conduct of the British gentleman that must secure this moral power for the British Officer', resonates throughout *The Newcomes* as Thackeray questions the extent to which civil ideals of gentlemanliness are appropriate or sustainable within a military context. He focuses this debate through the two oppositional strands within the colonel's formative reading.

---

[27] Colby, *Thackeray's Canvass of Humanity*, p. 365.
[28] J. H. Stocqueler, *The British Officer: His Positions, Duties, Emoluments and Privileges* (London, 1851), pp. 1–2.

'THE COMPANY OF GENTLEMEN', PART 2: THE COLONEL'S READING OF MEN OF PEACE AND MEN OF WAR

The colonel is a composite figure, in which models of the military man from Thackeray's own life and extensive reading of military histories are fused with eighteenth-century fictional men of sentiment. The character is based in part on Thackeray's stepfather, Major Carmichael Smyth, and on Thackeray's understanding of the British army in India through the many other East India men in his family's circle, as well on a varied literary legacy.[29]

Thackeray directly references a key genre through which a wider public engaged with the army through the eighteenth and nineteenth centuries (and beyond), the military memoir or personal narrative of exploits. In his use of the family name, Newcome, Thackeray recalls David Roberts's popular comic satire *The Military Adventures of Johnny Newcome, with an Account of His Campaigns on the Peninsular and in Pall Mall* (1815), which was followed by reprints, and sequels by Roberts and others, such as John Mitford's *The Adventures of Johnny Newcome in the Navy* (1818).[30] Roberts, having left the army due to spinal injury (he had previously lost an arm), drew on his own experiences as an officer in the Peninsular Wars. His Newcome joins the army as a means to a fine uniform and dashing reputation with the ladies. Johnny Newcome's family have new money through his father's banking fortune, which enables him to secure his social position through the purchase of successively senior officer commissions.[31] Though he is quick to complain about the inefficiencies

---

[29] Thackeray's daughter Anne Ritchie commented that her 'step-grandfather had many of Colonel Newcome's characteristics'. Quoted by MacMaster, 'Composition', p. 384. Peter Shillingsburg characterizes Thackeray as having 'both admired and condescended to' his military stepfather; *William Makepeace Thackeray: A Literary Life* (Basingstoke: Palgrave, 2001), p. 57.

[30] Neil Ramsey has considered the popularity of Roberts's poem and spin-offs, and the significance of Rowlandson's cartoons, arguing that they 'suggest a deflationary bodily response to war' (we see Johnny Newcome vomiting after cigar smoking, strutting in his tightly fitting uniform, and wracked by fever), 'one that reorders the masculine codes epitomised by Britain's military heroes'; 'The Comic View of Johnny Newcome's War', paper given at 'Contested Views: Visual Culture and the Revolutionary and Napoleonic Wars', Tate Britain, London, July 2012.

[31] The name was used in the Peninsular Wars to refer to inexperienced recruits; George Bell, who served under Wellington and went on to be one of the most experienced commanding officers in the Crimean War, remembers the improbable tales told by his captain as 'his playful way of amusing "Johnny Newcomes"'; *Soldier's Glory, being Rough Notes of an Old Soldier* (London: G. Bell and Sons, 1956), p. 7. Thackeray's use of the name as well as referencing the family's new money also tempers the behavioural example, which many readers drew from the colonel, sending up his often disastrous ignorance of the ways of the world.

of ordnance, and poor provision made for food, lodging, and travel, once he joins his regiment on the eve of the Battle of Salamanca, Johnny Newcome's patriotic fervour sufficiently overcomes his total inexperience. Though 'smelling powder for the first time' (as Thomas Rowlandson's accompanying cartoon satirically illustrates) Johnny Newcome is ready to take command when his captain falls, and, improbably for his first encounter of active service, leads his men well, as 'British valour everywhere prevailed.'[32] Those Victorian readers able to compare these two military Newcomes would have seen even more clearly the extent to which Thackeray's Newcome departs from previous representations, which Mitford satirizes, of aristocratic officers following a code of glamour, blood, and honour, and innovates in the presentation of the military man as a man of feeling.

Earlier in his career Thackeray had levelled his own form of satire against the figure of the vain, puffed-up officer, in his spoof military memoir, *The Tremendous Adventures of Major Gahagan* (1838–9). In this he uses a similar comic technique to Mitford to deflate Gahagan's highly aggressive tall tales of his military prowess. Gahagan proudly introduces himself as having killed his brother in a duel over a toothpick case that Gahagan wrongly believes is his, and goes on to claim his position as a form (similar to the manly toughs of George Lawrence's work) of exemplary military man: 'I have been at more pitched battles, led more forlorn hopes, had more success among the fairer sex, drunk harder, read more, been a handsomer man than any now serving Her Majesty.'[33] In *The Luck of Barry Lyndon* (1844) Thackeray develops Gahagan's boastful pleasure in violence, here using Lyndon's unreliability to more subtly critique the aggressive values he expresses through his brawling and duelling, and his careers in the British and Prussian armies.[34]

Thackeray's inclusion of the opposite extreme of military character in his depiction of the eminently humane Dobbin (1847–8) and Newcome (1853–5) parallels a transformation of attitudes towards the military in the mid-nineteenth century. Colonel Newcome's personal literary heroes, as we have briefly seen, are eminent figures of eighteenth-century politeness and sensibility. The colonel's indispensable portable reading stacks up to a hefty pile: '"The Spectator", "Don Quixote", and "Sir Charles Grandison" formed a part of his travelling library' (p. 41).[35] Thackeray details the

---

[32] [David Roberts], *The Military Adventures of Johnny Newcome* (London, 1815), p. 69.
[33] William Makepeace Thackeray, *The Tremendous Adventures of Major Gahagan* (Milton Keynes: Amazon print on demand, 2013), p. 4.
[34] Stanley Kubric extended this technique in his 1975 film based on the book.
[35] In his 'best correspondent in the world' persona of Bashi Bozouk Thackeray sends up the impracticality of taking one's books to war: 'Were a man in my present position to

reasons for the colonel's choice of books: '"I read these, Sir," he used to say, "Because I like to be in the company of gentlemen; and Sir Roger de Coverly, and Sir Charles Grandison, and Don Quixote are the finest gentlemen in the world"' (p. 41). The effects of Colonel Newcome's reading of Samuel Richardson's novel are formative; Thackeray variously presents the colonel's 'gracious dignity' as Grandisonian behaviour (p. 209, p. 515). In *Sir Charles Grandison* (1753) Richardson self-consciously tried to address the question of 'What makes a good man?' This hero is presented as 'the example of a Man acting uniformly well thro' a variety of trying scenes' and a 'Man of TRUE HONOUR'.[36] In showing the triumph of male virtue Richardson strives, as John Mullan has shown, to revise the gendered implications of his earlier *Pamela* (1740), and *Clarissa* (1748), in which ideal feeling and behaviour is firmly the province of 'the fair sex'.[37] Richardson's hero offers an ideal in which right sentiment is always met by right action—charity, sacrifice of time and self-interest, and sage advice. He is a prelapsarian man of feeling, clear of suspicions of emotional luxuriousness later levelled at Mackenzie and others. By the late eighteenth century the celebration of sensibility was tempered by concerns about fine feeling as self-indulgence, as a heightened capacity to feel only unevenly translated into social action, often dissolving in a flood of tears cathartic to the weeper but rarely of benefit to the wept for.[38]

For Victorian readers, as Fred Kaplan has documented, Mackenzie's work presented an 'uncomfortable' 'glorification of sensibility', contributing

---

pretend that he carried books about with him, and like FREDERIC or NAPOLEON had a campaign library, he would be humbugging the public.' Bashi Bouzouk uses this to explain the difference in his writing style in the field compared to 'regular, careful, philosophical, ornate history, such as some of my other works have been'. 'Important from the Seat of War! Letters from the East by Our Own Bashi Bouzouk', *Punch*, 17 June 1854, p. 257. The differences in content and genre of war writing are also, as we shall see, a major concern of *The Newcomes*.

[36] Samuel Richardson, *Sir Charles Grandison* (Oxford: Oxford University Press, 1986), p. 4.
[37] John Mullan, *Sentiment and Sociability: The Language of Feeling in the Eighteenth Century* (Oxford: Oxford University Press, 1988), pp. 81–3.
[38] In 'The Effects of Religion on a Mind of Sensibility', Mackenzie, best known for *The Man of Feeling* (discussed in the Introduction), praised his own work for its 'power of awakening the finer feelings, which so remarkably distinguish the composition of a gentleman' (*The Mirror*, 19 June 1779). Here a capacity for 'finer feeling', irrespective of right action, becomes a defining characteristic of the gentleman. On the growing critique of the self-serving indulgences of sentimental responses in the later decades of the eighteenth century see G. J. Barker Benfield, *The Culture of Sensibility: Sex and Society in Eighteenth Century Britain* (Chicago: University of Chicago Press, 1992), and John Mullan, 'Sentimental Novels', in *The Cambridge Companion to the Eighteenth Century Novel*, ed. John Richetti (Cambridge: Cambridge University Press, 1996), pp. 236–54.

to 'the Romantic belief that the feelings are the source of joy rather than goodness'. Richardson, on the other hand, offered 'attractive moral paradigms' through the linking of feeling and ethics, so that moral feeling produced moral action.[39] Grandison embodies this moral sensibility, making him a popular figure with mid-Victorians including George Eliot, Alfred Tennyson, and Thomas Macaulay.[40] As a figure famous for his combination of right feeling with right action, Thackeray's referencing of Sir Charles Grandison makes a significant contribution to the broader debate about the role of feeling in military masculinity.

The colonel's prized books present a particularly pacifistic model of manliness to carry into battle. *Sir Charles Grandison* and *Don Quixote* famously explore the limitations of aristocratic codes of chivalry. The Don finally abandons chivalry and Sir Charles Grandison proves his gentlemanliness by holding to his 'principle not to engage in a duel' (p. 256): 'I had an early notion, that it was much more noble to forgive an injury than to resent it; and to give a life than to take it' (p. 261). Although his general uncle wants to make him a soldier and Sir Charles does enter one campaign as a volunteer, he has an aversion to the service, largely due to the close correlation between an officer's honour and his willingness to meet any challenge, and rejects fighting in both an official and a private capacity. Instead, Sir Charles selects words and letters as his weapon of choice 'as a man of honour should wish to do', rather 'than either to kill or maim any man' (p. 208). Both novels reject violence as a means of settling differences or asserting honour. This is the creed to which Newcome fully subscribes; he gives the following Grandisonian lesson to Clive:

> The kind Colonel further improved the occasion with his son; and told him out of his own experience many stories of quarrels, and duels, and wine;— how the wine had occasioned the brawls, and the foolish speech overnight the bloody meeting at morning; how he had known widows and orphans made by hot words uttered in idle orgies: how the truest honour was the manly confession of wrong; and the best courage the courage to avoid temptation. (p. 143)

Although *The Newcomes* includes the action of a duel, between the unwilling Lord Kew and an irate Frenchman who will not be placated,

---

[39] Fred Kaplan, *Sacred Tears: Sentimentality in Victorian Literature* (Princeton: Princeton University Press, 1987), p. 33.
[40] Gilmour, *The Ideal of the Gentleman*, p. 31. Gilmour adds that though Sir Charles Grandison was widely admired by Victorian authors, he is presented, like Colonel Newcome, as a loveable anachronism: 'In the Victorian novel he becomes a byword for a quaint and slightly comical antique courtesy, of the kind found in Thackeray's Colonel Newcome and Trollope's Squire Thorne', p. 32.

such behaviour, like boxing and stage-coaching, is presented as anachronistic in this 'more peaceable and polished' age (p. 105). Notwithstanding the sardonic tone of Thackeray's commentary on the transformation of aristocratic behaviour—'so much does the spirit of the age appear to equalise all ranks; so strongly has the good sense of society, to which in the end gentlemen of the very highest fashion must bow, put its veto upon practices and amusements with which our fathers were familiar' (pp. 105–6)—the novel captures the shift in attitudes through which by the mid-century duelling became socially unacceptable. As Donna T. Andrew has argued, the definition of gentlemanliness based on being 'challenge-able' and willing to fight a duel, which persisted throughout the eighteenth century, was widely repudiated in the Victorian period.[41] This rejection of one form of authorized killing coincided with an increased ambivalence about the business of soldiering.

Colonel Newcome evades questions from his nephew and niece about how many people he has killed in combat, turning their attention instead to a more ameliorative aspect of conflict: the heroism of an army surgeon who, when a fever broke out on a transport ship, 'devoted himself to the safety of the crew, and died himself' (p. 192). He continues with one of the novel's only descriptions of military action, with a paean to non-violent self-sacrificing courage: 'What heroism the doctors showed during the cholera in India; and what courage he had seen some of them exhibit in action; attending the wounded men under the hottest fire, and exposing themselves as readily as the bravest troops' (p. 192). Newcome, like Goodman's soldier patients discussed in the Introduction, makes a reparative narrative swerve away from supposedly ascendant impulses to kill and tell.[42] Thackeray's turn to plots of non-violent war heroism is typical of a range of narratives of the Crimean War period, in which the fathering or healing soldier is a recurrent feature. A rather different message, however, is explicit in Colonel Newcome's other favourite reading.

---

[41] Donna T. Andrew, 'The Code of Honour and its Critics: The Opposition to Duelling in England, 1700–1850', *Social History* 5.3 (1980), pp. 409–34, p. 415.

[42] See the discussion of bellicose 'ur-war stories' in the Introduction and Joanna Bourke's discussion of a dominant 'urge to kill and tell', fuelled by civilian curiosity, in her account of twentieth-century soldiers' high-blown tales of massacre as belonging to a longer tradition of aggressive war storytelling, *An Intimate History of Killing: Face to Face Killing in Twentieth Century Warfare* (London: Granta, 1999), p. 35. Bourke argues that 'since refusal to tell such stories might throw into doubt a man's status and virility, few fathers, husbands, or lovers were able to resist the temptation to conform to an active warrior stereotype', p. 36. This history is called into question by a competing tradition of avoiding civilian curiosity for kill tallies and a narrative swerve to amelioration, embodied by Colonel Newcome. I elaborate on soldiers' own preferences for gentle Crimean War stories in chapters 4 and 5.

Though he models himself on the pacifistic Sir Charles Grandison, the colonel's other cherished book is Robert Orme's *History of the Military Transactions of the British Nation in Indostan* (1763, 1778). Orme chronicled the activities of the East India Company in the eighteenth century, having served with the company through his career. He was instrumental in sending the 1757 military expedition headed by Robert Clive to Calcutta to avenge the alleged Black Hole incident of the previous year, in which over a hundred British prisoners of war were said to have died. In Patrick Brantlinger's description of it, Orme's history, as is typical of imperialist writing, 'turned violence and rapacity into virtues, treating acts of aggression as acts of necessity and self-defence'.[43]

Orme's book is formative to Colonel Newcome's career, and to the plot of the Newcomes. As a boy 'he had a great fancy for India; and Orme's History, containing the exploits of Clive and Lawrence, was his favourite book of all in his father's library' (p. 23). This is a more traditional model of soldierly reading, in which the reading of military exploits is a catalyst for a performance of them. Accounts of Clive in India continued to exert formative fascination throughout the nineteenth century. J. W. Milne, a soldier who served in a volunteer regiment in the Boer War and re-enlisted in 1914 and fought at the Somme, explained the significance of books available to him through his membership of the Mutual Improvement Association: 'I thus had access to the shelves of the library and I took from them such books to read as *Darkest Africa* and *Lord Clive in India*. The stirring tales of the defence of Arcot, and other thrilling incidents imbued a spirit in me to see such things as were told in these books for myself.'[44] Milne's account, and the one that Thackeray gives of Newcome's engagement with Orme, follows the model of instructive reading set out by Maria Edgeworth in her 1809 *Essays on Professional Education*:

> A species of reading, which may be disapproved of for other pupils, should be recommended to the young soldier. His imagination should be exalted by the adventurous and the marvellous. Stories of giants, and genii, and knights and tournaments, and 'pictured tales of vast heroic deeds', should feed his fancy. He should read accounts of ship-wrecks and hair-breadth scapes, voyages and travels, histories of adventures, beginning with Robinson

---

[43] Patrick Brantlinger, *Rule of Darkness: British Literature and Imperialism, 1830–1914* (Ithaca and London: Cornell University Press, 1988), p. 81.

[44] Quoted by Richard Holmes, *Soldiers* (London: Harper, 2011), p. 311, together with other accounts of reading that contributed to the desire to sign up in the First World War, such as that given by James Marshall-Cornwall: 'My early enthusiasm for a military career was stimulated by the books which I used to devour. They included Rudyard Kipling's earlier works which were then appearing, G. A. Henty's historical romances and W. H. Fitchett's *Deeds that Won the Empire*.'

Crusoe, the most interesting of all stories, and one which has sent many a youth to sea.[45]

For Colonel Newcome, Orme's account of the British army in India has just this effect; after reading it he 'would be contented with nothing but a uniform' (p. 23). Colonel Newcome imagines a continuation of this line of inspiration, planning, as one possible future, that his own Clive 'can go into the army, and emulate the glorious man after whom I named him' (p. 57). Near the close of the novel the family copy of Orme's history again becomes significant to the future of the Newcomes, as a later will of the colonel's stepmother is found inside the book. This will leaves property to his son Clive, old Mrs Newcome having apparently become reconciled to her soldier stepson having read Orme's celebration of military prowess. In his old age the colonel shows how memorized passages from this book have remained with him all his life. The section he selects for recitation delights in the triumph of British energy and might over the French and the Marathas, an Indian warrior caste, here called Morattoes:

> 'The two battalions advanced against each other cannonading, until the French, coming to a hollow way, imagined that the English would not venture to pass it. But Major Lawrence ordered the sepoys and artillery—the sepoys and artillery to halt and defend the convoy against the Morattoes'—Morattoes Orme calls 'em. Ho! ho! I could repeat whole pages, sir. (p. 758)

Thackeray produces Newcome's recollection with almost word for word accuracy. Orme's text goes on to describe the advance, celebrating the effects of English endurance and 'vivacity', surprising to Indian and French adversaries: 'the enemy, who expected the English to be fatigued with a long and harassing march, were so startled at the vivacity of this motion, that they only stayed to give one fire, and then ran away with the utmost precipitation'.[46] The narrative of English military pluck, as this selection shows, is engrained in the colonel's mind. What then are we to make of this schism? How do we read this fascination with apparently oppositional books; on the one hand the central text of eighteenth-century masculine sensibility advocating pacifism as the greatest form of courage, and on the other bloodthirsty military history celebrating imperial oppression?

---

[45] Quoted in Sharon Murphy, 'Imperial Reading? The East India Company's Lending Libraries for Soldiers, c. 1819–1834', *Book History* 12 (2009), pp. 74–99, p. 76.
[46] Robert Orme, *History of the Military Transactions of the British Nation in Indostan* (London, 1763), p. 284. Stewart Gordon's research offers a more balanced picture of Indian military history of the period covered by Orme; see, for example, his *New Cambridge History of India: Marathas, 1600–1818* (Cambridge: Cambridge University Press, 1993).

The conflicting messages of the colonel's formative reading point to the unresolved tensions within a new bourgeois model of military masculinity, which could embrace feeling and value domesticity and caring roles, such as the intimate father, but also needed to be capable of violently dispatching the enemy. The colonel's mixed literary heritage, which is so formative of his career and character, prepares him to be a military man (Orme) of feeling (Richardson et al.). Thackeray's gentle officer proved to be a popular figure in wartime. Colonel Newcome takes his place alongside a range of gentle heroes as a personal favourite of serving soldiers in the Crimea and beyond.

CAMPAIGN HEROES: BATTLEFIELD READING AND MILITARY MASCULINITY

The colonel's reading patterns reflect those of actual servicemen. In her work on the libraries established by the East India Company in the 1820s and 1830s, Sharon Murphy notes that supplied material was supplemented by personal collections, as 'soldiers, particularly officers, frequently brought a selection of books with them to India'.[47] Murphy notes that many library titles 'were evidently chosen as particularly appropriate for soldiers, either because they would contribute to their moral improvement or stimulate their desire for adventures in foreign lands'.[48] Many first-hand accounts, though, from those serving in the Crimean War, express different motivations for the selection of campaign reading material.

Charlotte Yonge's novels were unlikely favourites. As Susan Walton has noted, Yonge's novel *Heartsease* was the last book read by Lord Raglan, commander of the British army in the Crimean War, before his death in the campaign; it was lent to him by a naval captain who was a close friend.[49] Meanwhile *The Heir of Redclyffe*, Markovits points out, 'was the most requested novel among officers in the hospitals in the Crimea'.[50] Charlotte Yonge's brother Julian, serving in the 2nd battalion of the Rifle

---

[47] Murphy, 'Imperial Reading?', p. 77. Had Thackeray placed Colonel Newcome's East India career twenty or so years later, he could have pictured his hero borrowing another of his favourite reads, *Don Quixote*, from the company's library (see Murphy, p. 77, p. 87, for the popularity of this title).

[48] Murphy, 'Imperial Reading?', p. 84.

[49] Susan Walton, *Imagining Soldiers and Fathers in the Mid-Victorian Era: Charlotte Yonge's Models of Manliness* (Farnham: Ashgate, 2010), p. 13.

[50] Stefanie Markovits, *The Crimean War in the British Imagination* (Cambridge: Cambridge University Press, 2009), p. 78.

Brigade, was happy to report home that 'nearly all the men in his regiment had a copy'.[51] *The Heir of Redclyffe* features a plot of anger and aggression rerouted into healing and the surrender of selfishness; self-sacrifice, in the form of a willingness to preserve a former enemy's life at the expense of one's own, is central. This novel, like others of the period including *The Newcomes*, considers the question of what makes a gentleman, birth or behaviour, through a focus on touch and emotion. In Yonge's novel gentility is both social and tactile. The hero, Sir Guy, overcomes what he believes is a blood inheritance of violence, 'a strange ancestral enmity', through sacrificial nursing.[52] He risks and finally loses his life nursing his former rival back to health, as his patient puts it, 'there never was such a one for a sickroom' (p. 335) and 'never was there such a nurse as he' (p. 338). In his constant sickbed attendance, Guy contracts the fever and only saves his patient at the expense of his own life. In her study of Yonge, Alethea Hayter cites an example of 'an officer in the guards [who was] asked in a game of "Confessions" what his prime object in life was, [and] answered that it was to make himself like Guy Morville, hero of *The Heir of Redclyffe*'.[53]

As Walton argues, 'there is a particular significance in the esteem for *The Heir* among army officers encamped in the Crimean Peninsula: in spite of their profession, they had internalised an ideal of a contained, non-violent masculinity'.[54] For Colonel Newcome, the models of Sir Charles Grandison and Don Quixote are essential to his self-fashioning as a gentle military man; this strand within his battlefield reading, rather than being *in spite* of his military profession, is an essential component of it, one that sustains him on campaign. Like Newcome's reading choices, *The Heir of Redclyffe*, with its focus on the overcoming of ancestral violence through care for former enemies, offered soldiers a pacifistic model of exemplary manliness. Through their vocal enjoyment of Yonge's work fighting men could endorse, if not live by, the values of humanitarian compassion, aspiring to be 'like Guy Morville'. George Orwell offers an insightful reflection on later choices of wartime reading, inspired by E. M. Forster's description of his experience of reading 'Prufrock' and other early T. S. Eliot poems in 1917 and being heartened by work that was 'innocent of public spiritedness'. Orwell empathizes with Forster's selection: 'If I had been a soldier fighting in the Great War, I would sooner have got hold of

---

[51] Christabel Coleridge, *Charlotte Mary Yonge: Her Life and Letters* (London: Macmillan, 1903), p. 183.
[52] Charlotte Yonge, *The Heir of Redclyffe* (London: Macmillan, 1909), p. 323.
[53] Alethea Hayter, *Charlotte Yonge* (Plymouth: Northcote House, 1996), p. 2. I discuss Yonge's novel in more detail in 'Negotiating the Gentle-Man'.
[54] Walton, *Imagining Soldiers and Fathers*, p. 20.

Prufrock than *The First Hundred Thousand* or *Horatio Bottomley's Letters to the Boys in the Trenches*. I should have felt, like Mr Forster, that by simply standing aloof and keeping in touch with pre-war emotions, Eliot was carrying on the human heritage.'[55] Orwell's appreciation of battlefield reading as a means of fulfilling a need to 'keep in touch with pre-war emotions', indeed, with forms of feeling alien to the experience of warfare (following Forster he celebrates 'Prufrock' as a connection with a mundane, mildly disgusting world: 'What a relief it would have been at such a time to read about the hesitations of a middle-aged highbrow with a bald spot'[56]), perhaps, in part, explains the popularity of fiction featuring non-militaristic versions of masculinity, that question traditions of heroism.

The popularity of Yonge's work with military men suggests a different trajectory to military reading to that offered by conventionally militaristic accounts of 'do and die' (line 15), as represented by what stands as the most famous text of the period, Alfred Tennyson's 'The Charge of the Light Brigade'.[57] Tennyson famously reprinted his poem in a 'soldier's version' when a chaplain at the front requested copies: 'It is the greatest favourite of the soldiers—half are singing it and all want to have on black & white—so as to read—what has so taken them.'[58] Even this poem, usually seen as a straightforward patriotic valorization of military courage and self-sacrifice, incorporates, as Trudi Tate has shown, an unease with its own glamorization.[59] Tate argues that such unease is generated by a conflicted view of military masculinity, in which it is not clear how the values of an aristocratic code of martial honour, seen in glorious action and extermination in this poem, can be retained in a more democratic army of bourgeois efficiency. The aristocratic cavalry officers of the charge are shown to be outmoded at the same time as their courageous code is

---

[55] George Orwell, *Inside the Whale and Other Essays* (Harmondsworth: Penguin, 1962), pp. 46–7.
[56] Orwell, *Inside the Whale*, p. 47.
[57] *The Poems of Tennyson*, ed. Christopher Ricks, 3 vols (Harlow: Longman, 1987).
[58] Tennyson describes the chaplain's request in a letter to John Forster, 6 August 1855, quoted in Edgar Shannon and Christopher Ricks, ' "The Charge of the Light Brigade": The Creation of a Poem', *Studies in Bibliography* 38 (1985), pp. 1–44, p. 8.
[59] Trudi Tate, 'On Not Knowing Why: Memorialising the Light Brigade', in *Literature, Science, Psychoanalysis, 1830–1970: Essays in Honour of Gillian Beer*, ed. Helen Small and Trudi Tate (Oxford: Oxford University Press, 2003), pp. 160–80. Also counter to jingoistic readings, Daniel Hack has suggested that this poem presents a terminal response to the ethos of firm self-governance, offering a form of 'eroticised resistance to the demands of Victorian masculine self-discipline and the perceived marginalisation of the imagination in an increasingly utilitarian England', more readily attributed to Tennyson's explicitly 'exotic' poems: 'Thanks to their self-discipline... the soldiers in the Light Brigade achieve the death that Ulysses's weary men "stretched out beneath the pine" so obviously crave in "The Lotus Eaters"'; 'Wild Charges: The Afro-Haitian "Charge of the Light Brigade"', *Victorian Studies* 54.2 (2012), pp. 199–225, p. 218.

mourned. Thackeray's novel, as we have seen, navigates this difficult transition in ideals of military masculinity, and the unresolved conflict in the colonel's oppositional formative texts creates a similar unease to that observed by Tate in Tennyson's poem.[60] The novel's emphasis on the significance of soldiers' reading is continued in the various afterlives of *The Newcomes*. John Everett Millais's painting *Peace Concluded* (1856) depicts, in part, the competing forms of wartime reading as a returned Crimean officer reads the announcement of peace in *The Times*, having discarded a number of *The Newcomes* in its distinctive yellow wrapper. The selection of Thackeray's novel is an interesting one politically, given that Millais had originally intended for the painting to work as a critique of pampered officers sent home for 'urgent private affairs' or with minor injuries, while officers with less influence and soldiers of the ranks remained to face the fighting and dire conditions.[61] Millais's likely convalescent officer, though importantly we can't see any specific injury, reclines, swathed in rich fabrics and supported by his wife's embrace, passively watching the drama of the Russian bear chastened by the British lion as played out on his knee by his daughter's toy animals. In this context Thackeray's exemplary colonel, who has distinguished himself in numerous campaigns and is a champion of the vulnerable, supports the intended rebuke to the insufficiency, in some cases, of officer heroics in this war.

Millais's painting is framed by the officer's two choices of reading material: an instalment of Thackeray's novel to his right, and *The Times* in his left hand. The painting visualizes the same alternatives between an official and emotional account of war that Thackeray discusses in an early number of *The Newcomes*:

> Besides that official history which fills *Gazettes* and embroiders banners with names of victory, which gives moralists and enemies cause to cry out at English rapine; and enables patriots to boast of invincible British valour—besides the splendour and conquest, the wealth and glory, the crowned ambition, the conquered danger, the vast prize, and the blood freely shed in winning it—should not one remember the tears too? (p. 54)

---

[60] Ambivalence about the sufficiency of militarism in securing male identity is located even within the colonel's favourite celebrant version of bellicosity. Orme's enthusiasm for Clive of India is qualified by the biographical details of Clive's early attempts on his life, and suicide at age forty-nine.
[61] For discussions of the composition of Millais's painting and its initial conception as a direct critique, under the planned title 'Urgent Private Affairs', see Matthew Lalumia, *Realism and Politics in Victorian Art of the Crimean War* (Michigan: UMI Research Press, 1984), pp. 93–5, and Markvotis, *The Crimean War*, pp. 192–209.

Here Thackeray elaborates on his famous claim for the value of a domestic perspective on war in *Vanity Fair*: 'We do not claim to rank among the military novelists. Our place is with the non-combatants.'[62] In *The Newcomes* he extends the call for a more emotionally nuanced account of war to that offered by 'official history', one which will take account of the distress as well as the triumph. He presents a richer emotional history of conflict, which the novelist can offer (as the long serialization of *The Newcomes* demonstrates), as important to the tempering of jingoism. Millais's officer has laid down *The Newcomes* to read *The Times*'s report of the conclusion of the peace treaty. Importantly, though, we see him moving between official and unofficial history, and we can speculate, with the thought of Julian Yonge's regiment eagerly perusing *The Heir of Redclyffe*, about his appreciation of the alternative heroism offered by Thackeray's novel to that presented in the newspaper report.

The particularly gentle forms of heroism offered by *The Newcomes* and *The Heir of Redclyffe* are remarked in G. A. Lawrence's account of the reformative reading of his intensely violent hero, in *Guy Livingstone* (1857). Lawrence's novel, published a year after the cessation of the Crimean War, celebrates an aggressive model of masculinity founded on 'size and sinews' (p. 48). As discussed in the Introduction, the lifestyle of the dashing officer of heavy drinking, gaming, and womanizing is shown to have its limitations in its tragic consequences for all the novel's principal men. Livingstone is finally chastened through his loss of the woman he loves, and his physical excesses are, at least partially, revised by his account of gendered readerly affect:

> Very old and very young women, in the plenitude of their benevolence, are good enough to sympathize with any tale of woe, however absurdly exaggerated; but men, I think, are most moved by the simple and quiet sorrows... We yawn over the wailings of Werther and Raphael; but we ponder gravely over the last chapters of *The Heir of Redclyffe*; and feel a curious sensation in the throat—perhaps the slightest dimness of vision—when reading *The Newcomes*, how that noble old soldier crowned the chivalry of a stainless life, dying in the Grey Brother's gown.[63]

The kind nobility of Colonel Newcome is sufficient here to move the otherwise unmovable male. Livingstone's (almost) tearful response to the death of Colonel Newcome parallels the grief expressed by Thackeray's first readers, and Thackeray himself, over the death of this hero, and

---

[62] Thackeray, *Vanity Fair: A Novel Without a Hero* (Oxford: Oxford University Press, 1998), p. 361.
[63] George Lawrence, *Guy Livingstone, or Thorough* (London: The Daily Telegraph, no date), p. 337.

participates in a continuing celebration of the colonel's quiet power to generate sentimental response.

COLONEL NEWCOME IN THE FIRST WORLD WAR

The position of the colonel as Britain's favourite gentleman was confirmed in the early twentieth century. Enthusiasm for the colonel's character became eloquent again in a wide-ranging public debate about which actor was fit for the role when Michael Morton's adaptation of the novel was staged in 1906. In a style familiar from the 1850s reviews the colonel is deployed in wider discussions about commended forms of manliness and national character. Herbert Beerbohm Tree, most famous for his performances as charismatic villains, was controversially cast. A piece in *The Daily Mail* asked 'Should Mr Tree be Allowed to Play Colonel Newcome?', and began the discussion by recognizing the difficulty of representing 'a truly loveable man': 'how shall it be possible to put upon the stage that most tender and pathetic character in the whole of modern English literature, Colonel Newcome'.[64] The article continues with a sneering critique of Tree, in which the ability to present feeling is insidiously connected to national character: Colonel Newcome 'needs to be played with a depth of feeling which has never been displayed by Mr Tree. "Adsum" in that guttural accent which has become identified through the playing of characters such as Svengali and Fagin would border on the absurd.' Tree is, it seems, too 'guttural', and—so the not so subsumed subtext goes—insufficiently English (Tree was the son of a German emigrant father, and had anglicized his stage name by adding a partial translation of his father's name, Beerbohm) to play this hero of 'English literature'. The *World* responded to this controversy with a mischievous squib which played upon the 'shady' qualities, the word invoking race as well as the villains for which he was known, of Tree:

> Some folks are sighing
> And sadly crying
> That it must really be
> Dramatic quackery
> To tinker Thackeray
> And serve him up with Tree.
> But those who're sobbing
> With hearts a-throbbing

[64] H. A. Mitton, 'Should Mr Tree Be Allowed to Play Colonel Newcome?', *Daily Mail*, 18 May 1906. Held by Bristol University Theatre Collection, HBT/TB/000034.

> Might surely wait and see
> Though tears be blinding
> They might be finding
> Naught shady about Tree.[65]

Surely enough Tree made a triumph of the role, and was particularly commended for his performance of feeling. The *Evening Citizen* applauded his 'manly pathos', while the *Glasgow Record* proclaimed 'he has done nothing so absolutely beautiful as his study of Colonel Newcome. It is a vivid portraiture, mostly of golden devotion, entirely permeated by the spirit of this most loveable of fictional creations.'[66] Interviewed in the *Pall Mall Gazette* Tree emphasized the gentleness of this gentleman character, as well as his understanding of the significance of the colonel's national heritage: 'that fine old English gentleman, the gentlest of moderns, the lineal descendent of Don Quixote'.[67] He went on to confirm that heart rather than head governed his interpretation of the role: 'I don't know that I have *thought* so much about the colonel's character, as that I have *felt* it.'

This public debate around the 1906 stage adaptation shows a persistent valuation of manly feeling through the supposed high point of 'stiff upper lip' mentality. Here the colonel's capacity for emotion is invoked, surprisingly, as a matter of national pride. In an era of decreasing confidence in Britain's ability to retain its colonial 'possessions', the most gentle of soldiers remained a popular hero. Figured as an anachronism from his mid-Victorian inception, the colonel continued to channel collective cultural fantasies about a passed golden age of ideal gentlemanly character and manly feeling. If this 'fine old English gentleman' is old-fashioned, the emotional response to the character was very much ongoing, as Tree's testimony—'I have felt it'—shows.

Tree's success in this role was further confirmed a decade later when, in a revival during the First World War, the play achieved its greatest popularity. He toured Canada and the United States with the play in the winter of 1916–17, reaching the New Amsterdam Theatre, New York with it on 10 April 1917. Here he interpolated a toast to the British navy within the play to great applause, and added, 'And let us not forget our friends across the seas', to bring the house to a standing ovation.[68] The

---

[65] 'Umbrage and the Umbrageous', *World*, 22 May 1906. Held by Bristol University Theatre Collection, HBT/TB/000034.

[66] *Evening Citizen*, 18 September 1906; *Glasgow Record*, 18 September 1906. Held by Bristol University Theatre Collection, HBT/TB/000035.

[67] 'Interview with Mr Behrbohm Tree', *Pall Mall Gazette*, 17 May 1906. Held by Bristol University Theatre Collection, HBT/TB/000037.

[68] 'Sir Herbert Tree as Colonel Newcome', *The New York Times*, 11 April 1917.

New York Times echoed reviews of a decade earlier, praising 'Sir Herbert's portrait of the Colonel, a performance that is genuinely charming and alive with a heartiness that is as admirable as it is surprising'. Tree went on to appear in the role on a night in aid of mutilated soldiers at the Metropolitan Opera House.[69]

The playscript, of which a copy is held at the Drama Archive at Bristol University, confirms that playwright Morton considered the colonel's literary legacy to be essential to the delineation of his character; despite the pressure to abridge the substantial novel into a play-length script, Morton retained much of the colonel's discussion of his favourite books. The stage colonel's exclamation, 'Sir Roger de Coverly, Sir Charles Grandison, and Don Quixote are the finest gentlemen in the world!' is accompanied by a direction: 'moves over to table tinkering with various books'. The production's property plot is precise in the provision of three books, and so it is (just) possible that a sufficiently zealous props person may have secured a copy of Richardson's novel for use in this scene. In this way, the exemplary gentle man of the eighteenth century, Sir Charles Grandison, triumphs through a complex, contested history of preferred military reading, to become part of Newcome's travelling library again, and to appear in a benefit for First World War wounded soldiers.

While the conflict between a pacifistic model of military masculinity—which met the requirements of new bourgeois ideals of manly character at home and at war—and the realities of warfare remained unresolved, the emotional significance of the military man of feeling persisted, even, and especially, in times of conflict. Beerbohm Tree's deployment of Thackeray's colonel to benefit wounded soldiers in the First World War is a fitting legacy for a figure which embodied a wider cultural desire to transform narratives of war violence into domestic plots of care via the military man of feeling. An association between manliness and aggression persisted in some narratives of this period, as we have seen briefly here in texts such as Thackeray's *Barry Lyndon* and Lawrence's *Guy Livingstone*; and the muscular Christianity movement (as discussed in the next chapter) worked hard to establish a moral dimension to the manly tough. However, the inherently conflicted figure of the gentle soldier, as exemplified by Colonel Newcome, became a major cultural strategy for reconciling Victorian society to its participation in war.

---

[69] McMaster, 'Composition', p. 390.

2

Princes of War and of Peace

Secular and Spiritual Redemption in Dickens and Kingsley

The 'company of gentlemen' with which Thackeray's Colonel Newcome surrounded himself was expanded for readers in 1854 and 1855 by a circle of other literary military gentle men. Charles Dickens, a member with Thackeray of the Administrative Reform Association, responded to reports of dire conditions in the Crimea through the winter of 1854 with a Napoleonic narrative of sentimental soldiering, while Charles Kingsley wrote directly to the troops at Sebastopol and endeavoured to hearten them with the swashbuckling excesses of *Westward Ho!* (1855). This chapter draws out the continuities between Dickens's and Kingsley's Crimean War writings to see how the figure of the gentle soldier was mobilized in support of political and military reform, and to reconcile a self-styled civilized and Christian nation to its participation in war.

PRIVATE RICHARD DOUBLEDICK 'THE REDEEMED PROFLIGATE': PERSONAL AND ADMINISTRATIVE REFORM

The improbably named Private Richard Doubledick is the hero of Dickens's contribution to the 1854 Christmas number of his journal *Household Words*, 'Seven Poor Travellers'. Doubledick, a disgraced recruit to the ranks, features in a tale of soldierly rehabilitation, told through the story of his friendship with an exemplary officer, Taunton. In this seasonal offering Dickens rewrites class and national antagonism through a powerful celebration of the transformative nature of male friendship. The Christmas number participates in the wider coverage of the Crimean War in *Household Words*, which frequently draws upon a politicized presentation of gender, specifically a range of representations of appropriate soldierly masculinities, to mobilize its critique of the army system, and of the administration more widely.

'Seven Poor Travellers' was multi-authored in a style that had become familiar to readers in the three previous years since the inauguration of *Household Words*. This collaboration brought together short tales by Dickens, George Augustus Sala, Adelaide Anne Procter, Wilkie Collins, and Eliza Lynn Linton, under a loose framing device of the narratives told by those seeking refuge in an almshouse on Christmas eve. Dickens's traveller, having supplied the others with a festive meal, begins the storytelling with an account of his relative Private Doubledick. Doubledick has enlisted, in a familiar narrative of army recruitment, in desperation after a mysterious disgrace, which has prevented him from marrying his beloved fiancée, and lives as a soldier 'with a determination to be shot':

> There was not a more dissipated and reckless soldier in Chatham barracks, in the year 1799, than Private Richard Doubledick. He associated with the dregs of every regiment, he was as seldom sober as he could be, and was constantly under punishment.[1]

Doubledick, with an alacrity suitable to this condensed form of narrative, is swiftly reformed by his encounter with his commanding officer, Captain Taunton. Dickens's part of this number was reprinted in February 1855 in American journal *Harper's New Monthly Magazine* under a title which emphasized the redemptive Christmas message, 'The Redeemed Profligate'.[2] Readers of this issue were presented with a particularly clear line between Dickens's and Thackeray's expressions of soldierly gentleness, as the continuing serialization of *The Newcomes* immediately followed Dickens's tale.

The exemplary officer of Dickens's story, Captain Taunton, presents the belief that a military career can offer a democratic form of moral redemption by offering every soldier, even of the lowest rank, ready opportunities to regain their own self-respect, and earn that of their regiment. Through the powerfully charismatic figure of Taunton, Dickens deftly configures war as an opportunity for personal and social reformation. Doubledick's moral restoration is effected through his reaction to his captain, and their swiftly developing friendship:

> Now the captain of Richard Doubledick's company was a young gentleman not above five years his senior, whose eyes had an expression in them which affected Private Richard Doubledick in a very remarkable way. They were

---

[1] [Charles Dickens], 'The Seven Poor Travellers: The First', *Household Words*, vol. 10, Extra Christmas Number (25 December 1854), 573–82, p. 577.
[2] Charles Dickens, 'The Redeemed Profligate', *Harper's New Monthly Magazine*, vol. 10, no. 57 (February 1855), pp. 371–7.

bright, handsome, dark eyes... the only eyes now left in his narrowed world that Private Richard Doubledick could not stand. (p. 577)

F. A. Fraser chose to illustrate the reforming power of Taunton's gaze in the figure he produced for the 1871 collected edition of the Christmas numbers, as the single illustration for 'Seven Poor Travellers' (Figure 1). Fraser's illustration depicts both captain and private as men of fine feeling, taking the moment at which Doubledick begins to weep and physically documenting, in Taunton's upraised hand, the reaching out that redeems him. As with the officer ideal recommended in Stocqueler's military conduct books, discussed in the previous chapter, Taunton is attentive to the emotions of the men he commands, responding with sympathy and fellow feeling.

With a 'bursting heart' Richard asks Taunton to be the witness of his reformation, and Taunton agrees to be a 'watchful and a faithful one': 'I have heard from Private Doubledick's own lips, that he dropped down upon his knee, kissed that officer's hand, arose and went out of the light of the dark, bright, eyes, an altered man' (p. 578). Doubledick ruminates variously on the transformative effect of the man who 'saved me from ruin, made me a human creature, won me from infamy and shame. O God forever bless him!' (p. 579). Dickens's tale then follows the friendship of Doubledick and Taunton through the Napoleonic military campaigns of thirteen years. In 1801, Doubledick, who has been promoted to sergeant, is invariably 'close to' Taunton, 'ever at his side, firm as a rock, true as the sun' (p. 578). In an 1805 campaign against the French in India, Doubledick's heroism in saving the regimental colours and 'rescu[ing] his wounded Captain who was down' is rewarded by another promotion. Dickens is insistent on cataloguing Doubledick's promotions, at one point interrupting the narrative to list the ranks he has progressed through: 'Private, Corporal, Sergeant, Sergeant Major, Ensign... Lieutenant' (p. 579). By the end of the story Doubledick has become a major.

Dickens's emphasis on army promotion would have made immediate sense to regular readers of *Household Words*, who would have encountered Eustace Grenville Murray's article 'Army Interpreters' two weeks earlier in the 16 December issue. Murray provided several other articles for the journal, specifically on the Crimea, under his nom de plume 'The Roving Englishman'. His work provided part of *Household Words*'s substantial coverage of aspects of the conflict; the Dickens Journals Online index lists eighty-three articles for the journal in total under the heading 'Crimean War'.[3] These articles tend to focus, as Sabine Clemm has summarized in

---

[3] http://www.djo.org.uk.

Figure 1. F. A. Fraser, Captain Taunton, and Private Doubledick, 'Seven Poor Travellers', 1871, reprinted in the Library Edition of Dickens's works, 1911. Reproduced with permission from the Charles Dickens Museum.

her work on Dickens's journalism and ideas of nationhood, on the cultures and people of the Crimea and criticism of the British government for its handling of military matters.[4] Though overt comment on international politics was not the journal's usual mode, Grace Moore has shown how *Household Words* demonstrated clear support for the war in its early stages through a number of articles that explored Turkish civilization, refuting myths of Eastern barbarism, and some material inciting 'animosity against the Czar'.[5] Eliza Lynn's (later Lynn Linton) 'The True Story of the Nuns at Minsk', which was published on 13 May 1854, less than two months after Britain and France had formally joined with the Ottoman empire in the war against Russia, explicitly seeks to 'convert' those in Britain still partisan to the czar.[6] Once, though, the appalling conditions endured by the British army in the Crimea became apparent, the journal's coverage focused on the British government's mismanagement of the campaign, critiquing hierarchies and attitudes in the cabinet and the army.

Murray's 'Army Interpreters' opens with a scorching satirical account of a British blunder that results in the taking prisoner of Turkish allies in the mistake that they are Russian enemies. The interpreter is unable to understand them, as 'these stupid people', the report sarcastically comments, 'could not speak English'.[7] More darkly presented is the treatment of these prisoners:

> The affair occasioned a good deal of sparkling conversation, and gave birth to a joke of Cornet Lord Martingale's, which has quite made his reputation as a wit in the aristocratic regiment to which he belongs. 'We always shut up turkeys towards Christmas,' said his lordship; 'it makes them fatter for killing.' The point of the young peer's jest, however, was blunted by the haggard appearance of the prisoners, who having had nothing but salt pork served to them, had supported themselves merely on the bread which was given with it, according to a regulation which the interpreter had a dim idea was somehow or other connected with their religious tenets.

This example of witless aristocratic inhumanity is developed in a critique of the promotion system in public offices: 'Our public servants... are born, not made.' The piece closes with a warning to new entrants to Her Majesty's service hoping to advance through study and hard work: 'Let

---

[4] Sabine Clemm, *Dickens, Journalism and Nationhood: Mapping the World in Household Words* (London and New York: Routledge, 2009), p. 103.

[5] Grace Moore, *Dickens and Empire: Discourses of Class, Race and Colonialism in the Works of Charles Dickens* (Aldershot: Ashgate, 2004), p. 77.

[6] [Eliza Lynn], 'The True Story of the Nuns at Minsk', *Household Words*, vol. 9, no. 216 (13 May 1854), pp. 290–5, p. 290.

[7] [Eustace Clare Grenville Murray], 'Army Interpreters', *Household Words*, vol. 10, no. 247 (16 December 1854), pp. 431–2, p. 431.

him rather seek to enter the great British cousinocracy by marriage if he really wish to get on.'[8]

In this context the political impetus behind Doubledick's striking, and historically highly unlikely, progress from private to major is clear. Readers were encouraged to make a connection between Grenville Murray's 'Army Interpreters' and 'Seven Poor Travellers', by the immediate continuation from Murray's article—the final in its issue—into an advertisement for the special Christmas number.[9] More explicitly, both Dickens's tale and Murray's article participate in the wider campaign for administrative reform. Galvanized by Crimean mismanagement, the Administrative Reform Association was established four months after the publication of this Christmas number.

In his speech at the opening meeting of the Administrative Reform Association, Dickens explicitly linked William Howard Russell's Crimean dispatches for *The Times* to the widespread awareness of the campaign as a national disaster. He commended the paper's exposure of 'the ghastly absurdity of that vast labyrinth of misplaced men and misdirected things, which had made England unable to find on the face of the earth, an enemy one twentieth part so potent to effect the misery and ruin of her noble defenders as she has been herself'.[10] Dickens, as Markovits notes, admired Russell, whose reports clearly influenced Dickens's most famous response to Crimean mismanagement in his depictions of circumlocution in *Little Dorrit* (1855–7).[11] Though it doesn't have the profile of *Little Dorrit*, Dickens's 1854 Christmas tale is clearly concerned with reform on a national institutional level, as well as a personal one. Despite the historical unlikelihood of a cross-class friendship between captain and private, Dickens endorses a command model of moral influence and cross-rank sympathy through the exemplary figure of Taunton.

---

[8] [Murray], 'Army Interpreters', p. 432.

[9] The advert which follows that for 'Seven Poor Travellers' is for the continuing serialization of Elizabeth Gaskell's *North and South* (1854–5). Stefanie Markovits, *The Crimean War in the British Imagination* (Cambridge: Cambridge University Press, 2009), has made a convincing case that Gaskell's novel, published from 2 September 1854 to 27 January 1855, can best be understood within the context of the journal's Crimean War coverage. Markovits gives particular attention to the relationship between Gaskell's novel and Adelaide Anne Procter's numerous Crimean War poems, which explore the attractions of pacifism and ideas of just war, pp. 92–3. Proctor also contributed a story about a patriotic cowgirl to this 1854 Christmas number.

[10] 'Administrative Reform Association, 27 June, 1855', *The Speeches of Charles Dickens*, ed. K. J. Fielding (Oxford: Clarendon Press, 1960), pp. 197–208, p. 201.

[11] Dickens encouraged Russell to undertake a lecture tour on his return from the Crimea and later wrote to him: 'I have always followed you closely, and have always found new occasions to express my sense of what England owes you for your manly out-speaking and your brilliant description', quoted in Markovits, *The Crimean War*, p. 36.

Through Doubledick's promotion from common soldier to officer, Dickens is also determined to figure the army as a site of social aspiration, with opportunities for betterment through individual hard work and heroism, insisting that Ensign Richard Doubledick had 'risen through the ranks' (p. 578). One of the aims of the Administrative Reform Association was realized a decade and half later in the Cardwell reforms to overturn the system of bought commissions. This made army leadership a more accessible prospect to middle- and working-class men.[12] In the aftermath of the Crimean War, as Alan Skelley has shown, formal reforms were supplemented by a range of efforts to improve the education and quality of leisure time for ranking soldiers, with an emphasis on increasing the appeal of 'rational recreations' of reading rooms, lectures, etc. so that they became preferable to the canteen. These changes, and education reforms, were 'an important aspect of the army's transition from an earlier uncaring, fiercely disciplined body to a more humane organisation with greater provision for the welfare of its men'.[13] In the course of these reforms the qualities of the soldier of the ranks, and his capacity for self-discipline and self-help, came under scrutiny similar to that given to the working man in the approach to the 1867 Reform Act.[14] Dickens's presentation of Doubledick's military opportunities shows the more radical edge of administrative reform. While Thackeray's *The Newcomes* shares the association's middle-class emphasis on extending leadership, critiqued by Chartists as 'a palpable cheat', in the narrative of Doubledick's reclamation by kindness and professional advancement Dickens makes a broader classed case for working men's opportunity.[15] This topic was fresh in readers' minds as 1854 had begun

[12] Anthony Bruce, *The Purchase System in the British Army, 1660–1871* (London: Royal Historicial Society, 1980).
[13] Alan Ramsey Skelley, *The Victorian Army at Home: The Recruitment and Terms and Conditions of the British Regular, 1859–1899* (London: Croom Helm, 1977), p. 117.
[14] As Keith McClelland has shown, 'the axial figure' in the enfranchisement controversy was 'the "respectable working man": could he be trusted if he was to be given the vote? How was he to be differentiated from the "rough" or "unrespectable"?' These questions around trust and differentiation were, in part, resolved through a yoking of respectability with reason, with an emphasis on 'rational recreations' and temperance. 'England's Greatness, the Working Man', in *Defining the Victorian Nation: Class, Race, Gender and the British Reform Act of 1867*, ed. Catherine Hall, Keith McClelland, and Jane Rendall (Cambridge: Cambridge University Press, 2000), p. 72, p.115. Stefan Collini documents an increasing politicized emphasis on 'character' in this period, *Public Moralists: Political Thought and Intellectual Life in Britain, 1850–1930* (Oxford: Clarendon Press, 1991). Middle-class ideals of manly self discipline, forged to legitimate the increasing social power of that class, and an evangelically informed bourgeois emphasis on restraint and asceticism, were thus conceptually extended, with the vote, to a section of working-class men.
[15] 'The Chartists and the War', *The Empire*, 23 June 1855, p. 471. This description precedes the National Reform League's case against Parliament's taxing and military enlistment of those without a vote quoted in the Introduction.

with the queen's endorsement of proposals made by Lord John Russell, a close friend of Dickens's. The queen's speech opening parliament announced 'measures', which were to be postponed until 1867, 'for the amendment of the laws relating to the representation of the Commons in Parliament'.[16] Although the proposed Reform Bill had been quietly shelved on the outbreak of war, its impetus was channelled during the conflict into questions about administrative failings, army advancement, and the character of the working man, who emerged in reports of the bravery of common soldiers as a saviour of the nation. In celebrating Doubledick's character reformation and contribution to his country at war Dickens reassures his predominantly middle-class readership about the dependability of the working man and implicitly adds to the enfranchisement argument that those who fight for the country should be full voting citizens.

Dickens's expansive definition of a military masculinity, which can encompass deep feeling and tenderness in all ranks, works not to critique a militarized society per se, but to critique the inefficiencies of the current system. Peace campaigners (for different reasons to Chartists) were frustrated by the position of the Administrative Reform Association; they pointed to shared ground in exposing 'those who are now in administration' for 'squandering millions' but acknowledged a more fundamental difference in aims: 'We regret to find so many friends of Administrative Reform at the same time the friends of the present war.'[17] As advocates for peace mournfully acknowledged, the association did not oppose war itself but wanted to ensure a more effective waging of it. Counter to the effect we might expect of Dickens's Christmas narrative in which soldiers weep, express the intensity of their friendship, and mourn for one another, this narrative also campaigns for the greater efficiency of the war machine.

'SIDE BY SIDE IN ONE CAUSE': THE REMAKING OF ANGLO-FRENCH RELATIONS

Doubedick's military trajectory renegotiates class barriers and national antagonisms. 'Seven Poor Travellers' is engaged in a wider remaking of national attitudes, worked out through Doubledick's reaction to the suitably heroic French officer, a 'courageous, handsome, gallant officer of

---

[16] C. Dereli, *A War Culture in Action: A Study of the Literature of the Crimean War Period* (Bern: Peter Lang, 2003), p.18. See Dereli, chapter 1, for a detailed discussion of the rerouting of reform arguments after the outbreak of war.
[17] 'What Should the Advocates of Peace Do?', *The Empire*, 23 June 1855, p. 473. The article went on to ask 'with whom' 'can the friends of peace ally themselves?'.

five and thirty' (p. 578), who gives the command for the fire in which Taunton is killed. Doubledick becomes 'a lone, bereaved man' (p. 579), living only to deliver a packet of Taunton's hair to his mother and to avenge his friend's death through an encounter with this Frenchman. This plot is only briefly interrupted when Doubledick, having returned to his regiment, suffers a serious head injury. On regaining consciousness in a hospital in Brussels, 'it was so tranquil and so lovely, that he thought he had passed into another world. And he said in a faint voice, "Taunton are you near me?"' (p. 580). This death-longing reverie of physical proximity to the lost beloved is supplanted by a more conventional nursing romance plot of a type Florence Nightingale abhorred, as Doubledick's former fiancée, Mary, finds and heals him.[18] This redirection of Doubledick's emotional emphasis is variously unconvincing—he fails to remember that in his fever, 'at the point of death', he married Mary that he might call her 'Wife before he died' (p. 581).[19] Mary's arrival only creates a slight detour in the main plot line by which Doubledick will continue to develop his relationship with Taunton through an encounter with the French officer who gave the fatal command. While Doubledick receives some comfort in forming a posthumous brotherhood to Taunton, whose mother feels that 'in her bereavement' in Doubledick 'she had found a son' (p. 579), vengeance threatens to become Doubledick's predominant response to his loss: 'A new legend now began to circulate among our troops; and it was, that when he and the French officer came face to face once more, there would be weeping in France' (p. 579).

This promised revenge plot is a conventional accompanying narrative to the typical plot of wartime camaraderie, with roots reaching from classical antiquity. The power of the desire for vengeance is often the means by which the intensity of the bond between male friends and co-warriors is expressed. In Virgil's *Aeneid*, for example, Aeneas responds to

---

[18] In her 1859 *Notes on Nursing*, Nightingale attacks the proliferation of nurse romance plots in Crimean narratives: 'Popular novelists of recent days have invented ladies disappointed in love or fresh out of the drawing-room turning into the war hospitals to find their wounded lovers, and when found, forthwith abandoning their sick-ward for their lover, as might be expected. Yet in the estimation of the authors, these ladies were none the worse for that, but on the contrary were heroines of nursing'; *Notes on Nursing: What It is and What It is Not* (London: Duckworth, 1970), p. 75.

[19] The scene where Mary reminds Doubledick that she shares his name anticipates Eugene Wrayburn's similarly muted enthusiasm for what he believes will be a final act, again a reparative one which will correct past wrongs, of deathbed marriage to Lizzie in *Our Mutual Friend* (1864–5). The structures of a reluctant (or in Doubledick's case, apparently unconscious) marriage in contrast to an emotional enthusiasm for a beloved male friend are also paralleled. I have discussed Eugene's subdued capitulation to marriage and his explicit love for his boyhood friend Mortimer Lightwood in Holly Furneaux, *Queer Dickens: Erotics, Families, Masculinities* (Oxford: Oxford University Press, 2009), pp. 101–2.

the battle death of his beloved friend Pallas with bloodthirsty frenzy against the enemy (book 10), and in subsequent books he works to fulfil the duty laid on him by Pallas's father to avenge the death of his son (books 11 and 12). Similarly in Homer's *Iliad* Achilles is driven to avenge the death of Patroclus, whom he loves beyond all. Victorian war stories, however, take a determined turn away from the valorization of the revenge plot in classical epic. Through a convenient twist in Dickens's plot, Taunton's mother unknowingly becomes the guest of the French officer whose order killed her son, and Doubledick, on joining her, finds that his host is his cherished enemy. Doubledick's perplexity about how to react allows Dickens space to remake Anglo-French relations in a manner befitting the new alliance of these nations in the Crimean War.

Military co-operation between the British and the French was so novel that British officers and men made repeated slips of the tongue in which the French were conflated with the enemy. Famously Lord Raglan, who commanded the campaign and had served on the Duke of Wellington's staff during the Peninsular War of 1808–14 and lost an arm at Waterloo, would absentmindedly refer to the French, rather than the Russians, as the current enemy.[20] This kind of widespread confusion is cited in another *Household Words* piece a couple of weeks after 'Seven Poor Travellers', 'The Rampshire Militia'. This article presents a fictional account of the mustering of a volunteer force, including farm workers, such as Ned Barry: 'Ned Barry, for one, did not know who the enemy were, though he felt sure there was one coming—Rooshan or French, or somebody—to take Westerleigh, and burn down our house.'[21] In 'Seven Poor Travellers' Dickens reflects on the historical enmity between the countries as the narrator laments that in the aftermath of the Napoleonic conflicts, 'unhappily many deplorable duels had been fought between English and French officers, arising out of the recent wars' (p. 582).

On encountering the French officer, though, Doubledick's desire for vengeance immediately evaporates and he thanks the spirit of his departed friend for 'these better thoughts... rising in [his] mind' and for showing him 'the blessings of the altered time': 'It is from thee the whisper comes that this man did his duty as thou didst—and as I did, through thy guidance, which has wholly saved me, here on earth—and that he did no more' (p. 582). In this final moment of epiphany, Doubledick recognizes that rather than the further bloodshed of a vengeful duel, sincere

---

[20] Alastair Massie, *The National Army Museum Book of the Crimean War: The Untold Stories* (Basingstoke: Macmillan, 2005), p. 11.
[21] [Harriet Martineau and ?James Payn], 'The Rampshire Militia', *Household Words*, vol. 10, no. 251 (13 January 1855), pp. 505–11, p. 505.

friendship between the former enemies, and unqualified forgiveness, is the most fitting reaction to Taunton's death. In a highly idealized ending Dickens offers the vision of a friendship between these former adversaries that continues beyond death through future generations, who, like Doubledick and Taunton, recognize their bond through an unbreakable battlefield allegiance:

> The time has since come when the son of Major Richard Doubledick, and the son of that French officer, friends as their fathers were before them, fought side by side in one cause: with their respective nations, like long-divided brothers whom the better times have brought together, fast united. (p. 582)

This fraternal image of unity clearly had a political dimension in celebrating the Anglo-French military alliance and it is also informed by Dickens's own enthusiasm for French culture. As John Drew has shown, Dickens was particularly sensitive about the representation of the French during the Crimean War period. In October 1854 he held over G. A. Sala's comic article on French military dandyism, explaining to Wills that it came 'painfully upon the Battle Field accounts in *The Times*... I would rather say nothing about France unless I had plenty to say about its gallantry and spirit'.[22] In this explanation we can see how W. H. Russell's dispatches for *The Times* helped to shape the wider coverage of the war in periodicals like *Household Words*, informing that journal's critiques of mismanagement and Dickens's editorial decisions about appropriate content. Dickens preferred firmly Francophile material, publishing 'Our French Watering Place', a glowing account of Boulogne and the chivalry of her citizens, proud to billet troops free of charge, as the lead article of the 4 November issue, the day before the Battle of Inkerman. The conclusion of 'Our French Watering Place' anticipates that of 'Seven Poor Travellers', with a celebration of Anglo-French unity, praising the 'long and constant fusion of the two great nations there', which 'has taught each to like the other, and to learn from the other, and to rise superior to the absurd prejudices that have lingered among the weak and ignorant in both countries equally'.[23]

The celebration of this alliance was a particularly suitable sentiment to communicate to serving soldiers, and *Household Words* was a popular publication amongst the British army in the Crimea. Nathaniel Steevens of the Connaught Rangers, for example, says in his Crimean campaign

---

[22] Quoted in John M. L. Drew, *Dickens the Journalist* (Houndmills: Palgrave Macmillan, 2003), p. 117.
[23] [Charles Dickens], 'Our French Watering Place', *Household Words*, vol. 10, no. 241 (4 November 1854), pp. 265–70, p. 582.

reminiscences for January 1855, 'during this month I fortunately picked up several numbers of *Household Words*'.[24] This is a particular relief to Steevens, who commented repeatedly in earlier parts of the journal on the difficulty of getting any decent reading material. In May 1854, for example, he writes, 'we greatly felt the want of books to read; the few that could be purchased were trashy novels, and very dear'. He reiterates this in July 1854: 'We much felt the want of books to while away the many spare hours; and newspapers were most eagerly read and reread.'[25] This reference to the rereading of newspapers suggests a considerable multiplier effect at work, also suggested by the letters of Ernest Knight, a junior officer in the 77th Regiment, who discusses passing on copies of *Household Words*.[26] Improving supply routes to the Crimea, which Steevens also mentions in January 1855, make it just possible that one of the issues he was reading that month was the recent Christmas number. Though (sadly!) he doesn't pass comment on Doubledick and Taunton, he does at least give his impression of *Household Words*: 'I found this periodical to be very acceptable reading in leisure moments.'[27]

In Steevens's relief at receiving copies of *Household Words* we glimpse, as is typical of war narratives, the range of possible, potentially competing effects of Dickens's story. The figure of the military man of feeling was put to various uses, public and private; these ranged from calls for army and administrative reform, to making camp and battlefield life more manageable for individual soldiers. While such narratives participated in a wider debate that culminated in the significant reforms to army hierarchy in the decade after Dickens's death, they might also, for some readers, have called into question the value of conflict. While in many ways 'Seven Poor Travellers' straightforwardly supports the Administrative Reform Association case for the more effective waging of war, Dickens's moving emphasis on the power of male bonds, capable of overcoming a long history of national antagonism and reworking a private desire for

---

[24] Nathaniel Steevens, *The Crimean Campaign with 'The Connaught Rangers', 1854–1856* (London and Edinburgh: Griffith and Farran, 1878), p. 177.
[25] Steevens, *The Crimean Campaign*, pp. 23, pp. 62–3.
[26] Ernest Knight, to his father, 22 December 1854.
[27] Steevens, *The Crimean Campaign*, p. 177. Dickens's fiction was particularly popular reading for soldiers in this period. Dickens, alongside others including Jane Austen, Edward Bulwer-Lytton, and Henry Fielding, was named on a list of authors receiving the 'highest degree of popularity' in J. H. Lefroy's 1859 Report on the Regimental and Garrison Schools of the Army, and on Military Libraries and Reading Rooms (London: Stationary Office), cited in Sharon Murphy, '"Quite Incapable of Appreciating Books Written for Educated Readers": The Mid-Nineteenth Century British Soldier', in *A Return to the Common Reader: Print Culture and the Novel, 1850–1900*, ed. Beth Palmer and Adelene Buckland (Aldershot: Ashgate, 2011), pp. 121–32, p. 126.

vengeance, allows for more complex responses. The abrupt reversal, which the tale dramatizes, of the historic enmity with France into an unbreakable alliance exposes the arbitrary nature of military allegiance, and might call into question the new hostilities of the Crimean War, while Doubledick's poignant mourning of his beloved friend killed in action shows, unequivocally, its costs.

CHRISTMAS SENTIMENT AND THE 'ABSURDITY' OF THE CHRISTIAN SOLDIER

Dickens mobilized the gentle military man for a variety of reforms—personal, political, and spiritual. This combination of secular and spiritual reformation is particularly typical of his Christmas writings. Indeed, the 1854 number cites Dickens's best-known Christmas book of a decade earlier, *A Christmas Carol* (1843). The traveller who narrates the tale of Taunton and Doubledick reminds us that 'Christmas comes but once a year—which is unhappily too true, for when it begins to stay with us the whole year round, we shall make this earth a very different place', echoing the lesson that Scrooge has learnt: 'I will honour Christmas in my heart and try to keep it all the year.'[28] In 1854 the opportunity for moral redemption is presented not by supernatural experiences, but by a reformed, meritocratic army system. The number, then, constitutes a sentimental, fictional deployment of the arguments made in broader journalism in Dickens's periodicals, and beyond, at this time which called for administrative reform. By placing 'Seven Poor Travellers' in this context, the politics of seasonal sentiment are laid bare.

The political mobilization of 'gentle' Christmas feeling is more readily associated with Dickens's Christmas books of a decade earlier, such as the attack on utilitarian thought in *The Chimes* (1844). Sally Ledger discusses the particular resonance in the 'Hungry Forties' of Dickens's emphasis on the 'regenerating power of human fellowship'.[29] A radically redemptive sentimentality, where the experience of strong feeling is intended to incite real-world change whether through character reformation or charitable giving, is familiar within the context of Dickens's Christmas writings. As Ledger argues of the earlier Christmas books of the 1840s, '*A Christmas Carol*, *The Chimes*, and *The Haunted Man*, in particular, all seem to be

[28] Melisa Klimaszewski draws out this parallel in her edition of *The Seven Poor Travellers* (London: Hesperus, 2010), p. viii.
[29] Sally Ledger, 'Christmas', in *Charles Dickens in Context*, ed. Sally Ledger and Holly Furneaux (Cambridge: Cambridge University Press, 2011), pp. 178–93, p. 179.

designed to educate the social conscience of Dickens's popular readership: the deprivation and social disruption which lurk within these tales could only be assuaged by the awakening of Dickens's readership into benevolent action.'[30] Ledger uses the Countess of Blessington's response to hearing Dickens read *The Chimes* as evidence of the 'pragmatic purpose and effect' of this work. A tearful Blessington wrote: 'This book will melt hearts and open purse strings... I was embarrassed to meet the eyes of my servants, mine were so red with tears.'[31] Ledger notes that Lady Blessington's reference to the opening of purse strings captures the double effect of these writings in the marketplace, inspiring individual charity at the same time as generating a considerable commercial success.

Men are repeatedly moved to repentant tears by exemplary soldiers in Dickens's Christmas numbers (later instances are discussed in the next chapter). Doubledick's weeping under the steady moral power of Taunton's gaze, the moment captured in Fraser's illustration, is not merely an incitement to readerly emotional self-indulgence. As the trajectory of this narrative (like Scrooge's) suggests, powerful feeling is followed by transformative social action. 'It was', as Ledger argues, 'of paramount importance to Dickens' that 'such emotional outpourings should have an instrumental effect'.[32] As Valerie Purton summarizes, 'sentimentalism's "belief in virtue" underpinned many of the key social and political reforms of the eighteenth and nineteenth centuries'.[33] In his 1852 Preface to the First Cheap Edition of the Christmas books Dickens gives a general statement of his purpose of inciting reformation of individuals and, by extension, the nation here united as 'a Christian land': 'My purpose was, in a whimsical kind of masque which the good humour of the season justified, to awaken some loving and forbearing thoughts, never out of season in a Christian land.' In 'Seven Poor Travellers' these 'forbearing thoughts' are directed to former French enemies turned allies, with Doubledick's eventual brotherly feeling for the French officer who was immediately responsible for his beloved friend's death presenting a topical parable of Christian forgiveness.

Dickens was clearly committed to the secular questions of army and administrative reform, using sentimental narratives of military men of feeling for political ends. Through his selection of the gentle soldier as the hero of his 1854 Christmas number, however, he also participates in

---

[30] Ledger, 'Christmas', p. 180.
[31] Quoted by Sally Ledger, '"Don't be so melodramatic!" Dickens and the Affective Mode', *19: Interdisciplinary Studies in the Long Nineteenth Century* 4 (2007), pp. 1–13, p. 3.
[32] Ledger, 'Don't be so', p. 3.
[33] Valerie Purton, *Dickens and the Sentimental Tradition* (London: Anthem Press, 2012), p. xxv.

the particularly urgent contemporary debate about how far Christianity and soldiering were compatible. As one satire, published shortly after the Crimean War put it: 'Of all conceits mis-grafted on God's Word / A Christian soldier seems the most absurd.'[34] Philip Bailey's poem critiques the warmongering of press and pulpit during the Crimean War, asking 'What's war but murder legalised?' (p. 34). It presents a direct attack on the incompatibility of committing violence and one strand of biblical teaching, by straightforwardly detailing the bodily realities of soldiering:

> That Word commands us so to act in all things,
> As not to hurt another e'en in small things,
> To flee from anger, hatred, bloodshed, strife;
> To pray for, and to care for other's life.
> A Christian soldier's duty is to slay,
> Wound, harass, slaughter, hack in every way...
> He's told to love his enemies, don't scoff;
> He does so; and with rifles picks them off.
> He's told to do to all as he'd be done
> by, and therefore blows them from a gun.

This simple argument with its visceral emphasis on wounding and hacking is combined with an arrestingly prescient one, about how the ideal of British democracy (which in Bailey's view is a problematic one anyway, as giving 'dominion / to blind eyes, rude heads, and unripe opinion', p. 7) is used to legitimate aggressive expansionism. Bailey's poem also shows the way in which press and Church unite to reconcile a Christian nation to war. Bailey's poem, together with Leigh Hunt's 'Captain Sword and Captain Pen' of 1835, belong to an incipient genre of war protest poetry.[35] Hunt's poem and accompanying essay also use depictions of war brutalities to question the coherence of an idea of just, Christian war. Critiquing the reader for wanting to turn away from the physical horror of war, Hunt points to a broad social culpability for this violence: 'Oh! shrink not thou, reader! Thy part's in it too; / Has not thy praise made the thing they go through / Shocking to read of, but noble to do?'[36] In the poem's postscript Hunt reinvokes the controversial lines addressed to God in

---

[34] Philip James Bailey, *The Age: A Colloquial Satire* (London: Chapman and Hall, 1858), p. 17.
[35] Rodney Stenning Edgecombe describes 'Captain Sword and Captain Pen' as 'the first antiwar poem in the language, or at least the first antiwar poem of the kind Wilfred Owen would come to write—poems that directly address the issue of violence'; *Leigh Hunt and the Poetry of Fancy* (Cranbury, NJ: Associated University Presses, 1994), p. 135.
[36] Leigh Hunt, 'Captain Sword and Captain Pen' (London: Charles Gilpin, 1849, third edition), p. 47.

William Wordsworth's Waterloo poem, 'Thanksgiving Ode' (1816): 'Carnage is thy daughter.'[37] Hunt vehemently disagrees with Wordsworth's poem, taking the opposite position to his contemporary Thomas De Quincey, who also used these lines in his essay of martial defence, 'On War' (1848), which was reprinted in an expanded version in 1854 at the start of the Crimean War: 'amongst God's holiest instruments for the elevation of human nature, is "mutual slaughter" amongst men, yes, that "Carnage is God's daughter" [sic]'.[38] These texts participate in a widespread debate about the compatibility of Christianity and soldiering in the Victorian period, debates which focused further reaching concerns about whether civilized men can wage wars.

Memorializations of Captain Hedley Vicars, the man who became known as the Crimea's foremost soldier saint, show the intensity with which the term Christian soldier was promoted and contested. Vicars felt a full conviction of Christian faith only some years after he had joined the army aged seventeen. When his regiment, the 97th, was posted to the Crimea, he worked tirelessly to bring the soldiers of all ranks around him to faith. As well as in conversations, small gatherings for prayer and Bible reading, distributing tracts, and giving burial services in the absence of army chaplains, he embodied a vigorous practical Christianity of the kind promoted by figures like Thomas Hughes and Charles Kingsley. Vicars visited the sick and dying in the Crimean hospitals, and actively cared for the men of his regiment, donating his blankets and warm clothing and often sleeping outside so that less robust men could have the benefit of protection from the Crimean winter.[39] As his biographer and memorialist Catherine Marsh put it, Vicars 'devoted himself with almost fatherly interest to the welfare of his men'.[40]

Memorials of Vicars emphasize the quality of his soldiering, as well as his godliness. Leading his men in a charge which saved a bungled operation, Vicars, as was widely reported, killed two Russians before being cut down himself and shot. As J. K. Watson argues, 'his conduct as soldier seems to have been exemplary. This is always recorded, if only because it

---

[37] William Wordsworth, 'Thanksgiving Ode', *Shorter Poems, 1807–1820*, ed. Carl Ketcham (Ithaca: Cornell University Press, 1989), p. 188. Discussed by Hunt, 'Captain Sword and Captain Pen', postscript, pp. 9–10.

[38] *The Works of Thomas De Quincey*, ed. Grevel Lindop et al., 21 vols (London: Pickering and Chatto, 2003), vol. 20, p. 31. For a full discussion of this essay and the widespread (mis)quotation of Wordsworth's lines through the nineteenth century by authors including Byron and Ruskin see Philip Shaw, '"On War": De Quincey's Martial Sublime', *Romanticism* 19.1 (2003), pp. 19–30.

[39] Catherine Marsh, ed., *Memorials of Captain Hedley Vicars* (New York: 1857), see especially pp. 196–7.

[40] Marsh, *Memorials*, p. 186.

was seen as evidence that a man could be a Christian and a soldier.'[41] Importantly, though, Vicars did not believe that soldiering was a Christian life. He explicitly states that had his sense of religious calling come earlier he would not have joined the army: 'Had I loved Jesus when I was seventeen, or rather had the love of Jesus been then made known to my soul, I *certainly* should not have been a soldier; but as it is, death alone shall make me leave my colours.'[42] This perspective, though, was eclipsed by the use of Vicars's biography as an exemplar of the Christian soldier. In her bestselling life and letters, *Memorials of Hedley Vicars* (1856), Marsh presents his life as a means to assuage doubts about this potential oxymoron:

> There are those who, in the face of examples to the contrary, still maintain that entire devotion of the heart to God must withdraw a man from many of the active duties of life, and who would be prepared to concede that in making a good Christian you may spoil a good soldier. To them the subject of this memoir affords a fresh and ample refutation.[43]

Many were unpersuaded. As one, possibly Quaker, reviewer colourfully put it in 1856, 'Captain Vicars going forth from "precious communion with his Saviour", to bayonet poor Russian peasants, or pour infernal fire upon the deserted town of Sebastopol, is as violent and revolting contradiction, as that of John Newton, combining a similar exercise with the man-stealing and manacles of the African slave trade.' The reviewer describes soldiering as 'professional homicide' and concludes that 'the profession of a Christian and a soldier could not possibly be reconciled'.[44]

Christian opinion was deeply divided on this point; pacifism was a key component of Quaker belief and this group led the establishment of a broader, non-denominational peace movement through groups including

---

[41] J. K. Watson, *Soldiers and Saints: The Fighting Man and the Christian Life*, in *Masculinity and Spirituality in Victorian Culture*, ed. Andrew Bradstock, Sean Gill, Anne Hogan, and Sue Morgan (Basingstoke: Palgrave, 2000), pp. 10–26, p. 20.
[42] Marsh, *Memorials*, p. 126, original emphasis.
[43] Marsh, *Memorials*, p. viii.
[44] *Soldiership and Christianity* (London: Ward and Co, 1858), p. 9, p. 16. The review supports this position with arguments about the problematic suspension of conscience for men under military discipline. Trev Broughton has tracked republication of Vicars's memoirs in tract forms through later nineteenth-century conflicts, including the American Civil War; these often incorporated the subtitle 'The Christian Soldier'. Some readers, as she records, continued to object to this conjunction, including the Civil War diarist Mary Chestnut who reflected, following a reading of Vicars's life in December 1861, 'I do not believe a genuine follower of Christ can be a soldier.' For this and other critical voices see Broughton, 'The Life and Afterlives of Captain Hedley Vicars: Evangelical Biography and the Crimean War', *19: Interdisciplinary Studies in the Long Nineteenth Century* 20 (2015).

the Peace Society.[45] The first British peace association was established in May 1816, and as Ceadel has shown, 'by the summer of 1851 pacificism seemed to be on such a sharply rising trajectory of public sympathy as to have some prospect of eventually displacing defencism'.[46] *The Herald of Peace*, the publication of the Peace Society, for example, achieved a circulation of over 12,000 in 1850, while annual peace conferences, widely supported pacifist pledges, and talks by campaigners attracting audiences of 4,000, made for high visibility and dissemination of peace arguments in the early 1850s.[47] The Crimean War was the first major campaign fought by Britain in the context of an established, organized peace movement. Though the Peace Society and related organizations had little direct impact on foreign policy, the presence of a robust critique of war had significant cultural implications in denaturalizing older views of war as inevitable and questioning new apologias for war as ideologically or religiously just. The resistance to war of the Quaker-led Peace Society offered a direct challenge to the championing of the Christian soldier.[48]

In this period the idea and identity of the Christian soldier was fiercely embattled, a counterweight to the prevailing idea of Victorian Britain as entirely adjusted to its own militarism. In 'Seven Poor Travellers' Dickens endorses the Christian soldier, helping to reconcile readers belonging to 'a Christian land' to Britain's participation in the violence of warfare. Just as a more efficient prosecution of the war via administrative reform would help to alleviate the extremes of unnecessary soldierly suffering, making war more socially acceptable, the figure of the Christian soldier legitimated war as just, emphasizing compassion over aggression even in direct

---

[45] For a discussion of the origins and legacy of Quaker peace testimony, formalized in the declaration of 1660 after which 'no Quaker would knowingly engage in any livelihood or action which involved war or violence', see Meredith Baldwin Weddle, *Walking in the Way of Peace: Quaker Pacifism in the Seventeenth Century* (Oxford: Oxford University Press, 2001), p. 8.

[46] Martin Ceadel, *Semi-Detached Idealists: The British Peace Movement and International Relations, 1854–1945* (Oxford: Oxford University Press, 2000), p. 32. Ceadel uses the term pacificists for a larger group than the small minority committed to absolute pacifism, who believe that 'war can immediately and unconditionally be repudiated'. Pacificists strive for the future cessation of warfare via international and state reforms, during which a defensive force may be needed. Defencists consider robust national defence as the best deterrent, following, in short, the maxim 'if you want peace prepare for war', p. 7. For more detail of the peace optimism around the Great Exhibition, swiftly followed by a new wave of French invasion fears, the founding of the Militia Act, and increasing support for war against expansionist Russia see David Nicholls, 'Richard Cobden and the International Peace Congress Movement, 1848–1853', *Journal of British Studies* 30.4 (1991), pp. 351–76.

[47] See Ceadel, *Semi-Detached Idealists*, pp. 26–30.

[48] As Ceadel puts it, 'though this was to be the last war in which the government was to hold fast days, secularisation and political change had not yet gone far enough to allow non-Christian inspirations for pacifism wholly to supersede Christian ones', *Semi-Detached Idealists*, p. 42.

combat. Dickens predominantly presents Doubledick's transformation of heart in a secular, humanist way; his reconciliation with the French officer is attributed to the promptings of his beloved friend's spirit, rather than to any specifically religious experience. Significantly, however, Christ is directly invoked in the rerouting of the revenge plot as Doubledick silently 'forgave him in the name of the Divine Forgiver of injuries'. The Christian content of this narrative is also amplified by Dickens's closing frame for the number, in which the narrator walking on Christmas day is struck afresh by signs in the landscape confirming his Christianity; he feels 'surrounded' by 'Christmas sacredness', and, as is typical of Dickens's emphasis on a deeply merciful, Christ-centred theology, 'thought how the Founder of the time had never raised his benignant hand, save to bless and heal' (p. 608). The specific reparative case that Dickens makes in 'Seven Poor Travellers' for the Christian soldier can fully be seen through the close parallels it has with Charles Kingsley's Crimean War writings.

'BRAVE WORDS' AND KILLING WITH RIGHT FEELING

The Reverend Charles Kingsley devoted considerable energy to trying to reconcile faith and war during the Crimean conflict, both in his novel published during the war and his direct addresses to the troops. Kingsley was one of the foremost proponents of a vigorous, practical Christianity, which quickly became dubbed 'muscular Christianity'. In 1854 he wrote 'Brave Words for Brave Soldiers and Sailors' to be distributed to the army and navy besieging Sebastopol.[49] In this he anticipates their concern: 'We want to be sure that God's blessing is on our fighting and our killing' (p. 203), and provides reassurance that this is a just war. Using examples of biblical battles, Kingsley argues that:

> the Lord Jesus Christ is not only the Prince of Peace; He is the Prince of War too. He is the Lord of Hosts, the God of armies; and whosoever fights in a just war, against tyrants and oppressors, he is fighting on Christ's side, and Christ is fighting on his side; Christ is his Captain and his Leader, and he can be in no better service. Be sure of it; for the Bible tells you so.

---

[49] On Kingsley's writing of this pamphlet as a result of his discomfort at being an armchair spectator of the war see Tai Chun Ho, 'Civilian Poets and Poetry of the Crimean Conflict: The War at Home', PhD thesis, University of York, 2015, and Louise Lee, 'Deity in Dispatches: The Crimean Beginnings of Muscular Christianity', in Mark Knight and Louise Lee, eds, *Religion, Literature and the Imagination: Sacred Worlds* (London: Continuum, 2009), pp. 57–74.

He also presents both fighting men and Christ as men of deep feeling. He offers reassurance to soldiers disheartened by the sense that no one can fully sympathize with and understand them in the midst of the horrors, privations, and agony of war and cholera, 'nothing is so comforting, nothing so endearing, as sympathy, as to know that people feel for one. If one knows that, one can dare and do anything. If one feels that nobody cares for one's suffering or one's success, one is ready to lie down and die' (p. 199). He encourages them to be cheered by the care of 'a Friend in heaven who feels for every trouble of yours, better than your own mothers can feel for you, because He has been through it all already' (p. 202).

Things become a bit more complicated in Kingsley's exhortation: 'ask Him to make you true and good, patient, calm, prudent, honourable, obedient, gentle, even in the hottest of the fight' (p. 203). Even within the context of a just war sanctioned by a God prepared himself to war for justice, the idea that one might embody gentleness 'even in the hottest of the fight' is a stretch (p. 204). Kingsley works hard in the pamphlet and in his fiction of the Crimean War period to differentiate goodness and brutality even in the action of killing. He provides practical moral guidance on the avoidance of dissent between ranks, tale bearing, complaints, laziness, and disorder as 'the devil's work', and condemns rape and plunder of civilians as cursed by God (p. 208). But as 'all cruelty and brutality is doing the devil's work' (p. 208), the exercise of battlefield violence requires some special pleading: 'Fight the enemy in God's name—and strike home; but never have on your conscience the thought that you struck an unnecessary blow. You are to kill for the sake of victory, but never to kill for the sake of killing' (p. 209). Righteous killing requires a particular state of mind and heart, in which enemy brutalities are forgiven through the pattern of Christ's forgiveness for his murderers. Killing for the 'sake of victory' must not be in a spirit of vengeance (p. 209).

This is the principal lesson that Amyas Leigh, hero of Kingsley's novel *Westward Ho!*, published in the same month as 'Brave Words for Brave Soldiers', must learn. Like this pamphlet, copies of the novel were sent to the troops. In a parallel with the conjunction of commerce and Christian conviction in Dickens's Christmas writings, Kingsley intended *Westward Ho!* to be both profitable and propagandistic, a tale to 'make others fight' and to shore up his shaky finances.[50] Kingsley outlines the characteristics of the muscular Christian in his dedication of *Westward Ho!* to Rajah Sir

---

[50] Markovits, *The Crimean War*, p. 70; see Norman Vance on Kingsley's effort to ensure the book would be commercially successful, *The Sinews of the Spirit* (Cambridge: Cambridge University Press, 1985), p. 87.

James Brook and George Augustus Selwyn, to whom he ascribes 'that type of English virtue, at once Manful and Godly, Practical and Enthusiastic, Prudent and Self-Sacrificing'.[51] It seems that Amyas Leigh will similarly embody these characteristics. He is introduced as sharing the training of 'the old Persians "to speak the truth and draw the bow"' and possesses additional 'savage virtues' of 'enduring pain cheerfully, and of believing it to be the finest thing in the world to be a gentleman; by which word he had been taught to understand the careful habit of causing needless pain to no human being, poor or rich, and of taking pride in giving up his own pleasure for the sake of those who were weaker than himself' (p. 9). Though this system works well against school bullies—Amyas is known for 'doing justice among his school fellows with a heavy hand and succouring the oppressed and afflicted' (p. 10)—in Amyas's adult career Kingsley shows the complexity of judging what counts as a just war, and of deciding when pain can rightly be caused to others. The space of the novel allows for a recognition of the difficulties inherent in the philosophy that Kingsley presents as simple in his pamphlet to Crimean War soldiers—that right killing must be done with right feeling. The novel's demonstration of the strains of its own philosophy at least in part redeems the excesses for which it is usually remembered.

Westward Ho! is a celebratory tale of Elizabethan colonialism, with fortune-hunting adventures in South America and plenty of skirmishing against the hated Spanish Catholics, culminating in the British defeat of the Spanish armada. The book is characterized by racial stereotyping and fairly hysterical anti-Catholic sentiment, as noted by contemporary reviews. The *Athenaeum*, for example, suggested that *Westward Ho!* would 'rouse a spirit of religious hatred and bitter intolerance'.[52] The novel's rabid anti-Catholicism even gives Kingsley momentary pause as in one of the direct references to the current less glorious campaign in the Crimea ('our late boasting is a little silenced by Crimean disasters', p. 592) he must acknowledge all the 'Roman Catholics whose noble blood has stained every Crimean battlefield' (p. 61). Notably he addresses his 'Brave Words to Brave Men' 'alike to Roman Catholic and Protestant' (p. 199), recognizing the major contribution made by Catholic soldiers, especially in the Irish regiments. Powerful anti-Catholic feeling is an uncomfortable component of texts of the muscular Christian genre, cutting against their

---

[51] Charles Kingsley, *Westward Ho!* (Edinburgh: Birlinn, 2009), p. v. Vance describes these dedicatees as two 'aggressively manly Christians of his own day', *Sinews*, p. 86.
[52] *Athenaeum*, 31 March 1855, p. 376. See Dereli, *War Culture*, p. 147, for other reviews making this point.

messages of love and justice.[53] The Christianity in muscular Christianity is strictly of British Protestant variety.

Though the lessons Amyas learns do not temper the novel's antipathy to Catholics and Spaniards, they do raise questions about the problems of personal hatred, drawing attention to the questionable morality of all national, racial, and religious prejudice. Amyas's quest to the Indies is inspired by a plan to 'rescue' Rose, a beautiful local woman, dubbed the 'Rose of Torridge', beloved by all the local Devon men, including Amyas and his brother Frank. When Rose leaves with a charismatic Catholic Spanish nobleman, Don Guzman, the men of Devon form the 'Fellowship of the Rose', pursuing her to the Indies, and taking plenty of gold along the way. Though the hero's and the narrative's energies are dedicated to this quest, Kingsley directly critiques it as a 'fatal venture of mistaken chivalry' (p. 398). Rose is found to have married the Don by her own choice, and the 'Fellowship's' arrival only causes her disaster. In this expedition Amayas and his first mate (Salvation Yeo, a former prisoner of the Inquisition, whose Indian wife and baby have been killed by the Spanish) are given plenty of direct motivation for their racial and religious hatred. Both Amyas's beloved Rose and, even more precious to him, his dear brother Frank, are taken, tortured, and killed by the Inquisition. Amyas focuses his desire for vengeance onto the figure of Don Guzman, whom he holds responsible for their deaths. Consumed by his appetite for revenge, which translates into a masturbatory obsession with his sword, Amyas is unable to take communion, considering himself 'in love and charity with no man' (p. 630):

> He is moody, discontented, restless, even (for the first time in his life) peevish with his men. He can talk of nothing but Don Guzman; he can find no better employment, at every spare moment, than taking his sword out of his sheath, and handling it, fondling it, talking to it even, bidding it not to fail him in the day of vengeance... That one fixed thought of selfish vengeance has possessed his whole mind; he forgets England's present need, her past triumph, his own safety, everything but his beloved brother's blood. (p. 629)

[53] In Hedley Vicars's letters, for example, he expresses his distress at learning that Catholic nuns have begun as nursing volunteers in the Crimean hospitals. Though he is firmly committed to alleviating the suffering in army hospitals, and sensitive to the needs of Roman Catholic soldiers (e.g. Marsh, *Memorials*, p. 158), Vicars fears for the spiritual welfare of men who may be converted to Catholicism: 'I know enough of Popery to dread its artifices', Marsh, *Memorials*, p. 206. Similar exclusiveness is apparent in different branches of Protestantism. Church of England Kingsley was less than fully enthusiastic about Vicars as evangelical hero, likening the evangelical movement's championing of Vicars to 'geese who have unwittingly hatched a swan' (1858 preface for his late 1848 novel *Yeast: A Problem* (London: Everyman, 1976), p. 6).

Finally, having pursued the Don around the world, during the battles of the Spanish armada and beyond, Amyas meets his foe in the midst of a cataclysmic storm. As the Don's ship goes down, Amyas and Salvation Yeo are struck by a lightning bolt, which kills Yeo and blinds Amyas. The blind hero recognizes this as 'a just judgement on him for his wilfulness and ferocity' (p. 653), and is reconciled to God: 'I have been wilful and proud, and blasphemous and swollen with cruelty and pride; and God has brought me low for it, and cut me off from my evil delight. No more Spaniard-hunting for me now, my masters, God will send no such fools as I upon His errands' (p. 657). Asked if he repents of fighting Spaniards, Amyas answers, 'Not I: but of hating even the worst of them' (p. 657). His rehabilitation is completed through a strange vision in which he speaks to the drowned Don among the 'oar weed', 'the prawns and the crayfish and the rockling' (pp. 658–7), and accepts that his adversary loved Rose truly and that Frank and Rose have forgiven him:

> 'We are friends Don Guzman; God has judged our quarrel and not we.'
> Then he said, 'I sinned and I am punished', and I said, 'And, senor, so am I.'
> Then he held out his hand to me, and I stooped to take it, and awoke.
> (p. 659)

In showing his hero repeatedly erring and finally chastened, Kingsley recognizes the lived difficulties of the apparently simple advice he gave to the soldiers before Sebastopol: 'to kill for the sake of victory, but never to kill for the sake of killing'. War, as other fiction of the Crimean period similarly recognizes, ferments deep personal enmity as well as the more culturally and (for some) spiritually acceptable enmities between nations. In its case for the triumph of individual acts of love and forgiveness between members of opposing sides as the moral basis through which national enmities can be fought out and then safely defused, Kingsley's message is remarkably similar to that of Dickens's Crimean War Christmas writing. In 'Seven Poor Travellers' a practical parable of army reform is swiftly transformed into a spiritual lesson in line with Kingsley's, which requires the soldier to be a man of right feeling, and to reject the temptation to kill in anger.

The parallels between Dickens's and Kingsley's rejection of the military revenge plot point to the less explicit Christian humanism of Dickens's work. Some critical attention has rested upon Dickens's fairly affirming delineation of muscular Christianity in the Reverend Septimus Crisparkle of *Edwin Drood* (1870), although Dickens is better known for puncturing the hypocrisy and egotism of churchmen and self-promoting philanthropists, the latter represented in that novel by the overbearing

Honeythunder.[54] Despite his scepticism about the misapplication of the Gospel by Church and churchmen, in his Christmas writings Dickens repeatedly held up the possibility of personal and spiritual redemption interlinked with social reform.[55] The parallels between his and Kingsley's Crimean War writing draw our attention to the significance of the model of Christ (often overlooked in discussions of Dickens's work) in Dickens's parable for the remaking of military behaviour.

'SHOCKING IMAGES... OF COMPASSION AND MERCY': DICKENS'S AND KINGSLEY'S CHRISTIAN SOLDIERS

Dickens's regular readers had a clear precedent for Doubledick's moral transformation through army service in the soldier hero of Dickens's previous novel, *Bleak House* (1853). That novel's Trooper George anticipates the more detailed account of Doubledick's military reformation. Like Doubledick, who joins the army as a 'dissipated and reckless' character, George explains his enlistment: '[I] went away and 'listed, harum-scarum, making believe to think that I cared for nobody, no not I, and that nobody cared for me.'[56] George describes himself as an 'idle dragooning chap who was an encumbrance and a discredit to himself, excepting under discipline' (p. 846). For George the army fits with what he feels to be a vagabond lifestyle, which prevents him from marrying, and which means

---

[54] For a reading of Crisparkle as 'an exemplary muscular Christian', 'a cultural ideal of Anglo-Saxon vigour and virtue', see David Faulkner, 'The Confidence Man: Empire and the Deconstruction of Muscular Christianity in *The Mystery of Edwin Drood*', in Donald Hall, ed., *Muscular Christianity: Embodying the Victorian Age* (Cambridge: Cambridge University Press, 1994), pp. 175–93, p. 175.

[55] Dickens was also sceptical about the idea of holy war. He questions the religious motivation of the medieval crusades in *A Child's History of England*, pointing variously to greed, lack of other employment, love of adventure, and the appeal of sanctioned violence as inducements: 'All the Crusaders were not zealous Christians. Among them were vast numbers of restless, idle, profligate, and adventurous spirits of the time. Some became Crusaders for the love of change; some in the hope of plunder; some, because they had nothing to do at home; some because they did what the priests told them; some because they liked to see foreign countries; some because they were fond of knocking men about, and would as soon knock a Turk as a Christian', p. 58. As is characteristic of many Victorian writings on war, this critical perspective is contradicted in other parts of *A Child's History* by Dickens's racial supremicism—'the English Saxon character' 'has been the greatest character among the nations of the earth'—and imperialist enthusiasm for what he presents as the utopian global benefits of energetic Saxon expansionism: 'Wheresoever that race goes, there, law and industry, and safety for life and property, and all the good results of steady perseverance, are certain to arise', p. 27.

[56] Charles Dickens, *Bleak House* (London: Penguin, 1996), p. 845.

he can only be reconciled to the regular billet of the shooting gallery 'camp [ing] there, gipsy fashion' (p. 444). Despite his 'vagabond' disposition, his army career sees him promoted to sergeant, a rise from the ranks to the status of non-commissioned officer that suggests his diligence and capability.

Although the Crimean War was a significant turning point in perceptions of the soldier as worthwhile of humane treatment and having a capacity for admirable humanity despite the brutalization of war and of army life, Dickens's Trooper George demonstrates that these opinions were shifting, in line with a wider rethinking of the social role of the working man, prior to that war. In *Bleak House* Dickens anticipated the claims of the Administrative Reform Association for the superior efficiency of the middle and working classes, through the virtues attributed to George and his veteran friend Matthew Bagnet. These ex-military men exude 'efficiency, attention to detail, orderliness', qualities that, as Peck has pointed out, are 'entirely compatible with running a business'.[57] Like George, Matthew Bagnet's values are far from militaristic. 'An ex-artillery man, tall and upright' (p. 441), Bagnet speaks with some relief at having been able to leave the army after finding a talent for playing the bassoon. On Mrs Bagnet's advice he borrows one from his regimental bandmaster and practises it in the trenches, after years of failing with violin and then flute, which allows him an alternative livelihood playing theatres— together with his son, a drummer—and running a musical instrument shop. His phrase 'Discipline must be maintained' has a domestic rather than martial application, as it is used to support the fiction that he runs his household rather than the wiser Mrs Bagnet.

In *Bleak House*, as in his Crimean Christmas fiction, Dickens presents an army career as reforming to 'harum-scarum' characteristics of idleness, dissipation, and recklessness, largely through George's relationship with his commanding officer, for whom he cares deeply. As the various mysteries of the novel begin to resolve we learn that trooper George has nursed his captain through illness on campaign, a history of intimacy that the unscrupulous lawyer Tulkinghorn hopes to exploit: 'You served under Captain Hawdon at one time, and were his attendant in illness, and rendered him many little services, and were rather in his confidence' (p. 434). In a statement of fidelity that echoes the terms of the marriage service, George elaborates that he saved his captain from committing suicide:

---

[57] John Peck, *War, the Army and Victorian Literature* (Basingstoke: Palgrave, 1998), p. 108.

I have been at his right hand many a day when he was charging upon ruin full-gallop. I was with him when he was sick and well, rich and poor. I laid this hand upon him after he had run through everything and broken down everything beneath him—when he held a pistol to his head. (p. 348)

George's willingness to care for his captain in these extremities is extended after his army career through the physical and emotional care he offers to those suffering, across the social spectrum. In a materialization of the kind of juxtaposition with which this book is concerned, George's shooting gallery business becomes a makeshift hospital. George is assisted there by Phil Squod, one of the destitute, physically suffering men he takes in, who 'with his smoky gunpowder visage, at once acts as a nurse and works as armourer' (p. 732). Though Phil's skin is imbued with the residues of weaponry and George never shakes off his military bearing, these characters offer the kind of tender care also celebrated as the capacity of the novel's heroines. Many of Dickens's first British readers might have seen a continuity between *Bleak House*'s Sergeant George and the gentle soldiers of 'Seven Poor Travellers'. During 1854 *Bleak House* was published in translation in two Russian periodicals, *Sovremenik* (*The Contemporary*) and *Otechestvennye Zapinksi* (*Annals of the Fatherland*), giving those on the opposite side of the war an insight into Dickens's determinedly curative presentations of the military man.[58]

For Rowan Williams, speaking as the then Archbishop of Canterbury at the wreath-laying service at Westminster abbey on Dickens's bicentenary, *Bleak House* is Dickens's 'most profoundly theological' work. Williams made his case through the moving example of the dying Sir Leicester Dedlock 'holding open the possibility of forgiveness and restoration' to his erring wife. For Williams this is one of 'the strangest, most shocking images that Dickens ever gives us of compassion and mercy'.[59] Trooper George, in his democratic extension of care to all, offers a similarly strange vision of compassion. George has been a personal servant to Sir Leicester before his army career, and returns to care for Sir Leicester in his final illness so well that the baronet describes him as 'another self to me'. Indeed, George's care for Sir Leicester allows him to express that forgiveness for his wife—to which he calls George, his sister, and his housekeeper as witnesses: 'I revoke no disposition I have made in her favour...'

---

[58] Veronica Shapovalov, 'They Came from Bleak House', *Dostoevsky Studies* 9 (1988), pp. 202–7, p. 206. These translations were by V. Butszor and I. Biriler. Biriler's translation, Shapovalov records, was published as a separate book in 1855.

[59] Rowan Williams, Address, Westminster abbey, 8 Feb 2012. Available online at http://www.archbishopofcanterbury.org/articles.php/2347/archbishops-address-at-charles-dickens-wreathlaying-ceremony-at-westminster-abbey.

(p. 895). Williams sees this unconditional forgiveness as the strongest Christian statement in Dickens's writing. The baronet and trooper as exemplary men of feeling demonstrate the depth of Dickens's engagement with a Christian theology of boundless compassion. George can be seen, then, as an important part of Dickens's wider commitment to presenting the Christian soldier as a masculine ideal.

The project of delineating the Christian soldier was sufficiently problematic that Kingsley turned away from it in the novel he wrote after *Westward Ho!* In *Two Years Ago* (1857), which directly incorporates a Crimean War plot, the hero, Tom Thurnall, is not a soldier, but a doctor, who risks his life to save others in the cholera epidemic of 1853–4. Although Thurnall does eventually travel to the Crimean conflict (he hopes to work as a spy), his heroism has already been proved by his life-saving work at home. The novel presents a view of war as a bracing alternative to the supposedly enervating, degenerative effects of commerce and luxuriousness—'what can ever happen henceforth save infinite railroads and crystal palaces, peace and plenty, cockaigne and dillettantism to the end of time'—similar to that Kingsley expressed at the outbreak of the Crimean War, hoping it would despatch 'the dyspeptic unbelief, the insincere bigotry, the effeminate frivolity which paralyses our poetry as much as it does our action'.[60] In his battle with cholera Tom Thurnall finds a worthy object for vehement, crusading energy within a domestic context: 'I hate neglect, incapacity, idleness, ignorance, and all the disease and misery which spring out of that. There's my devil; and I can't help it for the life of me, going right at his throat, wherever I meet him!' (p. 212). As Norman Vance points out, 'Kingsley deliberately relinquished the opportunity to describe the heroism of war and to make the point that a truer heroism could be found at home, a tactic often deployed by the apologists of moral manliness' (p. 91). In this change of emphasis for his explicitly Crimean War novel, Kingsley recognizes the problems inherent in celebrating the Christian soldier and finds the muscular Christian working in humanitarian roles a more coherent figure. A swathe of writers of the period, including *The Times* correspondent William Howard Russell in his Crimean novel *The Adventures of Doctor Brady* (1868) and Dinah Craik in *A Life for a Life* (1859), made a similar move, making their heroes medical rather than military men. Reflecting on this phenomenon

---

[60] Charles Kingsley, *Two Years Ago* (London: Macmillan, 1889), p. 378; Kingsley, quoted in Jonathan Parry, *The Politics of Patriotism: English Liberalism, National Identity and Europe, 1830–1886* (Cambridge: Cambridge University Press, 2006), p. 218.

Markovits suggests that 'since suffering is the problem, the hero will be not a soldier but a doctor'.[61]

Two Years Ago does include a military man of feeling in its supporting cast of heroic men, the brokenhearted Major Campbell turned natural historian 'to drive away thought' (p. 241). Like Trooper George, but at the opposite end of the scales of class and rank, the major embodies a typical mid-Victorian combination of strength and delicacy: 'A right, self possessed, valiant soldier he looked; one who could be very loving to little innocents, and very terrible to full-grown knaves' (p. 240).[62] As with many descriptions of soldiers in the period (including Dickens's of George whose 'step too is measured and heavy, and would go well with a weighty clash and jingle of spurs. He is close-shaved now, but his mouth is set as if his upper lip had been for years familiar with a great moustache', p. 341), the profession is written into Campbell's physique, and his expression embodies the contest between military discipline and powerful feeling: 'His mouth was gentle as his eyes; but compressed, perhaps by the habit of command, perhaps by secret sorrow' (p. 239). Major Campbell sets aside his microscope to support Tom in the cholera epidemic, to offer aid to the unjustly jealous husband of the woman he loves, and then to fight in the Crimea. Variously described as combining the 'word of a Christian and a soldier' (p. 395, see also p. 291), he welcomes the war as an 'old soldier . . . who has been so long at his trade that he has got to take a strange pleasure in it' (p. 255). He quickly confirms that this 'strange pleasure' is not in killing: 'only in the chance of —— But I will not cast an unnecessary shadow over your bright soul' (p. 255). The major's pleasure in contemplating the chance of his own death is here only expressed as a shadowy unspeakability represented by a dash, but this longing is realized as he dies in the war with a note from the unattainable woman he loves in a silk bag 'lying next his heart', and is buried on Cathcart's Hill (p. 459).

---

[61] Markovits, *The Crimean War*, p. 32. Kingsley returns to a charismatic aggressive military hero in his historical novel *Hereward the Wake* (1866), again debating the compatibility of 'the rough fighting world' and the Christian chivalric ideal of 'gentle, very perfect knighthood' (London: Macmillan, 1895), p. 66. With the death of the hero, 'last of the old English', the balance between his prominent muscularity and only occasionally apparent Christianity is reversed in subsequent generations of 'new English' who endorse an alternative model of heroism: 'If others dare to be men of war, I dare more; for I dare to be a man of peace. Have patience with me and I will win for thee and for myself a renown more lasting, before God and man, than ever was won with lance', p. 373. As in *Westward Ho!* the historical setting allows Kingsley to align the novel's energies with the hero's endless willingness for vigorous battle, usually in a cause he perceives as just, and it is left to a reformative ending to briefly expose the contradictions within Christian soldiering.

[62] In his biography of Kingsley, Robert Barnard Martin describes Major Campbell via Thackeray as 'the patient Dobbin-like army man who loves hopelessly', *The Dust of Combat: A Life of Charles Kingsley* (London: Faber and Faber, 1959), p. 203.

Two Years Ago offers a sustained investigation into the varieties of masculine heroism. Set against the admiration, expressed by the novel's curate Frank Headley, of soldierly 'self-sacrifice'—'when he is needed, he will go and die that he may be of use to his country'—and the noble, if suicidally wilful, death of Major Campbell in the Crimea are 'other sorts of self-sacrifice, less showy' (p. 329). An answer is given to the question 'what can a man do more than die for his countrymen?': 'Live for them. It is a longer work, and therefore a more difficult and a nobler one' (p. 329). Though concerned in this immediate post-war period that such arguments 'may seem invidious' 'just now', Kingsley's 1857 novel makes a clear case for the domestic value of muscular Christianity as a response to epidemics and moral turpitude at home, retreating from the effortful endorsement of the combination of faith and fighting he'd made two years before.

LIBERAL WARRIORS

In both Dickens's and Kingsley's fiction the Christian soldier embodies a range of humanitarian values, compatible with the new liberal rhetoric of war. As Jonathan Parry puts it in his exploration of the development of a 'constitutional and humanitarian rhetoric' of defence in the second half of the nineteenth century, in the Crimean conflict 'the attempt to infuse Liberal politics with ethical righteousness had won its first victory—a war that was to kill over half a million people'.[63] Given the prevailing view of 'Britain's role as the defender of liberty, progress, fairness and self-government against brute aggression', representations of the ideal soldier as an antidote, rather than incitement, to 'brute aggression' supported the coherence of the liberal rationale for war.[64] As Parry points out, factors including the positive press coverage in the latter part of the war and the institution of the Victoria Cross to reward all ranks shifted perceptions of the army, 'once generally regarded as an arm of oppression and a taxpayer funded aristocratic bolthole': 'The war made the army appear a more respectable and even a Christian institution.'[65]

Prior to the Crimean War, as Michael Snape has shown, the army already incorporated Christian structures, including weekly public worship mandated under the Articles of War, and offered some religious provision through the Army Chaplain's Department. Shortages of company chaplains meant that many officers took on the roles for which

---

[63] Parry, *The Politics of Patriotism*, p. 6, p. 219.
[64] Parry, *The Politics of Patriotism*, p. 218.
[65] Parry, *The Politics of Patriotism*, p. 77.

Hedley Vicars later became famous, leading prayers, burial services, and 'promoting the religious well-being of their men'.[66] Civilian perceptions, however, of the soldier as 'an object of public sympathy' and 'a champion of Christian civilisation' developed during the Crimean War, as traditional stereotypes of the brutality and fecklessness of the regular soldier were challenged.[67] Authors like Dickens and Kingsley and other proponents of Christian militarism used representations of the Christian soldier to suggest the parity between military and civilian values in a predominantly Christian society, endorsing soldiering as a profession and recommending a broader model of energetic, socially curative manliness. While, as we have seen, opposing Christian peace arguments meant that the Christian soldier was a culturally contested figure, the humane qualities of that figure—reforming profligate soldiers, becoming reconciled to former enemies, nursing and working to improve sanitation, caring for children, etc.—were uncontroversial.

The gentle soldier was normalized to the extent that those, like G. A. Lawrence, writing about heroes who enjoyed the violence of battle, hunting, boxing, and street fighting alike, acknowledged themselves to be out of step. In his Crimean novel of 1859, *Sword and Gown*, Lawrence's ruthless Captain Royston Keene, a man of 'high play, and hard riding, and hard flirting (to give it a mild name), and hard drinking', eventually becomes a hero of the light brigade, dying in the infamous doomed charge.[68] As Vance argues, 'Lawrence's hard-bitten lawless adventurer is actually an unusual Crimean hero, for by the 1850s, the glamour of military achievement was often a starting point for the homily on Christian heroism and soldiers of the cross.'[69] Keene is a particularly unusual officer hero in his frank pleasure in violence as a release for 'passions' 'difficult to appease or subdue' (chapter 1), and in his turn away from the kind of moral command model exemplified by Dickens's Taunton and Kingsley's Amyas and promoted by military manuals. Lawrence questions the doctrine that officers will develop a mutually improving relationship with the men under their command. Instead, Keene 'had acquired to an unusual extent, the overbearing tone and demeanor which the habit of

---

[66] Michael Snape, *The Redcoat and Religion* (Abingdon: Routledge, 2005), p. 89.
[67] Snape, *Redcoat*, p. 76. As Snape documents, the Crimean War 'saw a dramatic rise in public expenditure on the soldier's ... religious needs', encompassing the extension of the army chaplain's department, the construction of chapel huts and chaplain's residences in military camps, and a tenfold increase in the production and distribution of religious literature. See also Olive Anderson, 'The Growth of Christian Militarism in Mid-Victorian Britain', *English Historical Review* 86 (1971), pp. 46–72.
[68] G. A. Lawrence, *Sword and Gown* (Middlesex: Echo, 2007), unpaginated, chapter 10. Subsequent references given by chapter.
[69] Vance, *Sinews*, p. 15.

having soldiers under them, is supposed to bring, too commonly, to modern centurions' (chapter 12); 'he was the strictest disciplinarian and looked upon his men as the merest machines' (chapter 11). Though described as 'The Cool Captain' by his regiment (chapter 1), Keene has an indefinable charisma, inspiring devotion amongst all that serve with him. In a remarkable departure from the representation of the beneficial influence of the caring, humane officer typical in the 1850s, he transmits his demonic bloodlust to his regiment on campaign in India: 'it seemed as if the devil that possessed him had gone out to the others too, for they all shouted in reply, not a cheery, honest hurra! but a hoarse, hungry roar, such as you hear in wild beasts' dens before feeding time' (chapter 11).[70] This account of the bestial, devilish violence of the British army—'We'll follow the captain anywhere—follow him to hell!' (chapter 11)—stands apart from contemporary representations.

Lawrence interrupts his narrative to recognize the cultural uneasiness provoked by the violence of war, especially unvarnished accounts of the supremacy of muscle power and the delights of stabbing and slashing he favours: 'There is a heavy run just now against the "physical force" doctrine...It is perfectly true that to thrash a prize-fighter unnecessarily is not a virtuous or a glorious action, but I contend that the capability of doing so is an admirable and enviable attribute. There are grades of physical as well as moral perfection; and, after all, the same Hand created both' (chapter 13). Though Lawrence nods to a possible defence for his character's excesses as a flexing of God-given muscles, and he shares Kingsley's frustrations with an 'advancing civilisation' that Lawrence presents as fitting men for little more than enjoying parlour games and caviare (chapter 13), there is little conceptually or theologically to ally his work to the scripture-based muscular Christian writing of Kingsley, and others like Thomas Hughes and F. D. Maurice with whom he was often grouped.[71] Lawrence's Captain Keene invokes Kingsley as a possible source of reformation: 'I think it might have done even *me* some good, when I was younger, to have talked for half an hour with the man who wrote "How Amyas threw his sword away"' (chapter 9, Amyas is applauded again in chapter 13). For a moment, even the decade's most brutal officer expresses the appeal of the personally and culturally ameliorative case for Christian soldiering, identifying the moment at which Amyas is purged of his bloodlust and rejects vengeful killing. In this

---

[70] Keene is similarly immoderate in a civilian context, only narrowly avoiding strangling a man who crosses him (chapter 12).

[71] Vance firmly distinguishes Lawrence from other writers popularly given a 'muscular Christian' tag, *Sinews*, p. 15.

denouement, as we have seen, Kingsley works hard to wrest the brawny pleasures of Amyas Leigh into line with the advice he gave the army and navy in the Crimea, finally transforming the joys of Spaniard-hating, plunder, and personal vendetta which drive *Westward Ho!* into a pointed reformist lesson. Lawrence's referencing here of Kingsley's Amyas parallels his 1855 invocation of Thackeray's Colonel Newcome, discussed in chapter 1, also a source of potential redemption for another aggressive soldier antihero. In presenting his enthusiasm for the '"physical force" doctrine' as an embattled position, rather than a norm, Lawrence responds to the cultural uneasiness with military violence that differently inspires the range of texts discussed here, concerned to make compatible civil ideals of the gentleman and martial ideals of the soldier.

The examples of morally exemplary and physically gentle soldiers, learning only to kill with right feeling and preferring to, variously, be reconciled or be killed rather than to kill, that abound in Dickens's and Kingsley's fiction and beyond, anticipate the twenty-first-century emphasis on the 'liberal warrior'. Julia Welland uses this term to describe how the soldier is 'familiarised and personalised' in British media and museums now; shown more frequently in civilian clothing than in uniform with weaponry, surrounded by friends and family, especially children, as part of the cultural concealment of war violence.[72] Representations of the liberal warrior have a longer history, directly linked to the self-presentation of Britain as a liberating power, aligned against autocracy. In the Crimean War this narrative of international intervention against Russia as an enemy to democracy and to the liberty of nations across Europe was particularly pronounced, as was the constellation of gentle British military heroes in published literature, and in soldiers' own accounts. The following two chapters consider a key component of the liberal warrior narrative—the soldier as tender protector of children. As Kingsley puts it in *Westward Ho!*, 'No man is lost who still is fond of little children' (p. 509), and again in *Two Years Ago*: 'the boy's heart cannot be in the wrong place while he is still so fond of little children' (p. 25). Major Campbell, 'one who could be very loving to little innocents', says of the

---

[72] Julia Welland, 'Liberal Warriors and the Concealment of Violence', Sensing War conference, London, 12–13 June 2014. In her work on the prioritization of the 'winning of local hearts and minds' in the work of ISAF (International Security Assistance Force) in counterinsurgency operations in Afghanistan, Welland argues that 'today, British soldiers similarly secure their innocence against claims of a "new imperialism" and their status as benevolent liberal warriors through an unhinging of the violence of the British Empire. Unlike the brutality of the Empire, contemporary interventions are [promoted as] in "partnership" with the local forces', 'Liberal Warriors and the Violent Colonial Logics of "Partnering and Advising"', *International Feminist Journal of Politics* (2014), pp. 1–19, p. 6.

possible nuisance of having lodgings near the school: 'What better music for a lonely old bachelor than children's voices' (p. 240). These sentiments derive from biblical texts including Matthew 19:14, Kingsley directly repeating the phrase 'little children' as given in the Authorized Version: 'But Jesus said, Suffer little children, and forbid them not, to come unto me: for of such is the kingdom of heaven', and Matthew 18:5, 'And whoso shall receive one such little child in my name receiveth me.'[73] Dickens emphasizes this part of Christ's teaching in the version of the New Testament he wrote for his children, detailing Jesus's naming of a little child as 'greatest in the Kingdom of Heaven', and continuing from the account given in Matthew 18, '"But whosoever hurts one of them, it were better for him that he had a millstone tied about his neck, and he were drowned in the depts of the sea"... Our Saviour loved the child and loved all children.'[74]

By applying a Christlike tenderness for children to their representations of soldiers, both Dickens and Kingsley continue their case for the Christian soldier. In their plots of soldiers adopting children on campaign—an important strand, as we shall see, of *Westward Ho!* and a recurrent narrative in Dickens's later Christmas fiction—the receiving rather than hurting of children is given a literal realization. To underscore the Christian content of this plot line the hero of Dickens's 1862 Christmas number who adopts an illegitimate toddler is called Corporal Théophile, which translates as lover of God. Plots of soldier adoption, more broadly though, offer powerful support to the image of the liberal warrior, engaged in a just, because liberal, war, an image popular during the Crimean War, its aftermath, and today.

---

[73] King James Version. See also Mark 9:37.
[74] Charles Dickens, *The Life of Our Lord* (London: Associated Newspapers, 1934), p. 55.

3

Children of the Regiment

Narratives of Battlefield Adoption

One of the quest narratives in Charles Kingsley's 1855 novel *Westward Ho!* is the burly gunner Salvation Yeo's search for the young girl he has promised to protect.[1] Yeo, Amyas's first mate and right-hand man, explains that the 'little maid', as he calls her, 'a little girl, a marvellously pretty child, of about six or seven', was entrusted to him by his former captain. On the run in the rainforest Yeo carries her, sings to her, collects blossoms of water for her to drink, makes posies for her hair and plaits sandals for her (p. 559). Having become separated from the beloved girl after this valiant attempt to sustain them in the South American jungle, Yeo is haunted by his broken promise, dreaming nightly of the child and feeling he 'shall go mad' if he doesn't find her (p. 148, p. 174). Similar plots of military men becoming adoptive parents as they care for neglected children encountered on campaigns or those displaced by war are surprisingly prevalent in mid-Victorian British literature and art. While exemplary officer figures (like Colonel Newcome, Captain Taunton, and Captain Amyas Leigh; see chapters 1 and 2) were often used to promote a more humane army system and a moral model of command, Kingsley and his contemporaries used adoption narratives to idealize soldiers of the ranks as Christian gentleman.

This chapter explores this persistent inflection of the idea of the regimental family to extend the question of why gentleness, tactile and emotional, is such a recurrent feature in representations of the regular soldier. It looks at the renegotiation of manly ideals along lines of class and nationhood, and considers debates about the relationship between military masculinity, domesticity, and the role of the father. Such plots continued to be highly popular in the late nineteenth century, persisting in the work of authors like John Strange Winter through the 1880s and 1890s, usually seen to be the heyday of the British empire, the stiff upper

---

[1] This novel is considered in the context of Kingsley's Crimean writings in chapter 2.

lip, and the literary portrayal of soldierly pluck and derring-do. In tracing the continuation of these plots through the late nineteenth century and into the twenty-first, the chapter considers how a particularly domesticated paternal ideal is ideologically mobilized in war narratives.

'FROM GREAT GUNS TO NEEDLES AND THREAD': THE SOLDIER AND THE DOMESTIC IDEAL

Both Kingsley and Dickens, as we have seen, made a straightforward connection, both scriptural and sentimental, between the care of children and personal reformation. Corporal Théophile, literally lover of God, of Dickens's 1862 Christmas number 'Somebody's Luggage', appears in a sequence of seasonal narratives of military adoption. In the subsequent two years of festive offerings in his journal *All the Year Round* (which superseded *Household Words* in 1859) Dickens was to follow Major Jemmy Jackman's adoption of an illegitimate infant in the Mrs Lirriper Christmas numbers of 1863 and 1864. In 'Somebody's Luggage' Dickens presents Théophile's paternal care for another illegitimate orphan as a natural extension of the regular soldier's capacity for homemaking.

As in 'Seven Poor Travellers', Dickens returns to a Francophile narrative of a military man of feeling for his contribution, under the heading 'His Boots', to a multi-authored Christmas number. Corporal Théophile is garrisoned in a Vauban fortress town on the French border, a training ground for Napoleon's 'Grand Army'. The French soldiers confound expectations of a strict division between military and domestic spheres, making themselves indispensable to the families with whom they are billeted:

> A swarm of brisk bright active bustling handy odd skirmishing fellows, able to turn to cleverly at anything, from a siege to a soup, from great guns to needles and thread, from the broad-sword exercise to slicing an onion, from making war to making omelettes.[2]

The potential threat of the town being overrun by a possibly unwelcome, hostile 'swarm' of soldiers is defused by the list of attributes that follows, particularly the alliterative 'brisk', 'bright', and 'bustling', which draws upon the language Dickens usually employs to describe the qualities of the 'little woman'. In contradistinction to their military activities, the soldiers produce modest (stereo)typically French working-class home cooking:

---

[2] Charles Dickens, 'Somebody's Luggage', in *The Christmas Stories*, ed. Ruth Glancy (London: Dent, 1996), p. 467.

nourishing soup and omelettes, featuring onion. The relative tactile delicacy—'from the broad-sword exercise to slicing an onion'—of the domestic skills of these 'handy' men is drawn out in the phrase 'from great guns to needles and thread', a neat summary of the kinds of juxtaposition with which this book is concerned. The homely aptitude of these soldiers is particularly perplexing to the story's other central figure, a bigoted Englishman who has never previously left the country but has now fled to France to more effectively sever his ties with his daughter who has had a child outside marriage:

> These fellows are billeted everywhere about... and to see them lighting the people's fires, boiling the people's pots, minding the people's babies, rocking the people's cradles, washing the people's greens, and making themselves generally useful, in every sort of unmilitary way, is most ridiculous! (p. 470)

The sequence of domestic verbs, 'lighting', 'boiling', 'minding', 'rocking', 'washing', offers a catalogue of activity not immediately associated with soldiering. While in the Englishman's narrow view these activities are comically and preposterously opposed to military masculinity, the narrative firmly places such skills as comfortably commensurate with army life:

> Was there not Private Valentine, in that very house, acting as sole housemaid, valet, cook, steward and nurse, in the family of his captain, Monsieur le Capitaine De la Cour—cleaning the floors, making the beds, doing the marketing, dressing the captain, dressing the dinners, dressing the salads and dressing the baby, all with equal readiness. (p. 470)

The romantically named Private Valentine (literally a military man of feeling) is placed in a context of regimental domesticity, with others of his troop similarly adept at housework, getting the groceries, and gardening. Dickens's reiterated descriptions of soldiers as men of 'the people'—'lighting the people's fires, boiling the people's pots' etc.—allies them with the intimate routines and concerns of working-class civilians, for whom they work selflessly. This illuminates the way in which representations of military domesticity work to erase the gap between state-directed actions of the army and the interests of the population.

An emphasis on domesticity is similarly apparent in soldiers' own descriptions of military life in letters and diaries. Across a broad range of conflicts and periods soldiers typically report developing their domestic skills as part of the experience of war. The conjunction of homeliness and soldiering was both political and personal. Soldiers became adept at the kind of tasks Dickens ascribes to Private Valentine—'housemaid, valet, cook, steward and nurse'—for reasons of expediency, and drew out continuities in routines and values between home and war as a form of what Michael Roper has called 'emotional survival'.[3] In terms of practical need, Madelyn Shaw and Lynne Zacek Bassett point out in their work on the American Civil War that 'self preservation in the military was considerably enhanced by self-sufficiency when it came to sewing, cooking and nursing, all skills in the female sphere in civilian life'.[4] In that war one senior officer, for example, sent a letter to the daughter of his aide-de-camp, teasing 'that her father is sitting on his blanket sewing a strap on his haversack. I think she ought to be here to do it.'[5] The first-hand accounts of British soldiers in the Crimean War regularly detail new endeavours in cooking and sewing, and more extended efforts at home-making. Audley Lempriere—a junior officer in the 77th Regiment, who is discussed in detail in the next chapter—wrote to his brother: 'The other day Leslie and myself made a most excellent plum pudding which I should not have thought of doing 3 months ago.'[6] He later reflects in a letter to a cousin on how his position requires him to develop housekeeping skills: 'I sent in for some currants, raisins and flour to make a plum pudding and for candles etc., as we are out of these luxuries. You will see therefore that amongst other things *this sort of life, besides teaching us the art of campaigning, teaches all the art of housekeeping*, and as I manage the accounts of our mess I have to send for things when they are wanted.'[7] Officers who survived into the later stages of the campaign, characterized by a static siege, could develop more elaborate 'art[s] of housekeeping'. George Roe, for instance, used his spare time and energy in attempting to cultivate a garden around his hut, using a combination of local flora and plants sent from home.[8] As we shall see in the following chapters, such work often included a significant component of emotional labour, as soldiers endeavoured to forge continuities between home and campaign life that could sustain them, others in their regiment, and their families.

A celebration of the domestic labour performed by soldiers was widespread in the histories, art, and literature of the period and frequently combined with detail of soldiers caring for children. Alexander Kinglake's history *Invasion of the Crimea* includes descriptions of the Rifle Brigade helping local women

---

[3] Michael Roper, *The Secret Battle: Emotional Survival in the Great War* (Manchester: Manchester University Press, 2009). I discuss Roper's work and reflect on soldiers' attempts to remain in touch with family via domestic practices in chapter 5.
[4] Madelyn Shaw and Lynne Zacek Bassett, *Homefront and Battlefield: Quilts and Context in the American Civil War* (Lowell, MA: American Textile History Museum, 2012), p. 141.
[5] Robert E. Loe to Louisa Washington, 9 August 1861, quoted by Shaw and Bassett, *Homefront and Battlefield*, p. 139.
[6] To Algernon, 25 May 1854, Hampshire Record Office, HRO 4M52/125.
[7] To Janey, 14 June 1854. Emphasis added.
[8] Roe's exchange of plants and horticultural news with his family is discussed in chapter 5 as part of a range of strategies for keeping in touch with home.

Children of the Regiment 91

with household work.[9] Similar behaviour was also observed in other regiments during the Crimean War, such as the 18th Irish, depicted in the assault on the Malakoff in a French painting (in the National Army Museum collection) which features a soldier feeding a baby from a bottle, while other members of the regiment get drunk or stand guard.[10] Such material, like Dickens's detailed descriptions of the homemaking of the French soldiery, disrupts an idea of a gendered separation of spheres.

Similarly, Thackeray's introduction of the year 1815 in his pre-Crimean War novel *Vanity Fair* extols soldierly childcare:

> When the soldier who drank at the village inn, not only drank, but paid his score; and Donald the Highlander, billeted in the Flemish farm-house, rocked the baby's cradle while Jean and Jeannette were out getting the hay. As our painters are bent on military subjects just now, I throw this out as a good subject for the pencil, to illustrate the principle of an honest English war.[11]

Here Thackeray generously acknowledges his source for this depiction in G. R. Gleig's *Story of the Battle of Waterloo*, which was published in 1847 and was a bestseller alongside *Vanity Fair*. Of all the material in Gleig Thackeray selects the homely aptitude of soldiers as his focus, drawing on this part of his account:

> It is recorded of the Highland Regiments in particular, that so completely had they become domesticated with the people on whom they were billeted, that it was no unusual thing to find a kilted warrior rocking the cradle while the mother of the little Fleming, which slept under its mountain of feathers, was abroad on her household affairs.[12]

Thackeray positions this vision of the caring, domesticated soldier as preferable to the heroic death and glory representations in some vogue at the time. Writing in *Punch* under the pseudonym of Professor Byles, Thackeray expresses revulsion in response to the military pictures exhibited at the Royal Academy in 1847, particularly the Battle of Meeanee by Edward Armitage. As Professor Byles says of the painting: 'In this extraordinary piece they are stabbing, kicking, cutting, slashing, and poking each other about all over the picture. A horrid sight! I like to see the British lion mild and good-humoured... not fierce, as Mr. Armitage has shown him.'[13] Reframing this somewhat double-edged critique in *Vanity Fair*

---

[9] Alexander Kinglake, *Invasion of the Crimea* (Edinburgh: Blackwood, 1863–80), vol. 2, p. 187.
[10] 'Épisode de l'assaut de la Tour Malakoff', NAM 1968-06-315-12.
[11] Thackeray, *Vanity Fair*, p. 336.
[12] G. R. Gleig, *Story of the Battle of Waterloo* (London: John Murray, 1847), p. 49.
[13] [William Makepeace Thackeray], *Punch*, 10 July 1847.

Thackeray proposes the image of the warrior rocking the cradle as a more appropriate subject for military art, which can 'illustrate the principle of an honest English war'. Thackeray's tone here is typically difficult to identify; the propagandistic formula 'honest English war' raises questions about the honesty of displacing soldiers' 'stabbing' 'and poking' with cradle-rocking. At the same time, as explored in more detail in chapter 1's reading of Thackeray's Colonel Newcome, Thackeray was himself drawn to gentle forms of war heroism, and to depictions of war that emphasized emotional losses and quiet victories of feeling and conscience over battle action. As we have seen, the 'cutting, slashing' school of military representation, exemplified by work by Armitage and G. A. Lawrence, was marginalized by the cultural predominance of gentle representations of the soldier. The domesticated 'British lion', 'mild and good humoured', was, as the sardonic inference behind the bluster of Professor Byles suggests, the much more likeable face of the British war machine.

Figures like Dickens's Théophile and Thackeray's cradle-rocking Highlanders rework the domestic ideal by carrying the bourgeois values of hearth, home, and family feeling into the public and professional context of the battlefield. These representations of military men of exemplary benevolence and domestic aptitude extend the work of figures like Thackeray's Colonel Newcome, and Dickens's and Kingsley's Christian soldiers, negotiating the increasingly apparent divide between civilian and military life. As Favret has suggested in the context of Romantic wars, repeated appeals to domestic sentiment had a strategic function as 'war is recast as the defence of women— mothers, sisters, wives—not the killing of other men'.[14] The shared investment in domesticity in literary and artistic representations of the Crimean War and in soldiers' own words and practices points to a development of a common structure of feeling; an emphasis on homeliness could make civilians feel better about national participation in war, and make soldiers' experience of war more manageable and communicable.

'ROUGH BUT KIND-HEARTED': SOLDIER ADOPTIONS AND THE REMAKING OF THE MILITARY GENTLEMAN

The Englishman in Dickens's 'Somebody's Luggage', whose reform is the central concern of this Christmas tale, is particularly fascinated and irritated by a particular case of domestic aptitude, in which Corporal

---

[14] Mary Favret, 'Coming Home: The Public Spaces of Romantic War', *Studies in Romanticism* 33.4 (1994), pp. 539–48, p. 543.

Théophile, a man of 'careful hands' (p. 476), cares for a disowned, illegitimate 'child of... no one', Bebelle. The corporal is billeted with the barber's family. Though the barber's wife receives a small stipend to look after the girl, she has been neglected until the corporal's arrival, when he takes her care upon himself: 'washing and dressing and brushing Bebelle... Always Corporal and always Bebelle. Never Corporal without Bebelle. Never Bebelle without Corporal' (p. 473). Dickens's story draws upon the summers he spent in 1853, 1854, and 1856 in Boulogne, where he observed the formation of the Northern Camp for the newly allied armies preparing for departure for the Crimea: 'It was wonderful... to behold about the streets the small French soldiers of the line seizing our Guards by the hand and embracing them.'[15] 'Somebody's Luggage' continues the work of Dickens's Crimean War Christmas fiction 'Seven Poor Travellers', remaking Anglo-French relations in a manner befitting this fledgling military alliance.

As in 'Seven Poor Travellers' Dickens's personal enthusiasm for French people informs the story. Dickens's representation of Théophile was inspired by his observation of the gentle childcare undertaken by a soldier of the ranks at the military camp in Boulogne, prior to the Crimean embarkation. Following this trip, in 1855 he noted the title 'Somebody's Luggage' in his *Book of Memoranda*: 'It was put into my head by seeing a French soldier acting as nurse to his master's—a Captain's—little baby girl, and washing her, and putting her to bed, and getting her up in the morning, with the greatest gravity and gentleness.'[16] On observing this type of inseparability between Théophile and Bebelle, Dickens's unlikeable Englishman exclaims, 'Why, confound the fellow, he is not her father!' (p. 472). The Englishman's landlady confirms this: 'He is not one of her relations. Not at all!' (p. 474), but contests the biological (il) logic in the Englishman's reading of the adoption: 'It is so genteel of him. The less relation, the more genteel' (p. 474). Dickens's emphasis on the gentility of this act (the landlady repeats the term 'genteel' three times in this conversation) translates the soldier's physical gentleness to the child into a measure of social worth, in a way typical of Victorian debates about what constitutes the gentleman.

Variously in 'Somebody's Luggage', gentlemanly status is accorded to those whose social standing is highest in terms of their benevolence, rather than their wealth, family, or profession. The caring but poor Monsieur

---

[15] Dickens to Forster, in John Forster, *Life of Dickens* (London: Chapman and Hall, 1874), vol. 3, p. 88.
[16] Dickens to Mrs Brown, 21 October 1862, quoted by Glancy, ed., *The Christmas Stories*, p. 449.

Mutuel, whose role in the tale is to approve the Englishman's interest in this adoption and his eventual reformation, is described as 'a gentleman in every thread of his cloudy linen, under whose wrinkled hand every grain in the quarter of an ounce of poor snuff in his poor little tin box became a gentleman's property' (p. 479). Dickens based this character on the kindly landlord of the houses he had rented in Boulogne, M. Beaucourt-Mutuel. In his article 'Our French Watering Place', and in his letters, Dickens celebrates the extraordinary benevolence and charity of this landlord, himself a military man of feeling, formerly a captain in the National Guard. In his biography of Dickens, John Forster records that Beaucourt-Mutuel preferred domestic serenity to military honours; on being offered a decoration by Captain Cavaignac, Beaucourt-Mutuel replied, 'No! It is enough for me that I have done my duty. I go to lay the first stone of a house upon a Property I have—that house shall be my decoration.'[17] Serendipitously the name Mutuel gestures towards the way the lives, of both the man and the character he inspired, are defined by the kind of benevolent social interconnectedness from which the Englishman in this Christmas number had hoped to distance himself. In this and other narratives of military adoption, the willingness to parent an unrelated child is synecdochic of a broader social manifesto for benevolence and interconnectedness (across divisions of class and nationality) between otherwise unrelated people. Dickens's Englishman who is described as having 'very little gentleness confounding the quality with weakness' (p. 472) must learn from the tender example of the corporal how to be a real gentle man, worthy, finally of Monsieur Mutuel's 'reverence' (p. 482).

The apparently simple story of 'Somebody's Luggage' performs substantial cultural work, exploring ideals of masculinity in ways that renegotiate traditional class values and national allegiances. Throughout there is a careful emphasis on the reciprocity of the benefit to both soldier and child. In a mode attentive to the emotional needs of the military man, the landlady intuits the mutual affective benefits of the partnership between Corporal Théophile and Bebelle: 'finding the poor unowned child in need of being loved, and finding himself in need of loving' (p. 475). That blood is not the only means of forming family is a lesson that, in the redemptive mode of the Christmas narratives, the Englishman must learn in order to reclaim his humanity. The Englishman must come to understand the benefit to both child and man in such a relationship, so that when the corporal unexpectedly dies a suitably heroic death, rescuing the villagers

---

[17] Forster, *Life*, vol. 3, p. 81.

from a terrible fire, he is ready to take on the care of Bebelle. In this the Englishman is explicitly inspired by the model of parenting he has observed: 'He made Bebelle's toilette with as accurate a remembrance as he could bring to bear on that work, of the way in which he had often seen the poor Corporal make it' (p. 481). Having learnt how to father from this tender military man, he leaves with Bebelle for England to find his 'forgiven' daughter (p. 481) and to experience family in a new way.

The somatic response modelled for the reader when the Englishman is moved to tears by the news of Corporal Théophile's death and is commended by M. Mutuel for his 'noble heart'—'I honour those emotions' says Mutuel (p. 497)—is not, or not merely, a self-indulgence in the pleasures of feeling for its own sake. In the trajectory of this narrative, as with Dickens's earlier transformative Christmas writings of Scrooge and Doubledick, powerful emotions incite social action.[18] Dickens's return to the military man as the reforming influence for social benevolence suggests that he wishes to inspire a change of heart and of attitudes towards the military. Dickens's depictions of gentle soldiers support post-Crimea army reforms, ongoing in 1862, that improved the service conditions and access to education of soldiers of the ranks. Dickens's working-class soldier heroes, from Trooper George of *Bleak House* onwards, also commend meritocratic forms of administration, and promote the reliability of the working man, an urgent topic within the context of reform to extend the franchise. Affirming narratives of military adoption by Dickens and his contemporaries offer a different way to celebrate the working-class soldier, hero of the 'thin red line' and 'soldiers' war'. Instead of emphasizing courage under fire, they present a socially palatable model of masculinity that transcends class categories: the military gentle man of feeling.

While Dickens clearly had a particular preoccupation with the plots of bachelor adoption and gentle soldiery, which he interweaves in Théophile's adoption of Bebelle, this Christmas number also speaks directly to a number of other highly popular representations of a child, usually a young girl, adopted by the military. Charlotte Yonge's Napoleonic adoption story *Kenneth, or The Rear Guard of the Grand Army* (1850) focuses on the retreat of the French army from their campaign in Russia through the freezing winter of 1812. Both Dickens's and Yonge's tales of the Napoleonic Grand Army offer plots of mutual saving, in which the soldiers who aid children are themselves spiritually and morally redeemed. These narratives share a renegotiation of class boundaries through the

---

[18] See chapter 2 for a fuller discussion of the politics of seasonal sentiment.

formation of adoptive families and rework historic national enmities, starring emotive French soldier heroes.

British images of the gentleness of French soldiers support a redrawing of lines of allegiance post-Waterloo, in readiness for the British/French/ Ottoman alliance in the Crimean War. Post-Crimean texts like 'Somebody's Luggage' also help to assuage anxieties about continuing French expansionism, which reached a peak in the invasion fears of 1859.[19] Brian Joseph Martin has argued that the reformed, more egalitarian systems of recruitment, integration, promotion, and training in the Revolutionary National Guard, which evolved into Napoleon's Grand Army, allowed ideals of fraternity to be realized between soldiers. This comparatively egalitarian structure appealed to those, like Dickens, frustrated by the hierarchies and barriers to progression, especially the purchase system, in the British army. Martin's study shows how French authors imaginatively capitalized on the expandability of military notions of family to present plots of co-parenting that drew parallels between Napoleonic and domestic loyalties. In his reading of Honoré de Balzac's *The Country Doctor* (1833) Martin focuses on the 'utopian postwar world' created around the veteran and adoptive father, Genestas, who parents the son of his dead comrade: 'in combining military and family duty, Genestas offers a new model of Napoleonic paternity for civilian society, where soldiers take responsibility for their children, and veterans forfeit warfare and guns for the welfare of their sons'.[20] Victor Hugo's French Revolution novel *Ninety Three* (1874), which explores the intersecting ethics of elective parenting, political idealism, morality, and faith through a sequence of adoption plots, draws a similar analogy between national and individual treatment of the child in need. Hugo documents that the revolutionary assembly declared 'childhood sacred in the orphan, whom it caused to be adopted by the country', and throughout the novel individual heroism or despotism is calculated by characters' responses to the three fatherless destitute children adopted by the Red Bonnet Battalion.[21] This adoption is instigated by the nursing baby girl's smile at the sergeant, at which 'a big tear rolled down his cheek and stopped at the end of his moustache, looking

---

[19] Accounts of previous conflicts, especially those in which the British proved victorious, could also provide reassurance in later, more uncertain conflicts, and as war evolved to incorporate troubling new tactics and technologies. John Peck, *War, the Army and Victorian Literature* (Basingstoke: Palgrave, 1998), p. 169, points out that during the Boer War there was a resurgence of Napoleonic and Crimean narratives.

[20] Brian Joseph Martin, *Napoleonic Friendship: Military Fraternity, Intimacy and Sexuality in Nineteenth Century France* (Durham, NH: University of New Hampshire Press, 2011), p. 214.

[21] Victor Hugo, *Ninety Three*, translated by Lowell Blair (New York: Bantam, 1962), p. 137.

like a pearl' (p. 13). On the other end of the political and class scale the characteristically pitiless aristocrat the Marquis de Lantenac is also redeemed by his capacity to feel for the children, particularly the infant girl Georgette, whose smile similarly moves him to tears: 'She smiled. That man of granite felt his eyes become moist' (p. 288). Hugo also elaborates on the ways in which elective affinity for a child can suspend structural differences and historical enmities:

> It is so easy to love a child! For what is he not forgiven? He is forgiven for being a lord, a prince, a king. The innocence of his age makes one forget the crimes of his race, his weakness makes one forget the exaggeration of his rank. He is so small that he is forgiven for being great. The slave forgives him for being a master. The old Negro idolizes the white infant. (pp. 94–5)

The expansiveness of French Revolutionary ideals of family and the Napoleonic army's reputation for fraternal feeling combined with widespread national assumptions about the French capacity for emotional expression to make the French soldier an ideal candidate for British visions of the military man of feeling. Seen as particularly equipped to embrace non-biological forms of family, the French soldier was a logical character choice in plots of adoption. Historians of emotion, such as Thomas Dixon, have suggested that British fears of French emotional excess as politically risky and tending to ferment revolution contributed to the development of a British national style of restrained feeling, which culminated in overlapping martial and civil ideals of the stiff upper lip.[22] In a wealth of mid-Victorian examples of approved soldierly feeling, an opposite impulse is apparent. In texts of soldier adoption, men of all ranks laugh and cry over their young charges, while providing tender nurture. Here the emotionally articulate French soldier is idealized for his ability to feel and care.

In their descriptions of an exemplary, emotive French soldiery Yonge and the historian Archibald Alison, by whose accounts she was inspired, picture Napoleon's army as more glorious in defeat, and in the last ditch defence of their fleeing comrades, than in victory. As with Thackeray's imaginative response to the details of soldierly care of children in Gleig's

---

[22] See Thomas Dixon, speaking on *Ian Hislop's Stiff Upper Lip: An Emotional History of Britain*, BBC2, episode 1, 2 October 2012, and Thomas Dixon, 'Forgotten Feelings: Our Emotional Past', *Huffington Post*, 1 Oct 2012: 'The bloody violence of that uprising [the French Revolution] was interpreted as the outcome of the cult of feeling. And the earliest versions of the idea that emotional restraint was an especially British trait appeared during the years that followed. The process had now begun of rewriting the national character in contrast with the revoltingly emotional French. Romance, enthusiasm, and strong feelings would have to go underground.' http://www.huffingtonpost.co.uk/thomas-dixon/british-stiff-upper-lip-our-emotional-past_b_1929511.html. Accessed 4 Nov 2014.

history, Yonge builds upon a suggestive short section in Alison's ten-volume *History of Europe during the French Revolution*, which details the retreat:

> In these moments of hopeless agony, all the varieties of character were exposed naked to view. Selfishness there exhibited in its baseness, and cowardice its meanness; while heroism seemed clothed with supernatural power, and generously cast a lustre over the character of humanity. Soldiers seized infants from their expiring mothers, and vowed to adopt them as their own: officers harnessed themselves to sledges, to extricate their wounded comrades; privates threw themselves on the snow beside their dying officers, and exposed themselves to captivity or death to solace their last moments. Women were seen lifting their children above their heads in the water, raising them as they sank, and even holding them aloft for some moments after they themselves were buried in the waves. An infant abandoned by its mother near the gate of Smolensko, and adopted by the soldiers, was saved by their care from the horrors of the Beresina; it was again seen at Wilna, again at the bridge at Kowno, and it finally escaped all horrors of the retreat.[23]

The selfishness and cowardice briefly mentioned are immediately displaced by an account of varieties of heroic care and sacrifice, and the military function of the army is eclipsed by the humanity of the individuals within it.[24] This is a typical trajectory in many nineteenth-century war narratives, which turn the focus from military violence to forms of rehabilitation, physical and emotional, necessitated by war.

Yonge's novel presents a particularly clear example of this transformative emphasis, through her focus on the cross-rank collective adoption of two children, Effie, age thirteen, and her brother, the eponymous Kenneth, nearly fifteen. Having lost their officer father, who is killed fighting for the Russian army in an early battle, the siblings are cast out into the snowy wilds of Russia by their flighty, and by this point desperate mother and her new French officer husband in the midst of the retreat. In this predicament they are saved by the cross-class care of an unlikely

---

[23] Archibald Alison, *History of Europe*, 10 vols (1833–43), vol. 8 (Edinburgh: Blackwood, 1840), p. 799.
[24] Yuval Harari, *The Ultimate Experience: Battlefield Revelations and the Making of Modern War Culture, 1450–2000* (Basingstoke: Palgrave, 2008) identifies military memoirs of the retreat from Russia as 'extreme disillusionment narratives', noting that, unlike in Alison's and Yonge's redemptive accounts, many Napoleonic soldiers witnessed the behaviour of their army as irredeemable: 'These narratives were particularly shocking because their almost unreadable descriptions of physical sufferings were not compensated for by *any* spiritual ideals, not even comradeship. Indeed the narratives usually described the moral collapse of the army in even greater detail than its physical collapse. According to many memoirs the *Grande Armee* became a decidedly unheroic mob of frightened, half crazed, and egotistical fugitives', pp. 277–8.

triumvirate of the French army, Colonel de Villaret and his nephew Lieutenant Louis de Chateauneuf, and a regular Breton soldier called Léon, a 'common soldier' as the officers describe him.[25] In their co-parenting the vertical structures of rank and class, as with those between Dickens's Corporal Théophile and the English gentleman, give way to a horizontal structure akin to brotherhood. Between them, these men by turns support, carry, and feed the children with what little food there is. Louis makes the ultimate sacrifice, giving Effie the last remaining morsel of food before dying himself of starvation. This, as Walton notes, is the scene selected for illustration as the frontispiece to the novel.[26] The forms of protection offered by these soldiers throughout are that of nurture rather than a military defence.

Yonge's brother, Julian, went on, as we have seen, to fight in the Crimean War. Walton suggests that in *Kenneth* Yonge aimed to write a book that would appeal to her brother and his friends and would 'instil the courageous characteristics she admired'.[27] More broadly, Yonge sought to make soldiering compatible with non-violent Tractarian ideals of masculinity, like those she was most famously to promote through the reformed behaviour of the aristocratic hero in *The Heir of Redclyffe*. In *Kenneth* her vision of masculine mercy and redemption takes in a broader class range. While the behaviour of the officers is clearly exemplary, Yonge also carefully details the gentle heroism of a rank and file soldier, Léon. Yonge's descriptions of the 'faithful care of the rough but kind-hearted Breton soldier' (p. 135) of 'rough but kind tones' (p. 75) highlight the juxtaposition of his qualities. Léon leaves behind a family who dread his 'learning the vices of the men among whom his lot was cast' and until the point in the campaign when he encounters Effie and Kenneth 'his good principles had been losing their force'. The children come by way, as he and the narrator see it, of battlefield salvation: 'Still his heart was not yet hardened, and he resolved, perhaps as a sort of atonement for past misdeeds, to protect these deserted children to the utmost of his power' (p. 77).

'These deserted children', and Effie in particular, have a civilizing effect. Long after the march Léon describes them as 'angelic messengers, sent to protect him during those dreadful days, at once from peril and temptation' (p. 325). He remembers Effie, in the language of the Victorian feminine ideal, as 'that little angel' (p. 319), a language also invoked by Dickens as

---

[25] Charlotte Yonge, *Kenneth, or The Rear-Guard of the Grand Army* (Leipzig: Tauchnitz, 1860), p. 91.
[26] Susan Walton, *Imagining Soldiers and Fathers in the Mid-Victorian Era: Charlotte Yonge's Models of Manliness* (Farnham: Ashgate, 2010), p. 78.
[27] Walton, *Imagining Soldiers*, p. 73.

the Englishman is reminded by Théophile's holding Bebelle aloft of the way he once lifted his own daughter in 'angel-flights' ('Somebody's Luggage', p. 472). Visual continuities are created by the illustrations to these texts, with their emphasis on the physical support provided to their angelic young heroines. Charles Green selects an intimate moment of Théophile holding Bebelle aloft as the only accompanying image for 'Somebody's Luggage' in the Illustrated Library Edition of 1874, while Effie is pictured lifted up by Louis in the illustration 'Crossing the Frozen River' (Figure 2).

Despite the battlefield context Effie still, quite implausibly, manages to be an angel in the house: 'Her little contrivances and arrangements would sometimes almost persuade her companions to imagine themselves comfortable, and certainly gave them many a pleasant feeling, recalling home in the midst of that desolate waste. And indeed her presence was of incalculable benefit to all, since it was that which chiefly served to preserve them from sinking into the selfish, desponding indifference which characterised so many of the other sufferers' (p. 97). In this narrative the benefits of benevolence are emphatically reciprocal. Furthermore they are socially transformative. In an important description of the way that Effie benefits from the collective care and affection of the cross-rank triumvirate, Léon is rendered a gentleman in both senses: 'she reaped the full benefit of the chivalrous courtesy of the true French gentleman' (p. 97).

Like Dickens, Yonge insists that character and acts (particularly tactile acts of care), rather than bloodline or professional rank, make the gentleman. By using the gentility of a soldier of the ranks to make this case these authors participate in a broader revision of attitudes to the so-called 'rank and file', and resist the stereotype still prevalent in this period of the brutalized soldier, incapable of finer feeling. Narratives of soldier adoption seize the possibilities offered by the family of choice for circumventing class categories; acts of elective parenting are shown to be available across classes while the adoptions represented create familial relationships between adults and children of different social backgrounds.[28] Dickens's Théophile, as a corporal, is a non-commissioned officer, having risen from the rank of private via his own endeavour. In his readiness to parent an illegitimate infant, literally the child of 'no one', he teaches the visiting wealthy Englishman that this is an appropriate response for any true

---

[28] Kath Weston uses the terminology 'families of choice' to question dominant 'procreative assumptions' about kinship, which ignore the much more varied histories of the family available. *Families We Choose: Lesbians, Gays, Kinship* (New York and Oxford: Columbia University Press, 1991), p. 17. Other important work in this field has been undertaken by Judith Butler, Jeffrey Weeks, Brian Heaphy and Catherine Donovan, Mary Bernstein and Renate Reimann and by Christopher Nealon.

Figure 2. Charles Green, Corporal Theophile, and Bebelle, 'Somebody's Luggage', 1874, reprinted in the Library Edition of Dickens's works, 1911. Reproduced with permission from the Charles Dickens Museum.

gentleman. Yonge's Léon is shown to be equally skilled in caring for children and as essential to their survival as the officers who share their parenting. The class barrier in *Kenneth*, however, is not fully dismantled by this life-preserving encounter between officer's children and common soldier. Though parented across ranks on the desperate retreat, having survived it Effie and Kenneth automatically become part of the family of the officers that care for them, with Effie dreaming of a marriage to Louis de Chateauneuf's younger brother that will formalize her relationship with this upper-class family.

BEAUTIFUL GIRLS OF THE REGIMENT: UNEVEN GENDERED REVISION

The military man's adoption of a prepubescent girl is such a staple of mid-Victorian fiction that novels such as Dinah Craik's *A Life for a Life* (1856) invoke the trope in passing as an index to the moral worth of the hero, an army doctor in this case. Having returned to Britain from the Crimean War, Craik's Doctor Urquhart becomes reflective on seeing a 'small creature, in curls', 'about the age of the poor wounded Russ, who might have been my own little adopted girl, by this time, if she had not died. I wish, sometimes, she had not died. My life would have been less lonely, could I have adopted that child.'[29] As is typical of such narratives, the benefit to the man is presented as at least as great as that to the child, the hoped for adoption seen as a salve to the child's war wounds and the adult's isolation. This potted history anticipates well-known fictions of an isolated civilian male being drawn back into love and community by the adoption of a vulnerable girl, including George Eliot's *Silas Marner* (1861), whose heroine Eppie echoes the name of Young's adopted Effie, and Anthony Trollope's *Dr Thorne* (1858).

Care for a dispossessed female child had a particular emotional and moral currency in nineteenth-century fiction. As Catherine Robson has shown, identification with and closeness to girls allowed Victorian men to connect to an idealized, imagined lost, version of themselves and to express their own vulnerability.[30] In his work on the First World War, Roper cites instances of returned soldiers becoming more actively involved in the routines of childcares, and suggests that this connection to a child's relative precariousness was particularly significant for soldiers: 'Veterans

---

[29] Dinah Craik, *A Life for a Life* (New York: Carleton, 1856), p. 114.
[30] Catherine Robson, *Men in Wonderland: The Lost Girlhood of the Victorian Gentleman* (Princeton: Princeton University Press, 2001), pp. 3–5.

could identify with the vulnerability of children, and often, having more adult experiences of sickness than others, could empathise with their ailments.'[31] By routinely featuring girls, soldier adoption plots harness the gendered ideology of the simultaneously curative and vulnerable female child and get around the narrative problem that boys of the regiment would typically become soldiers themselves. A. W. Cockerill uses the phrase 'sons of the brave' in his study of the historical use of child soldiers in the British army, many of them being literal sons as the young recruits of soldier fathers.[32] Unlike Craik's 'little Russ', however, in most plots of this kind the girl child does not die and instead develops into a sexually alluring woman, raising a narrative dilemma of a different kind.

George Gordon Byron's *Don Juan* (1818–24) offers a clear-sighted account of the erotic, exotic appeal of the beautiful rescued foreign girl, and of the emotional work done by the plot of battlefield adoption to offset war violence. Don Juan preserves a Turkish child, 'little Leila', 'the infant girl', 'a pure and living pearl' (Canto 8, 51, lines 404–8), 'as beautiful as May / A female child of ten years' (Canto 8, 91, lines 725–6), saving her from massacre by the Russian soldiers he is fighting with when the fortress of Ismail is stormed.[33] Don Juan's act is presented as combining 'courage and humanity' (Canto 8, 140, line 1114), he prizes the girl's safely over the medal he is awarded, and the poem goes on to document his unfailing care for Leila, who goes with him to England 'for

---

[31] Roper, *The Secret Battle*, p. 294. A similar observation is made in Johanna Spyri's 1880 novel *Heidi*, in which Heidi's grandfather (addressed here by another relative as Uncle) is well prepared to take on the care of his angelic young granddaughter and her disabled friend Clara, having learnt to nurse in the army:

'My dear Uncle,' she exclaimed, 'if I knew where you had learned to nurse I would at once send all the nurses I know to the same place that they might handle their patients in like manner. How do you come to know so much?'
Uncle smiled. 'I know more from experience than training', he answered, but as he spoke the smile died away and a look of sadness passed over his face. The vision rose before him of a face of suffering that he had known long years before, the face of a man lying crippled on his couch of pain, and unable to move a limb. The man had been his captain during the fierce fighting in Sicily; he had found him lying wounded and had carried him away, and after that the captain would suffer no one else near him, and Uncle had stayed and nursed him till his sufferings ended in death. It all came back to Uncle now, and it seemed natural to him to attend the sick Clara and to show her all those kindly attentions with which he had once been so familiar. (Chicago: Whitman, 1916, ebook 2014, pp. 183–4)

[32] A. W. Cockerill, *Sons of the Brave: The Story of Boy Soldiers* (London: Len Cooper, 1984). Cockerill documents that the Ordinance of 15 February 1645 authorized two drummers per company of 120 men; this job was usually performed by a boy, hence drummers received augmented pay 'because they needed more food to grow and soon grew out of their uniforms', pp. 28–9.

[33] George Gordon Byron, *Don Juan*, in *The Major Works* (Oxford: Oxford University Press, 2000).

she was homeless, houseless, helpless', the last of her family (Canto 8, 141, line 1122). The simple AB rhyme scheme reinforces the tears that seal his commitment to protect the child: 'And Juan wept / and made a vow to shield her, which he kept' (Canto 8, 141, lines 1127–8). His compassion for the beautiful girl is presented in the context of the effects of narratives of war: 'And one good action in the midst of crimes / is "quite refreshing"' (Canto 10, 90, lines 13–14).

> If here and there some transient trait of pity
> Was shown, and some more noble heart broke through
> Its bloody bond, and saved perhaps some pretty
> Child, or an aged helpless man or two—
> What's this in one annihilated city,
> Where thousand loves, and ties, and duties grew?
> (Canto 8, 124, lines 985–90)

Byron questions the narrative appeal of the 'one good action' that offsets war crimes, and exposes the affective logic by which the saved life outweighs the scales of mass annihilation of a 'thousand loves'. As is typical of the mixed messages of much nineteenth-century war writing, Byron celebrates Don Juan's attachment to his ward in rich emotive language *and* raises questions about the emotional power of this plot line to obscure the wider waste of war. This stanza draws out the affective contradiction that the celebration of the life spared has no effect on the willingness to wage war.[34] More clearly anti-war than the mid-Victorian soldier adoption narratives discussed in this chapter, Byron's *Don Juan* exposes the insufficiency of 'transient trait[s] of pity', while modelling the narrative

---

[34] *Don Juan*, in its careful exploration of the contradictions within war writing and particularizing of annihilation, has been recognized as unusually explicit in its critique of war. R. S White describes books 7 and 8 as 'some of the greatest anti-war poetry ever written', while acknowledging the contradictions in Byron's life and work; he was actively involved in the Greek war for independence and 'could write against wars of certain kinds while approving others', *Pacifism and English Literature: Minstrels of Peace* (Basingstoke: Palgrave, 2008), p. 188. Philip Shaw argues that 'Byron, of all Romantic poets, comes closest to conveying a sense of the cost of the war. The effectiveness of *Don Juan* comes from its insistence on the particularity of death', *Waterloo and the Romantic Imagination* (Basingstoke: Palgrave, 2002), p. 177. For further discussions of the ambivalence of Byron's war poetry, and his use of sieges to present the effects of war on the civilian population, see Simon Bainbridge, 'Of War and Taking Towns: Byron's Siege Poems', in Philip Shaw, ed., *Romantic Wars: Studies in Culture and Conflict, 1793–1822* (Aldershot: Ashgate, 2000), pp. 161–84, and Kate McLoughlin's argument that 'the discrepancy between the individual's lot and the large-scale unfolding of "events and situations"—is particularly marked in the siege cantos'; 'It becomes apparent that the exigencies of the military endeavour are inimical to the individual ordinary soldier's needs and, indeed, chances of survival', *Authoring War: The Literary Representation of War from the Iliad to Iraq* (Cambridge: Cambridge University Press, 2011), p. 172.

energy and readerly (and commercial) appeal of the military adoption plot as the ur-text of the 'more noble heart' breaking the 'bloody bond' of war.

Through pointed reference to the 'aged helpless man or two', a demographic his hero does not elect to rescue, Byron underlines the aesthetic appeal of the 'pretty child' as the beneficiary of acts of humane heroism. The fetishized value of a particular kind of life is reiterated in the next canto: 'That *one* life saved, especially if young / Or pretty is a thing to recollect / Far sweeter than the greenest laurels' (Canto 9, 34, lines 265–7). Byron makes explicit the valuing of some lives—more typically in Victorian narratives those of white, implicitly Christian, European girls—over others, anticipating Butler's critique of the devaluation of the lives of some populations as worth less to enable the prosecution of war.[35]

Byron's attention to Leila's physical beauty, exoticism, sexual appeal, and chastity—as, variously, a 'pure, living pearl', 'like a day-dawn she was young and pure' (Canto 12, 41, line 322), 'as beautiful as her own native land', 'the last bud of her race' (Canto 12, 29, lines 227–8)—raises concerns about how the sexually susceptible hero 'our friend Don Juan might command / Himself for five, four, three, or two year's space' (Canto 12, 29, lines 229–30). Expediently, given this rapidly shrinking space of time before Leila might become more wooed than ward, Don Juan sends her to an elderly lady for her education. The concerns Byron voices about the sexual appeal of the growing girl follow an account of the difficulties of understanding and defining their relationship: 'They formed a rather curious pair' (Canto 10, 57, line 452).

> Don Juan loved her, and she loved him, as
> Nor brother, father, sister, daughter love.
> I cannot tell exactly what it was. (Canto 10, 53, line 417–19)

Such uncertainties about how the bond between military man and adopted girl relate to conventional familial structures, and what to do with the girl child turned alluring young woman, are common in mid-Victorian incarnations of this plot. In Kingsley's *Westward Ho!* Salvation Yeo never finds the girl he thinks of as his 'little maid', though he does discover the beautiful Ayacanora, the woman she has become. Ayacanora is so attractive that Amyas thinks she might be a daughter of the lost Incas (p. 460).[36] When her identity is discovered and she half remembers Yeo,

---

[35] Judith Butler, *Frames of War: When is Life Grievable?* (London and New York: Verso, 2009).
[36] In fact she is European, daughter of a British father and Spanish mother, a heritage which causes the hero some anxiety due to her blood link to the race he hates most. Through her orphanhood and childhood in the South American jungle Ayacanora has become culturally and apparently racially hybridized, severed from a European heritage to which the novel works hard to reconnect her through her parenting by heroic English men.

she wants no more to do with him. Instead she instantly loves Amyas, to whom she slavishly devotes her life, initially entering his home as his 'daughter' (p. 569) and finally becoming his wife in his blindness. This uneasy, incestuous slippage from adoptive daughter to wife illustrates the problem that all these plots face of what to do with the child of the regiment when she grows up. The expected narrative trajectory by which the rescued girl becomes a wife is economically modelled in Kingsley's novel through the potted history of the lord mayor 'aged, but not changed, since he leaped from the window upon London Bridge into the roaring tide below, to rescue the infant who is now his wife' (p. 339). In Ayacanora's refusal to recognize the man who previously saved and parented her, Kingsley references her traumatic past of losing one adoptive father after another—'wild and bad everything. Ayacanora won't speak about that' (p. 557)—and seals off the innocence of Yeo's care for her in the jungle, keeping it entirely separate from her development into a desiring woman. Ayacanora's wildness and passion must, according to Kingsley's schema, be tamed via repatriation to Britain and codes, modelled by Amyas's mother, of British feminine patience, piety, and modesty. Ayacanora's immediate love for Amyas, of considerable wealth and social standing, rather than his working-class first mate, has an upward mobility that parallels Effie's attraction to Louis de Chateauneuf in Yonge's *Kenneth*. The rescued girls' romantic preferences expose the limitations to the social remaking of the rough, regular soldier via his gentle care.

All these narratives invest transformative feeling in the suffering body of an idealized young girl. John Everett Millais's Crimean War period painting *The Random Shot* or *L'enfant du Régiment* (1854–5, exhibited 1856) offered a particularly vivid representation of soldier adoption focused on the angelic beauty of a vulnerable girl child (Figure 3). This painting clearly inspired Dickens's 'Somebody's Luggage'. Like Millias's infant girl seen asleep on a soldier's tomb, Bebelle is found by the Englishman on Théophile's grave, taking comfort from it.

> A live child was lying on the ground asleep. Truly he had found something on the Corporal's grave to know it by, and the something was Bebelle... Bebelle lay sleeping, with her cheek touching it. A plain unpainted little wooden Cross was planted in the turf, and her short arm embraced this little Cross, as it had many a time embraced the Corporal's neck. (p. 479)

The physical detailing of the position of cheek and hand recalls Millais's image, in which the sleeping orphan (another cherubic girl child, complete

---

See C. J. Wee for a discussion of the 're-racination' of this orphan, 'Christian Manliness and National Identity: The Problematic Construction of a Racially "Pure" Nation', in *Muscular Christianity: Embodying the Victorian Age*, ed. Donald Hall (Cambridge: Cambridge University Press, 1994), pp. 66–88, pp. 82–4.

Figure 3. John Everett Millais, *The Random Shot* or *L'enfant du Régiment* (1854–5, exhibited 1856). Reproduced with permission from the Yale Centre for British Art.

with pale skin, pink cheeks, and blond hair) embraces the relics of a knight while recuperating from her war wound. Millais's image was itself inspired by Gaetano Donizetti's comic opera of 1840, *La Fille du Régiment*, which was revived in a run in London in 1856. This production was, as Markovits has shown, 'Crimea-inflected'; the lead was dressed in the costume of a *cantinière* (a woman who sold refreshment to the French troops), made familiar by Roger Fenton's recently exhibited photographs.[37] The backstory to Donizetti's opera is that the heroine, Marie, the illegitimate child of a French officer who is killed in the Napoleonic Wars, is found as an infant on the battlefield and adopted by his regiment, the 21st. The action of the opera takes place later when Marie is a young woman pledged only to marry a soldier of the 21st, as a partial fulfilment of the debt she feels she owes her regimental family.[38]

---

[37] Stefanie Markovits, *The Crimean War in the British Imagination* (Cambridge: Cambridge University Press, 2009), p. 202.
[38] See Amanda Holden, ed., *The New Penguin Opera Guide* (London: Penguin, 2001), p. 241 and Malcolm Warner, 'Notes on Millais' Use of Subjects from the Opera, 1851–54', *The Pre-Raphaelite Review* 2.1 (1978), pp. 73–6, p. 74.

In a period of worsening reports from the Crimea, Millais imagines a moment unnarrated in Donizetti's opera, of Marie's early history, injured as a child as a seemingly inevitable consequence of the professional hazard of her position as daughter of the regiment. By showing the soldiers who adopt Marie on active service (seen in flashes of colour through stone trellis work) Millais's vision is more complex than Dickens's. Though Bebelle loves to watch Théophile in military training exercises she is never required to follow him into actual battle. In Millais's painting, which juxtaposes the girl's injured, bandaged hand and evident exhaustion with the comfort of the military jacket turned blanket, there is a careful blending of vulnerability and care, danger and nurture.[39] The uniform she is wrapped in is that of a French grenadier's regiment, the stylized hand grenade insignia clearly visible on it making a direct reference to the war violence that characterizes the lives of her military family. The blood-red flaming grenades on the jacket nestle against the girl's sleeping body, with one hanging down and dangling ominously next to her exposed feet. Through the adoption backstory and the tender solicitude implied by the neat bandage on the girl's arm and the coat laid over her, the image does ask for a similar revision of military masculinity to that demanded by Dickens's tale. It also, though, vividly demonstrates the human cost of war by visiting it on the vulnerable body of a young girl. The painting draws out various tensions in the plot of soldier adoption; the girl's bandaged wound dramatizes the soldier as both a cause of, and a loving, gentle solution to the problem of war violence.

There is also an uncomfortable juxtaposition between Millais's *enfant*'s immaturity as she childishly clings to the stony muscled arm of the entombed knight, and the Donizetti backstory which interlinks adoption and marriage as the child of the regiment must become a wife of the regiment. This claustrophobic and psychically incestuous arrangement ensures that the regiment never loses its child, as the girl linked to it as daughter cannot pursue an exogamous marriage that would offer her a supplementary family, but instead endogamously formalizes and doubles her tie to the regimental family. In valuing a lifelong regimental commitment to a single woman, the incestuous charge of this plot also works to dissociate both regular soldiers and officers from an engrained stereotypical reputation for womanizing and romantic and familial faithlessness.

---

[39] Paul Barlow notes that the painting emphasizes 'the violating results of masculine heroism', a wider theme of Millais's work which also informs 'The Order of Release' and 'Peace Concluded', 'while the pictorial devices allow for constant transitions between rigidity and dissolution, coldness and warmth, comfort and threat', *Time Present and Time Past: The Art of John Everett Millais* (Aldershot: Ashgate, 2005), p. 61.

Dickens circumvents the dubious erotic currency while maintaining an unusual view of the soldier's impulses; Corporal Théophile fathers an illegitimate child, rather than 'fathering' offspring he will never meet. Dickens displaces the romance plot, emphasizing the paternal bond through the Englishman's training in parenting and the doubled adoption plot in which he takes up the fathering Théophile began, and restricting the relationship between Bebelle and Théophile to her earliest years via his untimely death. Yonge also turns aside a potential adoption-turned-marriage plot by having Eugène de Chateauneuf (the younger brother of the self-sacrificing Louis), who Effie instantly loves, killed at Waterloo. The steps taken here to avoid the position with which Donizetti's opera begins, that children of the regiment must become wives of the regiment, shows the difficulty of sustaining a narrative of soldier parenting as the regimental family fails to find alternative spaces for women, only accommodating young girls in need of care, or wives. While these plots require a revision of received wisdom about Victorian masculinity and ideas of family, demanding a much more nuanced understanding of the emotional and tactile components of fatherly feeling unlinked to biology, they do so by invoking conventional mythologies of ideal femininity. There is a significant asymmetry, then, in the revision of gender offered by this material, as characterizations of the adoptive military man legitimize his gentleness through an appeal to the civilizing effects of women, and especially young girls.

BOOTLES' BABY AND THE HIGH IMPERIAL POPULARITY OF SOLDIER ADOPTION

These limitations to the questioning of gender roles are particularly apparent in a novella by Henrietta Eliza Vaughan Stannard, writing under the pseudonym John Strange Winter. Her *Bootles' Baby: A Story of the Scarlet Lancers* (1885), which continues the popularity of the soldier adoption plot in the later Victorian period, sold over two million copies, was developed through a number of sequels, adapted for the stage, and later made into a film.[40] *Bootles' Baby* unabashedly rehearses the stereotype of the promiscuous army man in order to distinguish the exemplary Bootles, and draws upon the traditional romantic destiny of the child of the regiment in order to extend the interest in subsequent Bootles books.

---

[40] Owen Ashton, 'Henrietta Eliza Vaughan Stannard', *Oxford Dictionary of National Biography* (Oxford: Oxford University Press, 2004).

Captain Ferrers, commonly known as Bootles, becomes a father when a less principled officer in the regiment plants his baby girl in the captain's quarters, having refused to marry her mother. Bootles lives up to his reputation for a 'dashed kind heart' and 'softness of chawracter', as his best friend and fellow officer Lucy puts it, and refuses to send the baby to the workhouse, despite the taunts and warnings that he is encouraging the suspicion that he is her 'natural' father.[41] Bootles takes the infant's care upon himself, and names her Miss Mignon. Bootles reuses the name he gave to a woman he loved who was jilted and then died broken-hearted to invoke the tragic heroine of Goethe's *Wilhelm Meister's Apprenticeship* (1795–6):

> Miss Mignon's favourite plaything was Bootles himself—after Bootles, Lucy. People said it was wonderful, the depth of affection between the big soldier of thirty-five and the little dot of a child, scarcely two. Bootles she adored, and where Bootles was she would be, if by hook or by crook she could convey her small person into his presence. (p. 54)[42]

When asked by a commanding officer who she belongs to, Miss Mignon simply answers 'why to Bootles... Bootles is Bootles and I love him' (p. 58).

The account of this 'big soldier's' 'depth of affection' is rather different to the forms of military manliness predominantly associated with the expansion of the British empire, and with the genre of Boy's Own fiction most closely identified with it. Under the standard historiography feeling hardened in the later nineteenth century in order that Britain could operate, to use Michael Paris's terms, 'as an aggressively militant warrior nation'.[43] Joseph Bristow identifies an 'aggressive, ruthless' style as typical of a 'particular kind of late Victorian masculinity where feelings are increasingly taken for signs of weakness in grown up men'.[44] Dawson and Tosh document a move away from an endorsement of military men's domestic qualities (as celebrated in the first responses to General Henry Havelock's 1857 death in the Indian Mutiny but edited out of 1880s and 1890s Havelock biographies) in the period of New Imperialism: 'Imperial

---

[41] J. S., Winter [Henrietta Eliza Vaughan Stannard], *Bootles' Baby: A Story of the Scarlet Lancers* (London and New York: Warne, 1885, reprinted 1891), p. 26.

[42] Goethe's Mignon is also collectively parented, though less benevolently than Winter's Mignon, and her mysterious parentage was a source of fascination in many Victorian adaptations of the novel. Terence Cave places Winter's work within this context. *Mignon's Afterlives: Crossing Cultures from Goethe to the Twentyfirst Century* (Oxford: Oxford University Press, 2011).

[43] Michael Paris, *Warrior Nation: Images of War in British Popular Culture, 1850–2000* (London: Reaktion, 2000), p. 11.

[44] Joseph Bristow, *Empire Boys: Adventures in a Man's World* (London: Harper Collins, 1991), p. 36.

reputation was grounded in a small repertoire of masculine qualities, stoicism as in the death of General Gordon, steely self control exemplified by Kitchener, self-reliance in the case of Baden-Powell.'[45] The popularity of Winter's tales through this period suggest the competing cultural currency of a different valuation of gentle manly feeling as heroic, continuing the endorsement of a particularly tender model of military masculinity. Reviews of the novella series praised precisely this element of the Bootles stories, commending the 'fine and fresh portrayal of the feelings called into being by interest in babies', the treatment of 'children's character and their influence on men of the world'. John Ruskin described Winter as 'the author to whom we owe the most finished and faithful rendering ever yet given to the character of the British soldier'.[46] Similar views were expressed in response to Hugh Moss's 1887 four-act stage comedy adaptation of *Bootles' Baby*. As Carolyn Steedman summarizes, 'it was the contrast between "the tiny, helpless, dumb, starving infant, and the huge moustached spurred and gold-braided cavalryman" that was reckoned to make up so "fresh, ingenious and diverting" a stage picture'.[47]

Like the other materials discussed here, Winter presents the instinct to father as part of a generously expansive understanding of family. However, this series of books, structured around the implication that the feminine (in the shape of the abandoned girl baby) both requires male protection and is necessary for the military man's redemption, offers much less flexibility in its presentation of women's roles. Bootles is ably assisted in his care of Miss Mignon by Lucy, who 'proved himself a much better nurse than Bootles'. Lucy, having termed her 'La figlia del wreggimento' (p. 47), presents her to his colleagues: 'Mademoiselle Mignon bore the inspection calmly, conscious perhaps—as she was such a knowing little person—of the effect of her big blue star-like eyes under the white fur of her cap' (p. 48). The uneasy eroticism created by this presentation of an

---

[45] John Tosh, *A Man's Place: Masculinity and the Middle-Class Home in Victorian England* (New Haven and London: Yale University Press, 1999), pp. 174–5, for details of the shift in Havelock biography so that in later century versions his 'domestic life virtually disappears from view'; see Graham Dawson, *Soldier Heroes: British Literature, Empire and the Imagining of Masculinities* (London and New York: Routledge, 1994), pp. 135–50, p. 149.
[46] *Scotsman*, 17 Oct 1887; *Sheffield Telegraph*, 17 Nov 1886, John Ruskin, *The Daily Telegraph*, 17 Jan 1888. Collected in front material in John Strange Winter, *Bootles' Children* (London: F. V. White, 1888).
[47] Carolyn Steedman, *Strange Dislocations: Childhood and the Idea of Human Interiority, 1780–1930* (London: Virago, 1995), p. 147. Steedman quotes reviews in *The Era*, 12 May 1888 and *The Times*, 11 May 1888. She notes that reviews compared this moment to Mr Allworthy's care for foundling Tom Jones and the discovery of Eppie by Silas Marner, comparisons which placed Mignon's adoption within a wider literary framework of elective fatherhood.

attractive girl baby as knowing coquette is developed by the regiment's responses: '"What a pity she ain't twenty years older"', '"Pretty work she'll make in the regiment sixteen or seventeen years hence."' Though dismissed as 'an exceedingly old and threadbare regimental joke' (p. 48) the jest is continued in the sequel, *Mignon's Secret* (1886), in an uncomfortable 'comic' scene in which Lucy, or Lal as she calls him, repeatedly refers to the child as his sweetheart as they take tea in an approximation of adult courtship. As with the other representations considered here, the physical beauty of the girl is a factor in her value to the military men who care for her:

> Almost every head in the room was turned to watch the lovely child go to the table with the handsome soldier beside her... She was just eleven years old, tall and slim and full of grace as a kitten, with an exquisite little face, fair as a flower and framed in masses of waving, curling, golden hair. She was quite plainly dressed in a blue velvet frock, just the colour of her eyes, coming to her knees without a flounce or frill, her only ornament was a little gold brooch with the word 'Mignon' upon it—a brooch which had been Lucy's gift. What a lovely child she was, people whispered to one another. It was no wonder that Captain Lucy was so fond of her, and always declared he meant to marry her—no wonder at all.[48]

This long anticipated fantasy is fulfilled several books later in the series when Miss Mignon marries the now Major Lucy, her adoptive father's great friend, and her childhood nurse. In introducing *Mignon's Husband* (1887) Winter justifies the addition of five years to Mignon's age in the publication space of twelve months: 'This liberty has been taken in order to gratify the wish of a great number of persons in all parts of the world, that the matrimonial fate of Bootles' Baby may be decided.'[49]

Miss Mignon's relationship to the Scarlet Lancers has already been formalized by Bootles's marriage to the woman who turns out to be her mother. Sympathetic treatment is given to the 'fallen' women encountered (and usually swiftly married) by Bootles and the other military men of feeling he surrounds himself with through the novella sequence. In a number of examples that take in different ranks, the stereotypically faithless and brutal behaviour of one soldier is counterbalanced by the tender solicitude of another who makes reparation to the woman

---

[48] John Strange Winter, *Mignon's Secret* (London: F. V. White, 1886), p. 82. Steedman is perhaps thinking of descriptions like this when describing the 'stunning ingenuousness' with which Winter 'runs the gamut of pathos and paedophilia in her series of "Migon" novels', *Strange Dislocations*, p. 37.
[49] John Strange Winter, *Mignon's Husband* (London: F. V. White, 1887), p. 1.

wronged.[50] The reinscription of marriage, however, as woman's destiny in these narrative developments restricts the potential of the adoption narrative to restructure conventions of gender and the family, turning away from the possibility that family is not, or not necessarily, determined by the heterosexual structures of marriage and reproduction.

The Bootles sequence also points to class limitations in the expandability of the regimental family. In *Mignon's Secret* Lucy is loved both by the 'lovely' Mignon, who turns out to be the natal daughter of an officer and a gentlewoman, and the 'barrack brat' nicknamed Jack (p. 53), an angry dark-haired and dark-skinned working-class girl. Jack adores Lucy following his intervention against her stepmother's cruelty to her. Lucy's kindness to 'Private Henderson's little, ill used, worse than motherless lass' (p. 15) is an opportunity for further demonstration of 'his kindness to anything helpless or weak which was one of his greatest charms' (p. 47). Winter does show some sympathy for Jack's position, and gives her a redemptive death by drowning while saving Mignon, who she has pushed into the river in her terrible jealously of Lucy's preference for her. However, the privileged position of Mignon 'in all the beauty of her embroidered garments and the wealth of her golden hair' (p. 21) as the appropriate regimental adoptee is unchallenged. While the *Bootles* books continue the emphasis on the military man's capacity for sympathy, tenderness, and nurture, these qualities do little to challenge prevailing unequal structures of gender and class.

HEARTS AND MINDS: SOLDIERING AND SOCIAL WORK

The particular popularity of these narratives *during* war, and their persistence through the expansion of the British empire, suggests additional troubling ideological trajectories in this material. While the figure of the gentle soldier demands a reassessment of ideas about Victorian masculinity, and of military masculinity in particular, it does so by commending this figure as one that can be widely embraced. By socializing the soldier in this way, such images work to make the army a more respectable career choice and, more broadly, to imply the justice of war via its association with such noble figures. The protection of children works as an index of

---

[50] John Reed, 'Soldier Boy: Forming Masculinity in Adam Bede', *Studies in the Novel* 33.3 (2001), pp. 268–84 notes the 'dashing and sexually attractive' army officer as a hallmark of Winter's wider military fiction, p. 270. In the Bootles series, the ideal soldier's sexuality is firmly restricted to noble causes.

civilized army, firmly distinguishing these celebrated soldiers from a long, and continuing, tradition of marking the enemy as child murderers, or at least as a threat to children. Another short story by Winter, 'A Siege Baby' (1887), which sets the plot of elective parenting within the so-called Indian Mutiny of 1857, offers a characteristic portrayal of the brutality of the enemy, in this case the rising sepoys: 'Fever and famine thinned out the ranks of those who were still holding out against the cowardly foe who butchered little children and helpless babies in their thirst for blood.'[51] Visceral descriptions of the torture and killing of British children by rebelling Indian soldiers were a staple of British newspaper accounts, novels, and poetry. *The Times*, for example, gave a highly coloured report, complete with 'quivering flesh' and 'laughing' fiendishness: 'Children have been compelled to eat the quivering flesh of their murdered parents, after which they were literally torn asunder by the laughing fiends who surrounded them.'[52] Such descriptions drew upon a longstanding convention of representing the enemy as baby killers, dating back at least to the biblical account of Herod's massacre of the innocents (Matthew 2:13–18) and vivid reimaginings of that scene such as Rubens's famous paintings (1611–12, 1636–8).[53] Kingsley draws upon this tradition in giving a brief history of Salvation Yeo's tragic history, in which his American Indian wife and their child were killed by Spanish soldiers as he watched weeping:

---

[51] John Strange Winter, *A Siege Baby and Other Stories*, 2 vols (London: F. V. White, 1887), vol. 1, p. 41. 'A Siege Baby' offers a fascinating variation on Winters's much-worked theme of elective family. Here the siege baby's life is saved by her devoted Indian wet nurse, who darkens the infant's skin and passes her as her own child.

[52] *The Times*, 17 September 1857, quoted by Matthew Bevis, 'Fighting Talk: Victorian War Poetry', in *British and Irish War Poetry*, ed. Tim Kendall (Oxford: Oxford University Press, 2007), pp. 7–33, p. 21. Bevis puts this report in a context of wider, similarly lurid responses such as Martin Tupper's poem, which details 'the agonised wail of babies hewn piecemeal sickens the air'. Heather Streets, *Martial Races: The Military, Race, and Masculinity in British Imperial Culture* (Manchester: Manchester University Press, 2004) points out that representations of British soldiers as the heroic saviours of women and children worked 'to minimise criticism of the East India Company's failure to deal with the grievances of Indian soldiers and subjects'. 'This strategy had the effect of inciting heated emotions of revenge in Britain and allowed British forces incredible license to brutally crush the revolt', p. 11. For further discussions of the political uses of a rhetoric of sepoys' 'massacre of innocents' see Dawson, *Soldier Heroes*, pp. 90–8 and Patrick Brantlinger, *Rule of Darkness: British Literature and Imperialism, 1830–1914* (Ithaca and London: Cornell University Press, 1988), pp. 23–4.

[53] David Richards examines the referencing of Rubens's *Massacre of the Innocents* in John Singleton Copley's paintings to 'depict the French invasion as a war crime', *Masks of Difference: Cultural Representations in Literature, Anthropology and Art* (Cambridge: Cambridge University Press, 1994), p. 114.

No sooner was it Christened than, catching the babe by the heels, he dashed out its brains—oh! gentlemen! gentlemen!—against the ground, as if it had been a kitten; and so did they to several more innocents that night after they had Christened them; saying it was best for them to go to heaven while they were still sure thereof; and so marched us all for slaves, leaving the old folk and the wounded to die at leisure. (pp. 169–70)

Kingsley bluntly distinguishes between the inhumanity of an enemy who takes no care of the elderly and wounded and justifies mass murder of women and children, and the British 'gentlemen' Yeo addresses who extend kindness to these war victims, especially to beautiful threatened girls.

The trope of the enemy as child killers continued its momentum in the anti-'Hun' propaganda of the First World War, which depicted Germans skewering babies on their bayonets, and persists as Phillip Knightley shows in his account of the (later discredited) US media stories of Iraqi soldiers tossing babies out of incubators on the invasion of Kuwait.[54] At the 2012 British Military Tournament (8–9 December 2012, Earls Court, London) an enactment of the British army's work in Afghanistan used a backstory, regularly featured in British and US media accounts, that the Taliban had taken over a school as a base, stopping local children's education and causing them physical danger. These narratives deploy the emotive figure of the child to legitimize the actions of allied armies as offering protection to children, a recurrent trope, as Catherine Scott has shown. Scott notes the 'reliance on themes of lost innocence and lost childhood to justify war on terror policies', detailing the prevalence of references to 'innocent children' as victims of Saddam Hussein and the Taliban in George Bush's speeches and of the language of freedom in newspaper headlines and images showing 'liberated' children flying kites, playing football, and blowing bubbles. As a *USA Today* caption put it: 'Afghan boys enjoying the weather and their new found freedoms... Soccer was among amusements banned under the Taliban.'[55] Drawing out the close relationship

---

[54] Phillip Knightley, *The First Casualty: The War Correspondent as Hero and Myth-maker from the Crimea to Iraq* (London: Andre Deutsch, 2003), p. 486. Santanu Das includes some discussion of imagery of speared babies in anti-German war cartoons in 'An Ecstasy of Fumbling: Gas Warfare, 1914–18 and the Uses of Affect', in *The Edinburgh Companion to Twentieth-Century British and American War Literature*, ed. Adam Piette and Mark Rawlinson (Edinburgh: Edinburgh University Press, 2012), pp. 396–405, p. 398. *The Times* also included propagandistic reports of German soldiers cutting the hands and arms off children, 27 August 1914. Cited by John F. Williams, *German Anzacs and the First World War* (Sydney: University of New South Wales Press, 2003), p. 43.

[55] Catherine Scott, 'Rescue in the Age of Empire: Children, Masculinity, and the War on Terror', in Krista Hunt and Kim Rygiel, eds, *(En)gendering the War on Terror: War Stories and Camouflaged Politics* (London: Ashgate, 2006), pp. 97–117, p. 103. *USA Today*, 20 March 2002, quoted by Scott, p. 102.

between representations of war as a protection to children and an emphasis on gentle soldierly masculinity, Scott observes that these media reports also 'praised the high tech warrior as well as the nurturing soldier'.[56] Such reports take their force from the positioning of the child as the 'fantastic beneficiary of every political intervention', which Lee Edelman identifies as endemic in the US. Military acts taken in the name of protecting the futurity of the child become less contestable, and the cultural script that Edelman calls 'reproductive futurism' is strategically deployed (as in the examples above) to forestall a more critical response to war.[57]

Hysterical representations of the enemy as the other of allied humanitarianism provided the context for Operation Babylift, in which an estimated 3300 children were removed from Vietnam in 1975 at the end of the Vietnam War for adoption in the United States and in other countries including Canada and Australia. As President Gerald Ford was photographed meeting children from a plane at San Francisco airport, Vietnamese American journalist Tran Tuong Nhu questioned the case for the operation: 'What is this terror Americans feel that my people will devour children?'[58] Questions were also asked about the balance between motives of guilt, propaganda, a desire to rewrite the war as a narrative of care, and humanitarianism.[59] For some, the babylift was an extension of

[56] Scott, 'Rescue in the Age of Empire', p. 102.
[57] Lee Edelman, *No Future: Queer Theory and the Death Drive* (Durham and London: Duke University Press, 2004), p. 3. Though I have found Edelman's insistence that queer must be asocial and counter to the 'familiar familial narrativity of reproductive futurism' overly proscriptive (p. 17), his arguments about the cultural force of an appeal to the child to forestall debate apply very clearly to war propaganda.
[58] 'People and Events', historical resource accompanying the film *Daughter from Danang*, <http://www.pbs.org/wgbh/amex/daughter/peopleevents/e_babylift.html>. Accessed 4 Nov 2014.
[59] Gloria Emerson provided a compelling critique of the power of this operation to instil a 'self-congratulatory spirit, a feeling of winning something at last, the need to prove to ourselves what decent people we really are. It is almost forgotten during these excited, evangelical scenes at airports that it is this country that made so many Vietnamese into orphans, that destroyed villages ripping families apart, this country that sent young Vietnamese fathers to their deaths. Now we have decided the Vietnamese we will "save" and "love" must be very pliant, very helpless... Now the welfare of a few thousand children has become a most successful propaganda effort for us to defend and support the diseased government of Nguyen Van Thieu despite the opposition to him in the South. Babies are a nicer story than the 26 million craters we gave South Vietnam, nicer than the 100,000 amputees in that wretched country, more fun to read about than the 14 million acres of defoliated forest and the 800,000 acres that we bulldozed', 'Operation Babylift', *The New Republic*, 26 April 1975, pp. 8–10. Images of US soldiers' compassion for Vietnamese children also overwrote the history of local children working against the US army. See Emerson, *Winners and Losers* (New York: Random House, 1976), p. 91. Scott details more recent anxiety about children in war zones acting not as helpless victims or grateful recipients of aid but as hostile combatants, vividly documented in *Time* magazine's 2003

American imperialism, an act with parallels to war violence in the forcible movement and deracination of local populations.[60] More recently, clear examples of the use of forced military adoption as a tool of violence have emerged through the work of human rights groups to bring to trial military generals who kidnapped and then often adopted the children of political opponents in Argentina and El Salvador.[61] Nineteenth-century narratives of soldier adoption are not generally concerned with the child's deracination and cultural and political reprogramming; there may be a hint of such concern in Byron's mournful evocation of Leila as the last of her race, and his presentation of her refusal to relinquish her religion (Book 8, 141 and Book 10, 55–7). More typically, though, in line with British Victorians' prevalent belief in their cultural and racial superiority, assimilation into Englishness is presented as a desirable goal for figures like Kingsley's Ayacanora, and a happy ending for Dickens's and Yonge's European adoptees. Although these narratives make stark distinctions between enemy violence and allied humanitarianism, in ignoring or diminishing problematic questions raised by soldier adoption—such as whether children might better be raised by local civilians—this material exerts a propagandistic violence that reconciles readers to war as a form of humanitarian endeavour.

The presentation of military objectives as protecting the rights of children is another form of what Butler has critiqued as the 'spurious rationale of sexual politics' in the current discourses of US military intervention, in which there is a 'framing of sexual and feminist politics in the service of the war effort'.[62] Soldier adoption plots move the propagandistic portrayal from babies on bayonets to babes in arms. In

photo of a small Afghan boy with the caption 'Friend or Foe?', p. 111. Sara Fieldston's work looks at a broader history of North American adoption projects for children from overseas as part of an ideological resistance to Communism in the Cold War era, *Raising the World: Child Welfare in the American Century* (Cambridge, MA: Harvard University Press, 2015).

[60] See Statement on the Immorality of Bringing South Vietnamese Orphans to the United States, April 4, 1975, Viola W. Bernard Papers, Box 62, Folder 8, Archives and Special Collections, Augustus C. Long Library, Columbia University. Available at http://darkwing.uoregon.edu/~adoption/archive/SIBSVOUS.htm. Accessed 4 Nov 2014.

[61] 'Stolen Baby Hails "Liberating" Verdict', 6 July 2012, *BBC News*, http://www.bbc.co.uk/news/world-latin-america-18733415. Accessed 4 Nov 2014. 'Soldiers Stole Children during El Salvador's War', 22 Feb 2013, *USA Today*, <http://www.usatoday.com/story/news/world/2013/02/22/soldiers-children-el-salvador/1940533/>. Accessed 4 Nov 2014. My thanks to Alicia Vazquez for discussing this with me, and directing me to these reports.

[62] Butler, *Frames of War*, p. 26. Butler's is a recent voice in a wealth of feminist critique of the Bush administration's presentation of its interventions in Afghanistan as a defence of the rights of women. See also Hunt and Rygiel, eds, *(En)gendering the War on Terror*. Claire Duncanson surveys this body of work in *Forces for Good? Military Masculinities and Peacebuilding in Afghanistan and Iraq* (Basingstoke: Palgrave, 2013), introduction and chapter 1.

marking a determined break from the spectre of child killing as part of the atrocity of war, instead embracing a determined care for the vulnerable, these narratives have the power to overwrite and obscure the actual deaths of war, including those of children. Derek Gregory uses US Department of Defence photographs to assemble a collage of images, familiar from current media reports on war, of soldiers dispensing footballs, treats, medicine, warm clothing, holding aloft, and otherwise befriending the children local to areas of conflict. Gregory overlays these on a background of images of targeted streets and ruined homes to complete the composition, 'The Re-enchantment of War'.[63] He notes this re-enchantment takes place through a rhetoric of 'optic precision weapons and surgical strikes' by which 'death virtually disappears from the battle space, and the military prepares for its humanising "operations other than war"': 'The iconic figures that do appear on this artfully mediated ground of war are gentle soldiers and grateful recipients, actors in what the new US counter-insurgency doctrine describes as "armed social work".'[64]

The soldier as social worker is at the vanguard of battles for hearts and minds. As Julia Welland puts it in her exploration of the prevalence of the figure of the liberal warrior in twenty-first-century British and US representations of the military, 'when military intervention comes to be understood through the prism of compassion, it elicits something of a "writing out", or at least an obscuring, of the simultaneous presence of weaponry, violence and death'. Welland explores the political work of discourses of soldierly sympathy and care in counter-insurgency operations in Afghanistan, arguing that the 'announcement of compassion can work to conceal the ongoing violence and obscenity of war'.[65] This announcement, through which 'the soldier is reconstituted and reiterated as a good and

---

[63] Derek Gregory, 'War and Peace', *Transactions of the Institute of British Geographers* 35 (2010), pp. 154–86, pp. 164–5. Mark Rawlinson has examined camouflage, an object of cultural fascination in the twentieth century, as another technique through which war can be re-enchanted 'as a contest of tactical and technical invention', a re-enchantment that has become urgent 'in the face of evidence that it [war] is an unredeemable negation of humanity'. He looks at how authors critical of war have reversed the capacity of camouflage to redeem war as an exercise in human ingenuity and pluck, instead using it to point up rhetoric 'which makes war's core activity of hurting people less visible' and expose the trickery of 'latter-day Western propaganda about war-without-casualties', 'Camouflage and the Re-enchantment of Warfare', in *The Edinburgh Companion to Twentieth-Century British and American War Literature*, ed. Adam Piette and Mark Rawlinson (Edinburgh, Edinburgh University Press, 2012), pp. 356–65, p. 357, p. 356, p. 361. For another exploration of twentieth-century literary strategies through which violence is enchanted and disenchanted see Sarah Cole, 'Enchantment, Disenchantment, War, Literature', *PMLA* 124.5 (2009), pp. 1632–47.

[64] Gregory, 'War and Peace', p. 165.

[65] Julia Welland, 'Compassionate Soldiering and Comfort', forthcoming. See chapter 2 for a discussion of Welland's 'liberal warrior' terminology.

kind subjectivity despite any violences they may have engaged in' is, as Welland suggests, 'a highly comforting move' for soldiers themselves and for civilians who wish to endorse their work. There are continuities in the work performed by Victorian and present day representations of soldierly care for children. All these narratives attend to the humanity of the soldier, emphasizing his willingness to protect rather than harm. They reduce the perceived threat of the military man and his weaponry, effectively disarming him, to make the figures of the men themselves and the armies they represent less alarming.

The soldier turned tender adoptive father is, then, an unsettling figure. An entirely sceptical reading of representations of adoptive soldiering as enchanting violence, however, risks losing sight of the potentially transformative work of such material in contexts where the gentle soldier is far from a cultural norm, and preconceptions of soldierly masculinity rarely encompass empathy and nurture. While exposing the violent uses of a rhetoric of soldiering as social work, Gregory also acknowledges the recent resistance by some in the US to the concept that soldiers should be concerned with the well-being of civilians.[66] Duncanson has shown that efforts to move away from a combative approach in recent British army campaigns in Iraq and Afghanistan 'are often feminised and discredited, as when Brigadier Andrew Mackay's population-centred focus was dismissed by a senior Para as "fluffy" nonsense'.[67] Duncanson, as briefly seen in this book's Introduction, is concerned with the 'stickiness' of gender binaries that enmesh masculinity with warfare and violence. She argues that feminist scepticism about the deployment of 'regendered soldiers' and 'regendered militaries' enacts a violence of its own, by refusing the possibility that gentle ideals of soldiering might unpick the persistent binding of masculinity and violence, and change how war is viewed and waged.[68] This book suggests that the Victorian period offers a rich counter-history as a period in which the gentle soldier was widely celebrated. Although this is not the popular legacy of the Victorian soldier, a more fully fleshed understanding of the power of the military man of feeling in Victorian culture might help to unstick the stubborn conjunctions man/war/violence. The twenty-first-century gentle soldier is less a 'regendered' being than a continuation of a submerged history of masculine nurture within the military.

[66] Gregory quotes, among others, former Lieutenant-Colonel Ralph Peters's comments on the '"moral cowardice" of "the Obama Way of War" and its renewed commitment to a counterinsurgency doctrine that presumes the key to military success is "to hand out soccer balls to worm-eaten children"', 'War and Peace', p. 169.
[67] Duncanson, *Forces for Good*, p. 138.
[68] Duncanson, *Forces for Good*, p. 141, chapters 1 and 6.

On the one hand the material considered in this chapter supports a necessary rethinking of military masculinity as a form of manliness much more emotionally sensitive and complex than the stereotypes of the stoical, steely, and stiff upper-lipped Victorian soldier. It also presents the adoptive family as a powerful, potentially transformative example of the personal and social benefits of relationships across boundaries of class and nationality. On the other hand the same archive can be felt to work to make war more palatable, using a demilitarized male in the service of a militaristic agenda. I oscillate here between a hermeneutics of suspicion, through which the propagandistic power of the gentle soldier as enchanting violence becomes clear, and a reparative reading, which also recognizes that which is missed by the paranoid reading: that narratives of soldier adoption may also have the power to change perceptions and ultimately wars, reconfiguring assumptions about military masculinity and the behaviour of military men.

These mixed implications are also observable in soldiers' own investments in forms of fictive military kinship, both in fraternal bonds and in emotionally powerful designations of some men as trusted daddies and others as treasured children of the regiment. These familial languages draw on similar strategies to those used in published literature and art, undoing the hierarchies of rank in favour of familial organizations of relationship by feeling. As the following chapter explores, soldiers' accounts of their experience of regimental kinship present similarly mixed messages to the more polished literary material considered here. The child of the regiment has the capacity to challenge and extend our perceptions of the range of soldierly masculinity, showing the significance of domestic and family life and of emotional responsiveness to military men. Nurturing responses to this typically adorable figure, in both fiction and fact, can also obscure the willingness to cut and slash that is at the centre of the soldier's job description, working both personally and politically to make war more acceptable.

4

'Our poor Colonel loved him as if he had been his own son'

Family Feeling in the Crimea

Our loss was *severe* 60 men killed and wounded, and *seven officers*, of whom Colonel Egerton (a tall powerful man) and Captain Lempriere [of the] 77th [East Middlesex Regiment] were *killed*; the latter was very young, had just got his company and was about the *smallest* officer in the Army, a great *pet* of the Colonel's and termed by him his *child*; he was killed, poor fellow at the first attack in the rifle pit, the Colonel, *tho' wounded*, snatched him up in his arms and carried him off declaring 'they shall never take my child'; the Colonel then returned and in the second attack was killed.[1]

This is an account of the British attack on the rifle pits before besieged Sebastopol on 19 April 1855, and of the losses suffered in the attempt. It is one among many forms of memorial—written, verbal, material—produced by soldiers and civilians grieving the deaths of Colonel Thomas Graham Egerton and Captain Audley Lempriere. In this chapter I consider the range and intensity of responses to the death of Captain Audley Lempriere, who was widely known as 'the boy Captain'. I place the many poignant retellings of the paternal care of Colonel Egerton for the young man he termed 'his child' within a broader context of regimental family feeling. A network of emotional connections between home and campaign ground emerges, as grief is shared between the Lempriere family and the 77th Regiment.

Memorials for Lempriere comprise the archive for this chapter: his Crimean grave next to Egerton's, the tombstone in his home church, poetry written by officers and private soldiers, a remarkable memorial album produced by Lempriere's sister, and fond reminiscences by

---

[1] Letter of Nathaniel Steevens, 19 April 1855, NAM 1965-01-183-82. Original emphasis. This extract is reprinted in Alastair Massie, *The National Army Museum Book of the Crimean War: The Untold Stories* (Basingstoke: Macmillan, 2005), p. 183.

Lempriere's regiment and his family of his 'pet' pony. These are read within a context of Lempriere's own correspondence, and that of other officers and men of the 77th. In the shift in focus from published fiction to archival materials (much of it previously unexamined) this chapter attends to a different kind of cultural work. It is concerned with overlapping public and private structures of feeling, and the forms in which love and loss could be expressed by soldiers and civilians. The rich languages of emotion, and varied practices of mourning and memorial in response to the deaths of Lempriere and Egerton, blur an assumed divide between soldier and civilian, and public and private responses to the loss are intertwined. Feeling crosses ranks as officers and regular soldiers movingly express their loss in some similar ways.

SALVAGE WORK: A SHORT RISK ASSESSMENT

This chapter is concerned with a number of forms of recuperation. It continues to reclaim Victorian military manliness from an insufficient historiography, while using materials which were in themselves determinedly recuperative, in that they sought to offer comfort and consolation to the bereaved. Throughout this chapter, which in its focus on memorial is concerned with practices intended to make loss more manageable, I am aware of the caution of war novelist and Vietnam veteran Tim O'Brien:

> If at the end of a war story you feel uplifted, or if you feel that some small bit of rectitude has been salvaged from the larger waste, then you have been made the victim of a very old and terrible lie. There is no rectitude whatsoever.[2]

Responses to Lempriere's death are engaged, variously, in the politically risky business of salvage, as value (and sometimes even salvation) is found in the larger waste. Narratives circulated about Egerton's lifting of the small corpse from the field in part *because* they were uplifting for a range of different Victorian audiences, and they continue to be so. I am mindful also of the particular enchantments of this archive, as I feel the charisma of this loveable young man and the tingling joy of touching the small objects he hand-picked to send home. The paranoid/reparative methodology outlined in the Introduction structures my negotiation

---

[2] Tim O'Brien, *The Things They Carried* (New York: First Mariner, 2009, first published 1990), p. 65.

here of affectively complex materials, which generate, like much of the other material considered in this book, divergent and competing strands of interpretation.[3]

Sedgwick's work on reparative reading, concerned with 'how texts might help us to feel better and think differently', offers useful insight into the affective work of personal and public mourning.[4] Memorial responses, I argue, work reparatively in Sedgwick's terms as they strive to make the bereaved 'feel better and think differently' about their loss. Personal and public war memorials, for fellow soldiers, family, friends, and nation, are concerned with rectitude, and, in their consolatory function, have a particular ideological relationship to the practice of warfare. War memorials typically communicate a range of potentially contradictory meanings, as Jay Winter has argued in relation to monuments commemorating the dead of the First World War: 'While ambiguities of iconography and ritual are undeniably present in war memorials, and while they embody and proclaim a host of commemorative messages about war, they do not obliterate the simple truth that people die in war.'[5] Memorials of Lempriere incorporate both criticism and affirmation of war, provoking diverse affective reactions including grief and a painful sense of waste, celebration of the Good Death and of his character, a desire to connect with other mourners. They provide solace through powerful heroic and sentimental narratives, which overwrite some of the more troubling realities of the conflict, notably questions of officer privilege. The opportunity these eulogistic materials furnish for *feeling better* operates in a dual sense, as they offer comfort via an intense emotional encounter with the feelings of others, especially the grief-struck Egerton. Most often, as we shall see, soldiers and civilians alike affectively engage with loss, often in surprising ways, while at the same time, and more predictably, attempting to rationalize the deaths as a valuable part of the war effort and to celebrate them as exemplars of battlefield heroism. By overlaying a wide range of responses I look at the tensions produced within the heroic narrative by the frankness of the pain of loss expressed. I also attend to the mixed messages in Lempriere's telling of his own war via the letters he sent home.

---

[3] In the Introduction I use Sedgwick and Klein's work on positions to elaborate on the particular value, in reading war literature, of a critical practice that allows competing interpretations to coexist, overlapping and interrupting each other.
[4] This is Jason Edwards's helpful shorthand for Sedgwick's theories of what reparative reading might achieve, *Eve Kosofsky Sedgwick* (London and New York: Routledge, 2009), p. 107.
[5] Jay Winter, *Sites of Memory, Sites of Mourning: The Great War in European Cultural History* (Cambridge: Cambridge University Press, 1995), p. 78.

'REMARKABLY TALL' AND 'VERY MINUTE': REMAINS OF EGERTON AND LEMPRIERE

Lempriere and Egerton make a wonderfully odd pair. Both were the eldest sons of leading military men; General Sir Charles Egerton was Colonel of the 89th Foot, while Lempriere's father was a rear-admiral. Thomas Graham Egerton, the experienced commanding officer of the 77th (East Middlesex) Regiment of Foot, was a towering physical presence at 6 feet 8 inches. He had joined the 77th in 1829 and, having been commended in 1848 for 'energy, firmness and sound judgement' in dealing with post-election rioting in Montreal, took command of the regiment in 1850, with the purchase of his lieutenant-colonelcy.[6] He continued to distinguish himself throughout the Crimea, making important contributions at Alma and Inkerman; at the latter he and Lempriere were two of the nine officers of the 77th involved. After the 77th were instrumental in the capture of the castle of Balaclava, Egerton was deputed to receive the commandant's sword. In his memoir of the campaign Nathaniel Steevens reflects on Egerton's suitability for this honour with some enthusiasm: 'a finer specimen of a British officer could not have been found for this purpose for Colonel Egerton was a remarkably tall, soldierlike man.'[7] Lempriere, by contrast, had begun his army career when he joined the 77th as an ensign in December 1850, and was just twenty when he died. His rapid promotion through the officer ranks to become captain in the month before his death was a consequence of the extent of the losses in the Crimea. Lempriere stood under 5 feet in height, as his diminutive uniform, held at the National Army Museum, shows.[8] In a letter to his brother, in the month before his death, Lempriere records his weight as a mere 7 stones 6 pounds.[9] The war photographer Roger Fenton remembered him as 'very young and very minute'.[10]

The dispatches issued by Lord Raglan (General Commander-in-Chief, Army in the East) for the 27 April 1855 described Captain Lempriere as 'a very young but most promising officer', and detailed the loss of Egerton:

---

[6] Major H. H. Woollright, *Records of the 77th* (London: Gale and Polden, 1907), p. 61; Alastair Massie, ed., *A Most Desperate Undertaking: The National Army Museum Book of the Crimean War* (London: The National Army Museum, 2003), p. 259.

[7] Nathaniel Steevens, *The Crimean Campaign with 'The Connaught Rangers'*, *1854–1856* (London and Edinburgh: Griffith and Farran, 1878), p. 96.

[8] Massie, *Desperate Undertaking*, p. 260. Lempriere's coatee has a chest measurement of 31 inches and from nape to knees is just 30.5 inches long.

[9] 6 April 1855, HRO 4M52/125.

[10] Roger Fenton, letter to Grace Fenton, 24 April 1855, <http://rogerfenton.dmu.ac.uk>.

Colonel Egerton was an officer of superior merit, and conducted all his duties, whether in camp or in the field, in a manner highly to his own honour, and greatly to the advantage of the public, and Her Majesty's service could not have sustained a more severe loss, and it is so felt in this army and in the 77th, where he was much beloved and deeply lamented.[11]

Raglan's language imbues this loss with value by attributing strategic and heroic significance to the capture of the Russian rifle pits, known from then on as 'Egerton's pit'. Raglan describes the taking of the pits as a 'brilliant achievement', which was 'dearly bought by the sacrifice of Colonel Egerton, who was one of the best officers in the army, and looked up to by all'.[12] Military publications expanded upon the praise for Lempriere: 'A boy in years and stature, he behaved like a veteran soldier.'[13]

Such official commendation clearly had resonance for the bereaved both at the front and at home. These communities overlapped, as several of the officers of the 77th who were particular friends of Audley, notably Lieutenant Charles Ernest Knight (of Chawton House) and Captain Edward Chawner (Newton Valence Manor House), were also close neighbours of the Lempriere family when at home in Hampshire. The three families were major landowners in the Alton area.[14] Indeed, this familial closeness meant that Knight took on the unenviable task of communicating the news of Audley's death, much to the relief of his superior officer. Knight, understandably anxious about this duty, asks his mother to break the news to Lempriere's mother, 'as I should find it hard to word the letter'.[15] The continuing connection between the families is apparent from the inclusion in papers collected by the Lempriere family of a transcription, on black-edged mourning paper, of the *Daily News* announcement of Knight's death in camp from fever on 2 October 1855. Chawner was the only one of these three near-neighbours in the 77th to survive the campaign.

In a letter of condolence to Lempriere's family shortly after Audley's death, Chawner draws on the consolation offered by high-ranking praise, and details the burial arrangements:

---

[11] *The Military Obituary, 1855* (London: Parker, Furnivals and Parker, 1855), p. 23.
[12] Massie, *Desperate Undertaking*, p. 259.
[13] *Colburn's United Service Magazine and Naval and Military Journal*, part 2 (London: Hurst and Blackett, 1855), p. 175.
[14] [Charles] Ernest Knight, known as Ernest, was nephew to Jane Austen, whose brother Edward (Ernest's father) took the name of Knight after he became adoptive heir to the Knight family, who were distant cousins of the Austens. Chawton House is a five-minute walk from the now famous home (then known as Corner or Pond House) of Jane Austen in Chawton. For details of the estates see William White, *History, Gazetteer and Directory of the County of Hampshire* (London: William White and Simpkin Marshall, 1878), p. 10, p. 349.
[15] Major Clark Jervoise to Mrs Scote, 20 April 1855. The major expresses his 'great relief' at having been spared this 'most unpleasant task', NAM 2004-07-13, Notebook.

They were both buried together the day before yesterday and with them the men who fell that night. Egerton was held in such esteem throughout the army that Lord Raglan and staff and the generals of divisions &c attended the funeral, and Lempriere came in for his full share of regrets, as he was known to many of the staff. How I pity poor Lempriere! Was it not a horrible night's work? I dined last night with Sir George Brown, and he made me give him the whole account and amidst all his sorrow is delighted at the way the regiment behaved and said it was the most gallant thing done during the campaign.

This letter survives as part of a memorial notebook compiled by Lempriere's sister Ellen, who was sixteen at the time of her brother's death and is described in the 1851 census record, like other young ladies of her class, as 'scholar at home'.[16] The notebook, now held in the archives of the National Army Museum in London, brings together a range of contents including letters, sketches, pressed flowers, and other materials posted home by Audley, with mourning condolences, eulogies, and poetry written in response to his death by soldiers and family.

The Lempriere family notebook with its mixed media contents can be seen as an effort by those at home to connect with the physical phenomena of Captain Lempriere's life in the Crimea, a kind of posthumous effort to keep in touch with this beloved son/brother/cousin. The inclusion of material that Lempriere sent in letters as 'mementoes' of the battles and truces of the campaign—a scrap of Russian medal ribbon, violets from the slopes outside Sebastopol—allowed his family to touch some of the stuff of Lempriere's war experience. And Lempriere's sketches of camp and landscape enable his family to share his perspective of the campaign for these moments, giving an (albeit limited, carefully framed) insight into his view of the Crimea.[17] This lovingly preserved material also allows us to appreciate the conduits of feeling—emotional and tactile—between home and campaign. In his letters Lempriere regularly thanks his family for their own letters, and the things they have sent, including the local paper, clothing, and provisions; things that combined practical support with the news, routines, taste, and touch of home. The notebook's contents show, especially vividly, how soldiers at war also endeavoured to connect their families with some of their felt experience (Figure 4).

---

[16] Though the notebook is anonymous and does not include the compiler's personal recollections of Audley, annotations of transcribed letters such as 'From Capt. G. Lempriere to Papa' clearly position the compiler as a sibling of Audley Lempriere, and the notebook includes, without explanatory annotation, letters to Ellen. Lempriere also had a younger sister, Harriet, who was eleven when he died, and a younger brother, Algernon, who went on from Eton to study at Oxford during the period of Lempriere's Crimean campaign. For further details of the family's history see Kenneth Parry, *Pelham Place: A History* (London: de Lazlo Foundation, 2005), pp. 87–95.

[17] I discuss these materials and Lempriere's sketches in more detail in the next chapter.

Figure 4. Lempriere family notebook, cover and detail. Reproduced with permission from the National Army Museum.

These treasures are contained within a surprisingly modest-looking book, bound within undecorated brown covers and measuring 4 inches across and 5 high. The notebook became a double memorial as Ellen Lempriere turned it over and reused it when her other brother, Algernon, died nineteen years later. The contents comprise a range of written, drawn, and material objects produced by a range of different people. The compilation has similarities to album making, a popular pursuit of leisured women in the nineteenth century. It is significantly differentiated, though, from the album genre by what, in contrast, appears to be a determined rejection of ostentation. Given that the Lempriere family owned 50 acres and employed twenty people, the choice of material would not have been determined by cost. The notebook's modest appearance and relatively cheap material—the paper is very thin so pages occasionally bleed through onto their other side—suggests that it was compiled impromptu using whatever writing book came to hand, as a personal memorial intended to be seen only by Ellen herself or perhaps shared with immediate family rather than shown to visitors, as albums were, in a semi-public display of taste. Rather than commissioned pieces produced specifically for it, the process through which much album material was garnered, the notebook predominantly comprises transcriptions of letters, poems, etc. It has, then, a poignantly found quality, offering what feels like a reflection of Ellen's experience of mourning as she dedicates herself to gathering and re-presenting all material pertinent to her brother's death. The many expressions of loss and voices of condolence are assembled into a community of shared grief. The notebook, therefore, most closely overlaps with albums in drawing together a community of feeling, but is distinguished from album making by a disregard for the aesthetic quality of the incorporated material. Sentiment in this compilation, as is particularly apparent in the inclusion of poetry that ranges widely in its formal qualities, is always prioritized over craftsmanship.

Ellen Lempriere's labour in compiling this notebook is comparable to the often arduous 'work of mourning' examined by Drew Gilpin Faust as a widespread response to the losses of the American Civil War. In this different context, Faust considers a range of mourning work including the making of 'elaborate memorial volumes and scrapbooks' such as those produced by Henry Bowditch over six years as an 'extensive and therapeutic effort' in honour of his son Nathaniel who was killed in Virginia in 1863.[18] Faust is concerned with the emotional and practical effort required to survive war loss: 'Civil War fatalities belonged ultimately to the

---

[18] Drew Gilpin Faust, *This Republic of Suffering: Death and the American Civil War* (New York: Vintage, 2008), p. 170.

survivors; it was they who had to undertake the work not just of burial but also of consolation and mourning.' As she suggests, the labour of restoration and healing falls on 'families and communities' who must 'repair the rent in the domestic and social fabric'.[19]

Ellen Lempriere's emotional and practical labour of compilation in this notebook can also be understood, in psychoanalytic terms, as a reparative project. Extrapolating from Melanie Klein's account of a possible response to infant separation trauma, Sedgwick proposes a wider context, continuing through adulthood experiences of pain and loss, in which it becomes possible 'to use one's own resources to assemble or "repair" the murderous part-objects into something like a whole ... Once assembled to one's own specifications, the more satisfying object is available both to be identified with and to offer one nourishment and comfort in turn.'[20] In bringing together a plenitude of fragmentary, often repetitive, testimonies to her brother's life and death, Ellen succeeds in fashioning a potentially more sufficient document to her 'own specifications', which gestures towards completeness, 'something like a whole', to offer comfort. Ellen's thorough assembling of numbers of testimonies of her brother's final moments speaks to the closure and partial solace derived from information about the circumstances of a beloved's death in wartime.[21] These multiple accounts provide a way for the bereaved to realize the death, and produce a sense of wholeness in the narrative of Lempriere's contracted life.

Other Lempriere family memorial compilations—together with around eighty letters sent by Audley to his family during the Crimea campaign, his certificates of commission, reports from Eton, and earlier correspondence—are preserved in the Pelham papers (named for the family's Alton estate) at the Hampshire Record Office (HRO). Practices of consolation in these treasured family documents overlap significantly with public commemorations of Lempriere. In both the public—including newspaper reports, military dispatches, regimental records, published memoirs, and gravestone inscriptions—and private archives, emphasis is placed on Egerton's tender, familial response to Lempriere's death and on the physical characteristics and personal charisma of both men.

[19] Faust, *This Republic of Suffering*, p. 143, p. xiv.
[20] Eve Kosofsky Sedgwick, *Touching Feeling: Affect, Pedagogy, Performativity* (Durham and London: Duke University Press, 2003), p. 128.
[21] Winter documents the incredible efforts, mainly by volunteers, in the First World War to provide 'loved ones [with] the only solace that they believed could help: the truth, or that part of it which could be confirmed', *Sites of Memory*, p. 30, and Faust describes how similarly, in the American Civil War, 'the living searched in anxiety and even "phrensy" to provide endings for life narratives that stood incomplete, their meanings undefined', *This Republic of Suffering*, p. 267.

'I MUST SAVE MY POOR LITTLE BOY': CELEBRATED SOLDIERLY SENTIMENT

While the formal commendations of commanders and the sense of order provided by the military funeral for Egerton and Lempriere offered forms of consolation shared by soldiers and civilians, both constituencies also valued emotive language and descriptions that attempted to capture the intensity of felt response to these deaths. Ellen Lempriere's notebook also preserves Chawner's particularly moving account of Lempriere's death:

> Our gallant Colonel took him up in his arms and carried him under cover, crying out, 'Make way there for God's sake, I must save my poor little boy.' Poor fellow it turned me quite sick to think of it, he was such a favourite with us all, and our poor Colonel loved him as if he had been his own son.

Alongside this private correspondence the notebook also contains published newspaper reports of this event from *The Daily News* and *The Hampshire Chronicle*, the Lempriere family's local newspaper, which reprinted the piece:

> Captain Audley Lempriere, a lad in years and experience, the darling of his company and a general favourite in the regiment, also fell in the affair. He received a wound in the body, and on falling, Colonel Egerton caught him up in his arms as if he had been a child, and calling out 'Make way, men, while I carry my poor boy-captain away', took him to the trench in the rear.[22]

These newspapers and various public accounts emphasize the intensity of Egerton's response in the same way as private letters. The public reports recycle the language of private correspondence, incorporating versions of Egerton's reported speech.

Egerton's final act is unanimously presented as an exemplary form of the 'Good Death'. Faust argues that 'the Good Death was the foundation for the process of mourning carried on by survivors who used the last words and moments of the dead soldier as the basis for broader evaluation of his entire life'.[23] As Bourke has documented in her work on the First World War, last actions are in a hierarchy, with 'accidental' deaths (from a stray bullet on patrol, for example) or deaths from disease positioned as less heroic. The greatest heroism was attributed to those killed in action, especially the self-sacrificing deaths of those who 'offered their bodies to

---

[22] 'To the editor of the *Hampshire Chronicle*', NAM 2004-07-13, Notebook.
[23] Faust, *This Republic of Suffering*, p. 163.

save particular friends'.[24] This hierarchy is clearly visible in responses to Crimean War casualties. Ernest Knight, having died of illness, is not mentioned in the memorial pamphlet *Last of the Brave, or Resting Places of Our Fallen Heroes in the Crimea* (included in both Lempriere family collections for its mention of Lempriere), which eulogizes only those who died in action. By contrast, although Egerton is unable to save his favourite—in some versions, including Chawner's, he is directly presented as attempting this—his effort to do so imbues his subsequent death in direct action with particular heroism. Egerton's expression of grief and the partiality he shows for Lempriere, rather than being seen to be at variance with an expectation of stoicism, are celebrated as the ultimate narrative of the Good Death, providing the basis for glowing evaluations of the lives of both Egerton and Lempriere.

Many of the poems collected in the notebook present Egerton's final act of nurture as consolatory; like private letters and newspaper reports they emphasize Egerton's vocal expression, a form of famous last words, and the intensity of his felt response, in both tactile and emotional terms. A poem attributed to a private in the 77th, for example, includes the line 'the Colonel's arms his bier'. Another anonymous poem, 'In Memoriam', reflects on this moment at some length:

> ... At once his chief was nigh and said
> 'Faint not my gallant boy'
> And o'er him bent now helpless laid
> So late his pride and joy
> ... Within his stalwart arms the Chief
> His dying soldier caught
> And felt this [victory?] by such griefs
> Were all too dearly bought
> 'Make way men! While I bear my poor
> Boy-Captain from the field'
> He cried but knew that never more
> That death wound could be healed.
> And when he safely laid him down
> And gazed into his eyes
> A calm resigned look met his own
> And claimed his sympathies.
> 'And could you not be spared poor boy?'
> Were all the words he spoke...

---

[24] Joanna Bourke, *Dismembering the Male: Men's Bodies, Britain and the Great War* (London: Reaktion, 1996), pp. 247–9, p. 247.

The author attributes direct speech to Egerton; the poignant extrapolation 'And could you not be spared poor boy?' underlines the importance of the *expression* of deep feeling, while the direct address 'Make way my men...' presents this as grief communicable amongst the regimental community. The poem also celebrates the physicality of the colonel's response, taking comfort in the 'stalwart arms' that remove the dying Lempriere from the field. Here an explicit celebration of physical prowess combines with the components of deep affection and bodily intimacy characteristic of the many versions of this event. The poem registers an intensity of response—which shares characteristics with the erotic—when feeling is so thoroughly both affective and tactile. As Das has suggested in the context of the First World War, intimacies imbricated in experiences of survival, peril, loss, and mourning are rarely well understood through the limited vocabulary by which sexuality is categorized.[25] Instead a more nuanced appreciation of feeling is required, one that can begin to apprehend the varieties of comfort offered by tactility between soldiers, and by representations of touch and intimacy for their survivors. Notably consolation is also found (in the collected poetry and correspondence around the deaths of Egerton and Lempriere) in the posthumous proximity of the two bodies, buried side by side in the Sebastopol cemetery dedicated to the 77th.

N. A. Woods's published history of the Crimean War, gathered predominantly from his observations as a correspondent for *The Morning Herald*, presents this dramatic scene as part of a wider reflection on Egerton's character, particularly his capacity for gentleness. Woods reports the colonel as saying 'Don't give way, my boy; never give way', and then emphasizes the physicality of his final act of care for Lempriere, through active clauses: '*Taking him up* in his arms, Egerton *carried him back* to the shelter of the advanced trench, and as he *laid him gently down* Lempriere breathed his last.'[26] Woods eulogizes Egerton as 'a skilful soldier, accomplished scholar', 'with the bravery of an English officer united to those warm and gentle feelings which, except in the highest natures, so rarely long survive long practical acquaintance with the world'.[27] In Woods's

---

[25] Santanu Das, *Touch and Intimacy in First World War Literature* (Cambridge: Cambridge University Press, 2005), p. 118.
[26] N. A. Woods, *The Past Campaign: A Sketch of the War in the East*, 2 vols (London: Longman, 1855), p. 352, emphasis added.
[27] Woods, *The Past Campaign*, pp. 353–4. Accounts of Egerton's character and military command are almost uniformly positive. William Pechell, for example, a senior officer with the 77th, writes to his family in distress on learning of Egerton's death: 'To me it is the greatest misfortune that could happen, he was my best friend and the man I always looked to for advice and assistance in his double capacity of commanding officer and friend. His loss cannot be replaced...This is but a melancholy letter, but few know how much I liked Colonel Egerton and I trust the feeling was reciprocal', 20 April 1855. Private collection.

account, Egerton embodies a fascinating combination of physical power with delicate tactility; he unites the identities of soldier and scholar in a varied emotional life as brave military man and man of feeling.

Woods sees the preservation of 'warm and gentle feelings' as a rarity in the public lives of men, and a similar view has structured understandings of Victorian masculinity more broadly, and the Victorian military man in particular. Emotional literacy, however, was presented as central to a command model of moral management. As Stoqueler put it, 'It is the officer's duty to comfort the soldier in sickness and suffering, to console him in sorrow and affliction, to cheer him in toil and in the severe trials to which military life is exposed.'[28] Stoqueler's emphasis on 'comfort', consolation, and 'cheer' is one manifestation of the ways in which the reparative impulse can work to enable warfare, as the 'severe trials' of military life are made sustainable through a community of feeling. As is typical of such conduct manuals Stoqueler's advice is shaped by the regulation military manual, *The Queen's Regulations and Orders*, which each officer was obliged to study, own, and carry with him on foreign service. The *Regulations and Orders* contains advice on the friendly moral management of men, via an appeal to their best natures, including a caution against 'wounding the feelings' of those commanded: 'He is constantly to bear in mind that the confidence and affection of those who are placed under his charge are indispensable requisites towards the satisfactory exercise of his Command.'[29] This caring paternalist ideal conflicted with the harsh material conditions of regular soldiers' lives, which came under particular scrutiny during the Crimean War. Reforms to accommodation, discipline, recreation, health, and education followed. Officers who eschewed a model of care for their men—the Earl of Cardigan, for example, fresh back from commanding the ill-fated Charge of the Light Brigade, resisted reforms to the use of barracks over stables, assuring the House of Lords that reports of the discomforts of soldierly life

---

I am grateful to Marigold Somerset for permission to quote this material. George Willis (another officer in the 77th), exceptionally, offers a less glowing appraisal as he felt Egerton had prevented him from receiving a staff appointment. He writes to his family of having 'had another proof of Egerton's selfishness and injustice', 22 December 1854. He describes Egerton's death, however, as 'a great loss, for with all his faults he was a good and clever officer' and recalls 'Poor Little Lempriere' in familiar terms: 'a great favourite with us all—from his very small size we always called him "the Child" and there are few in the army out here who did not know or love "our Child"', 20 April 1855, NAM 2004-10-168-3.

[28] J. H. Stocqueler, *The British Officer: His Positions, Duties, Emoluments and Privileges* (London, 1851), p. 2. Stocqueler's work was discussed in chapter 2 as one source of inspiration for Thackeray's eminently gentle officer, Colonel Newcome.

[29] *The Queen's Regulations and Orders for the Army, 1844 (–54)* (London: Parker, Furnival and Parker, 1844), p. 117, p. 115.

were much exaggerated—began to look distinctly outmoded.[30] The balance of characteristics of both officers and men, then, gained particular cultural pertinence during the Crimean War, and continued to be debated in the decades thereafter.

Writers regularly commented on the apparently contradictory combination of characteristics, which Woods attributes to Egerton, that were required of both officers and men. James Fitzjames Stephen's famous 1864 essay 'Sentimentalism' for the *Cornhill Magazine* resists the assumption, typical in critiques of sentimentality, that 'tenderness goes with weakness'.[31] It points out that 'it is a common form for eulogistic biographers in the present day to speak of the "manly tenderness" of eminent men, to set forth their fondness for children and women, and to tell stories of their having cried over affecting scenes and the like'. The piece goes on to assert that 'the most energetic and the bravest of men have generally had a good deal of tenderness in them', and holds up heroes of the Peninsular War, Sir Charles Napier and his brother Sir William, as examples of this. Though Stephen is anxious about undisciplined and self-indulgent feeling, and his essay has tended to be read as an attack on the emasculating tendencies of 'wanton' sentiment, wartime emerges in his argument as a legitimate site for manly feeling as heightened emotions are merited by experiences that provide 'cause' 'for sadness'.[32] While Stephen restricts his examples of appropriately disciplined and sufficiently motivated feeling to aristocratic commanders, a similar amalgamation of bravery and tenderness was widely attributed to soldiers of the ranks during the Crimean War. *Lloyd's Weekly Newspaper*, for example, commented on the accounts of the Battle of Alma it published from letters of regular soldiers as full of 'feeling, tenderness, and valour'.[33] These juxtapositions reflect the 'contested versions' of martial manliness produced, as Walton puts it, by the 'difficulties which ensued when trying to reconcile a declining

---

[30] Alan Ramsey Skelley, *The Victorian Army at Home: The Recruitment and Terms and Conditions of the British Regular, 1859–1899* (London: Croom Helm, 1977), p. 34.

[31] [James Fitzjames Stephen], 'Sentimentalism', *Cornhill Magazine*, July 1864, pp. 65–75, p. 73. For a reading of this piece in a context of wider Victorian commentaries on feeling, and the appropriate response to feeling, see Carolyn Burdett, 'Introduction, Sentimentalities', New Agenda section, *Journal of Victorian Culture* 16.2 (2011), pp. 187–94, especially, and Burdett, 'Is Empathy the End of Sentimentality?', *Journal of Victorian Culture* 16.2 (2011), pp. 259–74.

[32] [Stephen], 'Sentimentalism', p. 70.

[33] 'Literature of the War', *Lloyd's Weekly Newspaper*, 12 November 1854. The enthusiasm for the emotive first-hand accounts of regular soldiers continued with the publication, a year later, of collected letters in *The War, or Voices from the Ranks* (London and New York: Routledge and Co., 1855).

investment in physical violence with the need to produce soldiers and empire builders'.[34]

The account of Egerton's response to his favoured second's death is characteristic of the range of actual and fictional narratives of the period, which circumvent this difficulty by transforming the plot of war violence into one of reparation and care. This impulse is apparent in a wider vogue for the expression of soldierly heroism via battlefield tales of practices more readily associated with the domestic sphere, including adoption and nursing (the subjects, respectively, of chapters 3 and 6 of this book). Egerton's deeply felt response—parental and nurturing as it is—is part of his heroism, and private and public accounts alike insistently celebrate it as such. Here, possessive parental feeling is not seen to be at odds with a public military role, rather, contrary to a gendered separate spheres model of public, non-domestic masculinity, powerful family feeling becomes a component of soldierly excellence. In fact, the mid-Victorian domestication of the military man is part of the wider reparative impulse that, paradoxically, by civilizing war allows it to remain culturally acceptable.

This rich archive of the tragedy of the 77th demonstrates the extent of the shift within the military, as well as in civilian society, to more bourgeois domestic values. The poignancy of the colonel's fatherly feeling resonated with soldiers of all classes, and with those grieving at home. In feeling for Lempriere as if for a son, Egerton, in a way particularly shaped by mid-Victorian ideals, intensified one of the most typical, long-standing modes of articulating intimacy in the military: the regimental family.

'OUR POOR COLONEL LOVED HIM AS IF HE HAD BEEN HIS OWN SON': FAMILIAL SENTIMENT

Regimental relationality overlapped with familial bonds in both metaphor and fact. It was usual for there to be family traditions within regiments, with members of a family, often across generations, joining the same division. When, for example, Lieutenant Frederick Peter Delme Radcliffe was killed while serving with the 23rd (Royal Welsh Fusiliers) Regiment of Foot at the Alma, his bravery there was recognized through the gift of a commission without purchase in the 23rd for his younger brother, Herbert.[35] Lines of familial feeling in regiments were variously structured. As well as being, in part, bonded by forms of blood relation, regiments

---

[34] Susan Walton, *Imagining Soldiers and Fathers in the Mid-Victorian Era: Charlotte Yonge's Models of Manliness* (Farnham: Ashgate, 2010), p. 2.
[35] Massie, *Desperate Undertaking*, p. 309.

continued and intensified existing social connections as evident in the constellation of three neighbouring Alton families in the 77th.

These actual familial and social ties were extended in a popular sense of blood brotherhood, albeit demarcated along lines of rank, between soldiers. The language of a 'band of brothers' so memorably evoked by Shakespeare's *Henry V*, and still resonant today (most notably in the book and TV series of that name), suggests the overlaying of lateral bonds of fraternity onto hierarchically organized relations of rank.[36] The different emotional quality of equal, reciprocal relationship suggested by brotherhood supplements, without supplanting, vertical lines within regiments. Major Clarke Jervoise's description of Lempriere's death, for example, deploys a conventional language: 'He was a great favourite with all his brother officers.'[37] This widely used terminology is reiterated on the memorial erected by Lempriere's family at their parish church, St Mary, Newton Valence: 'He enjoyed in a remarkable degree the confidence of those above him in command, and the esteem and affection of his brother officers and men.' References to the affection of 'brother officers' are common in letters of condolence sent by army personnel to mourning families, and in more public forms of commemoration, which suggests that the idea of a family-like regimental community offered a form of comfort to the bereaved at home. The memorial text chosen by the Lempriere family presents a particularly firm inscription of military hierarchy, and the term brother is carefully positioned to apply to the officers but not to the men. However, the range of material in the notebook, some of which is apparently written by rank and file soldiers, and wider recollections, suggest that the regard for Audley Lempriere as family extended beyond the officer class.

Among various poetic memorials to Lempriere collected in the notebook, there is one entitled 'Young Lempriere' that has the following annotation: 'Sent anonymously to Mrs W Lempriere of Pelham but supposed to have been written by a Private in the 77th Regiment who was an eyewitness of the event described.' This supposition is supported

---

[36] William Shakespeare, *Henry V* (4.3.60) in *The Norton Shakespeare*, ed. Stephen Greenblatt et al. (New York: Norton, 1997), p. 1500. In the closing documentary of the 2001 HBO series *Band of Brothers* many veterans of Easy Company's Second World War campaigns speak of their personal feeling of regimental brotherhood, or a sense which is 'more than family'. The series was inspired by Stephen Ambrose's book *Band of Brothers: E Company, 506th Regiment, 101st Airborne: From Normandy to Hitler's Eagle's Nest* (New York: Simon and Schuster, 1992). For a detailed account of the long cultural significance of military languages of fraternity see Brian Joseph Martin, *Napoleonic Friendship: Military Fraternity, Intimacy and Sexuality in Nineteenth Century France* (Durham, NH: University of New Hampshire Press, 2011).
[37] NAM 2004-07-13, Notebook.

by the unusual emphasis on the feelings of the men, including fear, inspiration, and love. The poem ends with a verse insisting on cross-ranks fraternal feeling:

> They loved him as a brother
> Their eyelids rained the tears
> And gladly they'd have died to save
> The goodly brave Lempriere.

Though leaning on a heroic poetic tradition of lauding the fallen, the sentiment here rings true with widespread accounts of the particular affection that soldiers of all ranks had for the young captain.[38] The varieties of family feeling for Lempriere experienced within the regiment—'they', the men, 'loved him as a brother', while Egerton, as Chawner puts it, 'loved him as if he had been his own son'—show the way in which a range of familial languages are invoked in wartime in order to articulate the quality of emotion between soldiers.

While Egerton's feeling for Lempriere provides a particularly poignant example of the intensity of experiences of regimental relationality, it is not unique. Other examples include Rowland 'Daddy' Hill, who became Commander-in-Chief of the British Army in 1828, and Colonel Thomas 'Daddy' Unett.[39] This affectionate informal term, which mimics the speech of a child, was comfortably applied to both these senior commanding officers. Unett, like Egerton, was one of the few experienced commanding officers in the Crimea, and he was seen as a father by the young men of his regiment. Unett died of his wounds on 15 September 1855, aged fifty-four, after leading an assault on the Redan. One lieutenant of his regiment, the 19th, reported the loss in a letter home:

---

[38] See, for example, a letter from a friend of the Lempriere family describing an encounter she had had with a soldier's wife who 'said they all loved him very much. When the regiment arrived at Liverpool where they embarked, the soldier's wives had to separate from their husbands, and many of these were left in very distressed circumstances, and she says that our dear Audley gave five shillings to every soldier's wife that was left behind', NAM 2004-07-13, Notebook.

[39] Michael Snape describes Daddy Hill as 'the most competent of Wellington's Peninsular Generals', 'remarkable for his humanitarian treatment of his men and for the mildness of his language and temper', *The Redcoat and Religion* (Abingdon: Routledge, 2005), p. 126. Gordon L. Teffeteller records that the name daddy was used as 'a term of appreciation for his benevolent concern for the common soldier', and suggests that this 'rather masked his ruthless combat qualities', 'Hill, Rowland, first Viscount Hill (1772–1842)', *Oxford Dictionary of National Biography* (Oxford: Oxford University Press, 2004); online edn, Jan 2011, <http://www.oxforddnb.com/view/article/13298>. T. F. J Collins documents that Colonel Unett was 'known affectionately by all ranks as "Daddy Unett"; he was a most popular and efficient commanding officer', 'The 19th Regiment at Drill, Chobham Camp, 1853', *Journal of the Society for Army Historical Research* 47 (1969), pp. 192–3.

138   *Military Men of Feeling*

> Our dear old Colonel Unett is gone, he was nearly shot to pieces, and though none were mortal, he was too old to get over it; I loved him like a father, for he was a father to his youngsters. He said to me the day before the attack, 'It's you boys that have mothers and sisters that I pity'; and he would have spared us all if he could have done so.[40]

Here the emotional attachments of regimental and actual family are interwoven, as Colonel Unett longs to preserve his boys, and protect their own mothers and sisters from grief. His is another exemplar of the Good Death, combining the same elements of self-sacrifice that endeavours to spare (younger) others and valiant action in the vanguard that circulate in narratives of Egerton's death. As was widely reported, Unett 'had to decide with Col. Windham who should take precedence in the attack. They tossed, and Col. Unett won. He had it in his power to say whether he would go first or follow Col. Windham. He looked at the shilling, turned it over, and said "My choice is made; I'll be the first man into the Redan."'[41] The lieutenant's letter, and the continuing addition of Daddy to Unett's name, supplements this record of bravery, presenting his expression of paternal feeling for his men 'the day before the attack' as a form of significant last words. Marsh's life of Hedley Vicars, whose own feeling for his men is presented as 'almost fatherly', as discussed in chapter 2, incorporates a mini-biography of Major Douglas Helkett, 4th Dragoons, who died in the Balaclava charge. As in accounts of Daddy Unett, Helkett's death acquires particular heroism through his paternal care for his men, and his dying thoughts of their families at home:

> His thoughtful and benevolent character had won for him the name of 'father of the regiment'. Brave as he was gentle, his gallant bearing was noticed even amidst the fury of that death charge. The last time he was seen, was on the field, fearfully wounded, holding out some bank notes to his men, with the characteristic words, 'Take them for the wives and widows at home.'[42]

Like Egerton, Unett and Helkett exhibit a heroic combination of bravery and gentleness, with the latter expressed especially clearly through the language of fatherliness. There has been some attention to the experience of 'maternal' feeling and care between soldiers in the absence of women, and the incorporation of supposedly feminine qualities into male

---

[40] *Naval and Military Records of Rugbeians* (London: 1864), p. 50.
[41] As reported in *The Times*, 27 September, 1855, p. 7, and 'Foreign Events', *Household Narrative*, 1855, p. 229.
[42] Catherine Marsh, ed., *Memorials of Captain Hedley Vicars* (New York: 1857), pp. 222–3.

behaviour in wartime.[43] It is apparent, however, from these examples that bonds between fathers and sons also provided a rich emotional vocabulary through which feeling amongst soldiers could be understood and described. Male-gendered domestic ideals of the caring daddy and beloved son provided sufficiently emotionally expansive models through which to express the desire to nurture, showing that care could be imagined in masculine terms. Expressions of familial feeling for Lempriere are indicative of personal strategies that soldiers used to maintain their sense of their own humanity during wartime, and which, for some, allowed the development of an identity as nurturing soldier. Sibling and parental love are appealed to as ideal and undissolvable relationships. Egerton's sense of Lempriere as his 'child' or 'his own son', as well as the more conventional trope of brotherly affection within the regiment, is emphasized in condolence letters to Lempriere's own parents and siblings. These letters use the overlapping structures of affection at home and at war as consolatory, drawing out the similarities, rather than the differences, between emotional experience in these spheres.

The blurring of civilian and military felt experience, and the significance of familial, domesticated feeling in wartime, is also apparent from the cross-ranks sentimental response to Lempriere's pony, Cherub. In a letter to his mother, Lempriere's aunt Maria recounts a 'most interesting visit, from Sergeant Wilson of the 77th Regiment now quartered in Jersey, he was Audley's Colour Sergeant'. Wilson, a non-commissioned officer, had walked to the family home in the (mistaken) belief that Admiral Lempriere, Audley's father, was visiting. He condoles feelingly with Lempriere's aunt:

> He spoke in raptures of his dear Captain Lempriere, and with tears in his eyes talked of his bravery; and repeated all the sad particulars of dear Audley's last moments. He described the deep sorrow felt by Colonel Egerton when he embraced him; three hours after he was also numbered among the dead. Wilson said 'if I could but see the Capt's dear little poney, how I would kiss him.'[44]

Wilson's testimony confirms the value of this much repeated story across ranks, and across the divide between regimental and civilian family. He

---

[43] Bourke notes instances, in the First World War, of the use of languages of mothering, including a quarter-master sergeant in France who 'reminded one man of a harassed but efficient mother of a reckless family', *Dismembering the Male*, p. 133. Walt Whitman played with the limitations of gendered languages of nurture, describing himself, amongst other things, as 'the mother man' in his nursing of American Civil War casualties, *Specimen Days and Collect* (Philadelphia: Ross Welsh, 1882–3).
[44] Maria Lempriere to Fanny Lempriere, HRO 4M52/128.

describes his understanding of Egerton's 'deep sorrow' at the same time as connecting, through the loss he shares with them, with Lempriere's grieving family. References to the 'dear little pony' also recur in Lempriere family accounts of meetings with those who served with Audley. Another aunt, Caroline, records in her diary a chance encounter with Colonel Norcote: 'Col. Norcote said when he was riding his big charger and Audley his little grey poney, he scarcely came above his elbow; he had quite tears in his eyes when speaking of him; he said he was more beloved than any other officer he knew.'[45] Like the conversation with Wilson, who also spoke with 'tears in his eyes', the exchange with Norcote combines first-hand testimony of Egerton's response with affecting reminiscences of Audley's smallest mount.

A strangely domesticated image emerges of the pony in camp. Colonel Dixon describes how 'Cherub was never tethered but ran about anywhere he liked. He used to peep into the men's tents and shake his head and snort at them and paw the ground with his forefeet and gallop off again to another part of the camp. Whenever he saw Audley in the distance he used to trot up to him directly and seem so fond of him and rub his nose against him.'[46] Clearly the regiment valued this affectionate presence; Cherub is capable, like many animals in wartime, of performing both practical and emotional work, including comic relief. Horses are often discussed feelingly in letters home from the Crimea; distress at the suffering and death of horses, which had often been with their owners for a long period, is common in letters written by those in the cavalry.[47] And a variety of animals were adopted as mascots and pets, providing a valuable subject of shared experience in letters home. Lieutenant-Colonel George Bell's letters home, for example, feature an adopted goose, who 'became a general favourite with all the soldiers. He was so very intelligent, and so fond of the men, he would walk up and down with the sentry at his post all the day.' Like Cherub, the goose is credited with an understanding of the domestic rhythms of camp life: 'Early in the morning he came nibbling at the door-cords to call me up or try to get in. As soon as I appeared, he bid me good-day most distinctly in his own way, and then sat down to await his breakfast of barley thrown into a dish of water.'[48]

---

[45] Caroline Lempriere, Pages from my Diary, 27 Jan 1857, HRO 4M52/129.
[46] Caroline Lempriere, Pages from my Diary, 10 Feb 1857, HRO 4M52/129.
[47] See variously in Glenn Fisher, ed., *Crimean Cavalry Letters* (Stroud: Army Records Society, 2011), including Edward Fisher Rowe (4th Dragoon Guards), who was not given to sentiment in his letters, but writes home on the death of his horse, 'my poor, dear gallant "Jack" is freed from his troubles and misery, and I can't help crying at his loss', p. 145.
[48] George Bell, *Soldier's Glory, being Rough Notes of an Old Soldier* (London: G. Bell and Sons, 1956), p. 203.

Bell clearly appreciates the companionship of the morning greeting, and the continuities with the routines and behaviour of pets at home. Lempriere's Aunt Caroline learns from Captain Jordan that Cherub, similarly, was a great favourite with the men, who took on the responsibility and cost of feeding in order to keep the animal with the regiment:

> At one time Audley said he could not keep him any more, as he had a large horse and did not want the poney; but the men said it should not be sold and that they would keep it for him at their own expense, which they did, they fed it themselves and he rode it whenever he liked. When he was walking about the different camps it used to follow him like a dog, even in and out of the tents! And the men were all so fond of it.

Cherub's faithful, doglike presence is clearly important enough for the men to invest their limited resources in keeping him as a pet of the regiment, a term also used to describe Audley himself, as in Steevens's account. The cross-ranks response to Cherub, in part because he 'is like a dog', is instructive about the dynamics of the feeling for Audley, in part because he is like a child. Both figures offer a clear line of continuity with home experiences, allowing a continuation of identities and feelings—of caring for pets and children—to continue in wartime.

Clearly opportunities for sentiment, more readily associated with the domestic sphere, were welcome in wartime. The ways in which this feeling is directed, however, have more complex implications, as the powerful narrative of Lempriere's death variously reflects and shapes attitudes towards the war. The presentation of Audley as a child overwrites more difficult realities, such as his fierce ambition and (often enthusiastic) participation in the violence of warfare, to transform him into an entirely mournable casualty. In mythologizing Lempriere as the 'boy captain' the complexities of his character are flattened, and the experiences of the actual children on campaign with the 77th are neatly elided.

THE LIMITS TO SENTIMENT

Lempriere's less sentimental response to his pony, which he is quite willing to sell, points to the differences between the feelings both 'pets' (Audley and Cherub) evoke in others, and Audley's own emotional experience. From Lempriere's letters to his family, a more complex character emerges. He is delightful, engaging, for example, in a lively correspondence with his youngest sister Harriet, aged ten at the time, about her prowess in battledore and his fears that she will beat him at the game on his return; he carefully remembers family birthdays and the ailments of correspondents. And he is commendable, giving up an opportunity for leave so that older officers with families can see their children.[49] In these ways he manages to live up to the hyperbole of eulogy, his letters providing much to confirm 'the excellence and amiability of his character' as it was recorded on the family memorial at Newton Valence church. He is also an extremely ambitious young man, and a highly privileged one. Anxious to get his promotion to captain, he is glad to go over the heads of more experienced officers who can't afford to purchase theirs.[50] While Cherub takes on a mythologized role after Audley's death, through which emotion can be cathected and articulated, Audley's own comments on horses throughout his letters are of a much more practical nature. A keen huntsman—much of his correspondence with his brother Algernon involves the exchange of hunting tips and news—he also proves, aided by his light weight, a successful jockey in the various horse races organized for the entertainment of officers in the Crimea. Various letters—including those from Fanny Duberly, herself a fine horsewoman who insisted on remaining with her captain husband throughout the Crimea—comment on Audley's prowess at the races.[51] In these sports of the elite we see the gap between the Crimean experience of officers and men, as wealthy gentry continued to race and hunt at the front, with some believing, outmodedly, that these skills uniquely equipped them for a combat in which they would act as hunt riders.[52] Although officers and men shared

---

[49] See, for example, 'To Harriet' portion of family letter, 6 May 1854, HRO 4M52/125.

[50] He is particularly frank about his ambitions for promotion in letters to his father. On 19 March 1855, exactly a month before his death, he writes to celebrate his captaincy: 'I must say I am wonderfully lucky—an Ensign, Lieut and Captn in the short space [of] only one month—for on the 10th August last year I was an ensign and now I am a Captain. It was very good of you helping me to purchase my company. I have gone over Wellington's and Richards's heads.' In a previous letter to his father he had speculated on this outcome: 'I am not sure that Richards and Wellington and Cordon are for purchase. If they are not I may go over their heads wh[ich] would be a great lift.' Elsewhere he writes proudly: 'I believe I *am* the youngest captain out here' (23 March 1855). HRO 4M52/126.

[51] Transcript of letter from Mrs Henry Duberly to her sister Mrs Ward, 21 April 1855, HRO 4M52/128. Helen Rappaport offers an account of the elaborate recreation of British sporting pursuits by the wealthiest officer class in the Crimea once weather conditions and supply lines improved in the spring of 1855. Pursuits included fishing, hunting, cricket, bathing, and sightseeing parties as well as races. *No Place for Ladies: The Untold Story of Women in the Crimean War* (London: Aurum, 2007), chapter 12.

[52] *Punch* parodied the ignorance of officers who approached the Crimea as a sociable hunt season in a cartoon of 15 April 1854. Others, such as the military historian Alexander Kinglake, held onto a traditional view that the hunt provided valuable battle training: 'The will of a horseman to move forward... is singularly strengthened by the education of the hunting field', *Invasion of the Crimea*, vol. 2 (Edinburgh: Blackwood, 1874), p. 334. I am grateful to Rachel Bates for these references.

the griefs and losses of the campaign, the men had little opportunity to enjoy pleasurable leisure pursuits as a relief from duty.

Differences in experience between ranks are brought into even sharper relief by a comparison of the officers' sense of Lempriere as 'our child', and their apparent indifference to the actual children of the regiment. Private Daniel Casey, also of the 77th Regiment, promoted to sergeant during the campaign, writes home of his concerns for the seventeen wives of the regiment (two of sergeants and fifteen of other ranks) who accompanied them to Crimea, especially those who delivered children there: 'Mrs Kelly was put to bed yesterday of a son. That makes us now three or four young children in the regiment: and those poor children are miserable in this country.'[53] Casey's letters are in contrast to Lempriere's and those of his circle, which do not mention those children, 'on the strength'; nor do they refer to another category of actual children at the centre of regimental life—the drummer boys.

The 77th embarked for the Crimea with thirteen drummers, many of whom, given the conventional recruitment of boys and teenagers in this role, were likely to have been younger than Lempriere.[54] Indeed, one of the regiment's drummers, fifteen-year-old Thomas McGill, distinguished himself during the attack on the rifle pits, as reported by William Howard Russell: 'A drummer boy of the 77th engaged in the melée with a young bugler of the enemy, took his bugle and made him prisoner—a little piece of juvenile gallantry for which he was well rewarded.'[55] As Massie notes McGill received official recognition in being presented with the French medal for valour.[56] He did not, however, despite being the orderly bugler to Egerton, feature in any of the personal accounts of the attack written by officers of the 77th.

The figure of the drummer boy became popular in critiques of the management of this war, especially of the uneven treatment of officers and men. *Punch*, for example, featured a particularly small drummer boy in its satirical cartoon of 24 November 1855, 'The New Game of Follow My Leader'. The full-page sketch sends up the scandal of aristocratic officers, including prominent figures such as the Earl of Cardigan, receiving leave to return to Britain on flimsy pretexts. The bold boy poses the hopeless question to Raglan's replacement, General James Simpson: 'Please, General, may me and these other chaps have leave to go home

---

[53] Daniel Casey to his wife Mary, 7 August 1854, The National Archives, WO177/122.
[54] *Records of the 77th*, p. 67.
[55] William Howard Russell, *The British Expedition to the Crimea* (1858), quoted in Massie, *Desperate Undertaking*, p. 262.
[56] Massie, *Desperate Undertaking*, p. 262.

on *urgent private affairs?*'[57] The emotional appeal of this doughty, straight-talking little figure who petitions so simply on behalf of himself and the regular soldiers ranged behind him, makes him a perfect mouthpiece for *Punch*'s satire. Sentiment for these child soldiers continued to be critically deployed throughout the century, culminating, most famously, in Thomas Hardy's Boer War poem 'Drummer Hodge' (1899), originally published under the title 'The Dead Drummer'. 'Young Hodge', 'fresh from his Wessex home', knows nothing of the reasons for the war waged over the 'broad Karoo'.[58] His death, in ignorance, poignantly suggests the waste and costs of war, including vulnerable, unknowing children.

Though the drummer boys of the 77th Regiment were largely disregarded by their officers, the figure of the child soldier or child otherwise caught up in war had a powerful cultural leverage, which delivers the critical edge to *Punch*'s sketch and Hardy's poem. As argued in the previous chapter, plots of children adopted by soldiers perform mixed cultural work, positioning care for, or killing of, the child at the centre of questions about the compatibility of war with ideals of a civilized and humane society. These texts draw upon a long history of popular emotional response to representations of an innocent child as a casualty of war. Felicia Hemans's 'Casabianca' (1826) exemplifies the affective appeal of the heroic if/because entirely pointless death of the child in war: 'the noblest thing that perished there / was that young faithful heart'. This poem, written in response to reports of the death of the ten-year-old son of the commander of the French flagship *L'Orient*, in the 1798 Battle of the Nile, was widely reprinted, recited, and parodied throughout the nineteenth century and beyond, widely disseminating, as Catherine Robson has shown, its emotionally resonant message of the child facing the fatality of war with 'brave despair'.[59]

Hardy's poem tempers the ostensibly celebratory tone adopted by Hemans; it does though, like memorials for Lempriere, incorporate a eulogy for innocent valour, and finds a sort of national value in the drummer boy's death as a 'portion of that unknown plain / Will Hodge forever be / His homely Northern breast and brain / Grow to some Southern tree'.[60] Though far from the jingoistic celebrations of war which Hardy wrote

---

[57] *Punch*, 24 November 1855, no. 750, vol. 29, p. 209.

[58] Thomas Hardy, 'Drummer Hodge', *The Collected Poems of Thomas Hardy* (Ware: Wordsworth, 1994), p. 83.

[59] Catherine Robson cites Hemans's explanatory note giving this context, *Heart Beats: Everyday Life and the Memorized Poem* (Princeton and Oxford: Princeton University Press, 2012), p. 92, and considers the difficulty of identifying whether the 'message' of this poem glorifies or critiques warfare.

[60] Hardy, 'Drummer Hodge', p. 83.

against in this poem, the gentle treatment of Drummer Hodge does recoup some meaning from his imagined death, and by extension all the actual deaths of the war. In death, Hodge makes part of the Velt 'forever England', as Rupert Brooke was to express it in his 1914 poem 'The Soldier'. The memorial function of Hardy's poem, like the range of testimonies about Lempriere's death, and the eulogistic genre of 'anthems for doomed youth' more broadly, relies, in part, on a version of what Wilfred Owen in 'Dulce et Decorum Est' (1917) would call 'the old Lie': it is a sweet and seemly thing to die for one's country.

By their reparative nature (a writing and reading of traumatic events in ways that can allow the reader to 'feel better') memorials of Lempriere participate in what O'Brien, post Vietnam, called 'a very old and terrible lie'. As we saw at the start of this chapter, O'Brien finds dangerous falsehood in the feeling that 'some small bit of rectitude has been salvaged from the larger waste'.[61] The powerful, sentimental narratives of the small captain and his pony as the darlings of the regiment, and of Lempriere's child-like form being carried from the field, eclipse larger questions of the value of this particular life/death, and all the losses of this war, and even the legitimacy of war itself. They also overwrite controversies particular to the Crimean War, about upper-class incompetence and systematic mismanagement, and about the uneven treatment of officers and men, the second category including the boys who went to the Crimea as drummers. In the eminently grievable deaths of Egerton and Lempriere, we see the unevenness with which different lives are attributed with value according to class (and nationality), so that, in Butler's terms, the 'grievable life' eclipses the loss of those whose lives were never culturally considered to count for as much.[62]

On the one hand, there is important work to be done in recognizing the emotional literacy of ranking soldiers and the clear overlaps between the experience of feeling between officers and men, as a crucial counter to ideas that military men of all ranks, but especially regular soldiers, were brutalized and incapable of fine feeling. There is also, though, a cost in recognizing the imaginative extent of the sense of a regimental family, as there were clearly classed limitations to this idea with some brothers-in-arms held more closely than others, and some 'children' of the regiment taking on great emotional significance while others were disregarded.

[61] O'Brien, *The Things They Carried*, p. 65.
[62] Judith Butler's *Precarious Life: The Power of Mourning and Violence* (London and New York: Verso, 2004) is inspired by her objection to 'the differential allocation of precariousness and grievability', p. 22. As she argues: 'Only under conditions in which the loss would matter does the value of life appear. Thus, grievability is a presupposition for the life that matters', p. 14.

In tempering the appealing, poignant memorial narratives circulated about Lempriere's life and death with some recognition of the complexity of his character, and of the class snobberies and inequalities prevalent in the British army in the Crimea, I try not to retell 'the old lies' which are bound up in the consolatory effects of this material. Reparative readings, of a kind that reclaim the military man from a legacy of historical and literary interpretation that has obscured his capacity for emotion, and thereby overlooked important continuities between military and civilian experience, are necessary to fully appreciate the richness and complexity of Victorian masculinity. However, these arguments can be valuably offset via a practice of paranoid, or suspicious, reading. A paranoid reading of this archive enables an essential critical suspicion of the unevenness with which war deaths are mourned, and of the fictiveness of narratives of the Good Death. Reparative reading, whilst seeing this, can also recognize the personal and cultural forms of recovery made possible by commemoration. As Sedgwick puts it, 'paranoia knows some things well and other things poorly'.[63] In this case, a paranoid reading knows well the ways in which old lies of noble sacrifice enable the continuity of war, but less well how the emotional power attached to a particular loss, presented as unacceptable through the emotive figure of the beloved child, might simultaneously trouble ideas of the value of war.

A blending or oscillation between reparative and paranoid modes recognizes that an either/or reading of the personal and cultural work performed by memorials of Lempriere is insufficient. The presentation of the exemplary military man of feeling in this archive neither straightforwardly romanticizes the nobility of war, nor does it offer a total critique of war's waste. The inflection of the feeling soldier as bereft at the death of his child, however, offers a particularly stark recognition of the losses endured in wartime, experienced with comparable intensity by military men and bereaved families at home. The emphasis on Lempriere as 'boy captain' can proffer a form of critique similar to that conveyed through sympathetic accounts of the powerlessness of drummer boys within the war machine. This movement between paranoid and reparative interpretative lines allows recognition of the emotional strategies by which war violence is recouped, and of the potential violence worked by any such recuperation. The next chapter extends the ethically complex consideration of salvage work, placing the Lempriere memorial album—the collaborative creative work of Ellen, her brother, and soldiers close to him—in a wider context of war material, soldier art, and souvenirs.

---

[63] Sedgwick, *Touching Feeling*, p. 130.

5

Sharing the Stuff of War

Soldier Art, Textiles, and Tactility

Soldiers' sensory pleasure at receiving the stuff of home is captured by John Luard's *A Welcome Arrival*, exhibited the year after the Crimean War ended. The painting shows three officers opening boxes, unpacking small domestic comforts, foodstuffs, a photograph of a loved one, a stripy knitted mitten. Their interaction with this material from home ranges across the senses. Responses encompass the visual, represented by one officer's close scrutiny of the small image, the tactile, the continued grasp of the knitted hand, the olfactory, in the smoked cigar and rising smoke, and the promise of gustatory sensation in the eatables and drinkables awaiting consumption. These homely everyday items bring welcome comfort to the hut, already a highly domesticated site. A cat relaxes in the warmth of the blazing hearth, and scenes from the illustrated press which paper the walls add decoration and insulation. This was a reassuring image of a war more famous for its mismanagement, including inadequate supply lines that left soldiers facing a freezing winter with insufficient shelter, clothing, and food (Figure 5).

Luard understood the emotional and practical significance of receiving a box from home, an event discussed in many officers' letters. He had left the army in 1854 to pursue an artistic career and *A Welcome Arrival* was inspired by a four-month Crimean visit to his brother, Richard, an officer in the 77th Regiment.[1] The painting gestures to the cycles of exchange between home and campaign.

As Roper has argued, boxes from home contributed importantly to soldiers' 'emotional survival'. In his work on the First World War Roper points out that the foodstuffs, reading material, and other personal objects sent to those at the front provided a powerful conduit to home. His examples include an army cook who 'used his mother's recipes, and

---

[1] See Matthew Lalumia, *Realism and Politics in Victorian Art of the Crimean War* (Michigan: UMI Research Press, 1984), pp. 101–2.

Figure 5. John Luard, *A Welcome Arrival*, 1857. Reproduced with permission from the National Army Museum.

prepared his men's food with the wooden spoon she had sent him', and of a mother who sent her soldier son wallpaper samples from the redecoration of their home.[2] As Roper puts it, this was the 'stuff of home itself, and it offered the most direct contact short of going on leave'. In attending closely to this stuff, Roper notes that in privileging the written word historians have 'overlooked the significance of these ordinary domestic objects'.[3] Soldiers' pleasure at receiving ordinary domestic objects creates a line of continuity across conflicts and time. Hetherington records the responses of members of the US Army in Afghanistan to receiving packages. As Specialist Kyle Steiner explains, 'getting things from anybody— your loved ones, your wife, your kids, your parents—that feeling was great'. He appreciates his mum's sending of novelty toys; another mother sends birthday brownies and silly hats: 'Everyone had a great time with that stuff... it was the thought. It was awesome... a great feeling, mail. It's the equivalent of being a four-year-old and running down the stairs for

---

[2] Michael Roper, *The Secret Battle: Emotional Survival in the Great War* (Manchester: Manchester University Press, 2009), p. 11, p. 10.
[3] Roper, *The Secret Battle*, p. 10.

Christmas.'[4] Steiner's comments capture the way parcels evoke domestic structures, a feeling of being like a child even within the fabric of the family home, 'running down the stairs', at a season firmly associated in his home country with family time and feeling. Arthur Gibbs, a young subaltern in the First World War, expressed a similar sentiment on receiving a box: 'I love undoing them and it's just as much fun as opening a Christmas stocking.'[5]

The emotional significance of receiving the stuff of home was already a feature of war in the mid-Victorian period. Receiving parcels was a regular occurrence for most officers, and the letters of the officers considered here are punctuated by a steady stream of thanks and special requests. Families of other ranks also, though less frequently, sent necessaries. Henry Blishen, a plasterer by trade before joining the Rifle Brigade, mentions that he 'would give worlds for' a 'few pills for diarrhoea, dysentery, and rheumatism' on 31 January 1855 and in April thanks his parents for sending them: 'I hope, please the Lord, I may be spared to reward you for your kindness' (15 April 1855).[6] Although Blishen's letters are often concerned with finances and with the small amounts of money he is able to send his parents, he also celebrates receiving a box from them: 'It was brought to me by a sergeant from Balaklava, on the 5th instant. I am at a loss to express my thanks for such kindness' (8 June 1855). Officers similarly registered the receipt of boxes and letters as emotional events.[7] Equally important, however, is the stuff sent in the opposite direction, home from war.

British soldiers' letters home were commonly supplemented by additional material that attempted an additional layer of communication. Soldiers of all ranks frequently included sketches of camp and hut and sent small objects in their letters, ranging from pressed flowers to scraps of Russian medal ribbon and talismans taken from the dead. Sketches of camp and surroundings and pieces of war material sent in letters home were often presented as a means through which soldiers could connect their families to their experience of war, or at least selected parts of that experience. Through such enclosures they created visual familiarity with shared scenes, and passed on some of their auditory and tactile experience through things like sheet music and flattened out bullets. This material

---

[4] Tim Hetherington, *Infidel* (London: Chris Boot, 2010), p. 125.
[5] Quoted by Roper, *The Secret Battle*, p. 95.
[6] Private collection. I am grateful to Laura Blishen for permission to quote this material.
[7] See, for example, Thomas Harvey to his younger brother William, 5 September 1855: 'Write to me as often as you possibly can. You don't know how fiercely we expect letters, and one from home of course makes the drum major's fingers [delivering them] in momentary jeopardy.' NAM 1997-07-47.

allowed soldiers and their families to participate in creative collaborative practices through which they could maintain shared cultures and a form of togetherness at a distance, and navigate experiences of fear, pain, and loss.

In examining these creative practices—from sketching to quilting, and the selection and repurposing of small objects by inclusion in letters home—the chapter endeavours to show the importance of a longer, multimedia history of soldier art, not restricted to the First World War or to the adaptation of weaponry. I build upon the definitions produced by the existing scholarship on trench art, notably by Nicholas Saunders and Jane Kimball, which focuses on items produced in and in response to the First World War. Saunders gives the following criteria: 'Any object made by soldiers, prisoners of war and civilians, from war materiel or any other material as long as object and maker are associated in time and space with armed conflict or its consequences.'[8] Kimball uses a similar definition, looking at how soldiers and civilians 'transformed materials designed to kill other human beings into an amazingly creative and diverse body of folk art that has been largely ignored... until recently'.[9] This quality of transformation is also characteristic, as we shall see, in the small war souvenir, posted home.

While Saunders and Kimball offer expansive definitions of trench art, most of their examples are works created from ammunition and weaponry, especially inscribed and ornamented shell cases from the First World War. Saunders traces a precursor to this creative use of ordnance in objects made from Russian cannonballs, which he sees as the 'most frequent[ly]' produced category in the Crimean War.[10] Kimball summarizes that 'war souvenirs from the Crimean War include inkwells made from cannon balls inscribed with the names of battles, pipes covered with regimental crests and various items made from horn as well as beadwork miser's purses', and the two photographs of objects she includes from this period are a cannonball inkwell and metal beaded purse with studding picking out Alma and Inkerman.[11] These selections place undue emphasis on

---

[8] Nicholas Saunders, *Trench Art* (Buckinghamshire: Shire, 2002), p. 4.
[9] Jane Kimball, *Trench Art: An Illustrated History* (Davis, CA: Silverpenny Press, 2004), p. xi.
[10] Nicholas Saunders, *Trench Art: Materialities and Memories of War* (Oxford: Berg, 2003), p. 23. Frederick Wilkinson makes a similar claim about objects produced during the Crimean War: 'One of the favourite items of this period was a cannon ball, solid or hollow, converted into an inkwell and mounted in some way', *Collecting Military Antiques* (London: Ward Lock, 1976), p. 123.
[11] Kimball, *Trench Art*, p. 7. The inkwell photographed was made by Arthur Coburn, First Officer on Royal Navy ship HMS *Wrangler*, from four cannonballs and shrapnel. These are mounted on an inkstand, which is inscribed with a dedication detailing the provenance and significance of the materials used: 'Presented to Wm Masters-Smith Esq.

soldiers' close interaction with one particular element of war material, reflecting and reinforcing perceptions that soldiers' predominant tactile experience was of handling weaponry and that the use of arms in battle was also the most affectively significant component of wartime. Attending to the softer materials of sketch paper, petals, and textiles, this chapter takes a similar approach to recent exhibitions that present a more richly textured account of the materiality of warfare. The American Civil War exhibition Homefront and Battlefield, for example, focused on fabric to trace the course of the war 'and the ways in which participants and their descendants remember it'. The curators follow the trajectory of cultural military history, suggesting that textiles 'offer a human quality to the narrative that is less readily available in the history of generals and battles'.[12] The exhibition featured a range of items produced and selected by soldiers and sent home, many of which referenced domestic experiences at home and front, including delicately made baby shoes and sketches of tent interiors.[13] Similarly the 2014 First World War Trench Art show at Compton Verney displayed the range of creative practices of soldiers, bringing beautifully carved shell cases together with embroidered flour bags and miniature productions, including a recreation of home within a matchbox. The matchbox opens to reveal a glimpse into ordinary home life; a kitchen table with seated male figure, standing woman figure churning butter, dog, and oven are made from wooden pieces, while pots and pans are drawn onto the back wall of the box.[14] This object, and the art and souvenirs considered in this chapter, strongly resonate with Saunders's vision of trench art as 'a unique mediator between men and women, between soldier and civilian, between individual and

from his affectionate nephew, a souvenir of Sebastopol and of the latter's promotion to the rank of Lieutenant Jan 14 1857. This inkstand made from shot picked up at Sebastopol polished and put together by an Engineer of H.M.S. Wrangler. The largest shot was picked up by me in the Warp Fort, the smaller ones in the Redan Malakoff. The piece of metal in the center is cut from the rigging of an unknown ship in Sebastopol Harbour. Arthur Cowburn, R. N. 1857', p. xiii.

[12] Madelyn Shaw and Lynne Zacek Bassett, *Homefront and Battlefield: Quilts and Context in the American Civil War* (Lowell, MA: American Textile History Museum, 2012), p. v. The exhibition opened at the American Textile History Museum on 30 June 2012.

[13] Confederate Officer Maxwell Clarke made a pair of baby shoes measuring four and a half inches from heel to toe for his daughter Mary Grace Clarke. The shoes comprise leather and woollen broadcloth, likely cut from Maxwell Clarke's own coat. Shaw and Bassett, *Homefront and Battlefield*, p. 167.

[14] The range of work displayed was broader than the exhibition's title, which referenced a more traditional approach to soldier art, 'Art from Ammunition: Trench Art from the First World War', Compton Verney, Warwickshire, opened 15 July 2014.

industrialised society, between the nations which fought the war and, perhaps most of all, between the living and the dead'.[15]

Thickly textured lines of two-way communication and shared affects between home and campaign disrupt the thesis, which sticks particularly stubbornly to understandings of Victorian warfare, of separate military and civilian spheres. Soldiers worked hard to resist a separation of spheres, finding resourceful methods for maintaining and creating connections between home and front. They often wrote home of new domestic skills learnt in wartime that connected them with the homemaking of mothers and sisters, and chose familial language to express intimacy. Military men also, as this chapter will show, repurposed battle material and produced art to send home, creating a shared material culture through which they could communicate some of their war experience. My arguments here build on those of previous chapters about the sharing of familial values and emotional structures between regiment and civilians. Culturally, mid-Victorian Britain was much more attached to presentations of the military man that showed his emotional life to be entirely compatible with the increasingly domesticated, bourgeois values of the period than to narratives that positioned war as an entirely transformative experience. This chapter participates in debates about the communicability of combatant experience, considering the sensory work done by exchanges of material between front and home that allowed soldiers to share at least part of the feeling, emotional and tactile, of war.

'YOU WILL GET A BETTER ACCOUNT OF ALL THAT IS GOING ON BY READING *THE TIMES*': WAYS OF TELLING

On the day of one of the bloodiest engagements of the campaign, the British attack on the Redan, Thomas Harvey tried to convey the magnitude of the awfulness he witnessed to his family: 'Take all the worst scenes you can and you would not, with them all put together, come across anything to equal this awful day' (8 September 1855). Eighteen-year-old Lieutenant Harvey, one of the youngest officers of the 77th who had been in the Crimea just three months at this point, gestures here to an experience beyond telling and imagining. The sentiment that his family could not gather enough 'worst scenes' from their experience 'to equal' his resonates with the features of military memoir emphasized by Yuval

---

[15] Saunders, *Materialities*, p. 15.

Harari. Harari has made an influential case for the emergence at the end of the eighteenth century for the modern understanding of war as absolutely transforming of self, revealing of truths unavailable to, and incommunicable to, civilians. He examines combatants' increasing emphasis on the incommunicability of war through typical formulations like 'it is impossible to describe it' and 'those who were not there cannot understand it'. The 'flesh-witnessing' of the combatant becomes the ultimate authority, Harari argues; physical presence, participation, and bodily endurance of war is privileged over mere 'eye-witnessing' or any other form of involvement, so the soldier becomes the beneficiary of truths of self and world that could never be fully communicated to civilians.[16] Harari suggests that the theory, advanced by Carl von Clausewitz and other tacticians, that war could not be understood by those without first-hand experience of it is accompanied by the powerful idea that civilians could not feel as intensely as combatants: 'Just as civilians could not experience horrors as intense as those of battle, so they could not experience love and joy as intense as those between comrades in arms.'[17] As seen, though, in the previous chapter, comrades in arms often selected the terms of familial relationships in order to draw continuities with civilian feeling, using languages of father/son bonds within the regiment which they and their families at home, in turn, found deeply comforting. This chapter extends the case for the communicability of experiences and feelings between combatant and civilian. Having suggested that scenes of the attack on the Redan were beyond his family members' imagining, Harvey goes on, nonetheless, in a later letter to try to fill in some details of the awfulness: 'I saw the ditch one mass of corruption fellows without eyes, grape in their head, and some without any legs. It was beastly' (17 September 1855). He frames these observations with discussion of a shared musical culture; this letter begins with a transcription of a regimental march. Throughout his letters, as we shall see, Harvey uses music and sketching to emphasize cultural continuities between himself and his family that persist through the tedium and trauma of the campaign, and he draws upon these media to further communicate his life at war.

Disclaimers of the type 'it cannot be described' or 'it is impossible to tell you' do appear in British soldiers' accounts and other eyewitness reports of the Crimean War. Kate McLoughlin identifies the rhetorical strategy of adynaton or impossibilia—'the stating of unfulfillable conditions' and 'the impossibility of addressing oneself adequately to the topic'—as a staple of

---

[16] Yuval Harari, *The Ultimate Experience: Battlefield Revelations and the Making of Modern War Culture, 1450–2000* (Basingstoke: Palgrave, 2008), p. 7.
[17] Harari, *The Ultimate Experience*, p. 230.

war writing.[18] Trudi Tate has shown that this was a common trope in first-hand accounts of entering the ruined city of Sebastopol.[19] As McLoughlin notes, 'paradoxically' adynaton makes 'big claims to inadequacy and diminution, large-scale confessions of smallness and ineptitude, of being unequal to the task'; 'each deployment of adynaton is a miniature may-day'.[20] The appeal to the untellable is, then, typically the beginning of a relation of traumatic experience and a form of emotional communication in itself.

A sense of 'smallness and ineptitude' and a recognition of the difference in scale between the individual's role and the magnitude of war, which might also be discussed through the language of the sublime, is recognized in soldiers' appeals to the newspapers to tell it better. Combatants in the Crimea regularly point their families to the press as a supplement to what they can report. Audley Lempriere, the young officer of the 77th introduced in the previous chapter, writes of the difficulty of making out an actual account of the bombardment of Sebastopol—he believes the French batteries were flawed, 'but whether that is true or not I do not know', and wonders about the Russian cessation of fire—and directs his family to their newspaper of choice: 'You will get a better account of all that is going on by reading *The Times*' (13 Oct 1854).[21] Soldiers' letters frequently comment that they can only get information about how the war is proceeding from the press. As William Pechell, another officer of the 77th, put it, 'we do not know the least here what goes on and look to *The Times* for Crimean News' (27 November 1854); 'we know less here of what goes on than you do at home, as *The Times* correspondent gets hold of everything'.[22] The lack of censorship laws during the Crimean War meant that *The Times* reporter William Howard Russell, and other early special correspondents, could give detailed accounts of military

---

[18] Kate McLoughlin, *Authoring War: The Literary Representation of War from the Iliad to Iraq* (Cambridge: Cambridge University Press, 2011), p. 156.
[19] Trudi Tate, 'Sevastopol: On the Fall of a City', *19: Interdisciplinary Studies in the Long Nineteenth Century* 20 (2015).
[20] McLoughlin, *Authoring War*, pp. 156–7.   [21] HRO 4M52/125.
[22] Pechell's letters are in a private collection. Referencing the Battle of Inkerman, Lempriere again invokes *The Times* to fill in the gaps: 'I will not fill up this letter with an account of it, as that is old news and you will have read good accounts of it in *The Times*. We admire that paper very much out here. I think the leading articles are so beautifully written in it, it is quite a pleasure reading them' (17 November 1854). See also George Roe: 'Do not forget to write to me often and if you would send me an occasional newspaper I would be obliged as strange as it may seem the Army out here learn nearly everything that is going on through the newspapers at home' (1 June 1855). Roe is confident that his family will have already heard what he can tell them of the weather and the waging of the war from their paper. Private collection. I am grateful to Patrick Roe for permission to quote this material.

engagements and of camp life.[23] The statement 'we know less here of what goes on than you do at home' is a reversal of what Harari identifies as a master narrative of modern military experience: 'the maxim that those who weren't there can't understand anything'.[24] The sense shared by Pechell and numbers of other combatant correspondents that their families would know more of the war via the copy produced by civilian reporters calls into question the ubiquity of this master narrative, suggesting instead that ideas of knowing and not knowing in wartime were carefully negotiated. By calling on newspapers to supply the gaps in their own correspondence soldiers could avoid describing traumatic events in detail, and emphasize the fragmentariness of the individual combatant's perception of war. At the same time, though, a circulation of press between home and front provided a valuable line of communication, helping soldiers and families to stay in touch with each other's worlds.

Pechell's correspondence, as is typical, is punctuated with thanks for the publications his family send and requests for more. Papers provide welcome news and reading material, which was hard to come by as discussed in chapter 1, and they generate a shared culture between front and home, with civilians and soldiers reading and discussing the same material. Local newspapers are in demand, with the Hampshire officers of the 77th sending requests and thanks for copies of the county paper, the *Hampshire Chronicle*. Soldiers also regularly contributed copy—verbal and visual—to the press and creatively engaged with publications through practices of interior decoration, embellishment, and collage. The newspaper— incorporating content produced by soldiers, containing news of war read by families and then sent to the Crimea, reread and creatively reused by soldiers as discussed in their letters home and in other representations of military life such as Luard's *A Welcome Arrival*—is one example of the thick connections and layers of communication between home and front. Luard's careful representations of pages of the *Illustrated London News* repurposed as wallpaper is indicative of the thoroughness of the overlaying of domestic material culture onto life in military camp; the painting also responded to the home front demand for insights into the everyday lives of soldiers.[25]

---

[23] See Rupert Furneaux, *The First War Correspondent: William Howard Russell* (London: Cassell and Company Limited, 1944) and Phillip Knightley, *The First Casualty: The War Correspondent as Hero and Myth-maker from the Crimea to Iraq* (London: Andre Deutsch, 2003).
[24] Harari, *The Ultimate Experience*, p. 240.
[25] See Lalumia on the growing popularity of artistic representations of domestic life in this period, which was extended during the Crimean War into a demand for homely images of soldiering, *Realism and Politics*, pp. 103–5.

Whilst, as Harari has argued, an increased emphasis on interiority and the significance of individual psychological response is a feature of modern warfare, so is a growing material and consumer culture through which soldiers and civilians could demonstrate and share emotional engagements with war.[26] The proliferation of illustrated newspapers and development of other new media, notably the photograph, gave new dimensions to the visual experience of war for both soldiers and civilians, as these items were circulated between home and front, in addition to personal sketches and small objects. Improved communications networks allowed for more immediate exchange between soldiers and those at home. Ideas of modern war as an intensely personal, ultimately unsharable experience are offset by a richly textured archive of letters and enclosures through which soldiers made a determined effort to communicate at least some parts of their experience. These efforts, often drawing on creative skills and involving a level of tactile communication via small pieces of war material, point to the value soldiers and civilians placed on creating lines of continuity between military and domestic life. The tactile quality of small items that soldiers selected and posted, many of which had a direct connection to the precarious fighting body, suggests a further reaching interpretation of 'flesh-witnessing', not perceived as exclusive to combatants but as extendable and shareable.

SKETCHING HOME: TO BRING 'YOU MORE FAMILIAR... THAN A PAGE OF FOOLSCAP WILL DO'

Pechell both invoked the press as a valuable source of campaign information and expressed scepticism about the way the papers represented life at the front. Reassuring scenes of camp life, like that produced by Luard, were popular in the illustrated press. Some objected to the overly comfortable impression of campaign life presented by images like that accompanying the *Illustrated London News* article 'Winter Dress for the Troops in the Crimea', 23 December 1854, which featured snugly clothed men and robust housing. This provided readers with a suitably reassuring vision in the pre-Christmas issue, despite the shortages the troops faced through this mismanaged first winter. Pechell wrote: 'I believe you all

---

[26] I am indebted here to Marian Füssel's suggestion that a closer attention to the material culture of war, in the case of his work the Seven Years War, shows the limitations of Harari's argument. 'Emotions in the Making: The Transformation of Battlefield Experiences during the Seven Years War (1756–1763)', paper given at Battlefield Emotions 1500–1850, Ghent, February 2014.

think we are living in houses with fur coats like the pictures in the *Illustrated London News*. We have neither and shall never have the houses, as there is no means of bringing them up. This ought to have been thought of in England and horses and carts sent out with them. Our tents have got very rotten with the snow and let in a good deal of water' (15 January 1855).[27] Although Pechell was critical of misleading images of domestic comfort, he also participated in the widespread endeavour to communicate the more homely side of military life, sharing his own representations of camp with friends and family.

The transcription of his letters made by his sisters records that on 12 February 1855 they received a line sketch of two tents, a stable, and kitchen. Unfortunately this sketch does not survive, but many do in the same genre of scenes of camp posted home.

The sketch of camp was a typical way through which soldiers attempted to communicate a part of their everyday life to families. Lempriere sent an idyllic scene of camp life to his sisters in the early part of the war on his route to the Crimea (Figure 6). The inclusion of horses peacefully cropping the grass reflects the family fascination with horses, a running theme in Lempriere's letters. He later sketches on a tiny slip of paper, enclosed with a letter, a miniature nostalgic record of his local Hampshire hunt. Lempriere's camp scene, evoking the horses and rolling hills of the grounds of his family's Hampshire estate, draws out the continuities between home and camp. Lempriere's version of the camp at Varna draws upon the conventions of picturesque landscape; another popular genre within the sketches home. The privately educated gentlemen who comprised the majority of the officer class had usually received some training in drawing. Standard subjects taught at the Royal Military Training College, Sandhurst, included military drawing and landscape drawing. Lempriere's report for 1852 shows that he passed these and all other standard subjects, and took additional lessons in fencing and music.[28]

Those less adept at drawing found means to include visual representations of camp. George Roe, an Irish officer of the 4th Regiment, sent his mother a floor plan in place of anything more elaborate: 'Above is a very rough sketch of the internal arrangement of my House, but you must excuse my ignorance of drawing. I will try and get a view of the outside and send it to you' (1 February 1856). By this late stage of the war

---

[27] Knight echoes this sentiment in a letter to his brother: 'People make an immense mistake when they think we are all comfortably hutted' (22 January 1855). HRO 39M89/F120.
[28] Half-yearly report of Gentleman Cadet Audley Lempriere, Royal Military College, November 1852, HRO 4M52/122. Lempriere studied there for a total of three years and five months, and received three decorations of merit and the report 'conduct exemplary'.

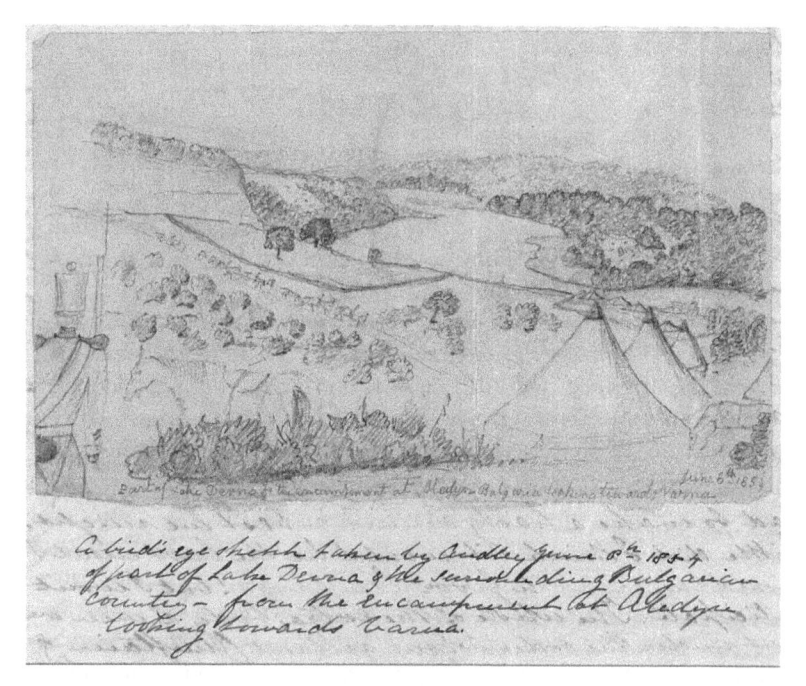

Figure 6. Lempriere family notebook, sketch of camp. Reproduced with permission from the National Army Museum.

accommodations were more established and Roe's plan indicates a fair approximation of home comforts including a porch, fireplace, and shelving as well as more portable furniture, reassuring his family that he was well equipped.[29] Roe is apologetic about his 'very rough sketch', and

---

[29] Accounts of homemaking contrivances are typical in war correspondence. Harvey describes his 'bedroom' as 'a finished concern': 'I got a very jolly table made with a hole in the centre for the tent pole to go through' (16 September 1855). Sketches that conveyed these improvised home comforts also feature in the correspondence sent from other conflicts. Julian Scott, a seventeen-year-old drummer boy in the American Civil War, sent his family a reassuring image of his lodgings during his convalescence at De Camp General Hospital, with the caption 'A copy of my tent on David's Island'. As Shaw and Bassett note, the 'tent he drew was a civilised place, clean and orderly', complete, like Roe's floor plan, with shelving, and with homely contents, 'stacks of books, binoculars, a potted plant, and a vase of flowers are scattered on a table covered by a patterned cloth ... a birdcage dangles from the rafter and a tame squirrel feeds atop a canvas partition', *Homefront and Battlefield*, p. 131. In the First World War E. L. Douglas-Fowles made a speciality of sketching home. In one example he endeavours to give 'a slight idea of our cellar in Loos'. The accompanying text identifies the men pictured concentrating on writing their letters home, while the drawing also picks out the candlelit table, laid with a checked cloth and piled with tins of provisions. See Roper, *The Secret Battle*, p. 107.

hopes to supply what he feels to be a deficiency by sending home a photograph 'view' of the hut and a likeness of himself 'but the man who makes them has had his equipment stolen' (20 October 1855). Pechell was more fortunate in being able to send photographs taken by Roger Fenton, the most famous of several photographers working in the Crimea. These photographs are similarly framed to many soldier sketches of camp, focusing on the more idyllic, domestic aspects of campaign life with inclusions of home comforts and domesticated animals:

> I send you some photographs which were done here the other day. Perekop and I are done just as I used to ride about all the winter. You will see the cuffs you sent me are put on the Regimental fur coat. I wore them all the winter to the admiration of everyone. The other photograph is five men of my company and myself as we went to the trenches, I moved my head while it was being done so the face is not clear. The little dog (Kalafat Jack) who came out with the regiment and was at Alma and Inkerman, is also in the picture but not very plain as he was in the shade. (17 May 1855)[30]

In his letter of a month later Pechell expresses his gladness that his family like the photos and thanks them for a box they have sent him. This indicates the speed of postal communication in the Crimea; by 1855 letters could reliably be expected within two weeks of postage.[31] References to cycles of exchange between soldiers and their families are typical of officers' letters in this war. The cuffs, or muffatees, sent for additional warmth which stand out in Fenton's photograph of Pechell (now in the collection of the National Army Museum) are a welcome comfort from home, and their use is recorded in the photograph which is then sent home.[32]

Photographs were a welcome way to supply the desire of those at home for insights into the experience of war. Roe's concern about the limitations of his drawing are paralleled in many officers' letters, which appreciate that

---

[30] Fenton was on a semi-official expedition supported by the British government which hoped to discredit Russell's criticisms through a more affirmative representation of the war. He made a speciality of 'Scenery of the Camps', and groups showing 'Military Life', which, as Natalie Houston has shown, offered reassuring images of life at the Crimean front, making them popular souvenirs for soldiers' families and a wider public, 'Reading the Victorian Souvenir: Sonnets and Photographs of the Crimean War', *Yale Journal of Criticism* 14.2 (2001), pp. 353–83. The *Athenaeum* expressed some dissatisfaction with the homeliness of Fenton's photographs: 'It is always sitting on broken baskets, and filling up cups, and smoking, and coming out of tents', quoted by Houston, p. 367.

[31] See Peter Boyden, *Tommy Atkins Letters: The History of the British Army Postal Service from 1795* (London: National Army Museum, 1990), p. 11. During 1855 three quarters of a million letters were sent through France to the British army and navy in the Crimea and 1.2 million were sent back to Britain, p. 10.

[32] 'Captain Pechell and men of the 77th (East Middlesex) Regiment of Foot in winter dress', NAM 1964-12-151-6-28.

their families would want a visual record, but express concern that their efforts might not be of a level to share with a wider social circle. George Willis, an officer of the 77th, wrote to his mother: 'I have some six or eight sketches to send by the first opportunity, but I have not seen any very striking scenery up here, so they are not very interesting. I am glad you liked the ones I sent to Mary, but it is not fair to show them as my productions unless you let them know I only commenced teaching myself a year ago' (31 August 1854).[33] Even skilled soldier artists expressed concerns about their abilities. Harvey was skilled in his favourite genre of 'views', seeking out atmospheric landscapes across the Crimea. Though he bemoaned his inability to draw figures—'they are like blots of ink upon the picture they are in' (6 July 1855)—his scenes were in much demand for other soldiers' letters.

Shortly after his first posting to Parkhurst military barracks, prior to his embarkation for the Crimea, Harvey explains to his family that he intends to adopt 'a good plan in writing to you to give you an occasional sketch of the places I have seen [as] the slightest sketch brings you more familiar with the places taken than a page of foolscap will do' (13 May 1854). Once established in the Crimea he undertakes to 'try to send a view by every letter if I can possibly find subjects. That is the most difficult thing because I am in a place which has been the subject of the sketches in the Illustrated for the last six months. It is therefore as you may suppose rather exhausted' (8 July 1855). Harvey's Crimean letters include small interpolated sketches within the prose, battlefield maps, and more carefully polished drawings. His correspondence is punctuated by commentary on the hunt for original scenes, appropriate art materials, and techniques of perspective and shading.

Though he has to adapt to the materials available, Harvey generally manages to maintain the chiaroscuro techniques he has learnt: 'Notwithstanding the hardness of the pencil I have produced some nice soft shading with the scraped side of the pencil, that though you can easily perceive a hardness through the whole picture it is much improved' (2 July 1855). On arrival at Balaclava he visits the bazaar to buy 'ammunition in the shape of penknives, pencils, and paper in order to give you some sketches of the trenches if possible' (3 June 1855). Bullets and incendiaries are exchanged for the ammunition of the artist's materials, and the trenches— a particularly dangerous and loathed element of this war for Harvey and many others—are transformed into productive subjects for drawing. Harvey explains that after showing a friend his sketch of the road of the

---

[33] NAM 2004-10-168-1.

trenches, 'the consequence was that he asked me to draw him it as he wished to send home the road that he walked every three days with so much danger to his personal identity' (6 July 1855). Sketches supplemented the communication of personally significant experience, clustering around sites of refuge, tents and huts, and of particular danger. In Harvey's formulation the sketch allows his friend to 'send home' a key part of his campaign. When posted to the trenches himself—described as 'that beastly place', 6 July 1855—Harvey draws the landscape, or failing that, figure sketches, as an occupation or diversion. He records being shot at having climbed the parapet 'to take a view of our new battery' (9 July 1855). The persona of soldier artist is a means of distancing himself and his family from often traumatic events at the same time as bringing those incidents into vivid proximity.

Harvey's concern with finding new subjects is related to the dual purpose of these drawings, intended both for his family and, he hopes, for the illustrated press. His family act as agents, advising him to produce 'exciting scenes' and passing these on to publishers. They succeed in placing two sketches, 'The Trenches at Midday' and 'The Road to the Trenches', in the *Illustrated Times* of 18 August 1855 and duly send Harvey a copy (Figure 7).[34] On 3 September 1855 he writes back in

Figure 7. Thomas Harvey, 'The Trenches at Midday', *Illustrated Times*, 18 August 1855. Reproduced from author's own collection.

[34] *Illustrated Times*, 18 August 1855, no. 11, p. 4.

celebratory mode: 'You can't think the pleasure it gives me to find the long expected sketches so well engraved in the *Illustrated Times*.' He goes on to detail the amendments made by the paper, which include 'cutting a foot off my legs. I don't mean depriving me of that member but shortening them that much', and gives a detailed critique of the opening image, knowing that his family have also looked closely at this paper. He is disappointed that this paper is no longer taken by the regiment's mess hut. On 6 October 1855 Harvey's 'Mules Carrying Gunpowder for the 21st' was published by the *Illustrated Times* with an atmospheric caption supplied by Harvey in the accompanying letter to his family: 'The whole of this ravine is so filled with shot and shell mostly from the Redan part from the crossfire of the Malakoff, that it is called in the spot the valley of death. I think that is exciting enough.' The paper picks up Harvey's echoing of phrases from Tennyson's poem about an earlier Crimean engagement to invest the siege with the dramatic energy of the campaign's battles. Although Harvey's stints on trench duty are peppered with incidents of personal danger—several times he reports being shot at when taking a vantage point from which to sketch—he puts this into the context of seeking sufficiently 'exciting scenes' for the press. He particularly aspires to the *Illustrated London News*: 'Although the Captains and great swells consider it a great thing to have my sketches in *The Times*, yet it was with a feeling as if I could not get them into the illustrated and I should like to show them I could' (16 September 1855). Harvey's publication ambitions offer a welcome distraction from other concerns and supply an inexhaustible subject for lively exchanges with his family.

Producing art gave Harvey a sense of purpose through the war, and allowed him to exercise agency in situations otherwise beyond his control, selecting views on trench duty for example. He reports appreciatively of other uses of art to reshape war narratives, commenting on the creative assembly of decorative illustrations on the walls of the mess, like that shown in Luard's painting:

> I saw this first picture of the 'Pens and Pencils' in our mess hut... We take the *Illustrated News* and all the papers and Captain Butts is very fond of posting them all around the Room so that now the hut is covered with pictures from *Illustrated* and *Punch* and in all the exciting scenes he will make them ridiculous. Somehow you must laugh when you see them. 'Explosion in the Trenches', well above the smoke of the Trenches he will stick some fat man as if he had been blown up. Another scene he has cut the figure of a man (in *Punch*) who is running after his hat in a frantic manner, he sticks this figure in a scene of Sentries on Guard in the Trenches and a smoking shell after him. In that manner pictures that you have seen 1000 times are still interesting. (2 July 1855)

The captain's work of collage transforms the 'exciting' into the 'ridiculous', a typical move in hut decoration. Captain Fred Dallas of the 46th Regiment recorded the confusion of visitors caused by the transposition of Russian and French generals in the pictures papering the walls, in which 'Prince Gortschikoff, appeared attired as a Highlander'.[35]

SMALL SOUVENIRS, AND RIFF ON A RUSSIAN RIBBON

Art and craft clearly presented opportunities for the reworking of difficult emotions in wartime. On hut walls fears of being blown up were transformed into comic cartoons, and opposing forces irreverently transformed into allies. Sketching home was also a convenient, widely available way (despite different ability levels) to share aspects of war with friends and family. Sketches are regularly supplemented by small objects, which augment the effort to communicate felt experience—handpicked things, selected and touched by soldiers, then by their families, and lovingly preserved.

Soldiers across ranks sent significant objects home. As a practice which did not require any specialist training or additional equipment, the main barrier to souvenir sending was cost. Young rifleman of the ranks Henry Blishen (whose pleasure at receiving a box from his family is discussed earlier in the chapter) sends low-cost items en route to the Crimea, some small Maltese figures, women and boy, gifted to specific family members (14 March 1854), and a worn Greek coin to illustrate his discussion of the difficulty of making purchases and changing money in Gallipoli: 'As a sample I enclose you a demi-piastre, value one halfpenny' (12 May 1854). The National Army Museum collection includes a 'splashed' (flattened out) lead Minié bullet, found in the cemetery outside Sevastopol. It was picked up by Private J. B. Robert when his brigade captured the cemetery on 18 June 1855, and sent home to his sister. In the accompanying note he explained he could only send one bullet home on account of its

---

[35] Quoted in Stefanie Markovits, *The Crimean War in the British Imagination* (Cambridge: Cambridge University Press, 2009), p. 172. The practice of decorating the mess and individual huts in this way is widely reported. See also Colonel Edward Cooper Hodge's description in an October 1855 letter of 'various scenes from *Punch* and the *Illustrated London News* depicted on the walls of my domicile', *Little Hodge: Being Extracts from the Diaries and Letters of Colonel Edward Cooper Hodge Written during the Crimean War, 1854–1856*, ed. Marquess of Anglesey (London: Leo Cooper, 1971), p. 131. My thanks to Flora Wilson for this reference.

heaviness making for expensive postage.[36] Cost was less of a concern for young officer Thomas Harvey, who sends his family a box including 'about 30 minie bullets in every shape and form after they had been fired', a map of Malta, crystals, and slippers (13 September 1855).

Objects particular to the geography and waging of war supplemented sketches in providing an insight into local conditions and key events. In the letter including the rough sketch of his hut, Roe links the sketch to other things he hopes to send home. After stating his plan to 'try and get a view of the outside [of my hut] and send it to you', Roe goes straight on: 'I will do my best and get you as many curiosities as I can but I fear everything is gone' (1 February 1856). Throughout his letters Roe is concerned with acquiring and sending material he believes will be of particular value to his family. He selects things in response to their enclosures, and as means of connecting, from a distance, with the rhythms of home life: 'I have got the violet you sent me in your last letter and will send you a flower from here as there are a few that grow about, but I do not know what they are called' (15 January 1855). Later that year he sends his mother 'a slip of one of the few flowers that grow here—I could not as yet manage to get a root—but will try, they do not seem to have any roots but are all stringy fibres. I am sure the garden looks beautiful now and with the fine summer which we read you have got you must be very pleasant' (27 July 1855). The received and sent flower reflects a lively continuous cycle of exchange between home and front, of which Luard's painting only captures one stage. Roe's effort to fulfil the commission for a root shows his family's aspiration to recreate his horticultural surroundings at home, as well as connecting him across the distance to his fondly remembered garden coming into its summer best.[37]

The enclosure of pressed flowers is a staple of soldiers' letters, so much so that Lempriere sends some gathered en route to the campaign with a self-consciousness about the relative worth of these keepsakes, determined by their proximity to the action of war:

> I enclose some Bulgarian wild flowers which I hope young Alice will duly prize and reverence, perhaps by and bye I may send you some that you will prize more 'flowers from the battlefield at Anapa' or something of that sort or 'flowers from the walls of Sebastopol' (20 July 1854).

---

[36] Alastair Massie, ed., *A Most Desperate Undertaking: The National Army Museum Book of the Crimean War* (London: The National Army Museum, 2003); NAM 1959-03-86.

[37] Homemaking at the front also included gardening. Pechell described his efforts in this line to his family: 'I went down yesterday afternoon with my cart and brought up some rose trees and flowers, I put them in all round my tent, but this morning they look very disconsolate, the chickens having scratched them all about' (29 May 1855).

Notwithstanding his somewhat caustic citing of the convention of prized petals, later he duly sends flora with accompanying military narratives: 'I have dried 2 Russian crocuses and two other flowers for you as a remembrance of the siege of Sebastopol' (15 October 1854). And like many other soldiers who send violets gathered during periods of truce, he later 'enclose(s) some violets that were picked within the Russian lines during the Armistice' (26 March 1855). Some of this flora has survived, as have some petals sent by a friend from around Lempriere's grave as a form of memorial, lovingly preserved within the covers of the scrapbook compiled by Lempriere's sister Ellen, also discussed in the previous chapter. In the context of his research on the First World War materials, Das reflects on the tactile process of archival work. He describes untucking a blue and white pressed flower from a letter sent to his wife by Private George Bennett: 'the process is intimate and unsettling'.[38] The personal narratives of these flowers, bound up in the events of the war they were removed from and of the military biographies of the men who sent them, gives them a powerful emotional resonance. This affect is amplified by the juxtaposition of the petals' fragility against the hard bulk of weapons and other war material, and by the survival of this delicate ephemeral material in contrast to the senders' shortened lives.

Also carefully preserved in the Lempriere family notebook is a cutting of about one centimetre square of red striped medal ribbon with the annotation: 'Audley cut off after the Battle of Inkerman from the breast of a dead Russian officer' (Figure 8). This ribbon carries an especially interesting tactile history, having passed from the body of the Russian through the hands of Lempriere and into those of his family. Since coming across it I have been wondering about the feelings—triumph, pride, sorrow, all of these, something else?—with which Lempriere sent it home. Lempriere's accompanying letter also survives in another archive (as part of the family collection at HRO), offering a rare opportunity to discern the affective work he explicitly attributed to this fragment of textile:

---

[38] Santanu Das, *Touch and Intimacy in First World War Literature* (Cambridge: Cambridge University Press, 2005), p. 15. Similarly Jay Winter pauses upon coming upon a pressed poppy in another First World War archive: '[Private] Stephen Allen (13th Battalion AF) had sent his mother a poppy growing in his dugout. In the files of the Australian War Memorial the poppy is still there, pressed into the letter', *Sites of Memory, Sites of Mourning: The Great War in European Cultural History* (Cambridge: Cambridge University Press, 1995), p. 40.

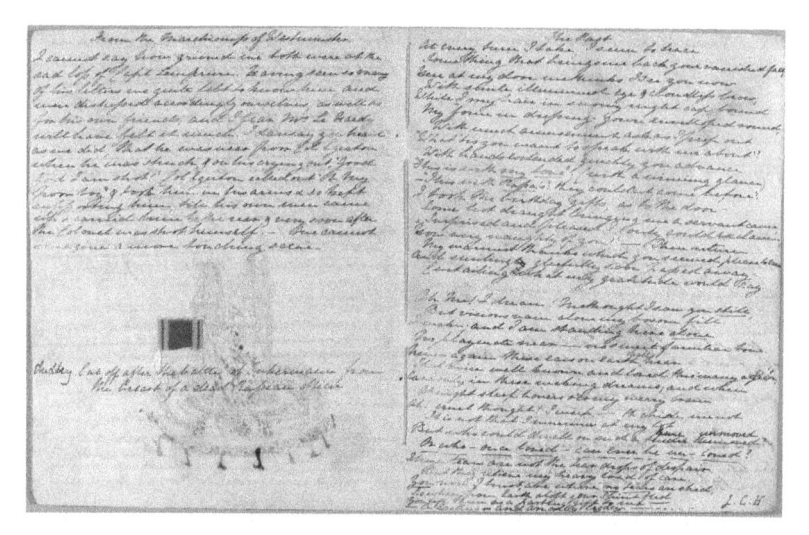

Figure 8. Lempriere family notebook, Russian medal ribbon and on facing page memorial poem 'The Past'. Reproduced with permission from the National Army Museum.

> My dear sister
> You see by the date of this that I have not forgotten to think of your birthday and to wish you *many many* happy returns of it. I enclose you a very small piece of ribbon taken from the body of a Russian officer after the battle of 'Alma' it will be a little memento of that engagement. I also send a piece for Harriet—I wrote to Dora and Eliza Knight and sent them each a piece in return for their notes you must tell me what they think of it. I think the ribbon must have been some order or else to commemorate some battle the Russian officer had been engaged in... (To Ellen, Heights Before Sebastopol, 22 December 1854)

The ribbon is sent as an appropriate gift to women, Lempriere's sisters and close family friends. It is a birthday present for Ellen, for whom he can't acquire much else at this point in the campaign (earlier, in Malta, en route to the Crimea, Lempriere sends some gold jewellery to a cousin on her birthday). It is a form of 'return' for notes received, a continuation of the clearly valued correspondence with the Knights, a local family. And it is presented as a talking point—'you must tell me what they think of it'—as part of keeping open communications with home.

This resourceful gift doubles as a 'memento', a souvenir of a particular battle. It offers a personalized alternative to mass-produced commemorative items that had become a feature of modern warfare. Minimal cost 'vivat' ribbons were particularly popular during the Seven Years War, while cheap ceramics formed a major commercial response to Waterloo and to the Crimea.[39] Soldiers' acquisition of more personal keepsakes is a typical wartime activity. Observing the recovery of effects in the First World War Lord Northcliffe noted the recurrence of items like 'a trench ring made of the aluminium of an enemy fuze' and pieces of German shell and was told that 'nearly every soldier carries a souvenir... The relatives at home set great store on these little treasures.'[40] Lempriere's presentation of the ribbon as a 'little memento' of Alma connects it with his less grisly selection of flowers in 'remembrance of the siege of Sebastopol'. Roe similarly uses the language of 'memento' or 'curiosity' for the items he sends home. These terms indicate that the primary value of these objects is personal and emotional rather than monetary, distinguishing these small souvenirs from spoils or plunder. In her work on the collections assembled by British soldiers in China in the period around the British plundering of the Summer Palace in 1860, Katrina Hill has shown that 'soldiers used terms like "trophy", "specimen", or "souvenir" loosely, often to rationalise acts of theft'.[41] The terms 'curiosity', 'relic', and 'memento' also recur in the accounts she discusses. Lempriere's language determinedly miniaturizes the item: 'a very small piece', a 'little memento'. In practical terms the ribbon is converted into something eminently mailable, and its emotional significance is also transformed through the act of sending it home.

Ellen understandably misremembers the ribbon as being from Inkerman, the more recent major battle, rather than Alma, immediately undoing and reworking the ribbon's specificity as a marker for a particular event. Alma, though, had a particular significance for Lempriere as his first experience of a major battle. His letter to his mother after it registers mixed feelings, combining exhilaration, 'our Artillery played into them most beautifully', 'it was a most exciting days [sic] work', and melancholy, a word he repeats:

> Yesterday after the battle I went over the ground in front of this battery where the 23rd suffered so much and it was a most melancholy and awful

---

[39] On the thousands of designs of vivat ribbons produced during the Seven Years War and bought and worn by all sections of society see Eva Gilloi, *Monarchy, Myth and Material Culture in Germany, 1750–1950* (Cambridge: Cambridge University Press, 2011), p. 26. The NAM collection incorporates a wealth of Crimean War commemorative mugs, including one which misattributes heroism to its subject, who was not present at the battle depicted, 'Sergeant Davis defending the Colours at Inkerman', NAM 1999-01-144. For further detail of this mug see Massie, ed., *Desperate Undertaking*, p. 144. Other examples of Crimea mass-produced ceramics include an alliance 'frog mug', NAM 1998-02-170, jugs, NAM 1962-11-181-1 and NAM 1961-03-25, and 'The Battle of Alma' relish pots, NAM 1960-12-10.
[40] Quoted by Kimball, *Trench Art*, p. 34.
[41] Katrina Hill, 'Collecting on Campaign: British Soldiers in China during the Opium Wars', *Journal of the History of Collections* 25.2 (2013), pp. 227–52, p. 228.

sight to see these poor officers, some of whom I knew well, lying dead with the ground under them saturated with their blood, their cold deathlike features and clenched hands and bleeding wounds, they were lying close under the battery and the Russians picked them out owing to their brilliant uniforms which made them so conspicuous, it made me feel very melancholy and made one think that if it had pleased God you might have been in the same state. (21 September 1854)

Lempriere characteristically moves from first to second person, to avoid spelling out that he 'might have been in the same state'. The ribbon offers another form of distancing, firmly marking the battle as past and survived; as Susan Stewart puts it, 'we do not need or desire souvenirs of events that are repeatable'.[42] Stewart's theorization of the affective work performed by souvenirs is useful in thinking through the way that Lempriere uses the ribbon to navigate 'most melancholy and awful sight[s]'. The ribbon memento allows a kind of domestication of the battle's horrors, especially in Audley's act of sending it home parcelled out into sections for loved female recipients (the letter details four separate pieces intended respectively for Ellen, Harriet, Dora, and Eliza). The souvenir, Stewart points out, 'domesticates on the level of its operation: external experience is internalised; the beast is taken home'.[43] While the 'distress flares', as McLoughlin puts it, of a rhetoric of the impossibility of describing war indicate overwhelming experience, the selection of fragments that supplement communications domesticates the sublime. In these small souvenirs the awfulness of magnitude and scale is reduced to that which can be contained within an envelope, and then within the family home, a scrap, at least, of war that becomes graspable. The diminutive language that characterizes Audley's letter—'very small', 'little'—shows the process of miniaturization through which souvenirs transform experience, from public to private, or, in Stewart's terms, from 'exterior to interior': 'The souvenir reduces the public, the monumental, the 3D into the miniature, that which can be enveloped by the body, or into 2D representation, that which can be appropriated within the privatised view of the individual subject.'[44] In this 'very small piece' Audley strategically compresses the

---

[42] Susan Stewart, *On Longing: Narratives of the Miniature, the Gigantic, the Souvenir, the Collection* (Durham and London: Duke University Press, 1993), p. 135.
[43] Stewart, *On Longing*, p. 134.
[44] Stewart, *On Longing*, p. 137. Saunders considers the tradition of 'representing miniature versions of the latest weapons of war' in trench art from the Napoleonic period onwards, 'perhaps a psychological reduction of danger through miniaturisation', *Materialities*, p. 22. This impulse can also be seen in the remaking of enemy weaponry into small wearable objects, like the First World War trench rings discussed above.

scale of losses, moving the experience from the monumental to the quietly domestic, a curio for sisters and friends to discuss.

Roe's letters provide particular insight into the acquisition of Crimean War souvenirs. Like the British soldiers in China who sought mementos of great cities and were 'anxious to obtain strange presents for their friends at home', he is concerned to supply his family with sufficiently interesting items.[45] Writing ruefully to his sister Kate of the British army restrictions on plunder, he explains: 'I will try to get you some Russian memento as occasionally we get something to buy out in the country which the Turks go and rob from the houses and then sell them to us as we are not allowed to get things ourselves' (7 August 1855). He explains the process by which scraps of ribbon like those Lempriere sent to his sisters and friends might be obtained: 'Tell Mama I shall try and get some Russian things for her but the only chance is to go after a flag of truce (which thank goodness occurs now seldom) and as they carry their dead away take a ribbon or medal off their breast' (21 July 1855). The connection between Lempriere and the dead Russian medal wearer is likely, then, a mediated one, in that he stands in for the other Russians Lempriere has likely killed at Alma, rather than having been killed by him. Notably Lempriere evacuates his own agency of acquisition through the passive formulation 'taken from the body'; sister Ellen introduces the more active and aggressive description, 'Audley cut off'.

The positioning of this ribbon in the notebook offers a particularly vivid example of the way in which its compilation transforms the emotional significance of each piece, making new relationships between them, and inserting the individual contents into an overarching, grand narrative of the mourning of Lempriere's death. In her work on women's album making in the nineteenth century, Patricia di Bello suggests that albums offer a particularly vivid demonstration of Roland Barthes's theory of the text as 'a multi-dimensional space in which a variety of writings none of them original blend and clash'. The features that di Bello identifies as particularly interesting about albums, 'poised as they are between being a reading and writing practice', are equally applicable to this scrapbook:

> [Albums] offer evidence of texts (visual and verbal) having been read or looked at in a particular context, that of the album pages, within specific sequences and juxtapositions, but also in the context of the domestic rituals in which albums were used.[46]

---

[45] Hill, 'Collecting on Campaign', p. 236.
[46] Patrizia di Bello, 'Mrs Birkbeck's Album: The Hand-Written and the Printed in Early Nineteenth-Century Feminine Culture', *19: Interdisciplinary Studies in the Long Nineteenth Century* 1 (2005), pp. 1–36, p. 7.

Within the context of the Lempriere notebook, the meaning of the Russian medal ribbon is newly inflected both through the context of surrounding materials and through that of the affective experience of reading it as part of a memorial project. In this memorial compendium, the ribbon records two life histories: the Russian's and Audley's. Here, as part of a document of mourning, its meaning is shifted or extended from trophy or souvenir to be part of the fabric of loss. Indeed, the ribbon is pasted onto a space on a page below a letter of condolence, and facing one of the memorial poems to Lempriere, entitled 'The Past'. Here, the foreshortened futures of the dead Russian officer and the dead English officer are brought together in a way that suggests, as Ellen may or may not have intended, the waste of war; for a moment the casualties on each side are balanced one for one.

Production of a memorial book was often part of the work of mourning, an endeavour that bears out Joy Damousi's arguments about the mourning of war dead as a potentially 'active, dynamic, and creative process, rather than one that negates activism'. Damousi also considers the ways in which mourners 'resisted the loss of memory of their own particular sacrifice in grieving their sons and husbands'.[47] Mourning albums or scrapbooks, like that compiled by Ellen Lempriere, are documents of a sacrifice shared by soldiers and their families. By incorporating materials produced and selected by the lost beloved, and often by his grieving military friends, the work of memorial making was also a form of creative collaboration. Ellen and Audley Lempriere and those close to him in the Crimean campaign work together to tell his war, in a way that offers comfort to those that survive it.

Creative collaboration with loved ones at home was also a strategy of emotional survival for those at war. Thomas Harvey's narration of awfulness he thought beyond his families' imagining in the final attack on the Redan is reached, as briefly seen earlier in the chapter, via his enclosure of regimental music:

> I have written down a March of the 34th Regiment which I think you could arrange for the flute to play the air and the violin ditto an octave higher, the parts being supported sufficiently by Loo's accomplished paw on the piano, but copy it first or she will blow me up for having put 2 tails to the notes. (17 September 1855)

---

[47] See chapter 4's discussion of Faust's phrase 'the work of mourning'. Joy Damousi's work refers to the experience of First World War losses in Australia, *The Labour of Loss: Mourning, Memory and Wartime Bereavement in Australia* (Cambridge: Cambridge University Press, 1999), p. 2.

Harvey envisages an ensemble of his own instrument (the flute), violin (presumably played by cousin Em, the letter's recipient), with piano accompaniment from his sister Loo. His cousin's and sister's skills are required to bring the raw material of his transcription to fruition. As with the reworked *Punch* cartoon that transforms being 'blown up' into a comic scene for shared enjoyment inside the regimental mess hut, Harvey resignifies this phrase. His instruction to Em in order to avoid his sister's explosive response to shoddy work defuses the threat of more deadly incendiaries. Harvey's characteristically colourful use of slang here shifts a real risk of war to one of gentle domestic scolding. Having opened the letter with this vision of shared family creative practice, he offers a couple of weakly comic anecdotes about organ playing which he admits are not to the purpose, and then finally describes the horror of the aftermath of the attack: 'When a dead man with goggle eyes and grinning mouth is pitched down at your feet and left there until the next day you don't like it.' Harvey's explicit collaboration with his cousin and sister to produce music that bridges the gap between war and home—the regimental march arranged for familial ensemble and drawing room performance—is his way into telling the more visceral events of war far beyond his family's experience. Earlier in the campaign he also turns to his musical skills to confirm the continuities with his home identity.

> I was seized with a mad fit the other day. I wished to see if I could compose as usual and immediately wrote down a pretty tune for two flutes. I won't say more because the piano accompaniment which I added was a miserable one, but only fancy the idea of attempting it at all. (7 July 1855)

Although Harvey presents this as an eccentric activity in wartime—'a mad fit', 'fancy the idea of attempting it at all'—his explanation, 'I wished to see if I could compose as usual', suggests that music offered a connection to his pre-war self. This chamber composition, the kind of intimate, small-scale piece that could be performed by family members in the drawing room, offers a direct link back to Harvey's domestic musical practices. In the context of Harvey's concern about whether composing is a skill he has lost, we can detect his relief in the immediacy of the creative response. He finds himself capable in these unfamiliar conditions of producing a 'pretty tune', even if the piano accompaniment was less satisfactory, 'a miserable one'. Within the context of the family's specialisms, this comment can also be read as deferential to sister's Loo's more 'accomplished paw' at the piano. Like sketching, music offered Harvey both welcome creative distraction and a means through which he could reinforce connections between his soldierly and familial identity.

Roe also uses music, together with objects, to connect with his family: 'I have got a piece of music which I took out of Sebastopol which I will send home to you it will put you in mind of me and show you I had not forgotten you although far away—I have also got some other little things which I shall try and send by the first opportunity' (5 October 1855). Here the music acts not as a memento of the allies' entry into the besieged city but as a double-sided reminder of family feeling, with those at home put 'in mind' of Roe who himself is mindful of them. His next letter details the contents of the parcel he has sent from Sebastopol:

> The basket is a nice little one, the sensor and the picture I got in a chapel, the cap is one the Russian officers wear when cadets serving in the ranks. The smaller charm with the figure of Our Saviour on it I cut off a Russian's neck in the Redan. I have also got a musket, helmet and coat but I could not send them now. I hope you will like them and I wish they were much better. (12 October 1855)

Although Roe, in common with his contemporaries, is generally untroubled about the ethics of plunder, his use of a similar diminutive language to that employed by Lempriere—'some other little things', 'a nice little one'—suggests an attempt to minimize the implications of whole-scale looting, possibly for commercial gain, to the more domestic level of souvenir hunting for family consumption alone.

These objects are on a different scale to the financially valuable Sebastopol bell George Willis manages to ship home to his family. Asking his sister to take good care of it, he explains that all other bells in the city have been secured as 'plunder' by the artillery, and that 'there is only one other in the Army belonging to an individual that I know of, and I have been offered as much as twenty pounds for it' (12 July 1856). Willis's correspondence offers a good indication of the range of motivations for souvenir hunting, from expediency—such as his letter detailing the Battle of Alma which is written on looted Russian paper: 'I have no other paper than this taken out of a Russian drill book one of the men brought me' (21 September 1854)—to money making, to the recording of personally significant events. The National Army Museum collection includes an icon, described in the catalogues as having been 'taken by' Willis 'from the body of a Russian soldier killed at the Battle of the Tchernaya'.[48] Cast entirely in brass, the icon measures 5.5 cm square and opens to reveal a central inside panel of Virgin and Child, while the folding doors are each engraved with saints. A small folded square on top accommodates a

---

[48] NAM 1994-01-1-320.

fastening thread. The brass is rubbed smooth in places through wear, presumably by the Russian soldier and then by Willis in carrying it.

Like the active description of Willis taking the icon straight from the dead Russian in the NAM catalogue, Roe cheerfully claims his direct role in acquiring the Christian charm. Roe gives the object a physical immediacy, of a kind Lempriere's letter avoids, in the powerful narrative of having 'cut [it] off a Russian's neck in the Redan'. His phrase 'the figure of Our Saviour' recognizes a faith shared with the dead Russian, and the biblical detail of the icon taken by Willis offers a particularly clear material confirmation of Christianity in common. Religious allegiance caused widespread unease amongst the British during a campaign which could not be straightforwardly positioned as a holy war, as Britain was allied with mainly Muslim Turkey against Christian Russia. The collective 'Our Saviour' refers both to the culture shared by Roe's family and religious community and to that of the Russian, offering a potentially mournful glimpse into the lost humanity of the enemy body in the Redan. The term 'cut off' (also used by Ellen Lempriere) conveys something of the violence of the battle for the Redan, and the action in proximity to the Russian neck perhaps suggests the cutting off of heads as well as charms. Ellen Lempriere's annotation details the bodiliness of the Russian in a way that her brother avoids; while Lempriere uses the passive construction and fairly neutral description 'taken from the body of' in the accompanying letter, in Ellen's memorial notebook this is transformed into 'from the breast of a dead Russian officer', the same language Roe uses in explaining how medals of the Russian dead might be 'taken from their breast'.

The selection of material worn close to the body, and cut from the vulnerable and erogenous zones of breast and neck, perhaps offers a similarly emotive substitution for the taking of a body part as war spoil. As Simon Harrison has shown, the use of human remains as trophies in conflicts between those deemed civilized nations was taboo throughout the nineteenth century: 'soldiers seem to have drawn a moral boundary preventing them from using as souvenirs the body parts of opponents with whom they understood themselves as sharing racial identity or kinship'.[49] Some sense of kinship is present in Roe's acknowledgement of shared faith with the dead Russian soldier, even as he cuts the crucifix from his corpse. This taboo prevailed when the adversaries were white European but was

---

[49] Simon Harrison, 'Skulls and Scientific Collecting in the Victorian Military: Keeping the Enemy Dead in British Frontier Warfare', *Comparative Studies in Society and History* 50.1 (2008), pp. 285–303, p. 289. Harrison places these arguments in a longer history of the connection between the taking of body part trophies and racism in *Dark Trophies: Hunting and the Enemy Body in Modern War* (New York and Oxford: Berghahn, 2012), see especially pp. 4–5.

suspended in wars against so-called 'barbarous' nations, and the British army in Africa engaged in scalping, and the taking of, particularly, skulls, ears, and teeth as prizes.[50] In her work on twentieth-century warfare Bourke presents the taking of body part trophies as part of the brutal pleasure of killing. She sees these, together with material reshaped by war like 'bent bayonets and rifles', as symbolic souvenirs, prized not for any exchange value, but for their ability to support a culturally expected performance of aggressive masculinity, 'to bolster wild stories they had told their loved ones' and 'as proof that a man had seen active combat and had thus proved himself on the field of battle'.[51] Bourke's interpretation helps to tease out the implications of Roe's use of aggressive language, 'I cut off a Russian's neck in the Redan', as an assertion of direct militancy, but it doesn't account for the more complicated range of emotions suggested by the shared culture and reciprocity with the Russian adversary recognized in Roe's collective language 'our Saviour'. Lempriere's contextualization of the ribbon trophy more thoroughly contradicts Bourke's thesis, showing the range of emotions—including discomfort with combat, remorse, and possibly grief, as well as exhilaration—that could attach to battle souvenirs. Far from using the ribbon to 'bolster wild stories' of his experience at Alma, Lempriere distances its acquisition from his own actions in the battle through passive constructions, and presents it as part of his narrative of distress on witnessing the aftermath of battle, 'taken from the body of a Russian officer *after* the battle of Alma'. He goes on to humanize the adversary to whom it belonged, speculating on the order or battle award for which it may have been given. Ellen Lempriere's incorporation of the ribbon into a memorial album further extends its affects in two competing ways; the more active, aggressive language she uses does present it as a proof of Audley's battlefield prowess but, at the same time, its contextualization gives it a more mournful resonance as a marker of precarious life. The afterlife of this Russian ribbon points to the complex and sometimes competing range of affective responses that war souvenirs generated for soldiers and their families.

Some patterns emerge amongst the range of narratives attributed to this diverse body of Crimean War souvenirs. Small postable things are usually presented with an object history that connects them directly to the soldier's own campaign and/or to significant events of the war. Clearly

---

[50] Harrison notes that 'on the rare occasions when these colonial practices came to public attention in metropolitan Britain, they caused public scandal and considerable official embarrassment', citing Queen Victoria's outrage at General Kitchener's appropriation of the skull of the Mahdi, 'Skulls', p. 291.

[51] Joanna Bourke, *An Intimate History of Killing: Face to Face Killing in Twentieth Century Warfare* (London: Granta, 1999), p. 34, p. 39.

availability was the major determinant of what was sent, but within a limited range of battlefield material it is clear that objects directly involved in the war, and particularly those transformed by it, are presented as of special interest. In his consideration of a material culture shared by combatants and civilians in the Seven Years War Marian Füssel cites a letter sent by a soldier celebrating his survival to his father:

> My musket was hit by a grape-shot bullet and cut off a quarter of its end. And I send you the end of the iron barrel and ask you to keep it for remembrance; by this we can see how the benevolence of God has led it away from me, because the bullet came close to my head but smashed iron instead of bones.[52]

This fragmented object, like many of those sent home in the Crimean War, is produced by the violence of war, and acts as a testimony to survival, a 'remembrance' of the precariousness of life in war. Also significant was the object's history of proximity to the body; both the living touch of the soldier sending it, and the posthumous touch of the enemy. Hill has shown that mandarin buttons were particularly prized by the British military in China, as they could only be won in close combat with a Chinese officer, and were therefore seen as proof of a man's bravery.[53] The buttons, like Russian medal ribbon and small crucifixes worn around the neck, could only be taken direct from the enemy's body, usually his corpse. The fleshly quality of some selected materials—taken from 'the breast' and 'the neck' of Russian dead—suggests a visceral attempt to extend a form of flesh-witnessing to those at home. The sharing of significant elements of war experience through sketches and small objects posted home offers an extension of eye witnessing and flesh witnessing that is at odds with arguments about the ultimate incommunicability of modern combat experience. The object histories attached to the items communicate some part of the horror of killing and the fear of being killed, while partly processing and distancing those affects as the material is domesticated. Sketches and souvenirs allowed soldiers to 'send home' (in the words of Harvey's friend who wants to 'send home' his perilous walk to the trenches) at least some part of the felt experience of war. They materialize the precariousness of war, and its losses, whether those are understood in a triumphalist or mournful way, or a combination of both.

---

[52] Johann Heinrich Ludewig Grotehenn to his father, translation by Marian Füssel, quoted by Füssel, 'Emotions in the Making'.
[53] Hill, 'Collecting on Campaign', p. 230. Bourke argues that objects worn close to the body, 'buttons, epaulettes, piccolos, medals, helmets', were particularly prized collectibles in the First World War, *An Intimate History of Killing*, p. 38.

TACTILE CONNECTIONS: MILITARY QUILTING

Materials taken from the soldier's body offer a form of flesh witnessing which is particularly pronounced in military patchworks using the fabric of uniforms. An account of soldierly sacrifice is typically attached to these colourful mid- to late Victorian patchworks, popularly known as Crimea quilts.[54] These objects acquire a special value through narratives of the fabric's proximity to the soldier's body and object histories that show the vulnerability of that fighting body. A number of nineteenth-century soldier-made coverlets and other patchwork objects are in the National Army Museum collection, including a patchwork and embroidered bed cover of the 17th (The Leicestershire) Regiment of Foot (NAM 1992-07-206-1), a fragment of a patchwork coverlet or counterpane made by an unknown British soldier, reputedly in India c.1880 (NAM 1981-12-34-1), and two intricate embroidered patchwork smoking caps worked by Colour Sergeant Joseph Fish of the Grenadier Guards during the Crimean War (NAM 1963-08-185-2 and -3). The 17th Regiment bedcover has a note attached: 'This coverlet was made by a soldier recovering from wounds during the Crimean War.' Though no further information is supplied which might help to verify this object biography, the clearly amateur production of the cover supports the accompanying note (Figure 9). The central panel design of the regimental colour, king's colour, and Leicester tiger (the regimental badge) incorporates some pieces of embroidered appliqué produced on pre-perforated canvas for easier stitching. While in scale and design the work is ambitious, measuring 140 by 162 cm and using tessellation of two sizes of diamonds of six colours of uniform fabric around the central panel, it has clearly been executed by inexperienced hands. Stitching in the patchwork varies in size and method, and the embroidery technique is improvised. The finished

---

[54] Strictly speaking none of the textiles considered here fulfils the definition of a quilt as comprising at least two layers held together through stitching on the face surface. These objects, though, are popularly referred to as quilts and often described as such in museum catalogues and exhibitions. This term, as demonstrated by the Victoria and Albert Museum show Quilts 1700–2010, has a particular emotional resonance, which explains its attachment to textiles beyond those that strictly qualify. As Christopher Breward notes in the exhibition book, narrative history and affective pull may take precedence over technical specifications: 'whether produced by men or women, the glory of a well made quilt lies in the resonance achieved between the emotional context of its making and the beauty of its finish', 'Serving Soldiers', in *Quilts, 1700–2010: Hidden Histories, Untold Stories* (London: V&A Publishing, 2010), p. 86. The exhibition included a beautiful military patchwork, possibly made by Private Francis Brayley when serving in India between 1864 and 1877. For further details of this provenance see Sue Prichard, 'Precision Patchwork: Nineteenth Century Military Quilts', *Textile History* 41, supplement 1 (2010), pp. 214–26.

Figure 9. Patchwork bedcover, 17th Regiment of Foot, *c.*1856. Reproduced with permission from the National Army Museum.

coverlet movingly inscribes the effort of its production, which combines with the attached note to invite those viewing it now to imagine the painstaking work of the unnamed wounded infantryman. The same narrative is attached to the Crimean War quilt held at the Tunbridge Wells Museum and Gallery. The quilt, comprising over 10,000 individual pieces, is said to have been the work of a soldier or soldiers wounded in the Crimean War.[55]

The attributions place these objects in a tradition, emerging in the mid-nineteenth century, of therapeutic patchwork. Needlework, in particular embroidery, was encouraged by the Temperance Association in their work with the British army through the latter half of the nineteenth century. Military exhibitions encouraged the cultivation of a range of handiwork, including quilting. The Great Exhibition of 1851 included more than thirty patchwork quilts submitted by military personnel and throughout the 1860s and 70s the army organized a number of soldiers' industrial exhibitions in Poona and Lucknow, India.[56] An 1873 issue of *The British Workman* featured Private Roberts who took up patchwork on giving up

---

[55] Ruth Kenny, Jeff McMillan, and Martin Myrone, *British Folk Art* (London: Tate, 2014), p. 120.
[56] See Janet Rae and Margaret Tucker, eds, *Quilt Treasures: The Quilters' Guild Heritage Search* (London: The Quilters' Guild, 1995), p. 170, and Prichard, 'Precision Patchwork'.

drink with the declaration 'I must be employed or I shall get into mischief.' As 'he had not been much accustomed to use of the needle' he began with pincushions but then achieved elaborate patchwork, including 'a beautiful quilt consisting of 14,000 pieces' pictured in the accompanying illustration. The journal presents Roberts as an inspiring case—'we wish to encourage such acts of "self-help"'—using a Smilesian ideology previously applied, as we shall see, to soldier patchwork in the Crimean War.[57]

Producing textiles provided a good distraction for hand and eye, offering a relief from the tedium of transport, siege, or convalescence. In December 1899 the *Graphic* printed a photograph of Rifleman Henry Paget knitting en route to the Boer War with the caption 'Life on Board a Troopship: A Favourite Occupation'.[58] The use of craftwork for therapeutic purposes was institutionally established by the First World War. Jeffrey Reznick has considered the curative workshops of that period, which were 'designed to create an atmosphere of contentment among the men', although there is evidence that this had mixed success with soldier patients often resenting such work.[59] During the Second World War patchwork was included in the occupational parcels of different kinds of handiwork sent by the war office to British POWs in overseas prison

---

[57] 'Another Patchwork Quilt', *The British Workman*, monthly, no. 216, February 1873, p. 152.

[58] Reprinted in Peter Boyden, Alan Guy, Marion Harding, eds, *Ashes and Blood: The British Army in South Africa, 1795–1914* (London: National Army Museum, 1999), p. 342. Private W. Ware sent his family a parcel from his posting in Cherat, India in May 1895, including a knitted gift of eight pairs of socks. He reports that 'there are about ½ of our Regiment that can knit'; 'I can tell you anyone can learn a lot of fancy ways if he likes to put himself about it. I can knit about 6 different ways alleady.' Ware uses his new skill, like Harvey with sketching and music, to retain a connection with family routines: 'In the first place there are four pairs for Arthur, two pairs with the grey feet, the reason I put grey feet in them is because walking two [sic] and fro and getting his feet wet out at the Moor I thought that coloured worsted might hurt him and the other two pairs of fancy ones will do for him on Sundays or do for a change after he has come home from work, but mother had better rinse them through in a drop of water before he can put them on as I soaked them in some native stuff to keep the colours from washing out and they shrunk up a lot but they will come alright after they have been worn a couple of times. The next two pairs of black ones is for Sam as I know working up in shorts he will want good socks, and now comes Earnest's two pairs I don't think he will be disappointed this time.' He is 'very sorry to see that Earnest was disappointed', presumably by a previous gift of overly small socks, 'but he must have grown a lot since I left home.' After an absence of three years, Ware keeps in vicarious touch, despite his physical distance from them, with his growing brothers, using the gift of knitted socks to show his thoughtfulness about his brothers' occupations and their daily routines, his solicitude for their bodily well-being and comfort (NAM 2001-09-77-2).

[59] Jeffrey Reznick, *Healing the Nation: Soldiers and the Culture of Caregiving in Britain During the Great War* (Manchester: Manchester University Press, 2004), p. 124, p. 128.

camps.[60] The recuperative associations of military patchwork place these objects within a long tradition of soldiers producing art as a form of survival; whether produced expediently by ill-provisioned prisoners of war as saleable, by serving soldiers using their art and collectables as an emotional lifeline to their families at home, or by convalescent soldiers surviving the pain and monotony of hospitalization.[61]

Another item in the NAM collection, a Crimean War patchwork draughtboard, cites a related narrative of immediacy with the soldier's body. In this cannily but simply produced object the backing doubles as a bag in which to keep the pieces (which remain almost complete, with only one counter lost over the estimated 160 years since the object was made). Ties allow for easy rolling and compact portability. The museum's catalogue provides the following detailed description:

> Board made from the uniforms worn by British soldiers and the pieces, twelve disks and eleven rectangles incised on top with a worm, made from bone. Reputedly made by soldiers during the Crimean War (1854–1856). Patchwork of 64 scarlet and white serge squares makes the board which is backed with white cotton and has a second backing sewn on to form a bag. (NAM, 1972-06-41-1)

This object is both a memorial, providing an afterlife for the no longer needed uniforms, and a lively object of camaraderie, pastiming, and likely gambling. Letters home from British soldiers in the Crimea often include accounts of pleasurable games of draughts and chess, although the correspondents are usually at pains to reassure their families that no gambling was involved. Like the range of soldier art considered here, the board raises questions about the connections between battlefront and home, military and civilian life, destabilizing any firm separation of these spheres. It is homely, allowing men on campaign to continue a typical family game they had likely played at home and learnt as children from parents or older siblings. At the same time the board is an intensely military product, made from the material to hand and likely as a response to the long periods of empty time, particularly during the siege of Sebastopol, which made gambling such an absorbing occupation.

The catalogue description 'made from the uniforms worn by British soldiers' adds an additional layer of tactile history, as the material moves from intimate proximity to soldiers' bodies, to maker's or makers' hands,

---

[60] For a more detailed discussion of the use of quilting by temperance and prison reformers and in soldiers' rehabilitation programmes see Prichard, 'Precision Patchwork'.

[61] For detail of art produced for sale or exchange by Napoleonic prisoners of war held in Britain see Kimball, *Trench Art*, p. 4.

to players' hands, to those who encounter it now. The identification of the material as from worn, used uniforms, suggests that it became surplus and available for reuse on the death of the wearers. This connects the board with powerful narratives circulated about military quilts produced from the uniforms of dead fellow soldiers. In an 1872 letter home from India, soldier Joseph Rawdon explained that he'd been working 'all of six years on and off to make the quilt from different uniforms, more than a few pieces from poor fellows that fought hard for their country and fell in the struggle'.[62] Rawdon presents his work as a form of memorial for the men who had previously worn material within it. In their discussion of Rawdon's work and the other Victorian military quilts catalogued during the Quilters' Guild Heritage Search, Janet Rae and Margaret Tucker suggest that pieces used were 'left over from uniform tailoring or uniform alteration. In some cases the cloth used came from the uniforms of soldiers who had died in battle.'[63] As Sue Prichard has shown, however, in the military quilts that survive from this period there was no evidence of the residue of use—no oil, powder, or blood—and it is more likely that the majority of materials came in the form of offcuts from regimental tailors.[64] The number of colours, taken from the relatively small fabric area of uniform facings (collars and cuffs) used in many military quilts, also make it unlikely that large, multicolour patchworks were predominantly produced by uniforms of the dead, although it is possible that some parts of the material were made available in this way. NAM's Leicestershire regiment coverlet, for example, incorporates large amounts of material from six colours. The regularity, however, with which this kind of story is attached to these objects shows the possible patriotic impulse for intimacy—proximity to the bodies of the heroic dead—and a desire for a rich narrative of the soldier maker's feeling, as the tactile experience of the detailed work of cutting, piecing, and stitching combines with the emotional project of memorializing dead comrades. Another typical narrative, that the quilt has been produced by a wounded soldier, again takes its force from the object's direct connection to the suffering body but this time to that of the heroic survivor maker. In these cases, the patchwork is also linked to a reassuring narrative of recuperation.

[62] Letter to Mr Bootland of Bradford, quoted by Rae and Tucker, *Quilt Treasures*, p. 177.
[63] Rae and Tucker, *Quilt Treasures*, p. 173.
[64] Prichard, 'Precision Patchwork', p. 218. The curators of the Homefront and Battlefield exhibition on textiles of the American Civil War found similarly that sections within quilts reputed to be made from uniforms had pieces that were actually too large to come from unpicked jackets. Shaw and Bassett, *Homefront and Battlefield*, p. 121. See also p. 186 for a discussion of the valuing of textile fragments that had 'touched the tragedy of the war', including uniforms worn by casualties and survivors, as a form of memorial.

A similarly emotive object history is attached to an intricate Crimean War tablecloth in NAM's holdings, described in the catalogue as 'scarlet, black, blue, yellow and white patches, reputedly cut from uniforms and made during the Crimean War (1854–1856) by drummer boys…' (NAM 1960-03-76-1). This beautiful, finely detailed object exhibits skilled piecing of layered small parts that produce an appearance of beading, and techniques of precise leather stamping that required specialist tools. The level of skill involved here differentiates it from many other soldier-produced patchworks. The draughtboard and several of the NAM patchwork pieces rely on basic utility stitches, such as plain, back, and whip stitch, and the canvas-work embroidery of the slightly difficult to identify Leicester tiger in the centre of the 17th Regiment coverlet is clearly the work of an amateur. The technical accomplishment, use of specialist equipment, and reliance on tiny pieces of thick cloth which act as beads and would be very difficult to keep hold of in camp conditions make it very unlikely that this was produced by drummer boys. Nonetheless the description gives this aesthetically striking object a similarly impressive sentimental biography. Drummer boys, as discussed in the previous chapter, had wide popular appeal as figures of sympathy, and were often used in the nineteenth century in critiques of the waste and senselessness of war. This attribution also continues the association of military patchwork with the regular soldier. While officers had readier access to drawing materials, and had often, like Lempriere and Harvey, received formal artistic training through a private education, soldiers of other ranks had to be more adaptive in the materials and skills they brought to art work. Patchwork produced by drummer boys, privates, and colour sergeants offers evidence of the perhaps unexpected range of tactile and aesthetic experience of the working-class Victorian soldier. The narratives attached to military patchworks provide insights into the ways in which soldier art is valued, variously by its producers, by the museums that preserve it, and by those viewing it now. Some feeling of proximity to the emotional life of the maker and/or the material is typically established by the catalogue description, which tends to ascribe at least the outline of a life story to at least one of these constituent parts (producer or fabric).

The patchwork done by Private Thomas Walker as he convalesced from a head wound in the Fort Pitt military hospital at Chatham made for a rich narrative relationship between soldier maker and textile, which was widely circulated in the contemporary press. The details known about Walker perhaps suggest a fuller accompanying narrative for the anonymous Leicestershire Regiment coverlet and the Tunbridge Wells quilt also supposed to have been made by a convalescent soldier or soldiers recovering from Crimean War wounds. Walker, of the 95th Regiment, was severely injured at the Battle of Inkerman. He met the queen during a series of royal visits to the wounded, and she described him in her journal as 'a most extraordinary case, a shell having burst on his head, the whole upper part of which was exfoliating, & would come away! Yet he looked well in the face, & said he did not suffer, only at times from giddiness. The Dr says he will entirely recover.'[65] *The Times* identified Walker as 'perhaps the most extraordinary case' among the wounded soldiers visited by the queen: he 'has been in hospital nearly 12 months, during which time he had 13 pieces of his skull removed by Doctor Parry... Her Majesty has seen him on every occasion of her visits, and has sent him a present of 10l.'[66]

An 1856 portrait by Thomas Wood, now in the collection of the Royal College of Surgeons, depicts Walker propped up in bed making a vibrantly coloured quilt using the red, black, white, and gold of army uniforms (Figure 10). *Cassell's Illustrated Family Paper* produced an engraving of Wood's painting, with which they included some details of how Walker had learnt to quilt in hospital with help from a fellow soldier's wife. As Glenn Fisher has documented, Walker's father was a brewer's servant and his own trade or calling was recorded on his attestation papers when he joined the 95th in 1850 as 'a hawker'. These papers also show that he was able to sign his own name.[67] Although Walker seems to have learnt patchwork in hospital, the report in *Cassell's* suggests that he drew on his existing skills in hawking goods, to turn his sickbed work into a successful commercial enterprise:

> He has employed much of his time whilst in hospital, and relieved the tedium of his confinement, in making patchwork rugs and table covers from the scarlet cloth and facings of soldiers' jackets. In the manufacture of these he has exhibited so much taste and ingenuity that her majesty was pleased to select one for which she generously sent him £10; another large one has also been purchased from him, and he is now engaged in the making of a third, and still more handsome large rug, besides some pretty table covers, which he hopes to be able to dispose of to some charitably inclined persons. It deserves to be recorded to Walker's credit that he has given six pounds of her Majesty's donation to his relatives, who are in distressed circumstances, and £1 to the wife of a fellow patient who has assisted him in his work.[68]

---

[65] Queen Victoria's Journal, The Royal Archives, 19 June 1855, vol. 39, p. 343.
[66] Visit of Her Majesty to the Military Hospitals at Chatham', *The Times*, 17 April 1856, p. 12.
[67] Glenn Fisher, 'Thomas Walker 95th Regiment', *The War Correspondent, Journal of the Crimean War Research Society* 26.3 (2008), pp. 23–4. Walker made an apparently full recovery, working as a labourer in Buckinghamshire, marrying, and having one son. He died in 1889 aged sixty-two.
[68] *Cassell's Illustrated Family Paper*, 5 July 1856, p. 212.

Figure 10. Thomas William Wood, *Portrait of Private Thomas Walker*, 1856. Reproduced with permission from the Hunterian Museum at the Royal College of Surgeons.

Although, sadly, the queen's Walker quilt does not survive as part of the Royal Collection, the archive at Windsor does demonstrate that the queen continued to be interested in Walker's work and well-being. Following the queen's Chatham hospital visits, an update on Walker's condition was sent to Colonel Phipps, keeper of the Privy Purse who advised the queen on her engagement with the war: 'About ten days ago Dr Parry extracted a large piece of his skull very skilfully. He is going on very well & amuses himself by making a patch work quilt of bits of cloth from soldiers coats, trousers and facings. He has shown great ingenuity in the devices he has chosen & does it very nicely.'[69]

Colonel Eden's commendation here of Walker's 'ingenuity' of design and nicety of work is echoed by *Cassell's* report of Walker's 'taste and ingenuity' and his continuing endeavour to produce 'still more handsome' items, and by the emphasis in Wood's painting on the neatness and delicacy of execution, as Walker carefully stitches together small triangles of material to produce perfectly interlocking particoloured lines. This celebration of Walker's dextrous needlework and aesthetic skill gives a new dimension to the more conventional soldierly heroics signalled by his battle wound. At the same time, these accounts work to reassure non-combatants about the rehabilitation of the wounded soldier, quickly returned to productivity and industry. *Cassell's* detailing of the monies Walker received and passed on for his work brings his narrative into the wider story of self-help and improvement promoted by the journal. Founder John Cassell welcomed content 'illustrative of the triumph of religion, temperance, morality, industry, energy and self-control over idleness, apathy, intemperance and habitual self-indulgence'.[70] In presenting Walker as a case study of soldierly excellence, the journal overlapped with temperance organizations and army industrial exhibitions in commending craftwork over less productive pastimes, and contributed to wider debates about the working man's capacity for self-help and his contribution to national well-being. The curation of Wood's painting in the Victoria and Albert Museum's Quilts show drew out another strand of reassurance, contextualizing it as a 'propaganda portrait designed to allay public concerns over hospital conditions for soldiers'.

THE (DIS)COMFORT OF SALVAGE WORK

Wood's painting of Walker concentrated on his patchwork offers a variety of forms of comfort. This is an image of exemplary hospital hygiene and surgical skill; snowy white linens suggest an improbably high standard of

---

[69] Colonel Eden to Colonel Phipps, 4 November 1855. Royal Archives VIC/MAIN/F/3/115.
[70] S. Nowell-Smith, *The House of Cassell, 1848–1958* (London: Cassell & Co., 1958), p. 42.

ward cleanliness, and the head wound, recorded on the card above Walker's bed, has been treated through the dexterity of Staff Surgeon Parry (an interpretation of the painting emphasized through its presentation to the Royal College of Surgeons by the artist's nephew). Walker's own skilled production shows the wounded soldier swiftly rehabilitated into useful work. In producing a coverlet, which acts as a blanket over his feet during production, the patient is shown as useful to himself and other invalids, making one of the many necessaries which mismanagement of the war had rendered scarce. Walker's useful craftwork anticipates the specialized production of care equipment, such as splints, bandages, and even artificial limbs, by convalescent soldiers during the First World War.[71] Beyond the practical implications, the image also offers a transformation of the violence of war apparent in Walker's head wound, as the trappings of militarism in the bold colours of the uniform are literally fragmented and remade into a form that gives comfort. The threat of the uniform is undone as it becomes a blanket to warm and cheer the convalescent soldier, a parallel with the reuse of soldier's jacket as child's coverlet in Millais *L'enfant du Régiment* discussed in chapter 3. This transformation of material is continued by Walker's activity, exchanging gun and bayonet for needle and thread.

Undercutting the various reassurances offered by this image of the turning of uniforms into objects of comfort and the transformation of the invalid into supposedly cheerful, productive worker, Private Walker's expression is less than content. The inscrutability of Walker's face in Wood's painting perhaps registers an ambivalence about soldiers' feelings towards such work. Though the queen recites the reassurance he 'said he did not suffer' in her journal, and *Cassell's* reports that Walker had borne much suffering 'with cheerful resignation', the expression Wood gives Walker does not necessarily confirm these assessments. Wood presents Walker's feelings about his position and his supposedly therapeutic work as unreadable. Similarly troubling is the positioning of the scissors in Walker's lap with their point directed to the centre of his crotch, uncomfortably suggesting emasculation, even castration, by invalidism and the craftwork of the sickbed. This pointed reminder of the wounds suffered by Walker is extended by the surplus of available scrap uniforms, in which we can perhaps glimpse the life and death narratives of those soldiers killed by the conflict that Walker narrowly survived. Wood's painting is not quite a reassuring image of military hospital propaganda. Instead it resonates with forms of uneasiness typically produced by the reclaiming of war materials

---

[71] Reznick, *Healing the Nation*, p. 126.

in trench art. The domestication of war material via repurposing is often incomplete, whether in the classic examples of First World War shell cases turned into flower vases, gas canisters becoming dinner gongs, or in a Crimean gift of Russian ribbon sent on a sister's birthday. Saunders describes the dissonance between the layered uses of the war material in trench art as ironic, as an unsettling residue of violence remains amongst the homeliness of these reclaimed objects.[72]

As with many textual responses to war, a distinguishing feature of soldier art is its combination of recuperative and troubling affects. Often the remaking of material that had been used to wound and is closely associated with death and loss is directly reparative. In an extension of the biblical celebration of the remaking of swords into ploughshares (Isaiah 2:3–4), weaponry is reformed into domestic objects, cannonballs into paperweights, and the uniforms and decorations of the dead are refashioned into the often comforting contexts of the quilt, coverlet, or family scrapbook. Stewart describes quilt making and embroidery as 'salvage crafts'.[73] This description is particularly applicable to military quilting, especially of the explicitly recuperative kind produced by the convalescing Thomas Walker, and to art and souvenirs composed of salvaged war materiel. The work of salvage applies here both to material and to producer, who may be, at best, therapeutically salved, and perhaps even experience salvation from the horrors of war by the imaginative remaking of war materials. For many of the soldiers considered here, that remaking—whether in sketch, music, small souvenir, or patchwork—allowed the 'beast [of war] to be taken home'. These forms, though, did not entirely defang that beast, deriving their value from the precariousness of the lives of the soldier producers.

---

[72] Saunders sees shell case art as 'redolent with irony'. Ambiguities of meaning are produced by differences between military use and designs associated with peace, as in the often pastoral patterning of shell case vases, and by the transitions of use. A particularly vivid example is the repurposing of expended shells struck as gas alarms, used after the war as domestic dinner gongs to the presumed horror of veterans who associated the sound with the terror of a gas attack. *Materialities*, p. 72, and chapter 5.
[73] Stewart, *On Longing*, p. 139.

6
Reparative Soldiering and its Limits
Cultures of Male Care-Giving

This final chapter attends to the most literally reparative form of war work, soldier nursing. It examines the limits of the cultural work performed by the military man of feeling. The chapter follows the gentle soldier narrative to its ultimate development in accounts of men sacrificing themselves to save and nurse fellow soldiers, and traces an abrupt termination of these ameliorative representations in the treatment of the actual soldiers who provided physical care for each other in the Crimean War as hospital orderlies. In this war, for the first time, the insufficiencies of the British army's medical system became a public concern and the army's responsibility for the physical care of soldiers became culturally necessary. In the absence of adequate medical care and the presence of a vocal press, wounding—the elided core activity of war—slips disconcertingly back into view. Here I consider the reasons why an upper middle-class woman nursing heroine was presented as the solution to the problems of military medicine in the Crimean War, and look at how, in the decades that followed, a narrative of the humane and civilized soldier was escalated through the development of a medical corps with both practical and propagandistic applications. The chapter is concerned with recognizing the elision of working-class male care in the Crimean hospitals and reclaiming the tactile and emotional history of the soldier orderly.

'HE IS LIKE A BROTHER OR A FATHER TO ME, AND NURSES ME MOST TENDERLY': NARRATIVES OF SOLDIER NURSING

Charlotte Yonge's immediately post-Crimean war novel, *The Young Stepmother* (serialized 1856–60), expands upon popular contemporary narratives of the military man of feeling as a reparative figure. Gilbert Kendall, the morally and physically weak stepson, achieves reformation through a short army career and his self-sacrificing nursing of a wounded fellow soldier after they narrowly survive the Charge of the Light Brigade. Via this plot a character previously 'loved for his weakness', 'boyish, sensitive, dependent and shrinking', is transformed into a 'hero who had dared the deadly ride and borne his friend through the storm of shot and shell' (p. 355). This man-making (the 'marked manly features' of Gilbert's corpse will be noted, p. 355) is effected via an extension of Gilbert's best qualities at home, of emotional sensitivity and physical gentleness to the sick, into an arena where those skills become unambiguously heroic. His little brother summarizes the news home from the Crimea: 'Gilbert shot two Russians, and saved Cousin Fred.'[1] As Gilbert drags his shelled cousin from the battlefield, deaf to his entreaties to 'relinquish his hold, and not peril himself for a life already past rescue', he fires defensively on some approaching Russians 'to lay two of the number prostrate, and deter the rest from repeating the attack' (p. 322). His shooting is presented as a protective necessity rather than an exhilarating or inevitable consequence of the charge, which is only detailed in its aftermath. Though 'prostrated' himself by these efforts, his own wounds, and a delicate constitution, Gilbert survives long enough to nurse Fred back to health. As a commanding officer confirms, 'Fred had had a hard struggle for his life, and had only been saved by Gilbert's unremitting care by day and night' (p. 335). Gilbert is equipped for this by his domestic nursing of his dying grandmother; he was 'useful and kind' in her sickroom (p. 283) and 'had exactly the gentle, bright manner best fitted to rouse and enliven. Nothing could be more irreproachable than his conduct, and his consideration and gentleness so much endeared him that he had never been so much at peace' (p. 272). An army career provides the opportunity for the ultimate exercise of 'unremitting care', through which Gilbert finally overcomes the weaknesses of character he fell into at home with danger to his siblings (notably he exposed his sister to an unsuitable courtship and then an unhappy marriage, and his little brother to fast company who press liquor upon the child).

Yonge presents Gilbert's redemptive nursing of Fred as bringing the cousins into a closer feeling of familial intimacy, drawing on the same languages of fraternity and paternity soldiers use (as discussed in chapter 4) to express their emotional connection. Gilbert describes Fred as 'like a brother or a father to me, and [he] nurses me most tenderly, when he ought to be nursed himself' (p. 342). The novel also follows a widespread deflection of war violence via narratives of care. The emphasis is not on

---

[1] Charlotte Yonge, *The Young Stepmother* (London: Macmillan, 1899, first published in novel form 1861), p. 321.

Gilbert's killing of the enemy, only mentioned in a defensive context, but on the saving of life. This pattern is familiar from the celebration of Philip Sidney's humanitarianism, discussed in the Introduction, Thackeray's rerouting of an invitation to kill and tell into a tale of the self-sacrificing heroism of a military doctor (chapter 1), and through the range of other narratives discussed that transform the soldier into, variously, spiritual redeemer, adoptive father, or nurse. The middle-class army doctor also takes a prominent heroic place in fiction of this period. For instance, as noted in chapter 1, *The Times* correspondent Russell makes an army doctor the hero of his fictional account of the Crimea, *The Adventures of Doctor Brady*. With the inauguration of the Victoria Cross in 1856, an award for valour regardless of rank, medical officers received some formal recognition of their heroism for the first time. Three surgeons received the honour, the first being Regimental Surgeon Mouat in recognition for his bravery at the Battle of Balaclava, dressing the wounds of a lieutenant colonel under fire.[2] Yonge's 1865 novel, *The Clever Woman of the Family*, continues the wider cultural trajectory that her work exemplifies, towards the realignment of martial heroism with the preservation of life. Here Captain Alexander Keith receives a Victoria Cross after throwing a burning shell away from his wounded and immobile comrades at the siege of Delhi, saving them at the cost of part of his right hand. This incident is cited in discussions about what constitutes true heroism, as the erring heroine, Rachel Curtis, the title's 'clever woman', learns to 'call that a deed of heroism far greater than mounting a breach or leading a forlorn hope'.[3]

The Young Stepmother follows a pattern of mutually redemptive, reciprocal care well established by Yonge's most famous novel, *The Heir of Redclyffe*, which was discussed in chapter 1 for the popularity of its self-sacrificing nursing hero with Crimean war soldiers.[4] Fred, recovering from

---

[2] See Michael Brown, '"Like a Devoted Army": Medicine, Heroic Masculinity, and the Military Paradigm in Victorian Britain', *Journal of British Studies* 49.3 (2010), pp. 592–622, pp. 607–8 for the critique, as summarized by the *Lancet*, of the 'Omission of Honorary Awards to Military and Naval Surgeons' in the award of medals for the Peninsula and French Wars (*Lancet* 49, no. 1241, 12 June 1847), and the disparity between the British army system, under which medical personnel were not eligible for battle honours until 1898, and the French practice of formally rewarding army medics. See also Neil Cantlie, *A History of the Army Medical Department*, 2 vols (Edinburgh and London: Churchill Livingstone, 1974), vol. 2, p. 71 and Melvin Charles Smith, *Awarded for Valor: A History of the Victoria Cross and the Evolution of British Heroism* (Basingstoke: Palgrave, 2008).

[3] Charlotte Yonge, *The Clever Woman of the Family* (London: Virago, 1985), p. 82.

[4] Other nineteenth-century narratives of male nursing include a similar transition between nurse and patient roles, including Dickens's *Martin Chuzzlewit* (1844), when Mark Tapley nurses Martin in the American swamps and then succumbs to the same fever. I discuss this in Holly Furneaux, *Queer Dickens: Erotics, Families, Masculinities* (Oxford: Oxford University Press, 2009), chapter 5.

the amputation of his right arm, sleeps on the floor by Gilbert's bed to be in constant attendance (p. 347) and tries to return the care of the man who saved his life: 'I am doing my best for him, but my nursing is as lefthanded as my writing' (p. 342). Gilbert's father, hurrying to his deathbed, reports on cousin Fred's 'assiduous and affectionate attendance at a time when he is very little equal to exertion. They are like brothers together and I am sure nothing has been wanting to Gilbert that he could devise for his comfort' (p. 346). He adds that Fred 'looks very ill and suffering, but seems to have no thought but for Gilbert, and will not hear of leaving him; and, in truth, they cling together so affectionately, that I could not bear to urge their parting, even were Fred more fit to travel home alone' (p. 347).

The reciprocity of nursing establishes intimacy between Yonge's suffering soldiers and, as is typical of nursing narratives, both men are transformed, their vulnerability in the sickroom also offering an opportunity for moral recovery. The emphasis is less on the rehabilitation of the body than of character, and while Gilbert dies a hero his cousin is saved to become a steadier and more religious man. Fred is most notable prior to the war as a 'rattlepate' officer (p. 282), a likeable but somewhat flighty ladies' man whose youthful infatuation with the titular young stepmother is followed by a string of other loves. Following his recovery Fred goes on to complete his reformation through marriage to Emily, the latest of these, who is presented as a compassionate woman of good sense and fun who takes pity on his inability to tie a necktie: 'now could I let him go back again alone, when he came so helpless, and looking so dreadfully ill?' (p. 377). Emily helps Fred to recover from the loss of Gilbert, which he feels particularly keenly. Yonge roots this feeling in the reparative intimacy established through their nursing:

> These four months of mutual dependence had been even more endearing than the rescue of Fred's life on the battlefield; and he declared that Gilbert had done him more good than any one else. They had been so thrown together to make the 'religious sentiment' of the younger tell upon the warm thoughtless heart of the elder. They had been most fondly attached; and in his present state, reduced by wounds, and exhausted by watching, Fred was more overpowered than those more closely concerned. (p. 355)

Fred honours this attachment and formalizes the intense sense of family connection developed through their reciprocal nursing by naming his son Gilbert, 'since they can wish nothing better for him than to be like him' (p. 428).

Gilbert's own reformation is completed through a change he makes to his will, empowering his father to complete the long-projected improvement of the unsanitary tenements owned by the family. This, 'the best deed of poor Gilbert's life' (p. 357), further shifts the emphasis from war heroics to a Kingsley-like domestic heroism of sanitary reform and care for the poor in the building of model cottages and almshouse. This conclusion has clear affinities to Kingsley's case for the relative worth of the less glamorous valour of domestic reform in his Crimean novel, discussed in chapter 2, *Two Years Ago*. Yonge repeatedly affirms the significance of this act in the making of Gilbert's heroism, and those resistant to the father's reforms are referred to the sacrifice of the son: 'His son got his death fighting for his queen and his country a year ago, and on his death-bed bade him do his best to drive the fever from your doors, and shelter you and save you from the union in your old age' (p. 396).

The personally and socially reparative soldier nursing plot of Yonge's *The Young Stepmother* incorporates a range of the characteristics of the military man of feeling documented in the preceding chapters. Gilbert and Fred are shown to be physically gentle and emotionally responsive, experiencing intense familial feelings of connection and bereavement. Martial and domestic qualities are presented as entirely compatible, and Gilbert's ultimate heroism is his intervention in improved living conditions for the poor of his village rather than his participation in the Charge of the Light Brigade. As the Kendal family return home after Gilbert's death their parting vision is of the 'fortress of the holy warriors vowed to tenderness and heroism' (p. 359), a description that distils this novel's commitment, shared as we have seen with many other narratives of the Crimean War, to the compatibility of Christianity and soldiering. Through the nursing plot Yonge teases out a soldierly capacity for physical gentleness which helps to support the conjunction of 'tenderness and heroism' in her incarnation of 'holy warriors'. *The Young Stepmother* demonstrates the ameliorative work of the military man of feeling, reconciling civil and martial values through the presentation of war as an arena which deepens familial feeling, Christian faith, and commitment to forms of domestic social reform—improvements in sanitation and better living conditions for the poor—in ways that will strengthen and stabilize the nation.

Yonge's characterization and plotting variously parallels accounts of military men of feeling written by published authors and soldiers themselves. It resonates with, for example, the account of Lieutenant Douglas

MacGregor's nursing of Captain Hedley Vicars published in Marsh's bestselling memoir of the latter. Vicars narrowly survived carbon monoxide poisoning, a cause of death for several officers following the burning of charcoal fires to warm their tents. As Marsh reports it:

> Hedley was carried into the open air and laid on the snow. His men stood around him, wringing their hands. Eagerly as brothers, tenderly as mothers, some assisted the medical officer in chafing with snow the body of him they loved, in the hope of restoring vitality... A serious illness had followed the accident. During its continuance the kindest attentions were lavished upon him both by officers and men, and he was nursed with devoted tenderness by Lieutenant Douglas MacGregor, with whom of late his affection had been ripening into an affection almost brotherly.[5]

The power of feeling that could inform this language of brotherliness is made explicit in MacGregor's letter to his mother on Vicars's death in action, several months after his recovery from this accident. This letter, reprinted in Marsh's biography, is the most expressively distraught of the wide range of articulations of war bereavement I have encountered in my research. MacGregor writes,

> This is a dark and sorrowful day with me; my heart is wrung, my eyes red and hot with crying. I feel gloomy and sorrowful all together. My very dear friend Vicars was killed last night!... I know not how to live without him. He was my truest friend, my most cheerful companion, and my friendly adviser on all occasions... I loved that man as dearly as a brother: and it seems that I almost hear his voice sounding in my ears as he read (two days ago) the service... As I took [his] locket—sprinkled with his life blood—I cried so that I thought I would get ill.[6]

The physical intensity of this anguish, 'heart' 'wrung' with debilitating tears, goes beyond the register of Yonge's novel and that typically expressed by soldiers, even though, as we have seen, Victorian soldiers were often eloquent about their grief for others killed in war. MacGregor identifies Vicars's earlier illness as clarifying these feelings: 'I never knew how much I loved him until he was so nearly dying of the charcoal.' Having helped his beloved friend to recover, MacGregor imbues Vicars's survival of the accident with religious and martial significance: 'He [God] spared him from the horrible death of suffocation by charcoal, for a few months, that he may die a soldier's death.'[7] Marsh's account gives Vicars's

---

[5] Catherine Marsh, ed., *Memorials of Captain Hedley Vicars* (New York: Robert Carter and Brothers, 1857), p. 227. I discuss this text in the context of debates about the compatibility of Christianity and soldiering in chapter 2.
[6] Marsh, *Memorials*, pp. 279–82.   [7] Marsh, *Memorials*, p. 281, p. 280.

death an additional meaning in its transformative effect on his former nurse, similar to the effect Yonge describes of Gilbert's death on Fred. In the brief remainder of his life MacGregor continued Vicars's work of hospital ministry. In Marsh's telling,

> bright as the young survivor's Christian life had been before, it cleared into yet fuller lustre, in those six short months, ere his sun went down at noon. He regularly visited the hospitals, to read and pray with the sick and dying, and in every way sought to follow in the steps of that beloved friend, over whose grave he had wept with the strength of manly affection and the tenderness of a woman's love.[8]

Soldiering, nursing, and Christianity combine in both texts detailed here to produce exemplary narratives of life and death.

The nursing soldier offers an obvious extension to the cultural and political leverage of, variously, the liberal warrior, the gentle military man, and the Christian soldier. While narratives of individual and informal physical ministration were celebrated, like that of MacGregor and the other officers and men of the regiment for Vicars, the integral role of nursing in the role of the regular soldier up to and throughout the Crimean War was less culturally acceptable. Indeed the requirement that soldiers supply the role of nursing orderlies, a key part of the Crimean campaign for many servicemen, remains almost invisible. In the remainder of this chapter I consider this disjunction between the wealth of ameliorative narratives of physically gentle military men of all ranks and the decidedly unreparative reputation that has stuck to soldier orderlies as brutal and drunken. I ask why the applause for the tenderness of soldiers stops abruptly at this point, considering the intertwined histories of gender ideals and military reform.

(DIS)ORDERLY CARE? SOLDIER NURSES IN THE CRIMEAN WAR

J. A. Benwell's 1856 lithograph of Florence Nightingale in the military hospital at Scutari narrates the familiar gendered story of the heroic lady with the lamp (Figure 11). It continues to be read as a testimony to the power of the angelic iconography of Nightingale and the small group of women who supplemented the official military hospital staff in the Crimean War. A reproduction of the picture, in large scale (about 2 by 6 metres), forms a backdrop to the section of the National Army Museum dedicated to this conflict, in which visitors are invited to open up panels to

---

[8] Marsh, *Memorials*, p. 283.

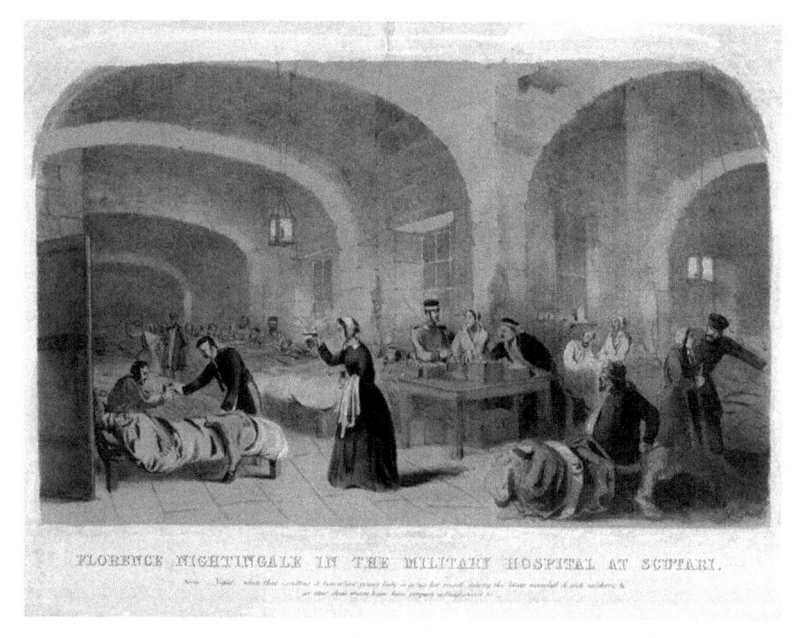

Figure 11. J. A. Benwell, *Florence Nightingale in the Military Hospital at Scutari*, 1856. Reproduced with permission from the National Army Museum.

learn more about Nightingale and hospital sanitation. Excellent art histories of the Crimean War by Matthew Lalumia and Ulrich Keller include it as part of their discussion of the representations of Nightingale. The figure in this image, though, who is most directly administering to a patient is not Nightingale but a soldier orderly, depicted in the bottom left-hand foreground, the two men's hands meeting as the orderly dispenses a drink. Though Nightingale is positioned in the centre of Benwell's composition, this interaction is also a focus of the image. The orderly and patient are watched closely by Nightingale, who directs the beams from her lamp to illuminate them.

Benwell is unusual in including the work of the orderly, a figure typically and, as we shall see, sometimes quite self-consciously omitted from visual representations of Crimean War hospitals, despite the reality that orderlies comprised the largest proportion of the hospital labour force. The system of using men of the ranks to staff the regimental hospital had long been the backbone of the army's medical strategy and remained so throughout the Crimean War, during which the insufficiencies of the system became clear. Dr Menzies, medical superintendent of Scutari hospital, recruited the entire hospital staff of 'ward-masters, ward orderlies, stewards, store keepers and cooks from the regimental details left behind at Scutari'.[9] He reported, 'I have secured an intelligent NCO, and a steady private and orderly to assist the purveyor in his duties; but as a general rule the regiments discarded all their bad characters with long crime sheets.'[10] This soldier staff performed the majority of hospital work throughout all the military and regimental hospitals during the campaign, including a range of patient care and domestic work usually described as nursing. As the 47th Regulation for the Management of Army Hospitals, current during the war, details: 'The duties of an orderly-man are to attend on the sick, administer their medicines, and comforts, keep their wards clean, and make himself generally useful.'[11] Accounts of the Crimean hospitals describe orderlies preparing and administering medicine, food, and drink, dressing wounds, changing, washing, and combing patients' clothing, bedding, and hair, fetching water, and cleaning the ward. This substantial contribution, however, has been entirely neglected in scholarly and popular histories of the period.

The Crimean War was the first time that the insufficiency of the system for nursing the army's wounded, as well as the inadequacy of supply lines and ordnance planning, was publicly exposed through a vocal press, notably Russell's dispatches for *The Times*. Though roundly blamed, the director general of the Army Medical Department, Dr Andrew Smith, had foreseen some of these difficulties, and after campaigning in vain for a larger staff of orderlies to be recruited, from the depots of the East India Company, he settled for reappointing retired servicemen. 370 men were employed in this way, but their reputation was for drinking rather than working, and as veterans mostly aged between forty and forty-five, they were physically unequal to the work.[12] As the majority of these men were required as ambulance drivers, only a small proportion were placed as orderlies in the general hospital at Scutari and many of these died immediately in the cholera epidemic. The orderly staff at Scutari was, therefore, almost entirely composed of men seconded, on command, from active regiments. The orderly pictured by Benwell was likely a convalescent soldier (probably Royal Artillery from his uniform), as during a time of active engagement commanders were reluctant to release members of their fit fighting force for hospital duty. Menzies's reports express frustration that the soldiers

---

[9] Cantlie, *History*, vol. 2, p. 20.   [10] Cantlie, *History*, vol. 2, p. 20.
[11] Quoted by Elizabeth Davis, *The Autobiography of Elizabeth Davis, A Balaclava Nurse*, ed. Jane Williams, 2 vols (London: Hurst and Blackett, 1857), vol. 2, p. 131.
[12] Cantlie, *History*, vol. 2, p. 12. As nurse Sarah Anne Terrot put it, 'some old pensioners sent out as orderlies did no better, in one respect worse, for their health universally gave way, and they soon became patients'. She describes one pensioner berating himself for his stupidity in taking up the role. *Nurse Sarah Anne with Florence Nightingale at Scutari*, ed. Robert Richardson (London: John Murray, 1977), p. 96.

seconded to him as orderlies had no experience of the work, and as soon as they had done the job long enough to become useful, they were returned to the ranks.[13] On her arrival at Scutari Nightingale took a similar view, writing to Lord Raglan, the British commander in the Crimea, requesting that soldiers who prove good orderlies be retained by the hospital.[14]

Though in this appeal Nightingale recognizes the possibility that properly trained and experienced soldiers could make good orderlies, she held a strong, strategic position about the undesirability of an all-male staff in military hospitals. Nightingale's 1859 book *Notes on Nursing*, in which she applied her Crimean experience to the domestic management of sick-rooms, famously opens with the statement, 'Every woman is a nurse.' Here she also states:

> I solemnly declare that I have seen or known of fatal accidents, such as suicides in *delirum tremens*, bleedings to death, dying patients dragged out of bed by drunken Medical Staff corps men, and many other things less patent and striking, which would not have happened in London civil hospitals nursed by women.[15]

The charges of drunkenness and thoughtless brutality recur throughout descriptions of male orderlies in the Crimea. Orderlies were typically criticized for mismanaging medicinal alcohol, either giving their patients too much out of misplaced kindness, or incompetence, or drinking it themselves. When members of the Catholic Sisters of Mercy arrived as nursing volunteers at Balaclava hospital, Sister Croke reported that there were 'two orderlies to each ward who are not at all pleased at the prospect of being soon deprived of the happiness of giving "spiritual consolation" to their patients in the shape of wine and brandy'.[16] The control of patient diets was taken over by the Sisters. In her post-Crimea report 'The introduction of Female Nursing into Military Hospitals in Peace and in War' Nightingale stipulates that wine not be left at patients' bedsides, lest it 'tempt' 'a dishonest comrade, or here or there, an orderly to drink it'.[17] The representation of soldier orderlies as drunken and needing careful

---

[13] Cantlie, *History*, vol. 2, p. 89. Cantlie describes 'the supply and control of the hospital orderlies' as the most frustrating of all the difficulties that Menzies as medical superintendent of Scutari had to contend with.

[14] Florence Nightingale to Lord Raglan, 8 January 1855, <http://www.nam.ac.uk/exhibitions/online-exhibitions/florence-nightingale>.

[15] Florence Nightingale, *Notes on Nursing: What It is and What It is Not* (London: Duckworth, 1970), p. 23.

[16] *The Crimean Journals of the Sisters of Mercy 1854–6*, ed. Maria Luddy (Portland, OR: Four Courts Press, 2004), p. 79.

[17] Florence Nightingale, *Subsidiary Notes as to the Introduction of Female Nursing into Military Hospitals in Peace and in War* (London: Harrison and Sons, 1858), p. 93.

direction from middle-class managers parallels concerns voiced in the run-up to the Second Reform Act about the working man's (in)ability to make a positive contribution to the strength and well-being of the nation.[18] The apparently innocent action Benwell captures, of the orderly handing a patient a cup, is a contested act of care. Here Nightingale herself holds back a glass of wine while, presumably, the orderly's basin contains less controversial refreshment. In this context Nightingale's gaze might not be one of benevolent approval (the kind of look associated with her popular legacy as ministering angel), but might instead be the scrutiny of a formidable reformer. The latter reading of Nightingale's overseeing of the orderly's interaction with the patient is supported by the caption beneath the image: 'Scene: Night, when that excellent and benevolent young lady is going her rounds among the brave wounded and sick soldiers, to see that their wants have been properly administered.'[19]

Benwell interweaves the two culturally dominant mythologies of Nightingale, as identified by Mary Poovey: feminine angel and aggressive reformer. As Poovey shows, these apparently competing narratives of Nightingale's heroism comfortably co-existed, as the modern nurse that Nightingale came to symbolize 'displaced anxieties' about a range of contemporary concerns, including developments in medicine and extensions of empire.[20] As Poovey argues of Nightingale's involvement in the Crimean War and then medical reform in British India, 'in the image of Florence Nightingale, as in the image of the Queen, the contradiction between an aggressive, economically interested war and the mother's curative tutelage of the child was symbolically resolved and the tensions it provoked could magically disappear'.[21] Nightingale's image in the Crimea as, simultaneously, a strong leader and angelic healer successfully displaced widespread anxieties about the administration of the army and the inadequacies of transport, supply, and medical care that the war

[18] See chapter 2 for a fuller discussion of the connections between changing attitudes to the working-class man, army reform, and franchise debates.
[19] This caption draws on widely circulated reports that present Nightingale as a cure both for soldiers' sufferings and for the inefficiencies of the Crimean military hospitals. See for example the very similar language used in *A History of the Russian War, Compiled and Arranged from the Most Authentic Sources* (Halifax: Milner and Soweby, 1860): 'Miss Nightingale, who, ending a day of untiring activity, would take a last look to ascertain whether any duty had been neglected, any urgent case forgotten, and solace unadministered', p. 333. Ulrich Keller finds Benwell the most appropriate pictorial chronicler of Nightingale, through this 'emphasis on organisation, administration, professional service'— 'no spiritual flirtation, no petting of the particular man', *The Ultimate Spectacle: A Visual History of the Crimean War* (Amsterdam: Gordon and Breach, 2001), p. 116.
[20] Mary Poovey, *Uneven Developments: The Ideological Work of Gender in Mid-Victorian England* (Chicago: University of Chicago Press, 1988), p. 174.
[21] Poovey, *Uneven Developments*, p. 197.

exposed. The voluntary nursing response attempted to alleviate the immediate problem of suffering, at the same time as a gendered ideology of women's unique ability to minister to the sick deflected attention from these structural problems, allowing the British public to feel better about the care for soldiers. Keller, observing the typical excision of male orderlies and surgeons in visual representations of the military hospitals in favour of intimate, homely scenes of soldiers tended by 'pretty self-sacrificing nurse[s]', identifies a 'culture of representation' as 'social communication, even social therapy of sorts. Precisely because it has so little to do with what happened at Scutari this therapy could be quite effective in England.'[22]

Although representations of the Crimean hospitals tended to present nursing as the reparative vocation of ministering women, this work was within the expected remit of all regular soldiers in this period and care arrangements had often been made with attention to the intimacies within regiments. When, after the Crimean War, Nightingale enquired how the military hospitals in Britain organized night nursing for severe cases, the Garrison Hospital at Chatham returned:

> When any case assumes such a character as to require more than the usual care and watching, a Requisition is immediately sent to the Commanding Officer of the Corps to which the man belongs for a steady, well-conducted soldier and who generally is the man's own comrade [so much the worse] to nurse him, and to attend upon him throughout his illness, but who is relieved by another as often as the Medical Officer in charge of the case considers necessary.[23]

Nightingale expresses her disapproval in parentheses of the hospital's policy, which derived from the view that a 'steady' soldier, especially one who had worked closely with the patient, his 'own comrade', would be well equipped for the role. Shared regimental history, a relationship based on identity in the regiment, and perhaps a personal friendship are all seen as advantageous in the appointment of a soldier nurse. Memoirs written by women nurses in the Crimean War record numerous examples of nursing comrades amongst the hospital patients, celebrating these personal, informal acts of care in a similar way to contemporary novels and soldier memoirs. The same nurses, however, were typically less approving of the patient care provided by the formalized system of soldier orderlies.

Sarah Anne Terrot, a volunteer in Nightingale's party working at the general hospital in Scutari, notes the incoherence in her own account in which soldier patients are heroes of nursing, with the same men taking the role of villainous orderlies on their convalescence. She records numerous

---

[22] Keller, *Ultimate Spectacle*, p. 113.   [23] Nightingale, *Subsidiary Notes*, p. 106.

instances of care between the ill, noting, for instance, that 'the patients who could walk used to... fetch flowers for their bedridden comrades' and reflecting that 'it was very touching to see the maimed waiting on and helping each other' (p. 93, p. 114). A Scotch artilleryman 'took a tender interest' in the consumptive 'gentle religious lad' in the bed beside him, and seeing his neighbour's critical state 'got up, dressed, and sat by and nursed him to the last' (p. 147). Another patient, Aslett, endangers his own recovery through his solicitude for others (p. 123, p. 151). From such behaviour, Terrot concludes that soldier patients were 'more noble patient, generous and unselfish than human nature generally is' (p. 152). Margaret Goodman, another lady nurse of Nightingale's party, reaches the same conclusion, commenting on the 'lasting and disinterested friendships' between soldiers who nurse one another: 'It was beautiful in many instances to observe their readiness to make any sacrifice for their comrade, and the tenderness with which, while they could scarcely drag about their feeble forms, they waited around his dying bed.'[24] Tenderness is a recurring term in these descriptions, recognizing soldiers' combination of emotional and physical responses to suffering comrades. Acknowledging the inconsistency in her views of soldier patients and orderlies, Terrot reflects: 'It may seem such conduct in the orderlies, considering that they were fellow-soldiers of the poor sufferers, was most unfeeling and inconsistent with the general character of the soldiers, and certainly all orderlies were not selfish and heartless, but on the whole they seemed very inferior to me in character than the other soldiers' (p. 95). Of the problems of making such character distinction given that soldiers often moved between the role of patient to orderly, Terrot merely says, 'I have seen men I thought well of as patients, on recovering and being made orderlies, show a negligence, hardness and indifference that surprised me' (p. 95). Like Nightingale, Terrot has a strategic stake in carving out nursing as a

---

[24] Margaret Goodman, *Experiences of an English Sister of Mercy* (London: Smith, Elder and Co, 1862), p. 152. Goodman gives a moving, detailed account of the self-sacrificing love between two regimental comrades, Valentine and his 'immense' red-bearded friend, who care for each other in the hospital, pp. 152–5. See also Fanny Margaret Taylor's discussion of patients' reciprocal 'great kindness to each other; men who had lost an arm would be seen helping others who had lost a leg to walk, then these in their turn would cut up the food, or help in other ways those who had lost their arm', and her account of the highlander entrusted with night watching of the sick patient in the next bed: 'She found him lying on his bed, his face turned towards the sick man, and one eye open watching him, ready to spring out of bed at the slightest movement; the lady laughed and said it was just like a cat watching its kitten: this was heard by the others, and the pair went by the name of cat and kitten among their comrades for a long time', *Eastern Hospitals and English Nurses: The Narrative of Twelve Months Experience in the Hospitals of Koulali and Scutari. By a Lady Volunteer* (London: Hurst and Blackett, 1857), p. 130, p. 132. Goodman is further discussed in the Introduction.

legitimate sphere for women's work, and despite her observations of exemplary informal nursing between patients, she states that 'it is an unnatural occupation for men, especially for young men, to have the care of sick and dying men' (p. 95). While differences between the conduct of orderlies are fleetingly acknowledged, Terrot's account is typical in placing the emphasis on the 'selfish and heartless'. This is the opposite representational strategy to that used in accounts of warring and wounded soldiering, including the many tales of comrades in arms nursing one another, in which aggression and brutality is eschewed in favour of accounts of self-sacrifice and gentleness.

The army's ability to treat its wounded had recently become a factor in discussions about whether war was compatible with civilization. In the essay that accompanied his 1835 anti-war poem 'Captain Sword and Captain Pen' (discussed in the context of debates about the compatibility of Christianity and war in chapter 2) Leigh Hunt presents the lack of medical care for soldiers as a principal horror of war; if war cannot be abolished, he argues, at least better provision for the wounded would reduce its abhorrence:

> Even if nothing else were to come of inquiries into the horrors of war, surely they would cry aloud for some better provision against their extremity after battle,—for some regulated and certain assistance to the wounded and agonized,—so that we might hear no longer of men left in cold and misery all night, writhing with torture,—of bodies stripped by prowlers, perhaps murderers,—and of frenzied men, the other day the darlings of their friends, dying, two and even several days after the battle, of famine! The field of Waterloo was not completely cleared of its dead and dying till nearly a week! Surely large companies of men should be organized for the sole purpose of assisting and clearing away the field after battle. They should be steady men, not lightly admitted, nor unpossessed of some knowledge of surgery, and they should be attached to the surgeon's staff. Both sides would respect them for their office, and keep them sacred from violence. Their duties would be too painful and useful to get them disrespected for not joining in the fight—and possibly, before long, they would help to do away their own necessity, by detailing what they beheld.[25]

Hunt's lurid, gothicized account of physical suffering, in which soldiers of all classes 'writh[e] with torture', are murdered and starved, transforms British pride in Waterloo into shame. He offers suggestions for the organization of a medical corps and anticipates objections, including one voiced in the Crimea, that men should fight not nurse. The horror

---

[25] Leigh Hunt, 'Captain Sword and Captain Pen' (London: Charles Gilpin, 1849, third edition), pp. 3–4.

produced by the spectacle of the battlefield aftermath, as outlined by Hunt, was a factor in work to mitigate the neglect of soldier wounded, a neglect which became increasingly unacceptable as the nineteenth century progressed. Henry Dunant was appalled by witnessing the aftermath of the 1859 Battle of Solferino and called for the formation of voluntary relief societies, a proposal that eventually resulted in the establishment of the International Committee of the Red Cross. Unlike Hunt, who suggested that such work might not only mitigate the atrocities of war but help to end combat through particularly harrowing witness, Dunant took the pragmatic position that such work would allow war to be waged 'in a manner humane and civilised'.[26] Mark Harrison points to the cultural and emotional effects of this organization as the Red Cross became a 'powerful symbol of benevolent neutrality, mitigating some of the horror of war for its survivors'.[27] The symbolic effects of medical relief organizations went beyond their practical applications, as institutions like the Red Cross helped to elide wounding as the core activity of warfare. As Scarry notes, there is a cultural consensus on this elision in the writing of war.[28] Other narratives, such as that of individual and institutional humanitarian care, displace wounding, even as disavowed injuring makes them necessary. In Hunt's and Dunant's horrified responses to untreated casualties we see the unacceptability of war when exposed as its principal act of wounding. While Hunt retains hope that the medical witnessing of suffering will help the case against war, Dunant and humanitarian organizations take the route of mitigating that horror.

In Britain during the Crimean War 'for the first time', as Harrison argues, 'medical care for servicemen became a matter of acute public concern'.[29] This concern arose from a combination of shifting sensibilities that increasingly recognized and applauded the humanity of the regular soldier, increased war reporting and newspaper audiences, and developments in medical science and higher expectations of treatment even for the

---

[26] John Hutchinson, *Champions of Charity: War and the Rise of the Red Cross* (Boulder: Westview Press, 1996), p. 19.
[27] Mark Harrison, 'War and Medicine in the Modern Era', in *War and Medicine* (London: Black Dog, 2008), pp. 10–27, p. 17. In his discussion of the Red Cross in the Franco-Prussian War of 1870–1, Bertrand Taithe argues that 'ostensibly "humanitarian" efforts were also an important form of mobilisation for the war', 'The practices of total war and of humanitarianism at war were closely related to one another', 'The Red Cross Flag in the Franco-Prussian War: Civilians, Humanitarians and War in the "Modern" Age', in *War, Medicine and Modernity*, ed. Roger Cooter, Mark Harrison, and Steve Sturdy (Sutton: Stroud, 1998), pp. 22–47, p. 24, p. 25.
[28] See Introduction for a more thorough discussion of Scarry's work on war rhetoric and ethics.
[29] Harrison, 'War and Medicine', p. 14.

poorest members of society. Chenery's sea-changing *Times* report, discussed in the Introduction, detailed the underpreparedness of the hospitals in Scutari, lacking nurses, dressers, and bandages, through a comparison with domestic arrangements for the indigent: 'the commonest appliances of a workhouse sick ward are wanting'. Chenery predicted that the failure to provide suffering soldiers with even the most basic medical care available to the poor at home would generate public outrage: 'It is with feelings of surprise and anger that the public will learn that no sufficient preparations have been made for the proper care of the wounded.'[30] A week later these 'feelings of surprise and anger' were exacerbated by Russell's report of the Battle of Alma, which highlighted the disparity—or 'disgraceful antithesis' as his emotive prose put it—between British and French treatment of the wounded: 'I could not see an English ambulance. Our men were sent to the sea, three miles distant, on jolting arabas or tedious litters. The French—I am tired of this disgraceful antithesis—had well appointed covered hospital vans to hold 10 or 12 men and their wounded were sent in much greater comfort than our poor fellows.'[31]

Such reports presented the lack of medical treatment of the soldiery as a cause for national shame, inciting a widespread response that included Nightingale's volunteer nursing initiative, the formation of a range of fundraising schemes including *The Times* Sick and Wounded Fund, and the knitting of mittens and socks and making of bandages in homes across Britain. Jane Williams, the editor of Elizabeth Davis's Crimean memoirs, the only published account by a working-class paid nurse, reflected on the cultural work of Nightingale's mission. Her 1857 postscript employs a form of paranoid/reparative interpretation:

> It has been said that one great object of the Government in sending out Miss Nightingale and the Female Nursing Staff, was to pacify the excitement of the public, and to turn away attention from the sufferings of the army as well as from the errors which had increased and multiplied them. This may possibly be true, for human motivations are often complicated and philanthropy and policy, were not, in this instance, inconsistent. (p. 291)

Williams's view of the compatibility of philanthropy and politics continues her insights into the connections between reported suffering, public sentiment, and national response. She details how accounts of 'sufferings

---

[30] [Thomas Chenery], 'The Crimea', *Times*, 12 October 1854, p. 7.
[31] [William Howard Russell], 'The War', *Times*, 20 October 1854, p. 7. For further discussion of the often emotive rather than factually accurate perception of the superiority of the French army's medical and transport infrastructure see Anthony Dawson, 'The French Army and British Army Crimean War Reforms', *19: Interdisciplinary Studies in the Long Nineteenth Century* 20 (2015).

inalienably incident to warlike operation' had generated 'surprise' and 'compassion', and these 'kindly feelings' were 'wrought' 'into a furious storm' by accounts of 'needless privation' (p. 228). As Williams's analysis suggests, the feelings produced by discomforting detailed knowledge of sufferings 'inalienably incident to wartime' could be productively rerouted into a critique of the specific mismanagements of this war, especially around the emotive topic of treatment of the sick and wounded. As with the work of the Administrative Reform Association (discussed in chapters 1 and 2) endeavours to improve hospital conditions mediate the possibility for anti-war feeling, transforming critique into campaigns for, arguably, a better war.

The War Office responded to the crisis by commissioning a thorough report on the conditions in hospitals in the Crimea and implementing changes in the provision of medical services which would later be developed into the Royal Army Medical Corps. On 11 June 1855 a royal warrant for the formation of the Medical Staff Corps was issued, recruiting civilians and men transferred from regiments exclusively for hospital work, and that November the first contingent of 300 men of the new corps arrived at Scutari to replace the regimental orderlies.[32] While many of these changes were too late to have much effect in the Crimean War, by the First World War the RAMC had become a source of national pride, used in propaganda material such as films in which staff courageously stretcher the wounded away under fire, which reassured the public about the care taken of soldiers.[33] As John Parrish puts it, 'the goals' of military

[32] Cantlie, *History*, vol. 2, pp. 149–50, p. 171. See also A. E. W. Miles, *The Accidental Birth of Military Medicine: The Origins of the Royal Army Medical Corps* (London: Civic Books, 2009). Changes in organization of ambulances, transport for medical supplies, hospital ships, and orderly staffing were suggested in the Hospital Commissioners Report of 1855, Cantlie, *History*, vol. 2, pp. 137–8. Taylor gives an account of the mixed success of the introduction of the new Medical Staff Corps: 'Their first appearance in the wards excited a feeling of great contempt from the military orderlies... They did not turn out well—at least they gave equally as much trouble as the others; and intemperance prevailed amongst them to quite as great an extent—12 of them, from this cause, on average, were each night placed in the guard-room at Balaclava. But there must always be an advantage in having men who, when trained, will remain in their place and not be liable to removal.' She goes on to discuss the increasing competence of this dedicated staff, *Eastern Hospitals and English Nurses*, pp. 323–4.
[33] The short 'Wonderful Organisation of the Royal Army Medical Corps' produced by the British Topical Committee for War Films in 1916, for example. The film is in the collection of the Imperial War Museum, IWM 133, and was shown as part of the War and Medicine exhibition, Wellcome, London, 2008. Ana Carden-Coyne argues that such films were part of media campaigns to 'defuse public anxiety' by promoting 'an image of the RAMC as a modern machine, capable of a speedy and painless evacuation'. She points also to the proliferation of First World War paintings, photographs, and posters showing soldiers receiving RAMC care, and quotes Lord Knutsford's letter of 10 November 1914 to *The Times* reassuring the public that the hospital arrangements 'are amazingly perfect... everywhere there prevails a tone of sympathy, kindness and gentleness, which makes one's heart

medicine 'are to maintain fighting strength and soldier morale, assuage the angst of citizens unwilling to accept the human cost of war, and meet a moral obligation to wounded warriors'.[34] These apparently humanitarian developments contribute to the acceptability of war, paradoxically allowing for greater levels of violence by meeting these with structures of treatment for the surviving participants. Culturally, army medical organizations perform ameliorative work similar to other narratives of the military man of feeling, legitimating war as sufficiently 'humane and civilised'. Also, like the figure of the liberal warrior, military medical corps reflect changing attitudes to war and the reduced acceptability of an expectation that soldiers should give their lives for their nation. Like other incarnations of the military man of feeling the work of organizations like the RAMC has dual, sometimes competing, effects and may have the potential to further incite thinking about the legitimacy of war.

In the Crimean War, prior to the establishment of a dedicated army medical corps which would illustrate the humanity of the army, at least to its own soldiers, the capacity of soldier orderlies for beneficial physical care was broadly discredited. Whatever their individual efforts, a system in which the fighting strength or weak convalescents must perform the physically demanding work of hospital nursing was clearly unsustainable. The systemic problems of using soldiers untrained in medical work, and overstretched by understaffing and long hours, clearly resulted in inadequate care. The insistence, however, in most first-hand accounts on aggregating all orderlies as incapable of the work, insensitive, and even brutal also reflects an emotional response to that insufficient system, namely deep shame.

Images of Nightingale worked to transform this shame into pride, displacing the working-class soldier orderlies who performed most of the hospital work with the 'magical', to use Poovey's word, iconography of a middle-class woman. As Elizabeth Barrett Browning noted, this was a 'retrograde' step, 'a revival old virtues':

> Since the siege of Troy and earlier, we have had princesses binding up wounds with their hands; it is strictly the woman's part and men understand it so. Every man is on his knees before ladies carrying lint, calling them 'angelic she's' whereas if they stir an inch as thinkers or artists from the

---

beat a little faster'. This letter is explicit about the heartening physical and emotional effects of witnessing tender care to the soldiery; 'Soldiers' Bodies in the War Machine', *War and Medicine* (London: Black Dog Publishing, 2008), pp. 66–83, pp. 75–6. See Brown for a discussion of the popularity of images such as 'A Non-Combatant Hero: An Army Doctor in the Firing Line' during the Boer War, '"Like a Devoted Army"', pp. 619–20.

[34] John Parrish, 'Preface', in *War and Medicine*, pp. iii–iv, p. iv.

beaten land (involving more good to general humanity than is involved in lint) the very same men would curse the impudence of the very same women... I do not consider the best use to which we can put a gifted and accomplished woman is to make her a hospital nurse.[35]

As Barrett Browning notes, conservative gendered ideals are deployed in the face of this national emergency. The iconography of Nightingale as the lady with the lamp and of the doomed manly chivalry of the Charge of the Light Brigade are the two things people now remember about the Crimean War. At opposite poles of the gender spectrum, these persistent popular legacies firmly divide men's and women's work. This gendered polarity gives a misleading impression of a period in which soldiers are widely celebrated for their gentleness, and individual accounts of male heroism focus on efforts to save rather than take life. It also places a deceptive emphasis on Nightingale's work as personally healing soldiers, rather than her legacy as hospital administrator and reformer.

The connections made between class, gender, and physical reparation in the popular image of an angelic Nightingale are similar in descriptions of Queen Victoria's engagement with wounded Crimean veterans. The queen was invested with a capacity for personally ministering to the sick soldiers. A letter in which she described her personal care for the soldiery, '*no one* takes a warmer interest or feels *more* for their sufferings, or admires their courage or heroism *more* than their Queen', was widely leaked, printed in the press, and posted onto the walls of the wards of hospitals across the Crimea.[36] Many commentators described the letter's effects as curative. As one volunteer nurse, Fanny Margaret Taylor, put it, these words caused 'such a thrill of gratitude and delight among the soldiers' (p. 242). Taylor goes on to describe how her patients also felt Victoria's care for them via the pages of the *Illustrated London News*, in which they saw the queen 'passing through hospital wards, and speaking gentle words to the sufferers there. They heard of her warm interest in all they did or suffered, and that no hand but her own was allowed to decorate their comrades who had returned home.'[37] The emphasis on the queen's

---

[35] Elizabeth Barret Browning to Anna Jameson, quoted in Helen Rappaport, *No Place for Ladies: The Untold Story of Women in the Crimean War* (London: Aurum, 2007), p. 232.

[36] *Morning Post*, 4 January 1855. Emphasis original. See Rachel Bates for a discussion of the dissemination of this letter, 'Curating the Crimea: The Cultural Afterlife of a Conflict', PhD thesis, University of Leicester, 2015, chapter 3.

[37] Taylor's impressions are confirmed by soldiers themselves. William Jowett, a lance corporal promoted to sergeant during the war, for example, records in his journal his response to hearing a dispatch from the queen read at parade: 'The language was beautiful. If I live, I will try to procure a copy of it', 2 November 1854, transcript online at <http://www.beeston-notts.co.uk/jowett3.shtml>. Accessed 10 January 2015.

personal presence, indeed the direct touch of her hand, is continued in prints and descriptions of the queen's distribution of Crimean medals in Horseguards. Though these were awarded to all who served in the Crimea, regardless of rank, the ceremony focused on awards to the wounded rank and file. As Rachel Bates has shown, visual and verbal accounts of this ceremony focus on the physical contact between queen and soldier. *The Times* report, for example, emphasizes the 'Royal hand' reaching out to all alike. The queen reflected on the significance of this touch in her journal: 'all touched my hand, the 1st time that a simple Private has touched the hand of his Sovereign, & that,—a Queen! I am proud of it,—proud of this tie which links the lowly brave to his Sovereign'.[38]

The appropriateness of the queen's touch continued a firm demarcation in the gendering of healing hands, which invoked biology to further legitimate nursing as strictly women's work. Mary Seacole, an experienced nurse who worked independently in the Crimea as victualler, innkeeper, and nurse after being turned down for Nightingale's party, frequently reflects on the informal nursing that soldiers provided to one another. She observes, for example, 'the Christian sympathy and brotherly love shown by the strong to the weak' at the sick wharf: 'The task was a trying one and familiarity, you might think, would have worn down their keener feelings of pity and sympathy; but it was not so.'[39] Seacole's war experience challenges her belief that 'only women know how to soothe and bless' sickbeds (p. 70), but she explains her continued championing of women's unique nursing skill through an appeal to physiology: 'Only women could have done more than they did who attended to this melancholy duty; and they, not because their hearts could be softer, but because their hands are moulded for this work' (p. 88, p. 90). In this Seacole and Nightingale, and those women who worked with the latter, find an unusual consensus. Terrot makes a very similar claim to Seacole about the hands best 'moulded for this work'. Terrot complains of the orderly assigned to her, describing him as 'an English ploughboy, with heavy horny hands from which the wounded used to shrink. He used to fetch and empty my water, and was fonder of pawing wounded limbs than their owners approved' (p. 121). Though she goes on to detail his qualities as an effective nurse, this orderly is disqualified by a physical heavy-handedness apparently shared by all soldiers of the ranks: 'men whose hands were hard and horny through labour—hands used once perhaps to the plough, and

---

[38] *Times*, 19 May 1855 and Queen Victoria's Journal, 18 May 1855, cited by Bates, 'Curating the Crimea', chapter 3.

[39] Mary Seacole, *The Wonderful Adventures of Mrs Seacole in Many Lands* (London: Penguin, 2005), p. 88.

more recently to the firelock—were not fitted to touch, bathe, and dress wounded limbs, however gentle and considerate their hearts might be' (p. 105). These arguments about bodily gender difference allows for recognition of the soldiers' emotional commitments to each other; their 'soft', 'gentle and considerate' hearts are contrasted with a physical incapacity for gentle handling to support the endeavour to make nursing a profession for respectable women. Goodman moves the emphasis from the haptic to the optic, she describes her 'watching for those trifles which only the eye of a woman was likely to observe, and yet were all important amidst so much sickness' (p. 177), delineating a uniquely feminine regime of surveillance advocated by Nightingale and captured by Benwell.

While the touch and attention of Nightingale and Victoria provided individual and national reparation after the shame of the British mismanagement of the war, the hands of the same private soldiers that Queen Victoria was so eager to touch were not recognized for their own healing power. The strategic editing of a public narrative of healing is especially clear in Jerry Barrett's oil study of Nightingale and her staff, *The Mission of Mercy* (now at the National Portrait Gallery) (Figure 12). Matthew Lalumia comments on the class significance of the changes Barrett made between the sketch for the painting and the finished piece. 'Whereas

Figure 12. Jerry Barrett, *The Mission of Mercy*, 1857. Reproduced with permission from the National Portrait Gallery.

military orderlies attended the wounded soldier at Nightingale's feet in the sketch, they were replaced in the painting by one of [Nightingale's] hospital nurses and Staff Surgeon Cruikshank.'[40] As Lalumia points out, through this change 'mid-Victorian viewers encountered a new definition of heroism suitable to the age in the form of enterprising individuals who set right the errors of government and the army. Nightingale and her crew demonstrated the capabilities of the British middle-classes to serve the nation in its most ambitious undertakings.'[41] Clearly only some forms of tactility, along lines of class and gender, were deemed culturally restorative.

'AS KIND... AS IF HE HAD BEEN HIS OWN CHILD': AN ALTERNATIVE HISTORY OF THE SOLDIER ORDERLY

Taylor's journal provides a clear view of the class ideology that underpinned the war effort of well-to-do women: '*Our orderlies* were a great deal of help to us; they were always most respectful and obedient, though, of course, they needed constant looking after. One of *our nurses* mistook their names, and always called them "Aldernies".' The orderlies, infantalized here, are at the bottom of a hierarchy, with those described as 'our nurses', the paid, experienced, but less educated working women recruited in addition to lady volunteers, placed just a little above the soldier staff.[42] These working women were also often accused of drunkenness and, occasionally, of brutality, in line with the established reputation of the hired domestic nurse memorably caricatured as Sairey

---

[40] Matthew Lalumia, *Realism and Politics in Victorian Art of the Crimean War* (Michigan: UMI Research Press, 1984), p. 88.
[41] Lalumia, *Realism and Politics*, p. 90.
[42] Anne Summers details the composition of the two official British parties of women nurses in the Crimean War, totalling approximately eighty-four women (although the recorded numbers vary slightly): 'working women with a variety of experience in paid nursing for the sick', Roman Catholic Sisters of Mercy from Ireland, and ladies 'without experience of paid employment or affiliation to any nursing institution', 'Pride and Prejudice: Ladies and Nurses in the Crimean War', *History Workshop Journal*, 16.1 (1983), pp. 33–56, p. 33. Summers details the social hierarchies within these groups. On numbers and different backgrounds of women nurses see also Mother Bridgeman's journal, in *The Crimean Journals of the Sisters of Mercy*, pp. 125–7. For further discussion of the negotiation of class and gender roles in the development of Victorian nursing see Arlene Young, '"Entirely a Woman's Question?": Class, Gender, and the Victorian Nurse', *Journal of Victorian Culture* 13.1 (2008), pp. 18–41.

Gamp in Dickens's *Martin Chuzzlewit*. In common with most journals written by lady nurses, Taylor extends the domestic ideology of the civilizing presence of the respectable, well-born woman to the military hospital, suggesting that the ladies exercised a beneficial influence on the paid women nurses, and that, in turn, 'under the sisters' and ladies' charge' the male, working-class orderly staff were transformed into an 'excellent set of nurses' (p. 122).

The journals of nurses in the Crimea, written by women from a range of classes and religious positions, offer valuable insights into work and relationships in the hospitals, including previously overlooked details of the contribution made by soldier orderlies. These journals are, of course, as much a reflection on each author's attitudes and characters as documentary evidence of conditions and working practices in the Crimean hospitals, and each has its own unique tone. Like Taylor many nurses of Nightingale's party are concerned with advocating women's unique nursing skills, using a discourse of women's civilizing mission. These journals and, to a greater extent, those of the Catholic Sisters of Mercy also draw upon Christian traditions of sacrifice and saviour as means through which their contributions to hospital work can be understood and endured. Despite their differences, a more complicated, often positive, picture of orderly care emerges across the spectrum of these nurses' journals. Elizabeth Davis, a paid nurse, gives a typically mixed impression of the attitude, character, and efficiency of soldiers working in the hospitals. Davis, experienced in hospital and domestic nursing, campaigned hard to be employed close to the front; she was given charge of the special diet kitchen at Balaclava hospital, with a daily working routine from 5 a.m. to midnight. She records the mixed quality of help she received from various orderlies. Initially she was assisted by 'a quiet, useful man', who became ill from the thick smoke and charcoal dust and was admitted to the hospital himself; Davis is less impressed by those who replaced him, whom she considered 'idle, tipsy fellows': 'I preferred going without such assistants and did all the work myself' (p. 156).

Though class prejudice strongly colours many of the first-hand accounts written by lady nurses, these do detail emotional connections between orderlies and patients. As well as recounting her frustration with careless, 'surly' orderlies (p. 141) and one negligent man in particular who is described as 'a brute' (p. 50), Taylor also details the many kindnesses of these soldier hospital staff. One patient, a dying young soldier called Algeo who was 'covered with abscesses and quite unable to move himself at all', elicits particular care; to him the 'orderlies were all kind', moving his bed outside to the shore of the Bosphorus, 'that the sea breeze might refresh him' (p. 149). As well as this general solicitude Taylor records the particular bond between one orderly, Dick, and the young patient:

> [Dick] was quite a character in his way—so rough and quaint; he looked as if he were just made to knock down a dozen Russians at once; but Dick was as kind to Algeo as if he had been his own child, and poor Algeo was so fond of him: it was strange to watch the affection between the rough, hard soldier and the dying boy. In the agony of death, just before he passed away, he called for Dick.
> 'Come here Dick; I want to kiss you, Dick.'
> And as Dick held him in his arms, the boy died.
> When the rough orderly told Sister _____ of it, the tears stood in his eyes. (p. 150)

The familial description, familiar throughout this book and also used to describe the particularly intense emotional connections formed in wartime nursing in Yonge's novel *The Young Stepmother*, registers the depth of Dick's feeling, also expressed in his tearful relation of this death. Although Taylor comments on the 'strange' experience of watching this affection, descriptions of orderlies showing feeling proliferate through the accounts left by women nurses. Taylor also recalls gentle teasing by orderlies of other young patients, including suggestions that they ask the lady nurse for sugar plums or plum pudding and that they should be at home with their mothers—'a bit of a chap like you ain't fit for such rough work' (p. 119)—and she gives an unusually detailed history of one orderly, Rooke, an eccentric, deeply saddened by news of the death of his wife, describing him as a 'capital nurse, full of rough kindness to the patients' (p. 120). Taylor also presents two men, Goody and N, as 'exceptions to the general rule concerning orderlies'. Goody is known for 'his willing spirit, his sobriety, industry and constant good humour; he was willing to help anybody, grumbling did not seem at all natural to him', and Taylor elaborates that 'they could be left and trusted very much. Their affection and attention to their patients were remarkable; they were as gentle as women' (p. 141). The simile is a typical one in efforts to describe manly gentleness, but the range of tender behaviour recorded, even of this class of men deemed brutal and careless by reputation, points to the redundancy of the gendered comparison.

The capacity of some orderlies for 'affection and attention' and 'rough kindness' has, however, been written out in existing histories. Cantlie, author of the most detailed history of Victorian army medicine, describes women nurses as 'trying to instil some degree of humanity in the rough and careless orderlies', and cites an extreme example at the opposite end of the scale from Algeo and Dick, of an orderly so desperate to get at his patient's money that he murders him.[43] The original account of the murderous, thieving orderly is from Terrot, whose reflections on the (in)coherence of the distinction she makes between exemplary patient nurses and brutal orderlies is discussed earlier in this chapter. While Terrot is generally critical of orderly care, her account is more mixed than Cantlie's selections suggest, and does include instances of humane orderlies, such as the heavy-handed but 'good-natured, patient, and attentive' ploughboy (p. 121) and the 'Flamingo': 'One especially (whom we called the Flamingo, from his brilliant red hair, moustache, and beard, which hung down over his chest) used to watch for us with anxiety and introduce us to the cases he thought required most attention' (p. 97).[44] Goodman also finds a balance between recording problems with orderlies' stealing and unreliability and instances throughout of orderlies fetching her in time to the bedsides of the dying. Counter to the typical representation of orderlies as needing careful scrutiny, she also gives examples of soldier nurses such as 'Black Tom' 'coming to the rescue' with practical solutions to problems (p. 164).

Sister Aloysius Doyle, one of the Catholic Sisters of Mercy, provides a particularly sympathetic account of the working conditions for orderlies and the resultant problems. She acknowledges that 'as a rule, the orderlies drink freely, when they can get it, to drown grief, they say. I must say their position is a very hard one. Their work is increasing and such work, death around them on every side, their own lives in continual danger; it is almost for them a continuation of the field of battle'.[45] As well as seeking to explain the reasons behind the stereotypical image of the drunken orderly, Sister Doyle's journal of her time at various Crimean hospitals shows the close relationships formed between orderlies and others working in the hospital, and the care that some of these deputed soldiers took in their work. Doyle describes, for instance, the distress of an orderly officer when an orderly he had worked closely with succumbs to cholera, and the risk taken by this officer in attending him: 'so devoted was his master that he came in every half hour to see him, and stood over him in the bed as if it was only a cold he had' (p. 22). She also transcribes a poem written by an orderly, after the death of another nurse in the group, Sister Winifred, and attached to the cross over her grave. It celebrates the sister as 'an angel of mercy' who left her home 'to bring to the soldiers sweet comfort and rest'

---

[43] Cantlie, *History*, vol. 2, pp. 124–5.
[44] Taylor records a similar incident of an orderly begging beef tea from the nurse with a 'tone of entreaty' for a particularly weak patient, as 'some of that stuff would do him good' (p. 45).
[45] *The Crimean Journals of the Sisters of Mercy*, p. 22.

(p. 40). The poem expresses the particularly difficult feeling of mourning in the midst of warfare, and the orderly's attachment of the manuscript to the cross marking the sister's grave is both recognition of her sacrifice and part of his work of bereavement. Mother Bridgeman notes in her own transcription of the poem that it is more notable for the 'circumstances under which it was found and the feeling it expresses' than for its formal properties, 'the metre, etc, is not the most faultless' (p. 244). The poem does display, though, a creative connection between form and content, echoing the shape of the cross to which it was attached in four stanzas of four lines. Like the memorials for Lempriere produced by men of the ranks, this poem is another response to the pain of loss offering further evidence for the emotional articulacy of regular soldiers.

Soldier orderlies, as well as patients, also creatively expressed feeling and relieved the monotony of hospital life through art and craft. Taylor includes a description of a ward where patients and orderlies are engaged in a range of handiwork and art:

> Some of the men were very clever at needlework and hemmed dozens of pocket-handkerchiefs and towels to be given to the invalids when going to England, or those going up again to the camp. They also mended hundreds of the blue jackets and trousers, the hospital outerclothing. There was one man six feet two high; he had been wounded in the foot, and was unable to put it to the ground for a long time: he made a dress for an officer's wife in the Crimea and made besides about thirty or forty sets of mosquito curtains. (p. 131)[46]

The production of practical necessities, which would be instituted in convalescent workshops by the First World War, is augmented by more elaborate and personal work, like the dress for an officer's wife. 'In this ward, too', Taylor records, 'was an orderly, who embroidered a pin cushion with beads, and it was really beautifully done; he gave it to the lady of his ward as a token of his gratitude' (p. 132). This 'beautiful' embroidered and beaded pincushion, made to register a particular feeling (albeit one, 'gratitude', identified in line with Taylor's ideology of women's improving influence), is indicative of the non-verbal, tactile ways in which soldiers also expressed themselves. The careful handicraft points to a wider range of experiences of touch than those typically imagined for the military man, many of whom (as also seen in the previous chapter) worked closely with textiles as well as with weaponry.

---

[46] Terrot also details the needlework of Scutari patients, including the dying young soldier Joe Martin: 'He was very fond of sewing, patching, etc., and used to show me his performances with childlike pleasure', p. 121.

A typical soldier's tactile experience also included, as outlined in chapter 3, the physical labour of homemaking, shopping, and cooking, and accounts of the Crimean War frequently comment in approving terms on the capacity of regular soldiers for domestic work. Soldiers deputed to orderly and fatigue duties had a particular remit in these areas. The diaries kept by the Sisters of Mercy detail orderlies and soldiers seconded for short-term help, taking pride in their domestic duties at Balaclava hospital and striving for more effective handiwork. Sister Doyle describes how she managed the kitchen with the help of 'three first class orderlies; besides a party of what are called fatigue men who come down every day from the "front" and are distributed wherever they are required':

> They were really anxious to do everything that could give us pleasure. They used to take great pleasure in having the kitchens very clean. One morning, when I went to see after the breakfast, I said, 'Really, Tom, the kitchen is beautifully clean.' 'Yes Ma'am, and we have the milk made as well.' Another day I was making some jelly and one of my orderlies said, 'Will you let me do it Ma'am?' He knew how anxious I was to have it clear, and it seemed to be his whole anxiety to succeed. When he had finished, he brought a tray of shapes, and I said, 'Really William, it's beautiful, I could not do it better myself.' 'Oh no, Ma'am it's not clear, not like the way you do. The boys could never do anything as neat as you.' This poor fellow was a big dragoon of six feet five. (p. 35)

Sister Doyle's emphasis on the commanding physicality of this soldier seems to register an incongruity with the dextrous, delicate work of handmaking 'beautiful' jelly, similar to Taylor's detailing of the height, six feet two, of the man who made a dress for an officer's wife. William's painstaking work to clarify the jelly for the nursing sister's pleasure resonates with Taylor's account of the effort made by an orderly in producing the 'beautiful' pincushion gift for 'his nurse'. Croke reports in her characteristically more caustic tone that 'it is most amusing just now to see three Royal Artillery peeling potatoes for the Sister of Mercy's dinner. They appeared as much in earnest as if they were besieging Sebastopol and had quite a military air' (p. 99). This commingling of martial and domestic qualities, the hallmark combination of the Victorian soldier hero, could cause some disquiet as well as humour. As Doyle puts it:

> Our fatigue men were from the cavalry regiments. They looked so respectable, I often felt a little delicate at asking them to do any dirty work. I gave one poor fellow a brush, soap and water and asked him if he would be kind enough to wash the kitchen table. He took off his coat and set to work. The table was long, and he commenced at the top and gave one rub to the bottom. I said 'Perhaps if you did not take such a long rub it might be

better.' 'Anything at all Ma'am, you tell me to do and I will do my best at it.' An officer came every evening to collect his men and he generally said, 'I hope Sister, you have no complaint to make.' We never had any. Very often these men had to go the same night to the trenches, or other places of danger. (p. 37)

Despite Doyle's feeling of delicacy, the learning of new domestic skills was a typical part of campaigning. Soldiers' aptitude for housework, craftwork, and the work of mourning combined with the development of nursing skills by those informally attending wounded colleagues or working as orderlies to make for a thorough overlapping of labour supposedly divided by gender.

Taylor names the three 'first class orderlies' who assist Sister M A[loysius]: 'James Brazil, of the 50th, Thomas Brennan of the 4th, and Peter McLoughlin, of the 14th Regiments'. She confirms their effectiveness, and their efforts to please and solicitude for the sisters: 'They all worked well together, and never was there a dispute among them; they vied with each other in gratitude and respect for the sisters. Often when a sister would be busying herself in the kitchen, an orderly would say, "Musha, Miss you'll kill yourself—let me do it"' (p. 319).[47] In testimony to the close relationships established with these long-term orderlies, the sisters' journals each record the distress expressed by these three men on their departure from the Crimea. As Croke put it, 'they were breaking their hearts, God bless them! Poor fellows, we owed them much of the little personal comfort we had' (p. 109).

These accounts challenge the conventional history that orderlies were the dregs of their regiments, 'bad characters with long crime sheets', as Dr Menzies put it, or as an officer described it to Goodman, 'invariably the worst men of their respective regiments who were found, to use his words, "Skulking in hospitals as orderlies, or in offices of that description, and therefore he hoped none considered the orderlies fair specimens of the English soldier"' (p. 142). In a parallel with Hunt's concern that a dedicated corps of carers might be 'disrespected for not joining in the fight', Terrot suggests that 'the orderlies felt themselves degraded at being in the comparative safety and comfort of the hospital instead of sharing the dangers and hardships of their comrades before Sebastopol' (p. 97). Elsewhere, however, she acknowledges the high risk and mortality rate of their work as many hospital staff contracted cholera and other fevers: 'The poor

---

[47] Taylor reserves particular praise for Brazil: 'He was ever at work, and apparently never tired—had always a pleasant, cheerful word for everyone; to overcome any difficulty was his determination, and his delight was to make matters easy for those with whom he worked', p. 320.

orderlies had little chance of escape. Confined to the crowded wards day and night, employed in carrying away the dead and in all the most trying parts of nursing' (p. 155). Hedley Vicars mourns a man of his regiment who contracted cholera in this way: 'Last night poor S_____ of my company, a fine, powerful young man, was admitted into hospital, he had been an orderly attending on cholera patients, and had therefore seen many die.'[48] Vicars's description of this 'fine, powerful young man' contradicts the typical narrative of orderlies as refuse of the regiment. The formal service history of Peter McLoughlin of the 14th Regiment, one of the men named by Taylor as an orderly at the general hospital, Balaclava, also suggests a different history. The regiment's muster rolls show that McLoughlin performed sustained service at the general hospital from April 1855 to March 1856, a year of work during which he acquired some skill in hospital duties, as the women nurses' approving reports attest.[49] He had no record of poor conduct, and while he was not in receipt of good conduct pay, one of the few men in the regiment who was, Benjamin Churchett, was also absent for the muster of June 1855 'attending the sick', and he received free rations for twenty-six days while working as a hospital orderly. Indeed, a large number of men of the 14th were sent on command as orderlies to the general hospital during this year, while others were listed as working as 'hospital fatigue' men, the term Sister Doyle uses for the soldiers who helped her in the hospital kitchen.

The gap between the received history of military orderly brutality and the wide cultural celebration of gentle soldiers shows the ways in which ideals of military masculinity are historically shaped, contingent on, particularly, military and political structures, as well as on broader attitudes towards gender and class. Narratives of voluntary acts of gentle heroism in wartime, including a self-sacrificing treatment of the wounded, were culturally important and continue to be so. The popularity of these narratives in the Crimean War period can be seen as part of Britain's coming to terms with its first major war in decades, a newly mechanized conflict which anticipated the far-reaching destruction and sense of loss and alienation usually associated with the First World War. They also, as we have seen, participate in debates about military and political reform that consider the social contribution of the working-class man, his well-being, and agency, and ultimately his enfranchisement. While individual acts of care by soldiers of the ranks were celebrated in fiction and first-hand accounts—Yonge's Leon, for example, or the anonymous soldier whose expression of brotherly grief for Lempriere in poetry was

---

[48] Marsh, *Memorials*, pp. 167–8.   [49] TNA, WO 12/3172.

proudly included in the Lempriere family album—the collective heroism attributed to working men of 'the thin red line' was firmly restricted to combat. Any idea of the heroism of the same soldiers risking their lives in cholera epidemics while fulfilling their duties as orderlies in military hospitals had no cultural purchase.

The national shame produced by the insufficiencies of army medicine combined with gendered and classed ideals of women as curative, ministering angels to invalidate soldiers' work in military hospitals. Civilian concerns about the physical well-being of soldiers and the possibility of a more humanitarian waging of war were met by a large-scale, institutionalized reparative effort by the formation of organizations like the RAMC and the Red Cross. These organizations also, paradoxically, allowed the horror of mass wounding—the bodily damage that made them necessary—to slip back out of view, as injuring as the core activity of war was replaced by ameliorative narratives of healing. In making the physical cost of war more acceptable and therefore allowing the continuation of war, these organizations magnify the culturally reparative effects of the figures of the Christian soldier, liberal warrior, soldier as social worker, nursing, and fathering soldier explored in this book. All, considered through a paranoid/reparative approach, share the dual effect of endorsing the value of humanitarianism while legitimating the wars that create the need for it. A cultural emphasis on the military man of feeling has competing effects, calling into question the valuing of aggression, and potentially of war itself, at the same time as making war acceptable. While this book as a whole has shown the cultural significance of narratives of reparative soldiering, this chapter complicates its trajectory by showing that not all acts of emotional or physical care were included in those narratives. It offers a recuperative history of the felt experience of working-class soldier orderlies, men like Peter McLoughlin, the Flamingo, William, and Dick.

Afterword

The Ballad of the Boy Captain

As a culmination of this research I had the great privilege to work with the year 5 and 6 students (ages nine to eleven) of Chawton and Selborne primary schools, the two schools closest to Audley Lempriere's home, to produce two original folk ballads recalling Lempriere's life and death. With project partners Hampshire Music Service, National Army Museum, and Hampshire Record Office, the students explored Lempriere's biography, detailed in chapter 4. Like this book, we focused on the felt history, emotional and tactile, of the Crimean War, and on the ways in which war narratives are revised and retold. The project aimed to extend the reach of this research, changing ideas about masculinity and war beyond the academy, thinking afresh about how to study combat, and alerting young people to the wealth of material they could explore in local and national archives. The project built upon the book's key findings about the emotional articulacy of the Victorian soldier, the thorough overlapping of military and civilian spheres, particularly through soldiers' creative efforts to share their war experience with those at home, and Victorian culture's privileging of the figure of the military man of feeling and of narratives that reroute injuring into forms of care. The project also endeavoured to test the value and limits of the approach to emotional military history documented in this book, and to consider, from a position of concerned scepticism about the political affirmations incorporated in much commemoration of war, which forms of memorial and afterlife are appropriate for military narratives. The ballads' performance brought together local historians, military historians, the press, and a broader interested public, and recordings and transcriptions of the work contribute to Lempriere's lasting legacy as part of the archive at Hampshire Record Office (HRO AV1556).

NAM's handling collection provided visceral experiences of heavy uniforms, scratchy blankets, impractically shaped knapsacks with chafing leather strapping, and wooden water bottles that when frozen had to be warmed next to the body. The students also considered the material Lempriere sent home to his sister, discussed in chapter 5. They had insightful responses to his sketches—'he makes it look nice, not scary, homely'—and the small objects particularly caught their curiosity. The scrap of medal ribbon provoked questions including 'was it part of a flag or uniform?', as did the purplish-red coloured petals from his grave—'was it blood on the page?', 'how did the flowers survive so long?' Students' highlights featured this tactile learning: 'Holding the objects' and feeling 'how uncomfortable war is when your [sic] fighting and when your terrified about what will happen'. We then looked at accounts of Egerton's response to Lempriere's death, something students also found memorable. The creation of family-like relationships between soldiers, central to this book's documenting of shared emotional structures between regiment and home, also resonated. One student recalled as her or his personal high point of the project: 'how he [Egerton] said when he was saving the boy "my child" when they weren't related'.

In a follow-up session we visited Hampshire Record Office, and the students gained insight into the process of archiving and preservation. They were especially engaged by the age, extent—'8 miles of shelving!'—and fragility of the records. One recorded as a highlight 'the way they repair all those documents. I couldn't believe how thin the Japanese tissue was. It felt like cobwebs.' Having thought about our own experience of touching part of this past—the textures of the documents, the difficulty or for some surprising ease of reading old handwriting, the sometimes disconcerting feeling of somehow connecting with the dead writer by holding their papers—we then worked directly with some of Lempriere's letters. In this context the small mementos selected by soldiers and sent home proved especially thought provoking, and were to feature in Selborne's ballad. A group transcribing Lempriere's letter to his sister Ellen in which he sends the Russian ribbon home suddenly recognized the connection: 'It was a birthday gift!' Others working on Lempriere's account of the Battle of Alma were not sure how he might have felt when sending it. They teased out the combination of emotions described, his triumph at the artillery 'playing into' the enemy, his distress in the aftermath, the awfulness of seeing the dead including men who had been his friends. The group noted the recurrence of the term 'melancholy', a word they found haunting and used in the writing of their ballad. Others looked at Aunt Caroline's account of Lempriere's pony Cherub, alongside another family album produced by the relatives of Colonel Norcote, with sketches of Norcote weeping over his injured horse Inky Boy, and a carefully preserved scrap of Inky Boy's tail. Possibly inspired also by Michael Morpurgo's *War Horse* (1982, itself poised between expressing

Afterword

and recuperating the horror of war and war loss), Chawton chose to tell their ballad from Cherub's perspective, using a traditional folk refrain, 'Oh poor old horse':

> **Chorus**: It's a lonely way along the track
> And I'm so melancholy
> Oh I wish my master was on my back
> Oh poor old horse

Working with Paul Sartin and Benji Kirkpatrick, members of the folk band Bellowhead, the students considered a history of military ballads. This rich tradition combines the patriotic excitement and promise of adventure in following the drum with laments for those left behind and for the perilous life of the departing soldier. They wrote and then performed their own ballads in front of the commemorative stone installed by Lempriere's family at St Mary's Church, Newton Valence, and an appreciative audience. We spoke about this layering of memorial and the forms of afterlife that continue Lempriere's biography, which does not end with the fatal shot in the rifle pits, with Colonel Egerton's lifting of the little body, with the black-edged letters and newspaper accounts, with his burial and grave in the cemetery of the 77th in the Crimea, with smooth marble in the family's church, nor with this book, nor, we hope, with the students' ballads, now recorded and archived with Lempriere's family papers.

The attempt to comprehend the feelings of Lempriere, his fellow soldiers, his family, and even his pony, left us with many questions unanswered; sometimes it was impossible to identify emotions or motivations not explicit in the written and material evidence. The project's emphasis on felt history—the sensory and affective experiences of those involved in the Crimean War and our own emotional and tactile interaction with the archive—did, however, lead to an understanding of the competing, contradictory emotions produced by war. This characterized students' responses to a final reflective activity in which they considered how British soldiers in the Crimea felt about their families, comrades, and the enemy. The last category produced the widest range of response, covering 'fear', 'anger', 'sadness', 'respect', 'they are the same as me', 'I could be friends with them after the war', feeling 'quite guilty to shoot' them, 'horrified', 'nervous', or 'annoyed'. As one student summed up: 'I feel like there would be different feelings towards the enemy. On one level, you would dislike them and want to kill them, but on another level there would be some respect and kindness because they are fellow soldiers.' Far from glorifying war, or finding in Lempriere an exemplary hero, the ballads proffer what I found a deeply moving account of the mixed 'different feelings' that war generates, particularly vulnerability and mourning. This emphasis on the competing emotions generated by various Lempriere memorial narratives continued the book's interest in contradictory affects, and in tracing the precedence of reparative affects in culturally preferred narratives of gentle soldiering. In the project I kept the same wary eye on the politically ameliorative effects of work invested in finding rectitude in war. The ballads are a practical, creative extension of the forms of salvage work explored in the book; as collaborative productions pieced from a material culture of war purposely shared by soldiers and civilians they take their place alongside mourning albums, regimental marches scored for family ensemble, and military patchworks.

I'd like to give the final word to Ellen Lempriere, as imagined by Selborne School:

> Chorus. Goodbye, goodbye boy captain, When shall we meet again?
> I'll miss you as a sister, and I'll miss you as a friend.
>
> v1. My name is Ellen Lempriere, my story I shall tell
> About my brother Audley, at Sebastopol he fell.
> Two brothers and two sisters, from Newton Valence came
> We rode and played together in happy childhood games.
>
> v2. Then Audley joined the army and he got the call to go
> He'll fight for Queen and Country, he has gone to fight the foe
> 'It's time to say goodbye', he said, 'We're travelling overseas,
> And with my best horse Cherub, it's time for me to leave'.
>
> v3. 'Dear Sister, Happy Birthday' my Audley wrote to me,
> 'I hope you like this ribbon that I sent from overseas'.
> The thought of him away from home is one I cannot bear
> I'll cherish all his sketches and the lock of Cherub's hair
>
> v4. The soldiers' coats got lost at sea so they were cold and bare
> They froze and starved in misery with lice all in their hair
> Some soldiers died of frostbite upon the blood-stained snow
> The warning of their comrades, 'Be careful where you go!'
>
> v5. Then Audley met with Egerton and he was very tall
> So they became the best of friends though Audley was so small
> He called him 'My Boy Captain' and helped him stay the course
> Through cold and bitter weather with Cherub, his pet horse
>
> v6. Bang, the gun shot sounded, the bullet pierced his heart
> Egerton knelt beside him and came to play his part
> Lifting him off the blood-soaked ground he carried him from harm
> Then Egerton met the same cruel fate and both the men lay calm.
>
> v7. A black-edged letter through the post it broke my heart to see
> For it was then I realised how much he meant to me
> Now all that I have left of him, to comfort my despair
> Are his sketches, letters, ribbon, and a lock of Cherub's hair.
>
> Final chorus. Goodbye, goodbye boy captain. We'll never meet again
> I'll love you as a sister and I'll love you 'till the end.

Bibliography

Adams, James Eli, *Dandies and Desert Saints: Styles of Victorian Masculinity* (Ithaca and London: Cornell University Press, 1995).
Adams, James Eli, *A History of Victorian Literature* (Oxford: Wiley-Blackwell, 2009).
Alison, Archibald, *History of Europe*, 10 vols, 1833–4, vol. 8 (Edinburgh: Blackwood, 1840).
Ambrose, Stephen, *Band of Brothers: E Company, 506th Regiment, 101st Airborne: From Normandy to Hitler's Eagle's Nest* (New York: Simon and Schuster, 1992).
Anderson, Olive, *A Liberal State at War: English Politics and Economics during the Crimean War* (London: Macmillan, 1967).
Anderson, Olive, 'The Growth of Christian Militarism in Mid-Victorian Britain', *English Historical Review* 86 (1971), pp. 46–72.
Andrew, Donna T., 'The Code of Honour and its Critics: The Opposition to Duelling in England, 1700–1850', *Social History* 5.3 (1980), pp. 409–34.
Anon., *The Queen's Regulations and Orders for the Army, 1844 (-54)* (London: Parker, Furnival and Parker, 1844).
Anon., 'Sentimentalism', *Critic* 6 (December 1847).
Anon., *The Military Obituary, 1855* (London: Parker, Furnivals and Parker, 1855).
Anon., 'Narrative of Parliament and Politics', *The Household Narrative of Current Events*, vol. 6, no. 5 (May 1855), pp. 97–110.
Anon., *The War, or Voices from the Ranks* (London and New York: Routledge and Co., 1855).
Anon., *Soldiership and Christianity* (London: Ward and Co., 1858).
Anon., *Naval and Military Records of Rugbeians* (London: Simpkin, 1864).
Ashton, Owen, 'Henrietta Eliza Vaughn Stannard', in *Oxford Dictionary of National Biography* (Oxford: Oxford University Press, 2004).
Bailey, Philip James, *The Age: A Colloquial Satire* (London: Chapman and Hall, 1858).
Bainbridge, Simon, 'Of War and Taking Towns: Byron's Siege Poems', in *Romantic Wars: Studies in Culture and Conflict, 1793–1822*, ed. Philip Shaw (Aldershot: Ashgate, 2000), pp. 161–84.
Baldwin Weddle, Meredith, *Walking in the Way of Peace: Quaker Pacifism in the Seventeenth Century* (Oxford: Oxford University Press, 2001).
Barker Benfield, G. J., *The Culture of Sensibility: Sex and Society in Eighteenth Century Britain* (Chicago: University of Chicago Press, 1992).
Barlow, Paul, *Time Present and Time Past: The Art of John Everett Millais* (Aldershot: Ashgate, 2005).
Bates, Rachel, 'Curating the Crimea: The Cultural Afterlife of a Conflict', PhD thesis, University of Leicester, 2015.
Bates, Rachel, Holly Furneaux, and Alastair Massie, eds, 'Charting the Crimean War: Contexts, Nationhood, Afterlives', *19: Interdisciplinary Perspectives on the Long Nineteenth Century* 20 (2015).

Bell, George, *Soldier's Glory, being Rough Notes of an Old Soldier* (London: G. Bell and Sons Ltd, 1956).
Bevis, Matthew, 'Fighting Talk: Victorian War Poetry', in *British and Irish War Poetry*, ed. Tim Kendall (Oxford: Oxford University Press, 2007), pp. 7–33.
Bourke, Joanna, *Dismembering the Male: Men's Bodies, Britain and the Great War* (London: Reaktion, 1996).
Bourke, Joanna, *An Intimate History of Killing: Face to Face Killing in Twentieth Century Warfare* (London: Granta, 1999).
Bourke, Joanna, *Wounding the World: How Military Violence and War Play Invade Our Lives* (London: Virago, 2014).
Bowden, Peter, Alan Guy, and Marion Harding, eds, *Ashes and Blood: The British Army in South Africa, 1795–1914* (London: National Army Museum, 1999).
Boyden, Peter, *Tommy Atkins' Letters: The History of the British Army Postal Service from 1795* (London: National Army Museum, 1990).
Brantlinger, Patrick, *Rule of Darkness: British Literature and Imperialism, 1830–1914* (Ithaca and London: Cornell University Press, 1988).
Breward, Christopher, *Quilts, 1700–2010: Hidden Histories, Untold Stories* (London: V&A Publishing, 2010).
Bristow, Joseph, *Empire Boys: Adventures in a Man's World* (London: Harper Collins, 1991).
Broughton, Trev, 'The Life and Afterlives of Captain Hedley Vicars: Evangelical Biography and the Crimean War', *19: Interdisciplinary Studies in the Long Nineteenth Century* 20 (2015).
Broughton, Trev Lynn and Helen Rogers, eds, *Gender and Fatherhood in the Nineteenth Century* (Basingstoke: Palgrave, 2007).
Brown, Michael, '"Like a Devoted Army": Medicine, Heroic Masculinity, and the Military Paradigm in Victorian Britain', *Journal of British Studies* 49.3 (2010), pp. 592–622.
Brownlie, Ian, 'Thoughts on Kind-Hearted Gunmen', in *Humanitarian Intervention and the United Nations*, ed. Richard B. Lillich (Charlottesville: University Press of Virginia, 1973), pp. 139–48.
Bruce, Anthony, *The Purchase System in the British Army, 1660–1871* (London: Royal Historical Society, 1980).
Burdett, Carolyn, 'Introduction, Sentimentalities', New Agenda section, *Journal of Victorian Culture* 16.2 (2011), pp. 187–94.
Butler, Judith, *Gender Trouble: Feminism and the Subversion of Identity* (London: Routledge, 1990).
Butler, Judith, *Precarious Life: The Power of Mourning and Violence* (London and New York: Verso, 2004).
Butler, Judith, *Frames of War: When is Life Grievable?* (London and New York: Verso, 2009).
Byron, George Gordon, 'Don Juan', in *The Major Works* (Oxford: Oxford University Press, 2000).
Cantlie, Neil, *A History of the Army Medical Department*, 2 vols (Edinburgh and London: Churchill Livingstone, 1974).

Carden-Coyne, Ana, 'Soldiers' Bodies in the War Machine', in *War and Medicine* (London: Black Dog Publishing, 2008), pp. 66–83.

Carlton, Charles, *Going to the Wars: The Experience of the British Civil Wars, 1638–1651* (London: Routledge, 1992).

Cave, Terence, *Mignon's Afterlives: Crossing Cultures from Goethe to the Twenty-First Century* (Oxford: Oxford University Press, 2011).

Ceadel, Martin, *Semi-Detached Idealists: The British Peace Movement and International Relations, 1854–1945* (Oxford: Oxford University Press, 2000).

Clemm, Sabine, *Dickens, Journalism and Nationhood: Mapping the World in Household Words* (London and New York: Routledge, 2009).

Cockburn, Cynthia, 'Gender Relations as Causal in Militarism and War: A Feminist Standpoint', in *Making Gender: Making War: Violence, Military and Peacekeeping Practices*, ed. Annica Kronsell and Erika Svedberg (London: Routledge, 2012), pp. 19–34.

Cockburn, Cynthia and Meliha Hubic, 'Gender and the Peacekeeping Military: A View from Bosnian Women's Organizations', in *The Postwar Moment: Militaries, Masculinities and International Peacekeeping*, ed. Cynthia Cockburn and Dubravka Zarkov (London: Lawrence & Wishart, 2012), pp. 103–21.

Cockerill, A. W., *Sons of the Brave: The Story of Boy Soldiers* (London: Len Cooper, 1984).

Colby, Robert, *Thackeray's Canvass of Humanity: An Author and His Public* (Columbus: Ohio State University Press, 1979).

Cole, Sarah, 'Enchantment, Disenchantment, War, Literature', *PMLA* 124.5 (2009), pp. 1632–47.

Coleridge, Christabel, *Charlotte Mary Yonge: Her Life and Letters* (London: Macmillan, 1903).

Colley, Linda, *Britons: Forging the Nation, 1707–1837* (London: Pimlico, 1992).

Collini, Stefan, *Public Moralists: Political Thought and Intellectual Life in Britain, 1850–1930* (Oxford: Clarendon Press, 1991).

Collins, Philip, *From Manly Tear to Stiff Upper Lip: The Victorians and Pathos* (Wellington, New Zealand: Victoria University Press, undated, based on a 1974 lecture).

Collins, T. F. J., 'The 19th Regiment at Drill, Chobham Camp, 1853', *Journal of the Society for Army Historical Research* 47 (1969), pp. 192–3.

Cooper Hodge, Edward, *Little Hodge: Being Extracts from the Diaries and Letters of Colonel Edward Cooper Hodge Written during the Crimean War, 1854–1856*, ed. Marquess of Anglesey (London: Leo Cooper, 1971).

Craik, Dinah, *A Life for a Life* (New York: Carleton, 1856).

Damousi, Joy, *The Labour of Loss: Mourning, Memory and Wartime Bereavement in Australia* (Cambridge: Cambridge University Press, 1999).

Das, Santanu, *Touch and Intimacy in First World War Literature* (Cambridge: Cambridge University Press, 2005).

Das, Santanu, 'An Ecstasy of Fumbling: Gas Warfare, 1914–18 and the Uses of Affect', in *The Edinburgh Companion to Twentieth-Century British and American War Literature*, ed. Adam Piette and Mark Rawlinson (Edinburgh: Edinburgh University Press, 2012), pp. 396–405.

Davis, Elizabeth, *The Autobiography of Elizabeth Davis, A Balaclava Nurse*, ed. Jane Williams, 2 vols (London: Hurst and Blackett, 1857).

Dawson, Anthony, 'The French Army and British Army Crimean War Reforms', *19: Interdisciplinary Studies in the Long Nineteenth Century* 20 (2015).

Dawson, Graham, *Soldier Heroes: British Literature, Empire and the Imagining of Masculinities* (London and New York: Routledge, 1994).

De Quincey, Thomas, *The Works of Thomas De Quincey*, ed. Grevel Lindop et al., 21 vols (London: Pickering and Chatto, 2003), vol. 20.

Dereli, C., *A War Culture in Action: A Study of the Literature of the Crimean War Period* (Bern: Peter Lang, 2003).

di Bello, Patrizia, 'Mrs Birkbeck's Album: The Hand-Written and the Printed in Early Nineteenth-Century Feminine Culture', *19: Interdisciplinary Studies in the Long Nineteenth Century* 1 (2005), pp. 1–36.

Dickens, Charles, 'Our French Watering Place', *Household Words*, vol. 10, no. 241 (4 November 1854), pp. 265–70.

Dickens, Charles, 'The Seven Poor Travellers: The First', *Household Words*, vol. 10, Extra Christmas Number (25 December 1854), pp. 573–82.

Dickens, Charles, 'The Redeemed Profligate', *Harper's New Monthly Magazine*, vol. 10, no. 57 (February 1855), pp. 371–7.

Dickens, Charles, *The Life of Our Lord* (London: Associated Newspapers, 1934).

Dickens, Charles, *Bleak House* (London: Penguin, 1996).

Dickens, Charles, 'Somebody's Luggage', in *The Christmas Stories*, ed. Ruth Glancy (London: Dent, 1996).

Dickens, Charles, *The Seven Poor Travellers*, ed. Melisa Klimaszewski (London: Hesperus, 2010).

Dickens, Charles, *A Child's History of England* (London: Odhams, no date).

Dixon, Thomas, 'Forgotten Feelings: Our Emotional Past', *Huffington Post*, 1 October 2012, http://www.huffingtonpost.co.uk/thomas-dixon/british-stiff-upper-lip-our-emotional-past_b_1929511.html.

Dixon, Thomas, 'The Tears of Mr Justice Willes', *Journal of Victorian Culture* 17.1 (2012), pp. 1–23.

Drew, John M. L., *Dickens the Journalist* (Houndmills: Palgrave Macmillan, 2003).

Dudink, Stefan and Karen Hagemann, 'Masculinity in Politics and War in the Age of Democratic Revolutions, 1750–1850', in *Masculinities in Politics and War: Gendering Modern History*, ed. Stefan Dudink, Karen Hagemann, and John Tosh (Manchester: Manchester University Press, 2004), pp. 3–21.

Duncanson, Claire, *Forces for Good? Military Masculinities and Peacebuilding in Afghanistan and Iraq* (Basingstoke: Palgrave, 2013).

Edelman, Lee, *No Future: Queer Theory and the Death Drive* (Durham and London: Duke University Press, 2004).

Edgecombe, Rodney Stenning, *Leigh Hunt and the Poetry of Fancy* (Cranbury, NJ: Associated University Presses, 1994).
Edwards, Jason, *Eve Kosofsky Sedgwick* (London and New York: Routledge, 2009).
Ellison, Julie, *Cato's Tears and the Making of Anglo-American Emotion* (Chicago: University of Chicago Press, 1999).
Emerson, Gloria, 'Operation Babylift', *The New Republic*, 26 April 1975, pp. 8–10.
Emerson, Gloria, *Winners and Losers* (New York: Random House, 1976).
Faulkner, David, 'The Confidence Man: Empire and the Deconstruction of Muscular Christianity in *The Mystery of Edwin Drood*', in *Muscular Christianity: Embodying the Victorian Age*, ed. Donald Hall (Cambridge: Cambridge University Press, 1994), pp. 175–93.
Faust, Drew Gilpin, *This Republic of Suffering: Death and the American Civil War* (New York: Vintage, 2008).
Favret, Mary, 'Coming Home: The Public Spaces of Romantic War', *Studies in Romanticism* 33.4 (1994), pp. 539–48.
Favret, Mary, *War at a Distance: Romanticism and the Making of Modern Wartime* (Princeton: Princeton University Press, 2010).
Ferguson, Niall, *The Pity of War* (London: Penguin, 1998).
Fielding, K. J., ed., 'Administrative Reform Association, 27 June, 1855', in *The Speeches of Charles Dickens* (Oxford: Clarendon Press, 1960), pp. 197–208.
Fieldston, Sara, *Raising the World: Child Welfare in the American Century* (Cambridge, MA: Harvard University Press, 2015).
Figes, Orlando, *Crimea* (London: Penguin, 2010).
Fisher, Glenn, 'Thomas Walker 95th Regiment', *The War Correspondent, Journal of the Crimean War Research Society* 26.3 (2008), pp. 23–4.
Fisher, Glenn, ed., *Crimean Cavalry Letters* (Stroud: Army Records Society, 2011).
Forster, John, *Life of Dickens*, 3 vols (London: Chapman and Hall, 1874).
Furneaux, Holly, *Queer Dickens: Erotics, Families, Masculinities* (Oxford: Oxford University Press, 2009).
Furneaux, Holly, 'Negotiating the Gentle-Man: Male Nursing and Class Conflict in the "High" Victorian Period', in *Conflict and Difference in Nineteenth Century Literature*, ed. Dinah Birch and Mark Llewellyn (Basingstoke: Palgrave, 2010), pp. 109–25.
Furneaux, Holly, 'Household Words and the Crimean War: Journalism, Fiction and Forms of Recuperation in Wartime', in *Charles Dickens and the Mid-Victorian Press*, ed. John Drew (Buckingham: University of Buckingham Press, 2013), pp. 245–60.
Furneaux, Rupert, *The First War Correspondent: William Howard Russell* (London: Cassell and Company Limited, 1944).
Füssel, Marian, 'Emotions in the Making: The Transformation of Battlefield Experiences during the Seven Years War (1756–1763)', paper given at Battlefield Emotions 1500–1850, Ghent, February 2014.
Gibbs, Philip, *Now it Can be Told* (New York: Harper, 1920).

Gilloi, Eva, *Monarchy, Myth and Material Culture in Germany, 1750–1950*, (Cambridge: Cambridge University Press, 2011).

Gilmour, Robin, *The Ideal of the Gentleman in the Victorian Novel* (London: Allen and Unwin, 1981).

Girouard, Mark, *The Return to Camelot: Chivalry and the English Gentleman* (Yale: Yale University Press, 1981).

Gleig, G. R., *Story of the Battle of Waterloo* (London: John Murray, 1847).

Goodman, Margaret, *An English Sister of Mercy* (London: Smith, Elder and Co, 1862).

Goodman, Margaret, *Experiences of an English Sister of Mercy* (London: Smith, Elder and Co, 1862).

Gordon, Stewart, *New Cambridge History of India: Marathas, 1600–1818* (Cambridge: Cambridge University Press, 1993).

Gregory, Derek, 'War and Peace', *Transactions of the Institute of British Geographers* 35 (2010), pp. 154–86.

Grenville Murray, Eustace Clare, 'Army Interpreters', *Household Words*, vol. X, no. 247 (16 December 1854), pp. 431–2.

Hack, Daniel, 'Wild Charges: The Afro-Haitian "Charge of the Light Brigade"', *Victorian Studies* 54.2 (2012), pp. 199–225.

Hall, Donald, *Fixing Patriarchy: Feminism and Mid-Victorian Male Novelists* (New York: New York University Press, 1997).

Hanson, Ingrid, *William Morris and the Uses of Violence, 1856–1890* (London: Anthem Press, 2013).

Harari, Yuval, *The Ultimate Experience: Battlefield Revelations and the Making of Modern War Culture, 1450–2000* (Basingstoke: Palgrave, 2008).

Hardy, Thomas, 'Drummer Hodge', in *The Collected Poems of Thomas Hardy* (Ware: Wordsworth, 1994).

Harrison, Mark, 'War and Medicine in the Modern Era', in *War and Medicine* (London: Black Dog Publishing, 2008), pp. 10–27.

Harrison, Simon, 'Skulls and Scientific Collecting in the Victorian Military: Keeping the Enemy Dead in British Frontier Warfare', *Comparative Studies in Society and History* 50.1 (2008), pp. 285–303.

Harrison, Simon, *Dark Trophies: Hunting and the Enemy Body in Modern War* (New York and Oxford: Berghahn, 2012).

Hayter, Alethea, *Charlotte Yonge* (Plymouth: Northcote House, 1996).

Hazlitt, William, *Sketches and Essays* (London: John Templeman, 1839, first published 1827).

Hetherington, Tim, *Infidel* (London: Chris Boot, 2010).

Hill, Katrina, 'Collecting on Campaign: British Soldiers in China during the Opium Wars', *Journal of the History of Collections* 25.2 (2013), pp. 227–52.

Ho, Tai Chun, 'Civilian Poets and Poetry of the Crimean Conflict: The War at Home', PhD thesis, University of York, 2015.

Hogg, James, 'The Adventures of Captain John Lochy', in *Altrive Tales* (Edinburgh: Edinburgh University Press, 2005), pp. 79–159.

Holden, Amanda, ed., *The New Penguin Opera Guide* (London: Penguin, 2001).

Holmes, Richard, *Soldiers* (London: Harper, 2011).
Homer, *The Iliad*, translated by E. V. Rieu (Oxford: Oxford University Press, 2003).
Houston, Natalie, 'Reading the Victorian Souvenir: Sonnets and Photographs of the Crimean War', *Yale Journal of Criticism* 14.2 (2001), pp. 353–83.
Hugo, Victor, *Ninety Three*, translated by Lowell Blair (New York: Bantam, 1962).
Hunt, Leigh, *Captain Sword and Captain Pen*, 3rd edn (London: Charles Gilpin, 1849).
Hutchings, Kimberly, 'Making Sense of Masculinity and War', *Men and Masculinities* 10.4 (2008), pp. 389–404.
Hutchinson, John, *Champions of Charity: War and the Rise of the Red Cross* (Boulder: Westview Press, 1996).
Kaplan, Fred, *Sacred Tears: Sentimentality in Victorian Literature* (Princeton: Princeton University Press, 1987).
Keegan, John, *The Face of Battle* (Pimlico: London, 2004).
Keller, Ulrich, *The Ultimate Spectacle: A Visual History of the Crimean War* (Amsterdam: Gordon and Breach, 2001).
Kennedy, Catriona, 'John Bull into Battle: Military Masculinity and the British Army Officer during the Napoleonic Wars', in *Gender, War and Politics: Transatlantic Perspectives, 1775–1830*, ed. Karen Hagerman, Giselda Mettele, and Jane Rendall (Basingstoke: Palgrave, 2010), pp. 127–46.
Kennedy, Catriona and Matthew McCormack, 'New Histories of Soldiering', in *Soldiering in Britain and Ireland, 1750–1850: Men of Arms*, ed. Catriona Kennedy and Matthew McCormack (Basingstoke: Palgrave, 2013), pp. 1–14.
Kenny, Ruth, Jeff McMillan, and Martin Myrone, *British Folk Art* (London: Tate, 2014).
Kerr, Paul, *The Crimean War* (London: Boxtree, 1997).
Kimball, Jane, *Trench Art: An Illustrated History* (Davis, CA: Silverpenny Press, 2004).
Kinglake, Alexander, *Invasion of the Crimea*, 8 vols (Edinburgh: Blackwood, 1863–88).
Kingsley, Charles, 'Brave Words for Brave Soldiers and Sailors', collected in *True Words for Brave Men* (London: Kegan Paul, 1885).
Kingsley, Charles, *Two Years Ago* (London: Macmillan, 1889).
Kingsley, Charles, *Hereward the Wake* (London: Macmillan, 1895).
Kingsley, Charles, *Yeast: A Problem* (London: Everyman, 1976).
Kingsley, Charles, *Westward Ho!* (Edinburgh: Birlinn, 2009).
Knightley, Phillip, *The First Casualty: The War Correspondent as Hero and Myth-Maker from the Crimea to Iraq* (London: Andre Deutsch, 2003).
Knott, Sarah, 'Sensibility and the American War for Independence', *American Historical Review* 10.9 (2004), pp. 19–41.
Kovitz, Marcia, 'The Roots of Military Masculinity', in *Military Masculinities: Identity and the State*, ed. Paul Highgate (Westport: Praeger, 2003), pp. 1–14.
Lalumia, Matthew, *Realism and Politics in Victorian Art of the Crimean War* (Michigan: UMI Research Press, 1984).

Lawrence, G. A., *Sword and Gown* (Teddington, Middx: Echo Library, 2007).
Lawrence, George, *Guy Livingstone, or Thorough* (London: The Daily Telegraph, no date).
Ledger, Sally, '"Don't be so melodramatic!" Dickens and the Affective Mode', *19: Interdisciplinary Studies in the Long Nineteenth Century* 4 (2007), pp. 1–13.
Ledger, Sally, 'Christmas', in *Charles Dickens in Context*, ed. Sally Ledger and Holly Furneaux (Cambridge: Cambridge University Press, 2011), pp. 178–93.
Lee, Louise, 'Deity in Dispatches: The Crimean Beginnings of Muscular Christianity', in Mark Knight and Louise Lee, eds, *Religion, Literature and the Imagination: Sacred Worlds* (London: Continuum, 2009), pp. 57–74.
Luddy, Maria, ed., *The Crimean Journals of the Sisters of Mercy, 1854–6* (Portland, OR: Four Courts Press, 2004).
Lund, Michael, *Reading Thackeray* (Detroit: Wayne State University Press, 1988).
Lynn, Eliza, 'The True Story of the Nuns at Minsk', in *Household Words*, vol. 9, no. 216 (13 May 1854), pp. 290–5.
Mackenzie, Henry, 'The Effects of Religion on a Mind of Sensibility', *The Mirror*, 19 June 1779.
McLoughlin, Kate, *Authoring War: The Literary Representation of War from the Iliad to Iraq* (Cambridge: Cambridge University Press, 2011).
MacMaster, R. D. 'Composition, Publication and Reception', in W. M. Thackeray, *The Newcomes*, ed. Peter Shillingsburg (Michigan: University of Michigan Press, 1996), pp. 371–90.
Markovits, Stefanie, *The Crimean War in the British Imagination* (Cambridge: Cambridge University Press, 2009).
Markwick, Margaret, *New Men in Trollope's Novels: Rewriting the Victorian Male* (Ashgate: Aldershot, 2007).
Marsh, Catherine, ed., *Memorials of Captain Hedley Vicars* (New York: Robert Carter and Brothers, 1857).
Martin, Brian Joseph, *Napoleonic Friendship: Military Fraternity, Intimacy and Sexuality in Nineteenth Century France* (Durham, NH: University of New Hampshire Press, 2011).
Martin, Robert Bernard, *The Dust of Combat: A Life of Charles Kingsley* (London: Faber and Faber, 1959).
Martineau, Harriet and James Payn, 'The Rampshire Militia', *Household Words*, vol. 10, no. 251 (13 January 1855), pp. 505–11.
Massie, Alastair, ed., *A Most Desperate Undertaking: The National Army Museum Book of the Crimean War* (London: The National Army Museum, 2003).
Massie, Alastair, *The National Army Museum Book of the Crimean War: The Untold Stories* (Basingstoke: Macmillan, 2005).
Meyer, Jessica, *Men of War: Masculinity in the First World War in Britain* (Basingstoke: Palgrave, 2009).
Miles, A. E. W., *The Accidental Birth of Military Medicine: The Origins of the Royal Army Medical Corps* (London: Civic Books, 2009).
Moore, Grace, *Dickens and Empire: Discourses of Class, Race and Colonialism in the Works of Charles Dickens* (Aldershot: Ashgate, 2004).

Mullan, John, *Sentiment and Sociability: The Language of Feeling in the Eighteenth Century* (Oxford: Oxford University Press, 1988).

Mullan, John, 'Sentimental Novels', in *The Cambridge Companion to the Eighteenth Century Novel*, ed. John Richetti (Cambridge: Cambridge University Press, 1996), pp. 236–54.

Murphy, Sharon, 'Imperial Reading? The East India Company's Lending Libraries for Soldiers, c. 1819–1834', *Book History* 12 (2009), pp. 74–99.

Murphy, Sharon, '"Quite Incapable of Appreciating Books Written for Educated Readers": The Mid-Nineteenth Century British Soldier', in *A Return to the Common Reader: Print Culture and the Novel, 1850–1900*, ed. Beth Palmer and Adelene Buckland (Aldershot: Ashgate, 2011), pp. 121–32.

Nicholls, David, 'Richard Cobden and the International Peace Congress Movement 1848–1853', *Journal of British Studies* 30.4 (1991), pp. 351–76.

Nightingale, Florence, *Subsidiary Notes as to the Introduction of Female Nursing into Military Hospitals in Peace and in War* (London: Harrison and Sons, 1858).

Nightingale, Florence, *Notes on Nursing: What it is and What it is Not* (London: Duckworth, 1970).

Nowell-Smith, S., *The House of Cassell, 1848–1958* (London: Cassell & Co, 1958).

O'Brien, Tim, *The Things They Carried* (New York: First Mariner, 2009, first published 1990).

Orme, Robert, *History of the Military Transactions of the British Nation in Indostan* (London: John Nourse, 1763).

Orwell, George, *Inside the Whale and Other Essays* (Harmondsworth: Penguin, 1962).

Paris, Michael, *Warrior Nation: Images of War in British Popular Culture, 1850–2000* (London: Reaktion, 2000).

Parrish, John, 'Preface', in *War and Medicine* (London: Black Dog Publishing, 2008), pp. iii–iv.

Parry, Jonathan, *The Politics of Patriotism: English Liberalism, National Identity and Europe, 1830–1886* (Cambridge: Cambridge University Press, 2006).

Parry, Kenneth, *Pelham Place: A History* (London: de Lazlo Foundation, 2005).

Peck, John, *War, the Army and Victorian Literature* (Basingstoke: Palgrave, 1998).

Poovey, Mary, *Uneven Developments: The Ideological Work of Gender in Mid-Victorian England* (Chicago: University of Chicago Press, 1988).

Praz, Mario, *The Hero in Eclipse in Victorian Fiction* (Oxford: Oxford University Press, 1956).

Prichard, Sue, 'Precision Patchwork: Nineteenth Century Military Quilts', *Textile History* 41, supplement 1 (2010), pp. 214–26.

Purton, Valerie, *Dickens and the Sentimental Tradition* (London: Anthem Press, 2012).

Rae, Janet and Margaret Tucker, eds, *Quilt Treasures: The Quilters' Guild Heritage Search* (London: The Quilters' Guild, 1995).

Ramsey, Neil, 'The Comic View of Johnny Newcome's War', paper given at Contested Views: Visual Culture and the Revolutionary and Napoleonic Wars, Tate Britain, London, July 2012.

Rappaport, Helen, *No Place for Ladies: The Untold Story of Women in the Crimean War* (London: Aurum, 2007).

Rawlinson, Mark, 'Camouflage and the Re-enchantment of Warfare', in *The Edinburgh Companion to Twentieth-Century British and American War Literature*, ed. Adam Piette and Mark Rawlinson (Edinburgh, Edinburgh University Press, 2012), pp. 356–65.

Reardon, Betty, *Sexism and the War System* (New York: Syracuse University Press, 1996).

Reed, John, 'Soldier Boy: Forming Masculinity in Adam Bede', *Studies in the Novel* 33.3 (2001), pp. 268–84.

Reed, John, 'The Victorians and War', in *The Cambridge Companion to War Writing*, ed. Kate McLoughlin (Cambridge: Cambridge University Press, 2009), pp. 135–47.

Reznick, Jeffrey, *Healing the Nation: Soldiers and the Culture of Caregiving in Britain during the Great War* (Manchester: Manchester University Press, 2004).

Richards, David, *Masks of Difference: Cultural Representations in Literature, Anthropology and Art* (Cambridge: Cambridge University Press, 1994).

Richardson, Samuel, *Sir Charles Grandison* (Oxford: Oxford University Press, 1986).

Roberts, David, *The Military Adventures of Johnny Newcome* (London: Patrick Martin, 1815).

Robson, Catherine, *Men in Wonderland: The Lost Girlhood of the Victorian Gentleman* (Princeton, NJ: Princeton University Press, 2001).

Robson, Catherine, *Heart Beats: Everyday Life and the Memorized Poem* (Princeton and Oxford: Princeton University Press, 2012).

Roper, Michael, *The Secret Battle: Emotional Survival in the Great War* (Manchester: Manchester University Press, 2009).

Russell, William Howard, *The British Expedition to the Crimea* (London: Routledge, 1858).

Sanders, Valerie, *The Tragi-Comedy of Victorian Fatherhood* (Cambridge: Cambridge University Press, 2009).

Saunders, Nicholas, *Trench Art* (Buckinghamshire: Shire, 2002).

Saunders, Nicholas, *Trench Art: Materialities and Memories of War* (Oxford: Berg, 2003).

Scarry, Elaine, *The Body in Pain: The Making and Unmaking of the World* (Oxford: Oxford University Press, 1985).

Scott, Catherine, 'Rescue in the Age of Empire: Children, Masculinity, and the War on Terror', in *(En)gendering the War on Terror: War Stories and Camouflaged Politics*, ed. Krista Hunt and Kim Rygiel (London: Ashgate, 2006), pp. 97–117.

Scott, Walter, *Waverley* (London: Penguin, 2011).

Seacole, Mary, *The Wonderful Adventures of Mrs Seacole in Many Lands* (London: Penguin, 2005).

Sedgwick, Eve Kosofsky, *Touching Feeling: Affect, Pedagogy, Performativity* (Durham and London: Duke University Press, 2003).

Bibliography

Shakespeare, William, *Henry V*, in *The Norton Shakespeare*, ed. Stephen Greenblatt et al. (New York: Norton, 1997).
Shannon, Edgar and Christopher Ricks, '"The Charge of the Light Brigade": The Creation of a Poem', *Studies in Bibliography* 38 (1985), pp. 1–44.
Shapovalov, Veronica, 'They Came From Bleak House', *Dostoevsky Studies* 9 (1988), pp. 202–7.
Shaw, Madelyn and Lynne Zacek Bassett, *Homefront and Battlefield: Quilts and Context in the American Civil War* (Lowell, MA: American Textile History Museum, 2012).
Shaw, Philip, *Waterloo and the Romantic Imagination* (Basingstoke: Palgrave, 2002).
Shaw, Philip, '"On War": De Quincey's Martial Sublime', *Romanticism* 19.1 (2003), pp. 19–30.
Shaw, Philip, *Sentiment and Suffering in Romantic Military Art* (Farnham: Ashgate, 2013).
Shaw, Philip, 'Wars of Seeing: Suffering and Sentiment in Joseph Wright's "The Dead Soldier"', in *Soldiering in Britain and Ireland, 1750–1850: Men of Arms*, ed. Catriona Kennedy and Matthew McCormack (Basingtoke: Palgrave, 2013), pp. 76–95.
Shillingsburg, Peter, *William Makepeace Thackeray: A Literary Life* (Basingstoke: Palgrave, 2001).
Shillingsburg, Peter L., 'Thackeray, William Makepeace (1811–1863)', *Oxford Dictionary of National Biography* (Oxford: Oxford University Press, 2004); online edn, October 2009, <http://www.oxforddnb.com/view/article/27155>.
Skelley, Alan Ramsey, *The Victorian Army at Home: The Recruitment and Terms and Conditions of the British Regular, 1859–1899* (London: Croom Helm, 1977).
Small, Hugo, *The Crimean War* (Stroud: Tempus, 2007).
Smiles, Samuel, *Self-Help* (Oxford: Oxford University Press, 2002).
Smith, Melvin Charles, *Awarded for Valor: A History of the Victoria Cross and the Evolution of British Heroism* (Basingstoke: Palgrave, 2008).
Snape, Michael, *The Redcoat and Religion* (Abingdon: Routledge, 2005).
Sontag, Susan, *Regarding the Pain of Others* (London: Penguin, 2004).
Spyri, Johanna, *Heidi* (Chicago: Whitman, 1916).
Steedman, Carolyn, *The Radical Soldier's Tale: John Pearman, 1819–1908* (London and New York: Routledge, 1988).
Steedman, Carolyn, *Strange Dislocations: Childhood and the Idea of Human Interiority, 1780–1930* (London: Virago, 1995).
Steevens, Nathaniel, *The Crimean Campaign with 'The Connaught Rangers', 1854–1856* (London and Edinburgh: Griffith and Farran, 1878).
Sterne, Lawrence, *The Life and Opinions of Tristram Shandy, Gentleman* (London: Penguin, 2003).
Stewart, Susan, *On Longing: Narratives of the Miniature, the Gigantic, the Souvenir, the Collection* (Durham and London: Duke University Press, 1993).
Stocqueler, J. H., *The British Officer: His Positions, Duties, Emoluments and Privileges* (London: Smith, Elder and Co., 1851).

Strange, Julie-Marie, *Fatherhood and the British Working Class, 1865–1914* (Cambridge: Cambridge University Press, 2015).

Streets, Heather, *Martial Races: The Military, Race, and Masculinity in British Imperial Culture* (Manchester: Manchester University Press, 2004).

Summers, Anne, 'Pride and Prejudice: Ladies and Nurses in the Crimean War', *History Workshop Journal* 16.1 (1983), pp. 33–56.

Taithe, Bertrand, 'The Red Cross Flag in the Franco-Prussian War: Civilians, Humanitarians and War in the "'Modern" Age', in *War, Medicine and Modernity*, ed. Roger Cooter, Mark Harrison, and Steve Sturdy (Sutton: Stroud, 1998), pp. 22–47.

Tate, Trudi, 'On Not Knowing Why: Memorialising the Light Brigade', in *Literature, Science, Psychoanalysis, 1830–1970: Essays in Honour of Gillian Beer*, ed. Helen Small and Trudi Tate (Oxford: Oxford University Press, 2003), pp. 160–80.

Tate, Trudi, 'Sevastopol: On the Fall of a City', *19: Interdisciplinary Studies in the Long Nineteenth Century* 20 (2015).

Taylor, Fanny Margaret, *Eastern Hospitals and English Nurses: The Narrative of Twelve Months Experience in the Hospitals of Koulali and Scutari. By a Lady Volunteer* (London: Hurst and Blackett, 1857).

Teffeteller, Gordon L., 'Hill, Rowland, first Viscount Hill (1772–1842)', in *Oxford Dictionary of National Biography* (Oxford: Oxford University Press, 2004).

Tennyson, Alfred, *The Poems of Tennyson*, ed. Christopher Ricks, 3 vols (Harlow: Longman, 1987).

Tennyson, Alfred, *Selected Poems*, ed. Christopher Ricks (London: Penguin, 2007).

Terrot, Sarah Anne, *Nurse Sarah Anne with Florence Nightingale at Scutari*, ed. Robert Richardson (London: John Murray, 1977).

Thackeray, William Makepeace, 'Important from the Seat of War! Letters from the East by Our Own Bashi Bouzouk', *Punch*, 17 June 1854.

Thackeray, William Makepeace, *The Newcomes* (London: Dent, 1994).

Thackeray, William Makepeace, *Vanity Fair: A Novel without a Hero* (Oxford: Oxford University Press, 1998).

Thackeray, William Makepeace, *The Tremendous Adventures of Major Gahagan* (Milton Keynes: Amazon print on demand, 2013).

Theweleit, Klaus, *Male Fantasies*, 2 vols (Minneapolis: University of Minnesota Press, 1987–9).

Tolstoy, Leo, *Sebastopol Sketches*, translated by David McDuff (London: Penguin, 1986).

Tolstoy, Leo, *War and Peace*, translated by Anthony Briggs (London: Penguin, 2007).

Tosh, John, *A Man's Place: Masculinity and the Middle-Class Home in Victorian England* (New Haven and London: Yale University Press, 1999).

Uglow, Jenny, *In These Times: Living in Britain through Napoleon's Wars* (London: Faber, 2014).

van Creveld, Martin, *Transformation of War* (New York: The Free Press, 1991).
Vance, Norman, *The Sinews of the Spirit* (Cambridge: Cambridge University Press, 1985).
Virgil, *The Aeneid*, translated by David West (Oxford: Oxford University Press, 2003).
Walton, Susan, *Imagining Soldiers and Fathers in the Mid-Victorian Era: Charlotte Yonge's Models of Manliness* (Farnham: Ashgate, 2010).
Warner, Malcolm, 'Notes on Millais' Use of Subjects from the Opera, 1851–54', *The Pre-Raphaelite Review* 2.1 (1978), pp. 73–6.
Watson, J. K., 'Soldiers and Saints: The Fighting Man and the Christian Life', in *Masculinity and Spirituality in Victorian Culture*, ed. Andrew Bradstock, Sean Gill, Anne Hogan, and Sue Morgan (Basingstoke: Palgrave, 2000), pp. 10–26.
Wee, C. J., 'Christian Manliness and National Identity: The Problematic Construction of a Racially "Pure" Nation', in *Muscular Christianity: Embodying the Victorian Age*, ed. Donald Hall (Cambridge: Cambridge University Press, 1994), pp. 66–88.
Weil, Simone, 'The Iliad, or The Poem of Force', first published 1940–1, translated by Mary McCarthy, *Chicago Review* 18.2 (1965), pp. 5–30.
Welland, Julia, 'Liberal Warriors and the Concealment of Violence', Sensing War conference, London, 12–13 June 2014.
Welland, Julia, 'Liberal Warriors and the Violent Colonial Logics of "Partnering and Advising"', *International Feminist Journal of Politics* (2014), pp. 1–19.
Weston, Kath, *Families We Choose: Lesbians, Gays, Kinship* (New York and Oxford: Columbia University Press, 1991).
White, R. S., *Pacifism and English Literature: Minstrels of Peace* (Basingstoke: Palgrave, 2008).
White, William, *History, Gazetteer and Directory of the County of Hampshire* (London: William White and Simpkin Marshall, 1878).
Whitman, Walt, *Specimen Days and Collect* (Philadelphia: Ross Welsh, 1882–3).
Wilkinson, Frederick, *Collecting Military Antiques* (London: Ward Lock, 1976).
Williams, John F., *German Anzacs and the First World War* (Sydney: University of New South Wales Press, 2003).
Williams, Rowan, Address, Westminster Abbey, 8 February 2012. Available online at http://www.archbishopofcanterbury.org/articles.php/2347/archbishops-address-at-charles-dickens-wreathlaying-ceremony-at-westminster-abbey.
Winter, Jay, *Sites of Memory, Sites of Mourning: The Great War in European Cultural History* (Cambridge: Cambridge University Press, 1995).
Winter, John Strange, *Bootles' Baby: A Story of the Scarlet Lancers* (London and New York: Warne, 1885, reprinted 1891).
Winter, John Strange, *Mignon's Secret* (London: F. V. White, 1886).
Winter, John Strange, *Mignon's Husband* (London: F. V. White, 1887).
Winter, John Strange, *A Siege Baby and Other Stories*, 2 vols (London: F. V. White, 1887).
Winter, John Strange, *Bootles' Children* (London: F. V. White, 1888).
Woods, N. A., *The Past Campaign: A Sketch of the War in the East*, 2 vols (London: Longman, 1855).

Woolf, Virginia, *Three Guineas*, in *A Room of One's Own and Three Guineas* (London: Hogarth, 1984).
Woollright, H. H., *Records of the 77th* (London: Gale and Polden, 1907).
Wordsworth, William, 'Thanksgiving Ode', in *Shorter Poems, 1807–1820*, ed. Carl Ketcham (Ithaca: Cornell University Press, 1989).
Yonge, Charlotte, *Kenneth, or The Rear-Guard of the Grand Army* (Leipzig: Tauchnitz, 1860).
Yonge, Charlotte, *The Young Stepmother* (London: Macmillan, 1899).
Yonge, Charlotte, *The Heir of Redclyffe* (London: Macmillan, 1909).
Yonge, Charlotte, *The Clever Woman of the Family* (London: Virago, 1985).
Young, Arlene, *Culture, Class and Gender in the Victorian Novel: Gentlemen, Gents and Working Women* (Basingstoke: Macmillan, 1999).
Young, Arlene, '"Entirely a Woman's Question?": Class, Gender, and the Victorian Nurse', *Journal of Victorian Culture* 13.1 (2008), pp. 18–41.

ARCHIVAL MATERIAL

Bristol University Theatre Collection
Hampshire Record Office
Imperial War Museum
The National Archives
National Army Museum
The Royal Archives

PERIODICALS, PAPERS, AND NEWS WEBSITES CITED

All The Year Round
Athenaeum
BBC News, <www.bbc.co.uk/news>
British Quarterly Review
Cassell's Illustrated Family Paper
Colburn's United Service Magazine and Naval and Military Journal
Cornhill Magazine
Daily Mail
The Daily Telegraph
Edinburgh Review
The Empire
Evening Citizen
Glasgow Record
Household Narrative
Household Words
Illustrated Times
Lloyd's Weekly Newspaper
The New York Times
Pall Mall Gazette

Punch
Sheffield Telegraph
Scotsman
The Times
USA Today, <www.usatoday.com>
World

OTHER WEBSITES

http://www.archbishopofcanterbury.org
http://www.bbc.co.uk
http://www.beeston-notts.co.uk/jowett3.shtml
http://www.djo.org.uk
http://www.nam.ac.uk/exhibitions/online-exhibitions/florence-nightingale
http://www.oxforddnb.com
http://www.pbs.org
http://rogerfenton.dmu.ac.uk

FILMS AND TV

Band of Brothers, HBO, 2001
Ian Hislop's Stiff Upper Lip: An Emotional History of Britain, BBC2, 2012

Index

Adams, James Eli 7, 30, 33–4
Administrative Reform Association 33, 35–6, 59–61, 78
adoption 37–8, 86, 87–120
 eroticization of adopted girl 105–6, 108–9, 111–13
 forced military adoption 116–17
 and gentlemanliness 88–9, 93–102, 106
 and race and nationhood 105–6, 117
affect 15, 20, 24–6, 104, 123, 144, 151–2, 165, 168, 170, 174, 186, 219–20; *see also* emotions
Afghanistan, *see* war in Afghanistan
albums 128, 169–70
Alison, Archibald 97–8
All the Year Round 88
Alma, battle of 124, 134, 166–7, 169, 172, 174, 202, 218
American Civil War 90, 128–9, 158
 Homefront and Battlefield exhibition 151
Andrew, Donna T. 43
animals at war, *see* horses, pets
Armitage, Edward 91
army medical system 187, 194–5, 203–4; *see also* Royal Army Medical Corps
Army reform, *see* Administrative Reform Association; Cardwell reforms; Crimean War and army reform

Bailey, Phillip 68
Bainbridge, Simon 104
Balaclava, battle of 6, 124, 138, 189; *see also* Charge of the Light Brigade
Balaclava hospital 196, 209, 213, 215
Balzac, Honoré de 96
band of brothers 136
Barrett, Jerry 207
Barrett Browning, Elizabeth 4, 204–5
Barthes, Roland 169
Bates, Rachel 206
battlefield reading
 Colonel Newcome's 40–6, 53
 soldiers' accounts of 44, 46–50, 64–5, 155
Bell, George 140–1
Benwell, J. A. 193–4, 197, 207
Bevis, Matthew 12, 25, 114

Bible 86, 114, 186
Blishen, Henry 149, 163
body part trophies 173–4
Boer Wars 144, 179
Bourke, Joanna 23, 43, 130, 174
boy captain, *see* Lempriere, Audley
Boy's Own fiction 110
Brantlinger, Patrick 44
Breward, Christopher 176
Bridgeman, Mother 212
Bristow, Joseph 110
British Military Tournament 115
Brooke, Rupert 144
brotherliness, *see* band of brothers, regimental family
Broughton, Trev 70
Brown, Michael 6, 25, 34
Brownlie, Ian 23
Burdett, Carolyn 134
Bush, George W. 115
Butler, Judith 22, 30, 105, 118, 145
Byron, George Gordon
 Don Juan 103–5, 117

camouflage 119
Cantlie, Neil 196, 203, 210–11
Carden-Coyne, Ana 203
Cardwell reforms 60
Carlyle, Thomas 34
Casey, Daniel 143
Cassell's Illustrated Family Paper 182–4, 185
Catholicism 74–5
Ceadel, Martin 71
Cervantes, Miguel de
 Don Quixote 42
Charge of the Light Brigade 83, 133, 188, 191, 205; *see also* Balaclava; Tennyson
chartism 7, 60, 61
Chawner, Edward 125–6, 130
Chawton primary school 217–20
Chenery, Thomas 7, 20, 202
Cherub 139–41, 218–20
children
 born at war 143
 as soldiers 103; *see also* drummer boys

children (cont.)
 soldiers as protectors of 2, 85–6, 90–1;
  see also adoption; liberal warrior
 soldiers as killers of 114–15
 as war casualties 144
China, British Army in 167, 175
chivalric revival 8
chivalry 7–9, 38, 42
cholera 73, 80–1, 195, 211, 214–15, 216
Christian soldiers 68–86, 191, 192–3
Christianity 67–86, 209; see also Catholics; Christian soldiers; Crimean War and religion; muscular Christianity; Quakers; Tractarians
class, see Crimean War, and class debates; gentlemanliness
Classical and Biblical accounts of battle 16
Clausewitz, Carl von 153
Clemm, Sabine 56, 58
Clive, Robert 44
Cobbett, William 37
Cockburn, Cynthia 14
Cockerill, A. W. 103
Colby, Robert 31, 35
Cole, Sarah 119
communicating war experience 149–50, 152–6, 159–75; see also incommunicability of war thesis; objects sent home; soldier art; souvenirs
Compton Verney 151
cooking 88–90
Coram, Thomas 37
Craik, Dinah
 A Life for a Life 81, 102
Creveld, Martin van 14
Crimean hospitals, see Balaclava, Scutari
Crimean War
 and army reform 7, 56–61, 95, 133–4; see also Administrative Reform Association
 background to 3–9
 battles, see Alma, Balaclava, Inkerman, Sebastopol
 and class debates 5–7, 33–5, 58–61, 78, 82
 and communication networks 20, 159
 critiques of mismanagement 33, 58–9, 64, 147, 195, 197, 203
 and liberalism 82, 85
 and national character 4–5
 and political reform 7, 58–61
 press coverage of 5–7, 20–1, 154–5
 see also *Cassell's Illustrated Family Paper*; *Illustrated London News*; *Illustrated Times*; *Household Narrative of Current Events*; *Household Words*; *Punch*; *The Times*
 and religion 5, 6, 69–86, 173
Crimean War nurses, see Croke, Mary Joseph; Davis, Elizabeth; Goodman, Margaret; Nightingale, Florence; Seacole, Mary; Sisters of Mercy; soldier nursing; Terrot, Sarah Anne
Croke, Sister Mary Joseph 196, 213, 214
crying
 see tears

Dallas, Fred 163
Damousi, Joy 170
dandies 30
Das, Santanu 14, 132, 165
Davis, Elizabeth 202, 209
Dawson, Graham 13, 14, 110–11
De Quincey, Thomas 69
death, see cholera; Good Death; medicine; memorial; mourning; wounding; wounds
Dereli, C. 61
di Bello, Patricia 169
Dickens, Charles
 A Child's History of England 9, 77
 A Christmas Carol 66
 Bleak House 77–80, 81
 Christmas writings 54–5, 66–7, 77; see also *A Christmas Carol*; 'Seven Poor Travellers'; 'Somebody's Luggage'
 Edwin Drood 76–7
 Little Dorrit 59
 'Our French Watering Place' 94
 Our Mutual Friend 62
 'Seven Poor Travellers' 54–67, 71–2, 76, 77, 88
 'Somebody's Luggage' 86, 88–95, 99–101, 106, 108–9
 The Life of Our Lord 86
 see also *All the Year Round*; *Household Narrative of Current Events*; *Household Words*
Dixon, Thomas 97
doctor heroes 80–2, 102, 189
domesticity 13, 87–92, 151–2, 213–14
 see also adoption; cooking; fatherliness; gardening; knitting; nursing; objects from home; objects sent home; sewing
Donizetti, Gaetano
 La Fille du Régiment 107–9

Index

Doyle, Sister M. Aloysius 211, 213–14
draughts 179
Drew, John 64
drummer boys 143–5, 181
Duberley, Fanny 142
duelling 17, 40, 42–3, 63
Dunant, Henry 201
Duncanson, Claire 14, 119

East India Company 44–6
Edelman, Lee 115
Edgeworth, Maria 44–5
Egerton, Thomas Graham 121–6, 129, 130–40, 218–20
Eliot, George 102
Eliot, T. S. 47–8
Emerson, Gloria 116–17
emotional survival 90, 147–8, 170, 179
emotions
  and command 133
  and ethics 21–2, 24
  history of 15, 24, 97, 187, 217
  masculine capacity for 16, 34–5, 38, 52, 97, 192, 212, 217
  mixed feelings 25–6, 50, 123, 167, 174, 186, 218–20
  and nationhood 97
  pre-war 48
  restraint 11, 34–5, 97
  see also emotional survival; mourning; regimental family; sensibility; shame; sympathy; tears
empire
  see imperial masculinity
enchantment of the archive 122
enchantment of violence 118–19
enfranchisement 7, 37, 60–1, 197, 215

families of choice 100, 113
  see also adoption
fatherliness 35–8, 88, 135–9, 210
  see also adoption; regimental family
Favret, Mary 20, 92
feeling
  see emotions, touch
Fenton, Roger 107, 124, 159
Fieldston, Sara 117
Figes, Orlando 3
First World War 215
  centenary 15
  Good Death 130–1
  memorials 123, 129
  popularity of *The Newcomes* during 52–3
  propaganda 115

Royal Army Medical Corps 203
soldier sketches 158
souvenirs 167
and stuff of home 147–9
therapeutic craftwork 179, 185
  see also trench art
Fisher, Glenn 182
flesh-witnessing 153, 175–6
Ford, Gerald 116
Forster, E. M. 47–8
Forster, John 94
Fort Pitt hospital 181–2
France and French soldiers 5, 61–6, 88–90, 93–4, 96–8, 108; *see also* French Revolution; Napoleon Bonaparte; Napoleonic Wars
Fraser, F. A. 56
fraternity, *see* band of brothers, regimental family
French Revolution 96–7
Freud, Sigmund 14
Füssel, Marian 175

gardening 90, 164
Gaskell, Elizabeth 59
gender roles 13–14, 41, 102–13, 119, 138–9, 193–208, 210, 214, 216; *see also* masculinity
gentlemanliness 27–38, 87, 93–5, 99–102
Gibbs, Philip 9
Gilmour, Robin 32, 42
Gilpin Faust, Drew 128–9, 130
Gleig, G. R. 91
Goethe, Johann Wolfgang von 110
Good Death 130–1, 138, 146
Goodman, Margaret 2, 3, 5, 9, 199, 207, 211, 214
Great War, *see* First World War
Green, Charles 100, 101
Gregory, Derek 118–19
grief, *see* grieveability; mourning
grieveability 145

Hack, Daniel 48
hands 93, 165, 179–80, 194, 206–7
  see also touch
Hanson, Ingrid 12
Hampshire Music Service 217
Hampshire Record Office 129, 217–18
Harari, Yuval 21, 23, 98, 152–3, 155–6
Hardy, Thomas 144–5
Harrison, Mark 201
Harrison, Simon 173–4

Index

Harvey, Thomas 152–3, 160–2, 164, 170–1, 175
Havelock, Henry 110–11
Hayter, Althea 47
Hazlitt, William 7–8
Helkett, Douglas 138
Hemens, Felicia 144
heroism 5–9, 19, 123, 205
  belligerent modes of 83–4
  and class 6–8, 99, 208, 216
  gentle and non-belligerent modes of 17, 23, 43, 48, 50, 80–3, 92, 98–9, 105, 135, 138, 191, 215–16
  and Good Death 130–1
  and nationhood 5
  see also chivalry; doctor heroes
Hetherington, Tim 24, 148–9
Hill, Katrina 167, 175
Hill, Rowland 'Daddy' 137
history of emotions
  see emotions
Ho, Tai Chun 16, 20
Hodge, Edward Cooper 163
Hogg, James
  'The Adventures of Captain John Lochy' 18–19
Holmes, Richard 44
homeliness *see* domesticity
Homer 16, 63
horses 140, 142, 157, 218–19
  see also Cherub
hospital orderlies, *see* soldier nursing
hospitals, *see* Crimean hospitals, Fort Pitt hospital
The Household Narrative of Current Events 33
Household Words 54–9, 63–5
Houston, Natalie 159
Hugo, Victor 96–7
Hunt, Leigh 68, 200–1, 214
hunting 142, 157
Hussein, Saddam 115
Hutchings, Kimberley 14

illness and injury, *see* cholera; medicine; wounds
Illustrated London News 162, 205
Illustrated Times 161–2
imperial masculinity 11–12, 87–8, 110–11
incommunicability of war thesis 153–6, 175
Indian Uprising or 'Mutiny' 8, 110, 114–15
Inkerman, battle of 6, 64, 165, 167, 124, 182
Iraq War 115, 119

Jervoise, Clarke 136
Johnny Newcome 39–40
Jowett, William 205

Kaplan, Fred 41
Keegan, John 15
Kimball, Jane 150
Kinglake, Alexander 90–1
Kingsley, Charles
  'Brave Words for Brave Soldiers and Sailors' 17, 72–3, 74
  Hereward the Wake 81
  Two Years Ago 80–2, 85–6, 190
  Westward Ho! 73–6, 84–6, 87, 105–6, 114–15
kinship, *see* adoption; families of choice; fatherliness; motherliness; regimental family
Kirkpatrick, Benji 219
Klein, Melanie 25, 129
Knight, [Charles] Ernest 65, 125, 131
Knightley, Phillip 115
knitting 178
Kovitz, Marcia 13

Lawrence, George
  Guy Livingstone, or Thorough 10–11, 50
  Sword and Gown 83–5
Ledger, Sally 66–7
Lempriere, Algernon 126, 128
Lempriere, Audley 90, 121–49, 154, 157, 164–70, 173–4, 217–20
  Audley's horse, *see* Cherub
Lempriere, Ellen 126–30, 166, 167, 169–70, 173–4, 220
Lempriere Harriet 126, 128, 141
liberal warriors 82–6, 118
looting, *see* plunder
loss, *see* mourning
Luard, John 147–8, 155
Lynn (Linton), Eliza 58

McCormack, Matthew 37
McGill, Thomas 143
MacGregor, Douglas 191–3
Mackenzie, Henry 19, 41–2
  The Man of Feeling 18
McLoughlin, Kate 1–2, 104, 153–4
McLoughlin, Peter 215
male nurses, *see* soldier nursing
man of feeling

Index

eighteenth-century models 17–19, 41
  see also sensibility
Markovits, Stefanie 6, 25, 46, 59, 81, 107
Marsh, Catherine 69–70, 138, 192–3
Martin, Brian Joseph 16, 23, 96
Martin, Robert Barnard 81
Marx, Karl 4
masculinity
  and domesticity, *see* domesticity
  and feeling, *see* emotion; touch
  and nurture, *see* fatherliness, nursing
  and performance, styles of 30
  and violence 13–14, 119, 174
  see also chivalry; gender roles; gentlemanliness; heroism; imperial masculinity; man of feeling; Victorian masculinity
Massie, Alastair 143
medicine, *see* army medical system; Crimean hospitals; doctor heroes; Fort Pitt hospital; nursing; Red Cross
mementos, *see* souvenirs
memorial 121–32, 136–7, 142, 165, 170, 179–80, 217, 219–20
memorial notebooks and scrapbooks 126–32, 165, 169–70, 174
Menzies, Dr Duncan 194–6, 214
military ballads 219
military conduct books 38, 133
military history
  see 'New Military History'; wars; war and ethics
military memoir 39–40, 98
military quilts, *see* soldier art
Millais, John Everett
  Peace Concluded 49–50
  The Random Shot or *L'enfant du Régiment* 106–8, 186
Milne, J. W. 44
Mitford, John 39
mixed feelings
  see emotions
Moore, Grace 58
Morpurgo, Michael 218–19
Morton, Michael 51–3
Moss, Hugh 111
motherliness 138–9
mourning 121–49, 169–70, 192–3, 212, 219–20
  work of 128–9, 170, 212
  see also memorial; memorial notebooks and scrapbooks

Mullan, John 41
Murphy, Sharon 46
Murray, Eustace Grenville 56
muscular Christianity 69–70, 72–6, 85

Napoleon Bonaparte 23, 96
Napoleonic Wars 96, 98
  representations of 56, 88, 91, 95–6, 107
  see also Waterloo
National Army Museum 91, 124, 126, 159, 163, 176, 193–4, 217–18
national attitudes 5, 82, 85, 96–7; *see also* France and French soldiers; Russia; Turkey
Nazi SS 23
'New military history' 15
Nhu, Tran Tuong 116
Nightingale, Florence 33, 62, 193–4, 196–8, 204–8
nursing, *see* Crimean War nurses; soldier nursing

objects from home 90, 126, 147–9, 159, 164
objects sent home 126, 149–52, 159, 163–75, 218
  flattened bullets 163–4
  flowers 164–5, 218
  icons 172–5
  Russian medal ribbon 165–70, 174–5, 218
O'Brien, Tim 122, 145
Operation Babylift 116–17
orderlies, *see* soldier nursing
Orme, Robert 44–5, 49
Orwell, George 47–8
Owen, Wilfred 144

pacifism, *see* peace campaigns
paranoid/reparative reading, *see* reparative reading
Paris, Michael 110
Parrish, John 203–4
Parry, Jonathan 82
patchwork, *see* soldier art
peace campaigns 61, 69–71
  see also war protest poetry
Pechell, William 132, 154–5, 156–7, 159, 164
Peck, John 33, 78
Penny, Edward
  The Marquis of Granby Giving Alms to a Sick Soldier and his Family 18
pets 139–41, 159
photographs 159

plunder 167, 172
  see also body part trophies
Political reform, *see* enfranchisement; Crimean War, and political reform
Poovey, Mary 197
precarity 22, 102–3, 145, 174–5, 186
Prichard, Sue 176, 179, 180
prisoners of war 178–9
Proctor, Adelaide Anne 59
Punch 5, 32, 41, 91, 142, 143–4, 162
Purton, Valerie 68

Quakers 70–1
Queen Victoria 182–4, 185, 205–7
The Queen's Regulations and Orders 133
quilts, *see* soldier art

Radcliffe, Frederick Peter Delme 135
Rae, Janet and Margaret Tucker 180
Raglan, Fitzroy 63, 124–5, 126
Ramsey, Neil 39
Rawdon, Joseph 180
Rawlinson, Mark 119
Reardon, Betty 14
Red Cross, International Committee 201, 216
Redan, assaults on 137–8, 152–3, 170, 172–3
Reed, John 25, 33, 113
re-enchantment of war, *see* enchantment of violence
reparative reading 25–6, 120, 122–3, 129, 145–6, 186, 202–3, 216
Reform Acts, *see* enfranchisement
regimental family 87, 96–9, 103, 120, 135–41, 188, 192, 210, 218
  see also adoption band of brothers
regimental mascots, *see* pets
Reznick, Jeffrey 178
rhetoric, *see* war rhetoric
Richardson, Samuel
  Sir Charles Grandison 17, 41–2
Robert, J. B. 163
Roberts, David 39–40
Robson, Catherine 26, 102, 144
Roe, George 90, 154, 157–9, 164, 169, 172–4
Roper, Michael 90, 102–3, 147–8, 158
Rowlandson, Thomas 39
Royal Army Medical Corps 203–4, 216
Rubens, Peter Paul 114
Ruskin, John 111
Russell, John 61

Russell, William Howard 59, 64, 80, 143, 155, 189, 195, 202
Russia 3, 5–7, 32, 49, 58, 63, 79, 85

sailors 6
Sala, G. A. 64
salvage work 122–3, 146, 186, 220
Sanders, Valerie 36
Sandhurst, Royal Military Training College 157
sanitary reform 83, 191
Sartin, Paul 219
Saunders, Nicholas 150, 151–2, 168, 186
Scarry, Elaine 22
Scott, Catherine 115–16
Scott, Walter
  Waverley 19
Scutari hospital 2, 33, 193–6, 198, 202, 203
Seacole, Mary 206
Sebastopol, siege of 121, 154, 162, 179;
  see also Redan, assaults on
Second World War 179
Sedgwick, Eve Kosofsky 25–6, 123, 129, 146
Selborne primary school 217–20
self-help 8, 60, 178, 184
sensibility 17–24, 33, 41, 67, 95
  see also sympathy, emotion, tears
sentimentality 134
separate spheres thesis 13, 91, 135, 139, 152–3
Seven Years War 175
77th Regiment 65, 90, 121–6, 133, 136–7, 139, 143, 152, 155
sewing 90, 176–8, 212
  see also soldier art; quilting and patchwork
Shakespeare, William 136
shame 4, 20–1, 200, 202, 204, 207, 216
Shaw, Madelyn and Lynne Zacek Bassett 90, 151, 158
Shaw, Philip 18, 104
Sidney, Philip 9
Sisters of Mercy 196, 209
  see also Bridgeman, Mother; Croke, Sister Mary Joseph; Doyle, Sister M. Aloysius
Skelley, Alan 60
Smiles, Samuel 8
Smith, Dr Andrew 195
Snape, Michael 6, 82–3
soldier art 150–86, 212

Index

collage 162–3
music 152, 171–2
quilting and patchwork 176–86
sketches 126–8, 149, 157–63, 218
soldier nursing 47, 78–9, 104, 187–216
  soldier orderlies 193–216
soldier poetry 131–2, 136–7, 212
soldiering and social work 113–20
  see also war narratives; enchantment of violence; liberal warrior
soldiers' reading, *see* battlefield reading
Sontag, Susan 21, 23
souvenirs 126, 150, 166–75
  see also body part trophies; objects sent home; plunder
Spyri, Johanna
  Heidi 103
Stannard, Henrietta Eliza Vaughan, *see* Winter, John Strange
Steedman, Carolyn 6, 111, 112
Steevens, Nathaniel 64–5, 121, 124
Stephen, James Fitzjames 134
Sterne, Lawrence
  Tristram Shandy 17–18, 37
Stewart, Susan 168, 186
stiff upper lip 11, 87–8, 97
  see also emotions, restraint.
Stocqueler, J. H. 38, 133
Streets, Heather 11, 114
Summers, Anne 208
suspicious reading, *see* reparative reading
sympathy 20–4, 37, 113, 118

tactility
  see touch
Taliban 115–16
Tate, Trudi 48, 154
Taylor, Fanny Margaret 199, 203, 205, 208–10, 212–14
tears 18, 40, 41, 67, 95, 96–7, 104, 139–40, 192–3, 210
temperance 177–8, 184
Tennyson, Alfred
  Maud 4, 25, 29–30
  'The Charge of the Light Brigade' 25, 48–9
Terrot, Sarah Anne 198–9, 206–7, 211, 214–15
Thackeray, William Makepeace
  'Important from the Seat of War! Letters from the East by Our Own Bashi Bouzouk' 32, 40–1
  The Luck of Barry Lyndon 40

The Newcomes 27–53
  adaptation of 51–3
  reception of 27–9, 51
  serialization of 32–3, 50, 55
  as Professor Byles in *Punch* 91–2
The Tremendous Adventures of Major Gahagan 40
Vanity Fair 28, 33–4, 50, 91–2
Theweleit, Klaus 14
The Times 7, 10, 20–1, 49–50, 59, 64, 114, 154, 182, 195, 202, 206;
  see also Chenery, Thomas; Russell, William Howard
Tolstoy, Leo
  Sebastopol Sketches 1, 21–2
  War and Peace 1, 21
Tosh, John 12, 36, 110–11
touch 47, 132–3, 206–8, 212–13
  and eroticism 132
  and learning 218
  and material touched by soldiers 122, 126, 163, 165, 175, 179–81
  see also nursing, soldier art
Tractarians 99
Tree, Herbert Beerbohm 51–3
trench art 150–1, 186, *see also* soldier art
Trollope, Anthony 27
Turkey 3, 5, 58

Unett, Thomas 'Daddy' 137–8
'urgent private affairs' 49, 142–3

Vance, Norman 80, 83
Vicars, Hedley 69–70, 75, 83, 138, 192–3, 215
Victoria and Albert Museum Quilts exhibition 176, 184
Victoria Cross 82, 189
Victorian masculinity
  scholarship on (summarized) 12–13
  stereotypes of 11, 15, 119–20, 133
  see also imperial masculinity; masculinity; heroism
Vietnam War 116–17
Virgil 16, 62–3
vulnerability 22, 102–3

Walker, Thomas 181–6
Walton, Susan 46, 47, 99, 134–5
war and ethics 20–4
war in Afghanistan 115–16, 118–19
  and stuff of home 148–9

war narratives
  ameliorative narratives 2, 22–3, 26, 43, 80–2, 98, 134–5, 187, 189, 191, 193, 204, 216
  see also Christian soldiers; doctor heroes; enchantment of violence; liberal warriors
  revenge narratives 62–3, 75–6
  ur–war story 1–2, 43
war protest poetry 68–9, 104–5
war rhetoric 2, 22, 82, 114, 118–19, 153–4, 168
Ware, W. 178
wars
  see American Civil War; Boer Wars; Crimean War; First World War; Indian Uprising or 'Mutiny'; Napoleonic Wars; Second World War; Seven Years War; war in Afghanistan
Waterloo 63, 109, 167, 200
Watson, J. K. 69–70
weeping
  see tears
Weil, Simone 15–16
Welland, Julia 85, 118–19
Wellington, Duke of 6
Weston, Kath 100

White, R. S. 104
Williams, Jane 202
Williams, Rowan 79–80
Willis, George 133, 160, 172–3
Winter, Jay 123, 129, 165
Winter, John Strange
  Bootles' Baby: A Story of the Scarlet Lancers 109–12
  Mignon's Husband 112
  Mignon's Secret 112–13
  'A Seige Baby' 114
Wood, Thomas 182–6
Woods, N. A. 132–3
Woolf, Virginia 13
Wordsworth, William 69
wounding 22, 68, 187, 201, 216
  see also wounds
wounds 181–5

Yonge, Charlotte
  The Clever Woman of the Family 189
  Heartsease 46
  The Heir of Redclyffe 46–7, 50, 99, 189
  Kenneth, or The Rear Guard of the Grand Army 95–102, 109
  The Young Stepmother 187–91
Yonge, Julian 46–7, 99
Young, Arlene 32